THE MACROECONOMIC MANAGEMENT OF FOREIGN AID

Opportunities and Pitfalls

Editors PETER ISARD, LESLIE LIPSCHITZ,
ALEXANDROS MOURMOURAS, BORIANA YONTCHEVA

INTERNATIONAL MONETARY FUND

Production: IMF MultiMedia Services Division
Cover design: Noel Albizo
Cover photo: Stephen Jaffe

Cataloging-in-Publication Data

The macroeconomic management of foreign aid : opportunities and pitfalls / editors, Peter Isard . . . [et al.] — [Washington, D.C. : International Monetary Fund, 2006].
p. cm.

ISBN 1-58906-520-4
"Presents the papers prepared for the seminar, which was hosted in Maputo by the Government of Mozambique during March 2005" — Pref.
Includes bibliographical references.

1. Economic assistance — Congresses. 2. Poverty — Congresses. 3. Fiscal policy — Congresses. 4. Foreign exchange rates — Congresses. I. Isard, Peter. II. International Monetary Fund.
HC60.M34 2006

Price: $28.00

Please send orders to:
International Monetary Fund, Publications Services
700 19th Street, N.W., Washington D.C. 20431, U.S.A.
Telephone: (202) 623-7430 Telefax: (202) 623-7201
Email: publications@imf.org
Internet: http://www.imf.org

recycled paper

Contents

The following symbols have been used in this book:
. . .   to indicate that data are not available;
–   between years or months (e.g., 1995–1996 or January–June) to indicate the years or months covered, including the beginning and ending years or months; and
/   between years (e.g., 1996/1997) to indicate a fiscal (financial) year.
"Billion" means a thousand million.
Dollars are U.S. dollars.
Minor discrepancies between constituent figures and totals are due to rounding.

Foreword

I am pleased to introduce this volume on *The Macroeconomic Management of Foreign Aid: Opportunities and Pitfalls*. As I indicated at the United Nations in September 2005, the IMF is a strong supporter of the Monterrey Consensus and is committed to helping countries meet the Millennium Development Goals. The IMF welcomes the recent pledges by the development community to support debt relief and provide a substantial increase in aid flows to low-income countries. Aid provides opportunities, but it also presents pitfalls. We need much more aid, but we also need smarter aid and smarter management of aid.

The IMF is centrally engaged in promoting policies that help countries achieve macroeconomic stability and high-quality growth—the surest and fastest route for reducing poverty. In support of these objectives, the IMF Institute took the lead in organizing a high-level seminar to raise awareness of the macroeconomic pitfalls and trade-offs that can arise in the wake of large new aid inflows. The seminar brought together senior African policymakers, experts from universities and development think tanks, and representatives of the IMF, World Bank, and aid-donor community. This volume presents the papers prepared for the seminar, which was hosted in Maputo by the Government of Mozambique during March 2005, and was cofinanced by the United Kingdom's Department for International Development (DFID) and Germany's Internationale Weiterbildung und Entwicklung gGmbH (InWEnt).

The Maputo seminar recognized the importance of taking maximum advantage of the exceptional opportunity that a significant increase in aid will provide. This will require careful macroeconomic management by aid recipients and supportive efforts by donors.

The papers in this volume address a range of relevant issues:

- The relationship between aid, growth, and poverty reduction.
- The potential for sizable increases in aid to adversely affect competitiveness, and how to avoid this.
- Concerns that aid flows that are volatile, unpredictable, and sometimes procyclical exacerbate macroeconomic stabilization difficulties.
- The impact of higher aid flows on the debt sustainability of recipients.

- The effect of aid on institutions and the political economy in recipient countries.

Ultimately, increased aid presents an opportunity to make major strides in reducing poverty. Improvement will require action by both aid donors and recipients. The IMF will play its part in helping countries manage increased aid flows so as to maintain macroeconomic stability, expand productive capacity, and seize the opportunity to raise standards of living.

I hope that the papers in this volume help in the process of resolving these critical issues. Certainly they open up for debate a number of profound questions that will continue to demand serious attention in the years ahead as we work toward meeting the Millennium Development Goals.

Rodrigo de Rato
Managing Director
International Monetary Fund

Preface

As part of its mandate to enhance the economic policymaking capacity of the Fund's member countries, the IMF Institute periodically organizes seminars at which high-level officials can discuss key policy issues with leading researchers and thinkers from academia and elsewhere. When well designed, the interactive nature of such events benefits both the policymakers and the subsequent research and thinking of the IMF and of outside experts.

Planning for the seminar on "Foreign Aid and Macroeconomic Management" began during the spring of 2004. With the international policy community strongly focused on the need for a large scaling-up of foreign aid and particularly concerned to address the plight of sub-Saharan Africa, the IMF Institute saw scope for a constructive discussion of issues relevant to ensuring that substantially more aid results in substantially more growth and less poverty. Although hardly anyone questions the formidable opportunity that a large increase in aid can provide in helping Africa accelerate growth and poverty reduction, it is critical for policymakers and donors to be well aware of the macroeconomic hazards that must be avoided to ensure that aid is used effectively.

By fall, the African Department of the IMF had agreed to lend its support to the organizing effort; the Government of Mozambique had graciously agreed to host the event and provide logistical support; the United Kingdom's Department for International Development (DFID) and Germany's Internationale Weiterbildung und Entwicklung gGmbH (InWEnt) had expressed strong interests in cofinancing; and an impressive group of experts had accepted invitations to give keynote addresses, present papers, or participate as session chairs or panelists.

In the event, the presentations and general interactions among ministers, central bank governors, and other high-level policymakers, aid donors, and outside experts succeeded remarkably in contributing to a deeper understanding of the key macroeconomic policy challenges associated with foreign aid. The decision to publish this volume reflected both the high quality of the papers prepared for the seminar and the numerous insightful perspectives that were provided during the presentations and general discussions. We have tried to capture many of the valuable perspectives in the overview chapter.

The organization of the seminar required substantial inputs from many people. Valuable contributions to the seminar program, including suggestions for paper presenters and session chairs, were received from Christopher Adam, Catherine Pattillo, and Arvind Subramanian. The African Department of the IMF provided suggestions for keynote speakers and high-level participants, and Mark Lewis did heavy duty in channeling an ongoing stream of logistical questions to appropriate staff in both the African Department and the offices of the IMF's resident representatives in Africa. Perry Perone, the IMF's resident representative in Mozambique, played a key role in liaising with the Mozambican authorities and making the initial arrangements for hotels and other facilities; and two members of his staff in Maputo—Emmy Bosten and Massiquina Calu—put in exhausting efforts over many weeks to ensure that the logistical arrangements worked smoothly. Many Mozambican government officials also devoted considerable time and energy to the organizational efforts. Antonio Laice supervised the government's team, which included Anabela Chambuca, Felix Massangai, Angelo Nhalidede, Manuel Paulo, Otilia Santos, Amilcar de Sousa, and Isabel Sumar.

We are also extremely grateful for the support received from others at the IMF Institute. Prior to the seminar, Eugenia Leonard and Olga Penova were extensively involved for several months—with valuable guidance from Nathalie Kerby-Lachnani and significant help from Jennifer Cook, Thomas Bonaker, Marie Therese Culp, and Deanna Kaufmann—in organizing materials, handling the communications with and administrative arrangements for participants, and dealing with the many frustrations of soliciting responses at long-distance from busy high-level officials. Following the seminar, we relied heavily on the careful and dedicated work of Martha Bonilla, who took charge of the editing and production of the book and recruited David Cheney to help with the editing. And Caryl McNeilly provided a very helpful set of reactions to a draft of the overview chapter.

The views expressed in these papers are those of the authors and do not necessarily represent those of any other institution.

—Peter Isard, Leslie Lipschitz, Alexandros Mourmouras,
Boriana Yontcheva

1

Foreign Aid and Macroeconomic Management

Overview and Synopsis of Key Lessons

PETER ISARD, LESLIE LIPSCHITZ, ALEXANDROS MOURMOURAS, AND BORIANA YONTCHEVA*

I. Introduction

Since the adoption of the Millennium Development Goals (MDGs) in 2000, the challenge of reducing poverty around the world has been more prominent on the agenda of the international community.[1] Relatively slow progress toward meeting the MDGs by the 2015 target date has added to the urgency of this effort. Two influential reports—the United Nations Millennium Project Report (the "Sachs Report") and the Commission for Africa Report (the "Blair Report")—envisage substantial increases in aid flows to poor countries, especially to countries in sub-Saharan Africa. The international community sees increases in aid, along with improvements in recipient policies and freer global trade, as necessary for global prosperity and poverty reduction.

While it seems clear that the MDGs cannot be met without a substantial scaling-up of foreign aid, historical experience provides reason to question whether

*The authors are IMF Institute staff members: Peter Isard, Senior Advisor; Leslie Lipschitz, Director; Alexandros Mourmouras, Division Chief; and Boriana Yontcheva, Economist.

[1] These goals, announced at the United Nations Millennium Summit in September 2000, set targets (in most cases for the period through 2015) for reducing poverty; achieving universal primary education; promoting gender equality and empowering women; reducing child mortality; improving maternal health; combating HIV/AIDS, malaria, and other diseases; ensuring environmental sustainability; and developing a global partnership for development. For details on the MDGs and the definitions of the concepts used, see United Nations (2003).

large increases in aid will translate into large strides toward the MDGs. Aid has indeed facilitated some remarkable successes in helping countries reconstruct or develop rapidly. Major beneficiaries have included the European recipients of Marshall Plan aid following the Second World War, Taiwan Province of China in the 1950s, Botswana and Korea in the 1960s, Indonesia in the 1970s, Bolivia and Ghana in the late 1980s, and Uganda and Vietnam in the 1990s. Aid has also been instrumental in eradicating certain diseases (e.g., river blindness) and clearly has the potential to facilitate large advances toward the MDGs for health and education. But the idea that countries can be lifted out of poverty simply by giving them more foreign aid belies half a century of experience.[2] To maximize the benefits of aid, policymakers and aid donors need to be aware of the important complementarities between aid, policies, and institutions, and to be cognizant of potential macroeconomic hazards to avoid.

The papers in this volume were prepared for a high-level seminar on "Foreign Aid and Macroeconomic Management," which was organized by the IMF Institute and the IMF's African Department, with cofinancing from the United Kingdom's Department for International Development (DFID) and Germany's Internationale Weiterbildung und Entwicklung gGmbH (InWEnt). The seminar was hosted in Maputo by the Government of Mozambique in March 2005. In opening the seminar, Prime Minister Luisa Dias Diogo emphasized that issues of macroeconomic management were complex and not conducive to simple solutions, that these issues were likely to become more challenging with a substantial scaling-up of aid, and that high-level seminars and other efforts aimed at strengthening the capacity for macroeconomic management were very important. Abdoulaye Bio-Tchané (IMF African Department) expressed similar views in his opening remarks, stressing the importance of strengthening not only the specific institutions of macroeconomic management but also the basic institutions and governance processes that support the rule of law.

The seminar brought together high-level African officials, experts from the academic community, and policymakers from the aid-donor community. While many issues relating to the efficient and effective management of aid were discussed in passing—for example, the scale of financial flows needed to meet the MDGs, and the short-run trade-offs between growth-enhancing infrastructure spending and social spending on health and education—the main focus of the seminar was on how to identify and forestall any adverse macroeconomic effects from a large-scale increase in aid flows. Do aid-receiving countries have the capacity to absorb a substantial scaling-up of aid flows? Does donor specification of the timing of spending and the precise sectoral allocation exacerbate the absorption problem? Could a substantial increase in aid shift relative prices in a way that would be detrimental to export competitiveness and longer-term growth prospects? What microeconomic constraints underlie the potential

[2] Easterly (2001).

macroeconomic hazards from scaling up aid? Will the scaling-up of aid exacerbate its volatility and unpredictability? What about the impact of higher aid flows on the debt sustainability of low-income recipients? And what is the effect of aid on institutions and the political economy in recipient countries?

This chapter provides a summary and synthesis of the perspectives that emerged from the papers and discussions in Maputo. Section II places the discussion of the macroeconomic hazards of aid in a broader context. It examines the nexus between aid, growth, and poverty reduction, which was the topic of the first session of the seminar. Section III of this chapter considers the issue of aid-induced Dutch disease—that is, the possible link between aid inflows and a deterioration of the recipient country's competitiveness in global markets—and the associated challenge of mitigating absorptive capacity constraints. It also addresses the trade-offs between different categories of aid-financed spending and the case for frontloading development assistance. This is followed by discussions of the volatility and unpredictability of aid in Section IV, and of debt sustainability and the choice between loans and grants in Section V. Section VI turns to the connection between aid and institutional quality along with the themes that rang through the three keynote speeches. Section VII summarizes the perspectives provided by the panelists in the final session of the seminar, and Section VIII pulls together the main policy messages that emerged from the discussions. The Appendix contains comments on some technical issues raised by the papers presented in Maputo.

II. Aid, Growth, and Poverty Reduction

Aid and Growth

The literature on the effectiveness of aid in promoting growth and poverty reduction is large and inconclusive: thus far, empirical studies have not found strong evidence of a robust and positive aid-growth relationship. The econometric work presented in Maputo provided new perspectives but did not lead to consensus on the effectiveness of aid in promoting growth. Some of the new evidence indicated that the relationship between certain types of aid and growth was more favorable than earlier literature had suggested; other empirical work painted a more pessimistic picture. The discussion was lively, and the debate remained unresolved.

The paper presented by Steven Radelet (Center for Global Development)[3] challenged the disappointing results of most aid effectiveness studies by questioning the appropriateness of basing analysis on an aggregate of all types of aid, which is the standard approach used in the literature. The authors (Radelet, Clemens, and Bhavnani) stress that many types of aid either are given for worthy

[3] Chapter 2 of this volume.

causes that have little to do with economic growth (e.g., humanitarian relief after floods, earthquakes, or other natural disasters; and aid to help democracy) or contribute to growth with long lags that short-run data cannot capture (e.g., spending on education and health). By contrast, aid to fund basic infrastructure or to support agriculture and industry ought to elicit higher growth after fairly short time lags. The absence of a strong link between aid and growth in the findings of many studies may reflect the failure to distinguish between these different types of aid.

Radelet and his coauthors therefore disaggregate aid into three types: humanitarian assistance; early-impact aid to finance infrastructure and direct investments in agriculture and other sectors; and late-impact aid to finance investments in human and social capital. Worldwide, early-impact aid averaged about 2 ½ percent of recipient country GDP between 1973 and 2001, and about 5 percent of GDP in Africa. Drawing on previous work,[4] Radelet's paper reported strong and robust evidence that early-impact aid exerts a powerful effect on growth. For the typical recipient, a 1 percentage point of GDP increase in this type of aid produces an additional 0.31 percentage point of annual growth over a four-year period. This is two to three times higher than previously estimated. By contrast, Radelet and coauthors find no clear influence of long-impact aid on growth and a negative relationship between humanitarian relief and growth, as the latter category of aid is often triggered by adverse growth shocks. They also find that the effect of aid on growth is more pronounced in countries with stronger institutions and longer life expectancy.

Radelet argued that high aid-to-GDP ratios in Africa ought not to alarm us: they reflect low incomes rather than generous aid.[5] Crucially, however, the effect of aid on growth is subject to diminishing returns, so that raising aid beyond some point does not add appreciably to growth. He estimated that, for the typical country, the aid saturation point is 8–9 percent of GDP for early-impact aid; this corresponds approximately to 16–18 percent of GDP for total aid. For some countries, these results may be good news: they suggest that there is substantial room to scale up aid from present levels without bumping into severe capacity constraints. However, the influence of each additional dollar of aid will be lower than that of the previous dollar.

In discussing Radelet's paper, Arvind Subramanian (IMF Research Department) emphasized the need for caution in assessing the growth effects of large aid packages and challenged Radelet's findings based on evidence from Rajan and Subramanian (2005). The latter paper examines whether labor-intensive industries (those in which a poor, developing country should have a compara-

---

[4] Clemens, Radelet, and Bhavnani (2004).

[5] As Radelet noted, per capita aid in Africa is about $30 per person, or one-third of what Korea received during 1955–75 and about one-fourth of aid to Botswana during the last quarter century.

tive advantage) grow relatively more slowly than other industries in countries that receive more aid. It employs an empirical methodology that exploits variation both within countries and across countries, and finds that aid inflows systematically undermine the competitiveness of labor-intensive export sectors, as reflected in a decline in the share of labor-intensive and tradable goods industries in the manufacturing sector. This result is not surprising at the theoretical level; it is consistent with most conventional models and with recent independent work by Arellano and others (2005) based on a calibrated real business cycle general equilibrium model. But the Rajan and Subramanian paper is remarkable for the robustness of the detrimental allocative effects of aid and the finding that these may occur without appreciable changes in the real exchange rate. Any link between aid and reduced export competitiveness is extremely important, Subramanian argued, because export-led growth has been so central to most successful development strategies.

Several participants raised a separate challenge to Radelet's conclusions based on the notion that aid is *fungible*. If aid is fungible—that is, if recipient governments can reallocate domestic resources in response to aid inflows—attempts to channel it to specific projects or sectors will be frustrated, the composition of public spending will remain that favored by the government, and the intended growth effects of aid might not be realized. Fungibility would not be an issue if the government's objective were to maximize social welfare and if donors and recipients had completely coincident views on how to do so. But in many developing countries the composition of public spending is biased against the poor and against growth. One explanation (Olson, 1965) recognizes the political pressure incumbents face—even in democratic regimes—from organized interest groups. These groups have power to influence the allocation of public resources in their favor, which is welfare-reducing as far as the general public is concerned (Dixit, Grossman, and Helpman, 1997).

Radelet argued that his results amounted to evidence that aid was not fully fungible, since the estimated effects of different categories of aid on growth are very different, implying that aid intended for different purposes has dramatically different relationships with growth. Goodall Gondwe (Ministry of Finance, Malawi) and others voiced support for Radelet's finding, noting that finance ministers cannot completely circumvent the allocative conditions attached to aid.

Radelet's paper also provoked questions about methodology. T.N. Srinivasan (Yale University) wondered whether the use of cross-section regression analysis was the right approach for analyzing the effects of aid on growth. Most developing countries had done very well until the oil shock of the early 1970s. One could argue that the global environment changed around that time, and that the change has had an impact on the development process. In Srinivasan's view, changes in donors' objectives and recipients' capacities and interests in receiving aid can affect the relationship between aid and growth but are not captured in cross-section regressions.

Among others who commented on methodology, Tertius Zongo (Ambassador to the United States, Burkina Faso) noted that a careful appraisal of the growth effects of aid required evaluation of the effectiveness of public spending, and Nancy Birdsall (Center for Global Development) emphasized the importance of looking at the impacts on productivity in assessing whether the growth effects were sustainable. Aart Kraay (Development Research Group, World Bank) added the perspective that cross-country regressions assessed the effects of aid, both directly and through its interaction with policies, after controlling for a host of factors, including institutions; but they did not shed light on the effects of aid on institutions and policies. The channels through which aid matters for institutions and policies are not well understood, but are an important agenda for research.

Aid and Poverty Reduction

Along with analyzing the effectiveness of aid in promoting growth, economists have sought a better understanding of the link between aid and poverty alleviation. Aid can make a direct contribution to poverty reduction. It can also have an indirect effect through its impact on investment, employment, market opportunities, and institutions. Kraay's paper (Chapter 3) addresses the effects of aid on poverty using household survey data from a large sample of developing countries.[6] A key result, which is corroborated by other studies, is that growth is the overwhelmingly predominant force behind poverty reduction: 97 percent of the cross-country variation in changes in poverty can be attributed to cross-country differences in growth, and virtually none of the variation to changes in relative incomes. More controversial, perhaps, is the finding that the impact on poverty of pro-poor growth strategies that explicitly seek to speedily improve the quality of life for the poor is not much different from that of other growth strategies. The latter finding provoked David Bevan (Centre for the Study of African Economies, Oxford) to point out that different countries have very different income distributions. Bevan regarded the view that almost all poverty reduction comes from economic growth—and that the only way to reduce poverty is through the growth process—as a form of extreme pessimism about the feasibility of altering a country's income distribution. He acknowledged that income distributions may be heavily influenced by culture and institutions, but he was somewhat more sanguine about the possibility of change.

A second key result is that the contribution of aid to poverty reduction—both directly and through its effect on growth—is quantitatively small. In a ver-

[6] Kraay first calculates changes in an index of poverty (the headcount measure) and changes in income or consumption. He then decomposes changes in poverty into "growth" and "income distribution" components, and employs variance decompositions to ascertain the relative importance of these two components.

sion of Burnside and Dollar's (2000) cross-country regression, Kraay finds that only 4 percent of the variance in growth is explained by aid, either directly or through its interaction with the quality of policies. By contrast, policies by themselves account for 10 percent of the variation in growth and institutions account for another 7 percent, while more than 60 percent cannot be explained by the specified regression. This underscores the need to better understand the nonaid drivers of growth, including institutions and policies, and how aid can support them.

Along with many other economists, Kraay views governance problems as a significant constraint on growth and poverty reduction in Africa, noting the poor performance of sub-Saharan Africa on measures of governance and the lack of improvement in recent years. He advocates tackling these problems as part of the effort to scale up aid to the continent. He takes issue with the suggestion (e.g., by Sachs and others, 2004) that governance is not an important concern in thinking about scaling up aid to Africa. He also recommends more research on how aid effectiveness can be enhanced by linking aid allocations to measurable improvements in governance. And while the direct poverty-reducing effect of aid through income redistribution appears small, Kraay argues that aid can be successful in addressing *nonincome* poverty—including through public health and other social spending for which long-term growth effects are hard to quantify.

Poverty Traps

Underdevelopment and poverty tend to be persistent. Countries often stay in a vicious circle of poverty for a long time. This might be taken to suggest that poverty is an equilibrium state and that there are forces at work that keep a poor country from developing (Basu, 2000, p. 17). A variety of technological, economic, and political mechanisms can generate such poverty traps. Endogenous growth theory suggests several such channels, which are surveyed by Kraay. For example, financial market imperfections could combine with lumpy investment needs to keep a country's capital stock (broadly defined to include human and physical capital) inefficiently low. This could rob a country of the ability to exploit economies of scale, causing sub-par growth and persistent poverty (Galor and Zeira, 1993). A scaling-up of aid could help a country break free from a low-income equilibrium if the problem involves threshold expenditure needs combined with a lack of resources.

Kraay cites a number of econometric studies that have used a variety of methods and data to look for evidence that poverty traps arise from the existence of investment or savings thresholds that must be overcome. These studies cast doubt on the notion that financial imperfections in combination with lumpy investment needs are responsible for persistent poverty, or that poverty can generally be attributed to low saving by poor countries. As Radelet argued, however, the anecdotal evidence of poverty traps seems particularly strong for the landlocked countries of the Sahara desert, which have been among the poorest countries of the world for centuries and lack opportunities to produce agricultural goods or labor-intensive manufactures. Moreover, Kraay is sympathetic toward the idea that poverty traps could arise from governance problems or from internal or external conflicts. If the problems are conflicts, corruption, or rent seeking facilitated by weak institutions, the success of a "big push" for development would require that these challenges be addressed together with resource needs.

The presentations by Radelet, Kraay, and Subramanian provoked Leslie Lipschitz (IMF Institute) to pose a number of questions. What did Radelet's finding of diminishing returns imply about the aid levels envisaged in the United Nations Millennium Project Report and the Commission for Africa Report? Was the case for a large scaling-up of aid undermined by Kraay's finding that aid explains only a small part of economic growth? Could a big scaling-up of aid be justified if one accepted Kraay's evidence that growth failures could not be blamed on poverty traps caused by threshold expenditure needs? Did the adverse effects of aid on competitiveness, as reported by Subramanian, offset the positive short-run effects of aid found by Radelet?

The discussion of these questions helped generate clarity on several important points. Participants agreed that the urgency of scaling up aid to Africa does not depend on whether poverty traps are relevant or not. However, the absence of poverty traps combined with diminishing returns to aid suggests that substantially scaled-up aid is unlikely to have proportionately much larger growth benefits than small increases in aid; moreover, the detrimental competitiveness considerations raised by Subramanian were particularly relevant to large increases.[7] Also, as emphasized throughout the seminar, the effectiveness of aid depends on much more than its scale. Thus, while the available evidence does not imply that a large scaling-up of aid is a bad idea, it does suggest a need to question unfounded optimism based on the notion of favorable discontinuities in the aid-growth relationship, and to be aware of, and guard against, the various factors that could reduce the effectiveness of aid. While Africa needs and can use more aid, it is not likely that aid will deliver a growth miracle unless other enabling conditions are also in place.

[7] Some participants took issue with this assessment. They thought that saving and technological traps were important in Africa. Situmbeko Musokotwame (Ministry of Finance and National Planning, Zambia) suggested that a large scaling-up of aid for Africa could have effects analogous to those of the Marshall Plan for Europe after World War II. Others countered that Europe in 1945 was a very different place than Africa is today. In particular, although much of its hard infrastructure had been destroyed during the war, Europe still had in place all of the knowledge and much of the human capital and other soft infrastructure needed to make aid effective. Many African countries may have less capacity to absorb large quantities of aid.

III. Aid Hazards Part I: Dutch Disease

Sessions II and III of the seminar focused on the macroeconomic challenge of avoiding the potential hazard of Dutch disease. Participants also addressed the related challenge of expanding absorptive capacity to address the microeconomic underpinnings of Dutch disease, the trade-offs between different types of aid-financed spending, and the implications of frontloading development assistance.

Dutch Disease: Conceptual Frameworks and Evidence

The debate about aid-induced Dutch disease centers on concerns that large inflows of aid could act like natural resource discoveries, inducing a real appreciation of the currency—either through inflation or nominal exchange rate changes—and reducing the competitiveness of exports.[8] To the extent that aid is used to purchase nontradable goods and services that are in short supply, the aid-induced increase in demand drives up the prices of these nontradables and shifts resources out of traded goods sectors. This could hurt development: for many countries successful development strategies have relied on exports to global markets as an engine of diversification and growth. Export production has also been an important source of productivity gains through learning by doing and other positive external effects.

In theory, the effects of aid on the allocation of domestic resources will depend on how the aid is used. It is useful to consider a few stylized cases.

First, suppose aid is used to buy traded goods that would not otherwise have been purchased (owing, presumably, to a dearth of foreign currency). In this case the real resource transfer intended by the provision of aid is effected immediately, the available supply of traded goods is increased, and this should enhance consumption in the recipient country and production to the extent that the imported goods are complementary to domestic goods in the production process.[9] There is no inflationary effect or loss of competitiveness.

Second, suppose that the aid prompts an increase in government spending on nontraded goods, but that the supply of these goods is infinitely elastic over the relevant range of demand because of unemployed resources. Again, there will be no inflation or real appreciation, and the effects of the spending will be wholly

---

[8] Dutch disease refers to the adverse effects of booming natural resource sectors on manufacturing production and exports. See Corden (1984), Gelb (1988), and Agénor and Montiel (2000). Bulíř and Lane (2002) draw attention to the possibility of aid-induced Dutch disease in their discussion of the macroeconomic and fiscal implications of aid.

[9] Of course, to the extent that domestic goods compete with imports there may be some secondary detrimental impact, but this can be ignored here.

positive. A question arises in this case, however, as to whether the positive effects are related to aid *qua* aid, or simply to increased government spending. There has been no transfer of resources from abroad—that is, net imports have not increased (except perhaps as a secondary effect)—and the same positive effect on economic activity could have been achieved by simply monetizing an increase in government expenditure that succeeded in eliciting a real supply response.

Third, suppose the aid leads to spending on nontraded goods and a consequent increase in the relative price of these goods—that is, a real appreciation—along with a shift of productive resources from the traded-goods sector to firms producing nontraded goods. Again, to the extent that aid is spent on nontraded goods, it does not elicit any real resource transfer from abroad. The inflationary consequences depend on the stance of monetary policy. If the additional spending is supported by a monetization of the increased foreign exchange received as aid (thereby giving the central bank more reserves as a cushion against future balance of payments needs), the increase in the relative price of nontraded goods will come about through inflation. Alternatively, if the monetary effects of the additional government spending are sterilized by selling the foreign exchange, there will be no inflationary impact from money creation but the nominal value of domestic currency will appreciate. In either case there will be a loss of competitiveness.

Clearly, it is this third case that commands much of the attention in the debate about aid-induced Dutch disease. The papers of Bevan and Christopher Adam (Centre for the Study of African Economies, Oxford)[10] draw on earlier joint work with a dynamic general equilibrium model of the effects of aid-financed investment in infrastructure on the real exchange rate and competitiveness.[11] The simulations reported by Adam assume—in contrast to the work of Rajan and Subramanian (2005) and Arellano and others (2005)—that aid-induced spending enhances the productivity of private factors of production. Under this assumption, an aid-induced expansion of public investment can increase long-term welfare and growth in the export sector of the economy even if it is associated with some initial real appreciation. The effect of aid-financed public infrastructure on resource allocation and competitiveness depends on the nature of the associated productivity boost. If the productivity boost favors nontradables, it could offset the appreciation of the exchange rate and explain why Dutch disease is not observed. If, on the other hand, aid raises productivity in the production of nontraditional exports more than that in tra-

[10] Chapters 4 and 7.

[11] This model (Adam and Bevan, 2004) is calibrated to Ugandan data and features several production sectors, several factors of production, and learning-by-doing externalities à la Arrow (1962) and Matsuyama (1992). The economy is closed to capital flows other than aid, so that domestic saving plus the aid-financed current account deficit equals domestic investment in each period.

ditional exports and nontradables, it will likely boost the profitability of producing nontraditional exports and attract domestic resources into their production. In these circumstances, any adverse short-term effect on traditional exports will be offset over time by the growth of the nontraditional export sector, and the overall effect on growth will generally be positive.

In commenting on these results, a question was raised as to whether aid per se is relevant to the growth effects of government spending on nontraded infrastructure. As there is no net transfer of resources from abroad at the time of the spending increase, the spending and the subsequent productivity gains could as well be financed simply by domestic means—borrowing or monetization—without any difference in macroeconomic effects in that period. The only case in which a critical distinction arises between aid-financed and domestically financed infrastructure investment is when the level of foreign exchange reserves is so low as to constitute a threat to confidence and a disincentive to any bold policy action by the government.

Monetary and Fiscal Policy Responses to Aid Inflows and the Case of Ghana

The analysis of Dutch disease, and of the macroeconomic effects of aid more generally, is clarified by considering how monetary and fiscal policies respond to the aid. The paper presented by Andrew Berg (IMF Policy Development and Review Department)[12] uses a case study of Ghana to examine the macroeconomic policy responses to scaled-up aid inflows in 2001–03. The authors (Aiyar, Berg, Hussain, Mahone, and Roache) note that aid inflows rose during this period but were volatile and unpredictable, fluctuating by several percentage points of GDP from year to year. Aid exceeded predictions in 2001, followed by a sharp drop the next year and a greater-than-predicted resurgence in 2003. Ghana went into the three-year episode with relatively weak macroeconomic conditions, including high inflation and public debt, very low international reserves, and a large domestic financing requirement for the budget.

The government of Ghana adjusted its monetary and fiscal policies in response to the variability of aid, and the central bank accumulated substantial quantities of foreign exchange reserves. In 2001, the top priority was the achievement of macroeconomic stabilization. To this end, the authorities limited the budgetary spending of the aid surprise and sought to lower inflation by selling some of the foreign exchange in the market to strengthen the domestic currency and help reduce money growth. With reserves still fairly low at end–2001, the collapse of aid during 2002 led to an easing of monetary policy and a renewal of government borrowing from the central bank, as the fiscal position contracted by less than the aid decline. Following the consequent

[12] Chapter 5.

acceleration of currency depreciation and inflation, the authorities again confronted a need to stabilize. Having been stung by the sharp drop in aid during 2002, the authorities chose to build up their foreign exchange reserves by more than the aid surprise during 2003 and to mop up liquidity through sales of Treasury bills and an increase in reserve requirements for domestic banks. While the accumulation of a foreign exchange cushion was understandable in light of the volatility and unpredictability of aid, Ghana's macroeconomic policy might have been more successful during 2003—including in meeting the objective of bringing the domestic debt ratio down substantially—had the authorities been less aggressive in accumulating reserves.

Relaxing Absorptive Capacity Constraints

In considering the operational implications of the prospect of Dutch disease, it is critical to recognize that the macroeconomic problem of limited absorptive capacity is rooted in microeconomic frictions. Government spending programs should take into account the presence of these constraints, which requires sector- and even firm-specific information. As Bevan stresses, before additional resources are poured into priority sectors, judgments are needed as to whether existing resources are being used effectively; if they are not, the problems must be diagnosed and solved or else there is little point in scaling up aid to these sectors.

This raises the difficult question of how to recognize capacity constraints. Sometimes, constraints can be easily identified. A simple headcount might be adequate in assessing whether there are enough trained personnel to expand social services. In most cases, however, such assessments are more difficult: the existence of capacity constraints may only become clear after outcomes deteriorate, projects fail to deliver planned results, and resources are thus wasted. Bevan is pessimistic about the feasibility of forward-looking diagnoses. Ideally, inputs could be monitored closely, and capacity constraints identified ex ante through activity-based budgeting and other means. But in practice, these approaches are informationally demanding and are probably not easy to implement, especially in countries with limited capacity. The good news, according to Bevan, is that this is recognized in recent public expenditure management strategies that aim at satisficing rather than achieving best practice. And, as others noted, because aid is a process—with expenditures in any sector typically occurring in tranches over time—it is sometimes both feasible and desirable to make early and mid-course corrections in spending plans, based both on current results and a forward-looking assessment. This process of periodic forward-looking evaluation is similar to that used by monetary authorities in operating inflation targeting regimes.

One of the factors that contributes to absorptive capacity constraints is the lack of coordination in many aid-related activities, particularly in social services. The government, bilateral and multilateral donors, and international and domestic nongovernment organizations (NGOs) all deliver services in aid-recipient countries and compete for skilled personnel and other scarce human resources. This competition sometimes leads to either bottlenecks or inefficient allocations. A key challenge is to find ways in which aid can be used to remove bottlenecks while simultaneously allowing better utilization of spare capacity. An aid-financed program for building some critical roads, for example, can eliminate a bottleneck to marketing agricultural produce and allow more complete utilization of arable land and rural labor. Very large competing road projects, however, could result in excess demand for certain types of skills, suck resources out of the agricultural and export sectors, increase wages, and reduce international competitiveness. Clearly, finding an appropriate balance between these outcomes is essential to success.

Allocative Trade-Offs and the Frontloading of Aid

Estimates of the amount of aid required to achieve the MDGs must be regarded as highly tentative, given the deficiencies in our knowledge and the various factors that can influence the effectiveness of aid. Such estimates can nevertheless be informative, particularly to the extent that they shed light on the trade-offs among different types of aid-financed public spending and the implications of frontloading assistance to low-income countries. The paper presented by Mark Sundberg (Development Economics, World Bank)[13] explores these issues using an approach that is similar to that of Adam. The authors (Sundberg, Lofgren, and Bourguignon) calibrate a World Bank dynamic general equilibrium model to Ethiopian data and use it to assess alternative approaches to meeting the MDGs.[14] Meeting the MDGs requires both basic infrastructure and social services (health, education, and water sanitation). Spending on infrastructure helps achieve the objective of cutting in half (between 1990 and 2015) the proportion of people whose income is less than $1 a day. Social spending helps achieve the other MDGs. The paper considers the trade-offs between infrastructure and social spending as well as the implications of alternative time profiles for the various components of expenditure.

According to the simulations generated by Sundberg and his coauthors, the cost-minimizing strategy for achieving the MDGs turns out to combine a

[13] Chapter 6.

[14] Sundberg and others limit attention to the requirements for achieving the MDGs for poverty alleviation, education, mortality rates, and access to safe water and basic sanitation. Their model includes a considerable amount of sectoral detail and assumes that aid "works" in the sense of being channeled fully into spending on specified goods and services. Aid has supply and demand effects, including on productivity, real wages, relative prices, and competitiveness.

front-loaded expansion in infrastructure spending with constantly growing social spending. It also involves accelerating spending on education to increase skilled labor quickly, as human capital investments take a long time to mature. Implementing this strategy would require raising aid to $60 per capita or 40 percent of Ethiopia's GDP, roughly twice the level of aid per capita to sub-Saharan Africa in the early 1990s.

Seminar participants agreed on the need for careful analysis of the microeconomic and sectoral effects of aid to ensure that it helps the economy get on a path to higher productivity and, ultimately, self-sustaining growth out of aid dependence. It was also recognized that the difficulties of growing out of aid dependence in part reflected factors that discouraged private entrepreneurship. Alan Gelb (Development Policy, World Bank) noted that a multitude of factors raise the costs of private activity in Africa to high levels, including regulatory red tape and a range of indirect costs, such as lack of reliable power and logistics, inadequate port facilities, and security failures. He emphasized that there is considerable scope for African countries to reduce these regulatory and indirect business costs and raise the productivity of the nontradables sectors that provide services to export sectors. Some crude verification was provided by Sundberg's simulations of the implications of improving the productivity of public services at a rate of 2 percent annually: there was a huge benefit from the advance in public efficiency, because it improved the use of all resources, not just the effectiveness of aid. Gelb argued that if indirect business costs came down to levels seen in other countries, African firms could offset the effects on exports of any aid-induced real appreciation and raise wages by as much as 50 percent. What is worrying, in Gelb's view, is that we have seen so little progress in reducing these indirect costs over the past decade.

Seminar participants also agreed on the need to give policymakers more flexibility in allocating aid, and to guard against excessive aid-financed spending on "flavor-of-the-day" projects or sectors. Sundberg's study makes the point that there may be technical, microeconomic reasons why aid-financed infrastructure spending should be more frontloaded than social spending. Raising productivity in social sectors may be difficult, both because of the nature of the goods and services that these sectors produce and because of governance issues. In addition, a massive increase in social-sector spending would pose the risk of repressing nontraditional exports. The donor community must avoid putting all its aid money into sectors that cannot absorb it. Donors should coordinate and consult with each other and with policymakers in recipient countries to identify those areas where aid-financed spending can be used productively.

IV. Aid Hazards Part II: Volatility and Unpredictability

Absorptive capacity constraints and the prospect of Dutch disease raise the prospect that aid can be detrimental to macroeconomic performance unless its use is carefully planned and monitored. Efforts to plan the effective use of aid may be largely for naught, however, when aid flows are highly volatile and unpredictable. As emphasized by Goodall Gondwe, Manuel Chang (Ministry of Finance, Mozambique), Kassoum Karamoune (Ministry of Economics and Finance, Niger), and several other seminar participants, volatile and unpredictable aid flows cause major problems for budget management and macroeconomic stabilization in many countries. Unanticipated declines in aid confront policymakers with a choice between two unattractive options. They can adjust the scale of budget expenditures to the resources available. This is economically and politically costly as its forces policymakers to scale down, postpone, or abandon projects that are typically important for promoting growth and maintaining macroeconomic stability. Alternatively, they can continue financing essential spending through money creation or domestic borrowing, thereby putting macroeconomic stability at risk.

In addressing the hazards of volatile and unpredictable aid, the seminar focused on the empirical evidence, the causes of erratic flows, and various suggestions and initiatives for mitigating and dealing with the problems.

The Evidence

The volatility and unpredictability in aid disbursements is documented in the paper presented by Aleš Bulíř (IMF Policy Development and Review Department),[15] which takes a fresh look at the variability of aid relative to that of domestic fiscal revenues using annual data from a large number of developing countries.[16] The authors (Bulíř and Hamann) examine whether the statistical properties of aid have changed since the late 1990s, when several initiatives were introduced aimed at improving program design and implementation.[17] In addition to asking whether aid flows have become less variable and more predictable, they examine both the general cyclical properties of aid and the question of whether or not aid acts as a shock absorber or implicit insurance mechanism—in particular, whether it rises when countries are buffeted by negative shocks to GDP.

Bulíř and Hamann's findings may be summarized as follows.

First, aid has continued to be more volatile than domestic revenue: the aid-to-GDP ratio in the median aid-recipient country is significantly more

[15] Chapter 8.

[16] Relative variability is the ratio of the variance of aid to the variance of revenues, where aid and revenues are logs of detrended ratios to GDP.

[17] These included the enhanced Heavily Indebted Poor Countries (HIPC) Initiative; the sharpening diagnoses of poverty, broader participatory processes, and enhanced focus on macroeconomic policy design (all part of programs under the Poverty Reduction and Growth Facility); and ostensibly improvements in cooperation among donors.

volatile than the ratio of revenues to GDP.[18] Second, compared with the 1970s and 1980s, aid became more volatile in the 1990s and has remained so during the first half of the present decade. It thus appears that the delivery of aid has not been smoothed by the initiatives of the late 1990s.

A third finding is that aid unpredictability—as measured by the ratio of aid commitments to aid disbursements—has risen since the late 1990s. Actual aid delivery falls short of promises by more than 40 percent. Moreover, aid is more unpredictable the less developed is the recipient country. The finding that aid-recipient countries with higher incomes receive a larger share of promised aid than countries with lower incomes is disturbing: the poorest countries, which need aid the most, can least depend on aid actually arriving.

Bulíř and Hamann also ask whether aid has contributed to economic stability by smoothing out adverse income shocks in low-income countries. In fact, they find that aid is as likely to decrease as it is to increase in the wake of a negative GDP shock.

Several participants posed questions about the measurement of aid volatility. Bevan noted that relative aid volatility could increase because aid became more volatile or because domestic revenues became less volatile. A number of countries had shifted from extensive reliance on volatile trade tax revenues—which were affected by the terms of trade, weather, and other shocks—to broad-based sources of revenues such as value-added taxes, which were more stable. He was interested in how much of the increase in relative aid volatility reflected a reduction in revenue volatility rather than increase in aid volatility. Bulíř responded that about 75 percent of the increase in relative aid volatility was due to an increase in aid volatility and 25 percent due to a decline in revenue volatility.

Some participants took issue with Bulíř's choice of the aid-to-revenue ratio as the metric of aid volatility. Adam argued that there was no single appropriate measure of aid instability—several alternative measures could be useful depending on one's perspective. From the point of view of donors, aid volatility could be measured in terms of donor currency units, in relation to donor budgetary expenditure, or relative to donor GDP. From the point of view of recipients, aid volatility needed to be measured in relation to the overall volatility of the recipient's economy, which depends on trade and other shocks. From the recipient's side, the dominant question was whether adding aid to budgetary resources increased or decreased the smoothing problem faced by governments. Adam wondered whether focusing on the aid-to-domestic revenue ratio led analysts to miss any important covariance effects. Data measurement issues were also relevant. He asked whether the arrival of HIPC

[18] The extent to which aid volatility increases with the degree of aid dependency (as measured by the aid-to-GDP ratio) is, however, ambiguous and sensitive to the particular statistical techniques used.

completion points or other debt forgiveness or restructuring contributed to measured volatility.

Causes and Consequences

A number of factors can contribute to the volatility and unpredictability of aid disbursements in the short run—that is, within the budget year or the normal short-run cycle. The instability of donor commitments, or of donor disbursements relative to commitments, can reflect changes in technical evaluations or political priorities, the workings of donor budget mechanisms, or administrative bottlenecks. Short-run volatility can also arise from the failure of recipients to comply with the conditions specified in IMF-supported or other donor-supported programs.[19] IMF conditions are especially important as many donors base their disbursement decisions on whether or not the IMF signals that macroeconomic policies are on track. From that perspective, Gondwe argued that the quarterly frequency of signals from the IMF under some lending facilities was excessive and part of the volatility problem.

Delays in the arrival of budgeted aid cause mismatches between government receipts and planned expenditures. In many poor countries with shallow financial markets, such mismatches are difficult to manage. Short-run aid volatility then translates either into expenditure volatility—especially for those categories of spending that are relatively easy to postpone (e.g., repairs, maintenance, and investment)—or into additional money creation or debt issuance. As Gelb noted, postponement of spending is costly not only in a direct sense, but also because it weakens the general discipline of government operations, since spending units cannot be held responsible for meeting targets unless they have sufficient resources to carry out their tasks. And as Adam and several other participants emphasized, money creation and debt issuance can cause aid volatility to spill over into volatility in inflation, interest rates, and exchange rates.

As one way to gauge the welfare costs of the volatility, unpredictability, and procyclicality of aid, Arellano and others (2005) use a calibrated real business cycle model to estimate that households would be willing to forgo ¾ of 1 percent of their aid receipts if the remaining aid was provided in a constant stream. For countries where aid receipts are roughly one-fourth as large as GDP, this estimate is comparable in magnitude (as a percent of GDP) to estimates of the welfare cost of business cycle variability in the United States (see for comparison Lucas, 1987; and İmrohoroğlu, 1989). Households would be willing to sacrifice considerably more in exchange for a countercyclical aid stream that offsets the effects of productivity shocks.

[19] About one-half of aid volatility seems attributable to recipients' failure to meet policy conditions (Gelb and Eifert, 2005).

Longer-Term Aid Inconstancy

Careful planning to maximize the effectiveness of aid would be difficult even in the absence of short-run volatility and unpredictability. Bevan's overview paper focuses, inter alia, on longer-term aid inconstancy and provides perspectives on the policy issues it poses for aid-recipient countries. To provide a baseline for discussion, Bevan notes that in an ideal world, donors would precommit to reducing aid flows gradually over time as recipient countries developed, and recipients would have the flexibility to spend the aid when they saw fit. Decisions about whether to spend or save a particular aid flow would depend on whether the flow was permanent or transitory. In the long-run, the aid relationship would end.

The real world is different. Donors are not always able to deliver aid according to predetermined timetables, while recipients have limited flexibility to decide when to spend aid receipts. Donors are now challenged to raise transfers to help poor countries achieve the MDGs, which implies that there must ultimately be a correspondingly larger exit from aid. Bevan emphasizes that managing this particular type of aid inconstancy would be difficult even in the absence of short-run volatility. The reasons are familiar from the experiences that developing countries have had in managing surges of income from natural resources. Many countries have experienced resource-related income surges, have understood the transitory nature of these revenues, and have faced no external constraints on using them. Despite this, they have not always had the expertise to manage such flows effectively. Managing large aid inflows could give rise to similar or more pronounced challenges. Recipients have even less control over aid than over resource income and are sometimes forced to react to aid surges by reducing domestic taxes or raising expenditures, which can be problematic in the longer run.

Mitigating Aid Volatility Problems

Seminar participants discussed several types of measures that could mitigate the difficulties posed by the short-run volatility and unpredictability of aid. Donors could try harder to disburse aid according to agreed timetables and to improve coordination, while recipient countries could try harder to meet the conditions upon which disbursements often depend. In addition, aid recipients could be given more flexibility to decide whether to spend or save aid flows on the basis of judgments about the time profile of future aid flows and the capacity of the economy to absorb an increase in spending in the short run. Such judgments must be made on a case-by-case basis, taking into account country-specific information—including, inter alia, the historical relationship between aid commitments and disbursements.

Several participants reflected on Ghana's strategy during 2001–03—discussed in the paper presented by Berg—in responding to unanticipated fluctuations in aid. Ghana had chosen to avoid spending positive aid surprises in order to build reserves and help bring down inflation. Gelb wondered whether it made sense, as a general response to aid that is volatile and interferes with government operations, to always pursue a conservative fiscal policy, as Ghana had done. In his view, the case for treating positive aid surprises as temporary and negative aid surprises as permanent depended on many factors, including the level of a country's international reserves. Countries facing large and volatile aid inflows ought to build foreign exchange reserves and to strengthen fiscal accounts so as to provide cushions for governments to buffer transitory aid shocks and avoid major disruptions of spending plans.

Catherine Pattillo (IMF African Department) argued that more needed to be done to improve our understanding of the causes of aid instability and its consequences. She favored developing a body of case studies to ascertain the sources of aid volatility. Pinpointing the root causes of aid volatility—whether its was due to shifts in donors' political priorities, the failure of recipients to meet specific conditions, or administrative procedures—would matter a great deal for identifying solutions to the problem.

That said, Pattillo offered some thoughts on how donors and recipients could reduce aid volatility and its effects. On the donor side, she proposed dealing with breaches of conditionality by reducing future aid commitments rather than by imposing immediate aid cutbacks. This suggestion would reduce endogenous aid volatility but needed to be examined more thoroughly, and with consideration to the possibility of time inconsistency problems. A second suggestion was for donors to link their aid forecasts more closely to historical experience and to be more transparent with governments. Donors could also do more to coordinate their aid processes, for example, by agreeing to let one donor take the lead in providing aid to a particular sector and by pooling donor funds. And changes in the global aid architecture—for example, the International Financing Facility (IFF) where donors could create some type of endowment instrument by securitizing future aid commitments—also had the potential to make aid financing more predictable over the longer term.

Several participants stressed that the international community was taking steps to reduce the volatility and increase the predictability of aid. Peter Grant (DFID, United Kingdom) noted that bilateral donors have been moving toward long-term commitments of aid, which provide the basis for more predictable flows. For example, DFID is willing to go to a 10-year commitment period for aid to Rwanda. It will continue to attach conditions in certain areas critical to achieving poverty reduction and the MDGs, maintaining human rights and international treaty obligations, and ensuring the fiduciary responsibilities of donors. So in the new environment of long-term aid commitments, there will still be some residual volatility in aid disbursements ex post. But the reasons for which aid might be turned on and off will be clear and agreed upon ex ante. Finance ministers will know the conditions for disbursements and the implications of their policy decisions.

Speaking for the broader international community, Paul Isenman (Policy Coordination Division, Organisation for Economic Co-operation and Development (OECD)) reported on a ministerial level forum in Paris on aid effectiveness. Bilateral and multilateral donors, recipient countries, and civil society organizations had agreed on a Declaration that focuses on issues similar to those that seminar participants had raised.[20] The Declaration starts from government ownership; addresses the need for aid to be aligned with country priorities and systems, including budgetary systems; focuses on the need for harmonization and simplification of aid; emphasizes managing for development results; and also addresses the important need for mutual accountability. This represents a major effort by donors and recipient countries to move ahead in the spirit of mutual commitment and accountability to speed up implementation of what everyone agrees is needed to make aid more effective.

V. Debt Sustainability and the Issue of Loans Versus Grants

Discussions of the international aid architecture during recent years have revealed growing sentiment for providing less development assistance through concessional lending and more in the form of grants. This shift in sentiment has been motivated in large part by the failure of poor countries receiving concessional loans to achieve debt sustainability. Session V of the seminar addressed issues relevant to the loans versus grants debate. How can we better understand why recipients of highly concessional loans have run into debt sustainability problems? And what considerations should govern the choice between loans and grants?

Conceptual and Empirical Perspectives on Debt Sustainability

The paper presented by Bikas Joshi (IMF Policy Development and Review Department)[21] sheds considerable light on the debt sustainability problems of low-income countries since the early 1990s. The authors (Daseking and Joshi) show that whether the ratio of debt to exports becomes smaller or larger over time depends on whether the interest rate on external debt is less than or greater than the growth rate of exports. It also depends on the size of the non-interest current account deficit relative to exports, the extent to which the

[20] "Paris Declaration on Aid Effectiveness," by the OECD Working Party on Aid Effectiveness and Donor Practices (OECD, 2005). The Party comprises ministers, heads of aid agencies, and other senior officials from 60 donor and recipient countries and more than 50 donor organizations. The text of the Declaration and related information can be found at www.aidharmonization.org.

[21] Chapter 9.

noninterest current account deficit is financed by new debt, and the degree of concessionality of the new debt.[22]

Daseking and Joshi examine debt dynamics for 72 low-income countries during 1992–2003. With the average export growth rate of 8.1 percent a year far exceeding the average interest rate of 2.7 percent, the debt-to-exports ratio declined for the "average country" over the period even without accounting for debt relief. This "average" result, based on mean values, was, however, misleading, as the variance among countries was high. Indeed, application of the debt dynamics equation using the median values of relevant variables indicates that, in the absence of debt relief, the ratio of debt to exports for the "median country" could have remained stable only at a relatively high level, and the ratio of debt to GDP would have risen. For many countries, debt sustainability problems worsened, even though loans were highly concessional.

Loans Versus Grants: Basic Considerations

In light of these findings, Daseking and Joshi examine the various considerations in the loans versus grants debate and what needs to be done to achieve the MDGs without undermining debt sustainability. Grants have the obvious advantage of not contributing to the debt distress and forgiveness pressures historically associated with loans. Grants may be particularly appropriate for financing spending on basic social services and human capital investments that have returns with long gestation periods, or that borrowing governments cannot easily capture either directly or through additional tax revenue.

A key advantage of loans is that, *for a given net present value of assistance*, they allow a larger gross flow of resources than grants, which can be important for countries without access to private capital. A second attraction is that reflows from concessional loans can be used to help poor countries in the future. It has also been contended that loans force countries to determine that their projects are worth financing; this assists them in eventually overcoming informational barriers to accessing capital markets. Also, the need to service loans makes recipients more cautious about the use of these resources and gives them incentives to build debt management capacity.

Daseking and Joshi point out that the availability of larger gross resource flows can conceivably justify loans even if some projects fail ex post and require

[22] To develop a conceptual framework, Daseking and Joshi use a country's balance of payments accounting identity to decompose the sources of growth in its external debt. They separate the current account deficit into interest payments on external debt and the noninterest current account deficit; they divide the sources of financing of the current account deficit into debt-creating flows (such as bank loans or sovereign bonds) and non-debt-creating flows (such as foreign direct investment); and they manipulate these definitional identities to derive a "debt dynamics equation" for the net present value of debt as a ratio to exports.

debt forgiveness. This assumes, however, that the volume of lending makes it possible to raise poor countries' investment relative to what would be feasible with the amount of assistance available under a grants-only approach, and that in making decisions about debt relief, it is possible to distinguish between project failures that can be blamed on bad luck and those that are attributable to recipient country behavior. If there is moral hazard, a lend-and-forgive policy would be a problem.

Choosing the appropriate mix of loans and grants involves weighing the benefits of the larger gross flows that loans allow against the risks of future debt problems. Daseking and Joshi favor an approach that tailors the form of assistance to the characteristics of the projects and/or the recipient countries. Under a projects-based approach, grants might be relied upon to fund investments with high social returns but uncertain or delayed financial returns—such as spending on education and health. Loans might be used to fund projects that generate high and timely returns to the budget, such as infrastructure. But the rationale for such a projects-based approach is weakened to the extent that grants and loans are fungible. Moreover, a projects-based approach that tried to limit fungibility could be difficult to implement effectively and would risk compromising domestic ownership.

An alternative approach would base the mix of loans and grants on country characteristics. Donors would tailor the blend of aid to the needs and absorptive ability of the particular country. Under an algorithm proposed by Radelet and Chiang (2003), need would be based on economic and social indicators, while ability would be assessed in terms of growth prospects. Poorer countries would receive more grants, while faster-growing countries, and those with sounder policies and institutions, would receive more loans.[23] The country's debt sustainability and exposure to volatility would also be considered in the loans versus grants decision. An approach based on country characteristics is operationalized in the IMF's new debt sustainability framework for poor countries (IMF and IDA, 2004, 2005).[24]

[23] In comments during the seminar, Radelet suggested that the World Bank and regional development banks should switch to a grants-only approach in assisting extremely poor countries—those with per capita incomes below a threshold of about $400. These are countries that have been unable to sustain growth over the past several hundred years and that would have difficulty repaying loans. An IDA-type window should be used for countries with per capita incomes between, say, $400 and $1,000, and countries with higher incomes should receive regular IBRD loans. Radelet would treat China and India as special cases—they would be considered for IDA or IBRD loans, not grants.

[24] As detailed by Daseking and Joshi, this framework consists of (i) indicative debt-burden thresholds that are linked to the quality of a country's policies and institutions; and (ii) standardized, forward-looking analysis of a country's external debt and debt-service dynamics, including sensitivity tests to examine the implications for debt sustainability given plausible shocks. On the basis of these assessments, the framework tailors the loan versus grant decision to a country's risk of debt distress.

Loans Versus Grants: Additional Considerations

In commenting on the loans versus grants issue, Srinivasan thought that the analytical framework of the Daseking-Joshi paper was incomplete. In particular, as Charles Soludo (Central Bank of Nigeria) had emphasized in his keynote address (see Section VI of this chapter), the effectiveness of aid depended on deeper political economy issues that had to do with commitment to future actions on the parts of donors and recipients, along with the capacity to design and implement policies that delivered development. Loans established an extended relationship in which recipients made decisions about whether or not to default and donors decided what to do with loan repayments. Whether grants had a different effect than loans depended on whether or not there was an expectation that grants would be given repeatedly to create an intertemporal resource flow comparable to that of loans. In Srinivasan's view, if a country had leadership committed to development and a team of experts who could design and deliver it, and if the donor and recipient agreed on the objectives of development, the choice between grants and loans was irrelevant.

Gelb offered a different perspective on the loans versus grants issue. In providing loans to a country, donors were taking a bet on the recipient's long-term growth. This made development lending a form of quasi-equity investment, even though the loan contract did not formally recognize that. Within the International Development Association (IDA), the compact was that countries that succeed in growing and moving up to middle-income status would pay back, thereby providing an enhanced volume of resources and easing the burden on donors. By contrast, the type of algorithm proposed by Radelet and Chiang (2003) might have led to grant aid for China had it been implemented several decades ago, when Africa was richer than Asia. Gelb saw the IDA framework as a pragmatic way of dealing with the difficulty of predicting how well countries would perform ex ante and keeping debt service low for countries that remained poor.

Peter Heller (IMF Fiscal Affairs Department), Famara Jatta (Central Bank of The Gambia), and Radelet raised the issue of the recurring costs associated with aid. Projects financed with either loans or grants often involve ongoing operations and maintenance outlays that need to be incorporated into the analysis. Heller also emphasized that whether or not donors get more leverage out of loans depends on whether the loans are repaid. Subramanian argued that the arithmetic of debt distress suggested, on average, a very low rate of return on loan-financed projects.

Peter Grant noted that bilateral donors had already shifted from loans to grants, and that the current loan/grant shift in World Bank policy meant that many of the poorest countries were on a grants-only basis in IDA.[25] The

[25] While eligibility for IDA assistance is based on income, the decision between loans and grants is based on a country's risk of debt distress (not income), with countries assessed as having high risks of distress receiving only grants and those at moderate risk of distress receiving 50 percent loans and 50 percent grants.

remaining question was whether concessional loans should survive. He agreed with Radelet that it was critical for donors to give the same rigor to grants as they do to loans, and to make grants go through the budget just as much as loans. Grant also thought that the key consideration in the grants versus loans decision ought to be debt sustainability rather than recipient countries' income levels.

Berg noted that unlike IDA and other multilateral and bilateral donors, the IMF had not—and would not—switch to grants, partly because of the nature of its funding. The IMF's role was to point out cases where countries had an increasing need for grants rather than loans. He took issue with Srinivasan's argument that the form of financing was irrelevant for countries that had ownership and a commitment to the right development agenda, since a country's development agenda might not work out for a number of reasons beyond its control. Berg agreed that it was important to consider both domestic debt and external debt when assessing debt sustainability and considering the grants versus loans question. In the new debt sustainability framework, domestic debt was integrated into the country analysis and influenced assessments of whether a country was at high, moderate, or low risk of debt distress. But domestic debt should not be a major consideration in financing decisions by IDA, as there were incentive issues that would be problematic if countries received grants when they had higher domestic debt. External debt from IDA was cheaper than domestic debt, and there were situations in which countries might find it attractive to borrow from IDA and use the funds to retire their domestic debts.

In concluding the session, Birdsall agreed that a country-specific approach made a lot of sense. She also sided with Bevan in arguing that there were grounds for doubting whether a larger volume of aid would be forthcoming under loans than under grants. The loans versus grants question related mainly to IDA resources, not to funding from the IMF, where grants were not feasible, or from bilaterals, which had already moved almost completely to grants. In the case of IDA, with a 10-year grace period and a 40-year repayment period, Birdsall was inclined to view cash flow as almost equally constraining for loans and for grants.

Birdsall stressed that, regardless of whether the resource transfers were loans or grants, it was important to consider whether the transfers were effective, whether they were adding to volatility or not, and whether they implied recurring costs for the budget. She also felt that recipient countries should focus on increasing the accountability of the donors, more than anything else, in considering choices between grants and loans. Did grants invite more or less accountability, emphasis on benchmarks, and openness to evaluation? Finally, Birdsall proposed that the IMF, the World Bank, and bilateral donors devise creative financing approaches for reducing the vulnerability of countries that were extremely poor, small, and subject to exchange rate risks. Reflecting Gelb's analysis, she favored a more flexible pricing of loans—offering recipients financial instruments that would amount effectively to grants under some contingencies but include repayment provisions if countries became able to afford repayments. Similarly, contingent forms of debt relief arrangements could be designed for countries that have graduated from HIPC, whereby adverse exogenous shocks (such as tsunamis) could trigger automatic suspension of debt service.

VI. Aid, Institutions, and Growth

The vital need for good governance and strong economic institutions has become a prominent theme in discussions of the determinants of economic growth and development. Issues relevant to this theme were explored in Session VI of the seminar, which asked: What do we know about the links between institutions and growth and about the determinants of institutional change? Does aid have a tendency to weaken institutions that are important for growth? And could aid be used effectively to strengthen institutions? In addition, each of the seminar's three keynote speakers, in addressing the challenges of economic development, focused on important directions for strengthening institutions or institutional approaches.

Institutions and Growth

Following the stimulus provided by Douglass North,[26] economists have devoted considerable efforts over the past decade to expanding our knowledge about the relationships between institutions and growth. There are many types of economic and political institutions, broadly defined to include the formal and informal constraints (rules, laws, constitutions, conventions) that shape the incentive structure for economic, political, and social behavior. The growing availability, often at high frequencies, of data on economic and political institutions in recent years has made it possible to begin characterizing the nature and strength of institutions in quantitative terms. Theoretical and empirical studies have yielded important insights into the importance of institutions for growth. It is generally agreed, for example, that while rapid growth over periods of several years may be achievable without strong institutions, sustained growth over decades requires effective institutions to protect property rights and provide incentives for saving, investment, and entrepreneurship. As stressed in the paper by Simon Johnson (IMF Research Department) and Subramanian,[27] "broad economic institutions"—defined as institutions that protect against expropriation by the state or powerful elites, and that ensure that contracts between private parties are enforced—are essential if people are to entrust their savings to financial intermediaries and invest in human and physical capital.

[26] North (1990).

[27] Chapter 10.

Johnson and Subramanian distinguish between economic and political institutions and examine their interactions. Political institutions—defined as the laws, rules, and other practices that determine how people acquire and utilize political power—can help explain why economic institutions are more or less effective. Good economic institutions are more likely to emerge when rents from natural resources or other sources are limited and when political institutions are representative, allowing broad sharing of political power, including with people who own capital. But we know less about the sequencing of political and economic institutional development. In some countries, economic institutions improve first, followed by political institutions. In other cases, strong political institutions lead to effective economic institutions. Overall, Johnson and Subramanian find little correlation between economic and political institutions. In Africa, democratic institutions have strengthened recently, but it is not clear whether this will translate into better economic institutions.

As a crude quantitative perspective, Johnson and Subramanian report that estimates based on existing measures of institutional development suggest that raising the quality of institutions in sub-Saharan Africa to that of developing countries in Asia would increase per capita income by 80 percent. They also note that institutional weaknesses help explain macroeconomic instability and crises. Weak political institutions hurt the economy by exacerbating distributional conflicts and aggravating instability. Strong political institutions allow the burdens of adjustment to be distributed broadly, which is conducive to political and economic stability and prosperity.

Determinants of Institutional Change

Given that institutions are a key determinant of growth, it is important to improve our understanding of how they can be changed for the better. Johnson and Subramanian argue that institutions tend to evolve slowly but are not predetermined. Institutional change depends on decisions made by those holding political power, which depends, in turn, on their self-interest, concern for the general welfare, or other motivations. The ease with which institutions evolve also depends on economic conditions. Higher growth facilitates institutional adaptation by permitting, for example, more compensation to be paid to those who lose from various reforms. Moreover, economic stagnation can lead to change in political institutions, through both the voting process and other political actions, such as strikes and uprisings.

From the perspective of aid donors and the international community, it is relevant to consider the extent to which outside forces, including conditions attached to foreign assistance, can help strengthen economic and political institutions. Johnson and Subramanian are skeptical of the efficacy of external interventions in facilitating institutional change. External mechanisms are effective in that regard only if they are compatible with domestic political and economic cost-benefit considerations (see also Dixit, 2003). The European Union's (EU) accession process is an example of such a mechanism because the benefits of integration into an economic union provide powerful incentives for candidate countries to undertake comprehensive political and economic reforms. By contrast, as Johnson and Subramanian argue, the ability of outsiders to influence institutions in Africa and Latin America is likely to be more limited, since an anchor similar to the EU is missing.

Aid and Institutions

While Johnson and Subramanian are pessimistic about the scope for outside interventions to effect institutional change, other seminar participants pointed to channels through which aid might have significant effects on institutions, both for worse and for better. Bevan's overview paper focuses on potential detrimental effects of aid on institutions, noting that large aid inflows could (i) adversely affect a government's domestic revenue effort, which could reduce the incentives of citizens to monitor its activities and weaken democratic accountability;[28] (ii) intensify rent seeking, just as rents from resource discoveries do; and (iii) create challenges for governments in managing good projects and ensuring that budgetary processes are not fragmented or impaired.

Seminar participants also focused on the possibility of using aid to reward countries that took measures to strengthen institutions and governance in addition to implementing sound macroeconomic policies. Radelet pointed out that there were many examples of performance-based aid, such as the U.S. Millennium Challenge Account, which links aid, among other things, to the quality of governance, as characterized by a list of indicators.

Given the importance of institutions for growth and development, donors can play an important role in helping low-income countries assess the quality of their institutions. Donors can help poor countries recognize and monitor how they compare with others in terms of the growing list of available institutional indicators. They can also encourage aid-recipient governments to be more open and more transparent in their policies, especially their public finances. These activities can be an important component of the international community's surveillance efforts aimed at helping low-income countries achieve and maintain macroeconomic stability and promote growth.

Bilateral and multilateral donors should be mindful of ways in which their policies may have adverse effects on institutional development. Radelet thought that the continuing financial relationships between the IMF and well-performing African countries hindered the development of these countries' institutional strengths. In his view there were about a dozen African countries

[28] Some authors (e.g., Clements and others, 2004) have argued that a switch to grant financing may have the effect of weakening governments' efforts to raise revenue.

that no longer needed IMF-supported programs and were using the IMF as an institutional crutch. Radelet sided with Soludo in arguing that the IMF needed to formulate better exit strategies and allow countries much more latitude in developing their own economic programs and moving forward. He appreciated that countries would encounter difficulties along the way, but considered that an acceptable price for institutional growth.

Radelet was also concerned that donor practices undermined recipient countries' budgetary processes, in part by hiring away the best people and by setting up project management units outside the budget. Moreover, he thought that there was inadequate attention to addressing structural matters related to the budget, such as transparency in accounting, publishing the budget on a regular basis, and hiring and training staff.

Radelet's concerns echoed a theme that others had voiced. In opening the seminar, Bio-Tchané had stressed the specific need to strengthen public expenditure management systems, noting that the Paris Declaration on Aid Effectiveness called for greater use of countries' national systems to disburse and monitor aid projects, as opposed to the parallel systems that many donors have set up.[29] Bio-Tchané understood that donors were worried about weak national systems and corruption on the side of recipient governments related to their receipt or use of aid revenues. But the real solution to these problems, in his view, lay in encouraging good governance; the practice of bypassing government institutions undermined domestic governance. The challenge for donors is to determine how they can avoid corruption when they come up against weak institutions without taking actions that further weaken those institutions.

A number of participants raised issues about the role of IMF conditionality. Jatta argued that sometimes conditionality did not adequately take into account local circumstances. He referred to safeguard missions that pressured the government to adopt international accounting standards, which was problematic because the accounting firms in his country had not yet moved to international standards. Other participants came to the defense of conditionality. Gondwe argued that without IMF and World Bank conditions, Africa would not have changed from what it was in the 1980s. Conditionality had been helpful to Mozambique and a number of other countries. While he was critical of cases in which there were too many conditions or in which the imposition of participatory procedures did not take into account the political realities in the countries, he disagreed with those who said that the role of the IMF should be revisited. In a world of integrated economies it was important that countries share experiences, and the IMF and World Bank are institutions that know about country experiences and should continue to sit with African policymakers to discuss sound macroeconomic management.

[29] Heller (2005) provides a detailed discussion of the challenges of managing the budget and the responsibilities of donors and recipients in an environment of scaled-up aid.

Birdsall agreed that in some respects the dialogue between the international financial institutions and African countries had worked quite well over a long period of time. But she also thought that creditors frequently weakened programs and undermined pressures to strengthen institutions by their unwillingness to enforce conditions. By not walking away from programs that were not working, creditors never really provided the incentives that might have mattered in subsequent rounds.

Gudrun Kochendörfer-Lucius (InWEnt, Germany) noted that a twofold strategy for promoting institutional change in Africa had been formulated a decade ago in discussions of technical assistance by the OECD Development Assistance Committee. Donors would provide training and technical assistance to build institutional capacity. But those discussions also arrived at the view that the quality of institutions was affected by the quality of the users of the institutions. This needed to be taken into account, as it naturally led to a focus on democratization and governance issues.

Strengthening the Institutional Capacity for Macroeconomic Management

The luncheon speech by Kochendörfer-Lucius addressed the central issue that Prime Minister Diogo had raised in her opening remarks: the challenge of strengthening the institutional capacity for macroeconomic policymaking. Kochendörfer-Lucius stressed that strong domestic institutions are critical for development, and that for many African countries, the effectiveness of scaled-up aid flows in support of the MDGs will depend on efforts to strengthen the human and institutional capacity to formulate and implement sound policies. Aid donors should consider the implications for technical assistance and training, especially training in the area of macroeconomic policymaking. Their efforts could benefit significantly from improving donor coordination and making better use of different donors' comparative advantages.

Kochendörfer-Lucius also argued that policy frameworks are unlikely to be successful if they are not home-grown and internalized. Accordingly, it is important not only that scaled-up aid flows be complemented with strong and systematic capacity-building efforts, but also that Africans play a central role in ensuring that training is tailored to individual country needs and draws as much as possible on local knowledge and expertise.

Development from Within

The interplay between the domestic political economy and outside forces in African institutional development was taken up in Soludo's speech. Soludo focused on the need for African countries to develop genuine ownership of good policies and for donors and creditors to provide more policy space to African countries. In addressing the challenges of home-grown development, he stressed that reforms were not sustainable in the absence of genuine ownership, and that donor-driven approaches emphasizing process and participation had not been effective in creating genuine ownership. Especially in heavily aid-dependent African countries, these approaches were used merely to promote Washington-driven economic policies. Africa needed ownership to be embedded in the domestic political process of each country and to bring donor programs into better alignment with country priorities. A strong political leadership and a cohesive core economic team were the most important ingredients in the success of recent reforms in Nigeria. A key challenge was to institutionalize change in the judiciary, the legislative branch, and other areas. Constitutional reform, an aggressive legislative agenda, and continuity of the economic team were needed to ensure that reforms were not reversed or slowed in the face of political change. Soludo also thought that donors needed to have strategies for exiting from aid; that technical assistance needed to be aligned better with domestic priorities; and that trade ought to be on the agenda. Countries' home-grown strategies needed to make tough choices and take into account the growing interdependence of the world economy, which made it impossible for African countries to isolate themselves from the global system.

The International Approach to Development

Donald Kaberuka (then Minister of Finance and Planning, Rwanda) focused his address on what we know about development. One of his themes was the need for a paradigm shift in the international community's approach to development. Poverty and underdevelopment did not have single causes; development was not simply a matter of resources or good governance, but rather involved complex, nonlinear, and country-specific processes. Countries grew and developed along different paths that depended on initial conditions, geography, history, and their political economies. A new approach is needed because poverty does not always respond to growth and because globalization has left part of humanity behind, in sub-Saharan Africa and in other parts of the developing world—even in countries that have been growing successfully.

A second theme in Kaberuka's address, echoing Soludo's earlier remarks, was the need for the IMF and other creditors and donors to provide more policy space to African countries. The IMF's Independent Evaluation Office (IEO) had issued a report on the prolonged use of IMF resources,[30] noting that lack of political commitment and poor governance were key factors in prolonging financial associations with the IMF, and highlighting the importance of ownership. To promote ownership, IMF-supported programs needed to provide more fiscal

[30] See IEO (2002). The IEO was constituted in 2001 to provide objective and independent evaluation on IMF performance. The IEO operates independently of IMF management and at arm's length from the IMF's Executive Board.

space and scope for alternative strategies.[31] Since 2002, when the international community reached the Monterrey Consensus on a new global approach to financing development, IMF and World Bank conditions had been streamlined, but political conditions imposed by bilateral donors had increased in complexity. The IMF also needed to become less timid in its surveillance in Africa and to provide more effective signaling on members' policies.

Kaberuka emphasized that there was progress on creating a new paradigm. The Washington Consensus had been replaced by the Monterrey Consensus, the essence of which was development from within, emphasizing country ownership, partnership, and mutual accountability as the basis for solving development problems. The new paradigm sought to replace conditions imposed by donors with home-grown policies for development, and sought to make Africans responsible for their own progress and prosperity. Kaberuka cautioned, however, that ownership needed to be complemented with improvements in the capacity to design and implement policies. In this regard, he made a special plea for giving greater emphasis to higher education and science in Africa. This would be good for development and also help reverse the brain drain from the continent. Besides human capital, capacity building also required addressing deficiencies in infrastructure, promoting common markets, and considering various trade and investment initiatives.

VII. Roundtable Discussion

The final session of the seminar featured four panelists who offered a range of views on how to improve the international financial architecture in general and the effectiveness of aid in particular. Srinivasan focused his remarks on the roles of global institutions. Most of the existing major intergovernmental organizations had been created in the aftermath of World War II. One of their important characteristics was universality of membership, regardless of the nature of country governments. National sovereignty was valued, and there was an implicit commitment not to use international economic organizations to interfere with the domestic political processes of any member state. A second important characteristic was institutional specialization. Each intergovernmental organization was given a clear mandate and the tools to pursue its mandate efficiently.

All that had changed over the past half century. International economic organizations had developed overlapping mandates without changing their tools, and the global institutional architecture was no longer functioning well. There was a need to sharply narrow and separate the mandates of the international financial institutions (IFIs) based on a clear statement of objectives. In Srinivasan's

[31] The IMF's 2005 review of PRGF program design addresses the issue of fiscal space; see IMF (2005).

view, the objectives boiled down to ensuring the stability of the international monetary and financial system, promoting economic development, and generating macroeconomic stability at the country level. The World Bank should provide financial assistance to developing countries that do not have access to international financial markets, but the design of development programs is largely a domestic issue, not an issue for the World Bank or the IMF. The Bank should support domestically grown and owned development programs, with resources committed for the longer term when there is mutual agreement on the programs. The IFIs should not be involved in financing those emerging market countries that can easily obtain resources from world capital markets. The IMF should focus exclusively on promoting global financial stability and providing advice on domestic macroeconomic stabilization through the Article IV consultation process; its role in low-income countries should not extend to structural adjustment issues. IMF financial assistance should be provided to countries facing temporary, exogenous shocks, but not to countries facing domestic, policy-induced shocks. In addition, the World Trade Organization should ensure that all countries have access to international trade on a level basis.

Srinivasan also expressed concerns about discussions that characterized the MDGs as a compact. In his view, the commitments involved were not clear and certainly not very firm, and there was no indication of what the penalties would be for failing to live up to commitments. There was too much rhetoric and not enough attention to the reality that power and income disparities would exist for many years to come, and that donors' objectives were unlikely to change suddenly.

Gondwe stressed the timely nature of the seminar in light of African countries' desire to accelerate economic growth, catch up with other regions, and participate more fully in the global economy. To meet these objectives, African countries needed to use aid effectively. More than a transfer of resources, aid was a package that also included transfers of technology and technical assistance and training. The real issue was not whether aid was useful, but how to maximize its effectiveness and accelerate growth. He agreed with the view that aid is subject to diminishing returns, but noted that aid to Africa was still well below the levels that various countries had benefited from in the past and encouraged more studies of the threshold levels at which the returns to aid become negative.

Gondwe hoped that the next high-level seminar would invite papers by ministries of finance in aid-recipient countries to complement the presentations by outside experts and representatives of aid donors. He noted that African countries are in the "enviable position" of no longer administering their economies alone. With frequent missions from the IMF and the World Bank, there is much expert advice and monitoring available to ensure that the problems of policies, institutions, and governance are being tackled. This puts

African countries in a position where aid can be used effectively if it arrives on time. The main challenge is that aid disbursements have been unpredictable and always less than the levels pledged, which creates major difficulties for ministers of finance. Gondwe hoped that the Paris Declaration on Aid Effectiveness would make a difference, but he was not very optimistic.

Soludo used his panel presentation to "dream dreams" and to predict that the international aid architecture as we know it today is on the way out. He criticized most of the Maputo discussions for focusing on "tinkering at the margins" of an aid system that was not working. This system had led to numerous declarations and statements of good intentions that were not being implemented. He predicted that donors and recipients would abandon the present aid relationship in the wake of the growing inequalities caused by globalization and the mounting of associated pressures from international crime (e.g., terrorism and traffic in arms and drugs) and immigration. Soludo favored replacing voluntary aid with mandatory international transfers funded by international taxes, such as the tax on air travel that the French and German governments had recently proposed.

Soludo also criticized discussions that viewed development as the only objective of aid. Such a characterization ignored the political dimensions of aid as an instrument of foreign policy and control. The nature of the current aid system created problems for recipient countries analogous to the recognized problems created by national welfare systems. Aid ought to be a temporary phase for developing countries rather than a way of life. Proceeds from mandatory globalization taxes should ensure that transfers from rich to poor countries are sufficient to provide the resources Africa needed to exit from poverty traps and its continued dependence on aid. There was also a need to rethink the role of trade in the exit strategy from the existing aid system. Together with greater economic integration would come closer political integration of African countries. Soludo felt that this was important, as many African states were not viable politically or economically. Africa needed to have its own debate on these issues.

Grant's observations on aid effectiveness struck a pragmatic middle ground between the views of aid optimists and aid pessimists. External aid could be useful in achieving its objectives of growth, poverty reduction, and humanitarian relief, but the macroeconomic risks were real. The potential hazards were not insurmountable, but it was not clear whether the Millennium Project had given them sufficient attention.

In looking ahead, Grant saw two key issues: the scale of resource transfers needed and the volatility and unpredictability of these transfers. On the former, DFID supported the scaling-up of aid to Africa and encouraged detailed, sector-by-sector studies to identify absorptive capacity constraints and consider where they can be relaxed. On volatility and unpredictability, the answer was improvements in mutual accountability. The aid relationship needed to become a genuine partnership among recipients and donors. DFID had revised its approach to conditions with the interests of recipients in mind. It wanted to support countries that were signing up to achieve the MDGs while holding them accountable for the pattern of spending to which they had committed. DFID also needed to retain the ability to meet fiduciary responsibilities and to insist that recipients comply with broader political commitments to international human rights and other conventions. The IMF and the World Bank had a responsibility to set appropriate program conditions and to provide practical advice on how to manage aid.[32]

During 2005, the United Kingdom was in the central role of having the presidencies of the Group of Eight and the European Union in the second half of the year, and the Commission for Africa Report had been generated in that context. The Report stressed the themes of capacity building and accountability as well as the need for a scaling-up of resources. In addition, the United Kingdom had made specific proposals for multilateral debt relief and for an International Finance Facility that would allow donors to frontload aid by borrowing in the international capital market against future aid commitments.

VIII. Concluding Policy Messages

The Maputo seminar revealed a widely shared consensus that downplaying the macroeconomic complications that can potentially arise from scaling up aid can be extremely dangerous for recipients and for the international aid system. While participants expressed different levels of concern about the macroeconomic hazards, the following broadly shared perspectives and policy conclusions emerged.

- Aid has produced some striking successes, but there are reasons to be concerned that a substantial scaling-up of aid may fail to elicit correspond-

[32] Musokotwame was concerned about the potential implications of the shifting composition of aid. In the past, project aid had allowed recipients to cushion important initiatives against volatility in program and budget support. The shift toward budget aid meant that such cushioning would become less feasible if donors suspended aid following negative IMF assessments of a country's macroeconomic policies. This raised the question of whether donors would totally align themselves with the indicators that the IMF used to assess macroeconomic performance, or whether they would be willing to differentiate their views from those of the IMF. In response, Grant noted that while DFID was moving in the direction of more budget support—in Africa, its target for budget support was 70 percent of aid allocations—the aim was to step back and put countries much more in the driver's seat in designing poverty reduction strategies. He did not expect the IMF to move away from the performance criteria that were set for arrangements with upper credit tranche conditionality. But there were differences between what DFID and the IMF were trying to deliver and corresponding differences in performance risks, so DFID was moving in the direction of setting its own performance standards; see DFID (2005).

ingly large increases in growth and reductions in poverty. One reason is that aid appears to be subject to diminishing returns, which makes it extremely important to increase absorptive capacity. Another is the prospect that Dutch disease may hurt export competitiveness, which has been the one proven channel of growth

- Policymakers should watch very carefully for early signs of absorptive capacity constraints, such as upward pressures on wages and the relative prices of nontraded goods and declines in the profitability of traded-goods sectors. These shifts should prompt a reevaluation of government spending, whether aid-financed or not, and perhaps also a reevaluation of monetary policy.
- The volatility, unpredictability, and procyclicality of aid pose major difficulties for recipient countries. Donors should allow recipients more flexibility in the timing of aid-financed expenditures. Recipients should build foreign exchange reserves and fiscal cushions to deal with aid volatility. They should be free to draw upon these resources when expenditure plans would otherwise be disrupted by aid shortfalls.
- Policymakers should adopt sensible and realistic spending plans consistent with their knowledge of absorptive capacity. They should be cognizant of the need to strike a balance between infrastructure development and spending on health and education, and they should not allow donor activity to be crowded into "flavor-of-the-day" sectors or to become inconsistent with an appropriate balance of overall spending.
- There is considerable scope for enhancing the competitiveness of Africa's exports through infrastructure investments and various initiatives to improve the delivery of services to business. Key issues in many African countries are reducing conflicts and improving governance and the attitude of governments toward business.

Good institutions and the sustained implementation of strong macroeconomic and structural policies are critical determinants of economic success. Well-designed policies are those that provide incentives for entrepreneurship and strengthen the supply responses of low-income economies to market signals. Countries that are able to exploit global markets will probably be the most successful in pursuing rapid sustainable growth and a lasting reduction of poverty.

Appendix. Sessions II and III: Comments on Technical Issues

This Appendix summarizes comments on a number of technical issues that were raised by participants during Sessions II and III.

Srinivasan made some general observations aimed at clarifying the nature of the evidence from cross-country regressions and simulation models. He noted that only a small proportion of firms in tradable-goods sectors are typically engaged in export activities, probably because of the fixed costs in entering export markets. If exporters have already incurred sunk costs, their short-run responses to unexpected shocks will be dampened. These considerations call into question empirical evidence based on sectoral averages or cross-country regression models and call for evidence based on firm-level responses. Regarding calibrated general equilibrium models, such as those presented by Adam and Sundberg, it is important to acknowledge that they rely less on data and more on modeling assumptions: while simulations produce clearer results, they are not necessarily more believable because they are less closely linked to data.

Srinivasan also thought it desirable to distinguish conceptually between concerning aid levels and those concerning volatility. Bevan, by contrast, did not think that the two could be cleanly separated. To him, a substantial scaling-up of the level of aid would also lead to a comparable increase in volatility. Srinivasan added that policy analyses relying on nonmonetary models alone were incomplete. Models that distinguish between tradable and nontradable goods yield important insights, but they may miss important responses of nominal variables under government control, which could be dangerous. One clear reference here is to the short-run phenomenon of exchange rate overshooting, as in Dornbusch (1976).

Seminar participants sought to reconcile concerns about aid-induced Dutch disease with the lack of clear evidence of aid-induced real appreciation.[33]

One possible explanation is the Adam-Bevan mechanism whereby aid enhances productivity and ameliorates short-term adverse effects of aid on competitiveness. Another is that macroeconomic policies could respond to aid inflows in a way that preempts a real appreciation of the currency. As illustrated by the Ghana case, aid inflows have no effects if they are saved. A third possibility, emphasized by Lamine Loum (former Prime Minister, Senegal) and Adam, is that historically, aid has often been part of a broader package that also includes policy reforms, such as devaluations and the removal of trade and other economic distortions. These considerations led to the question of whether analysis ought to ignore relative price effects and focus instead on the composition of production. Adam thought that was a sensible approach and that more effort should be devoted to developing appropriate measures of the relevant concepts of the structure of production.

Srinivasan provided another perspective on the issue, arguing that the lack of real exchange rate appreciation should not be surprising; it was easy to build pure trade models in which aid reduced the size of the tradable goods sector without any price (i.e., real exchange rate) effects. This is illustrated in Figure 1.1, which Srinivasan provided after the seminar. Production and consumption are initially

[33] It may be noted that Rajan and Subramanian (2005), in revising their paper since the seminar, report a new set of results that appears to be evidence of aid-induced real appreciation.

Figure 1.1. The Effects of Aid in a Trade Model

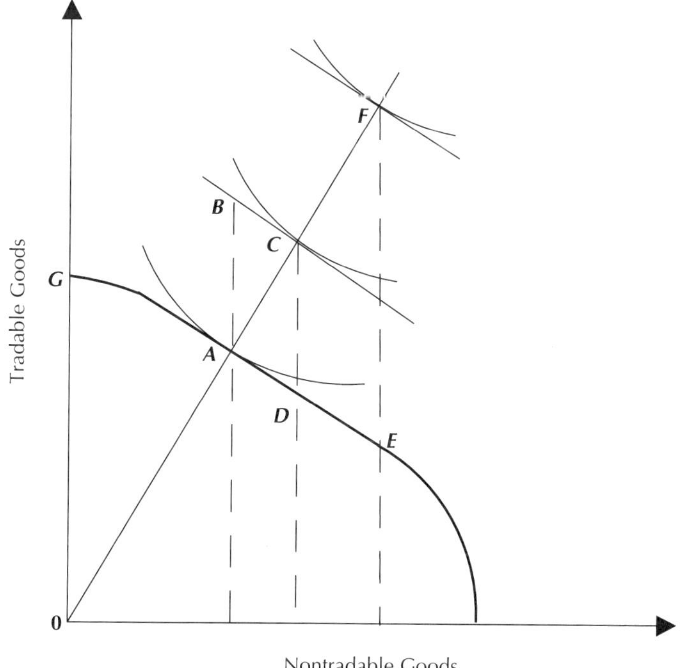

at point A on the linear segment of the production possibilities frontier, where the tradables and nontradables sectors are both subject to constant returns to scale at the margin. If consumer preferences are homothetic, the provision of an amount of aid sufficient to purchase the segment *AB* of additional tradable goods will lead to consumption at point C and production at point *D*, with no change in the relative price of tradables and nontradables (i.e., the real exchange rate, which is the constant slope of line segment *AE*). The maximum quantity of aid that can be absorbed by production changes without a change in the real exchange rate is *EF*, where *E* is the kink point in the production possibilities frontier.

Adam was asked about the empirical validity of the transfer paradox. He responded that evidence to support the classical transfer paradox was weak and that it was more relevant to focus on the income distribution effects of big relative price changes triggered by public expenditure decisions. Such changes may have important paradoxical effects for certain groups. Adam's paper alludes to an example from Uganda in which poor rural households that are net sellers of basic foods suffered real income losses in the aftermath of big supply-side boosts to output and associated relative price declines induced by aid-funded investments in roads.

References

Adam, Christopher S., and David L. Bevan, 2004, "Aid and the Supply Side: Public Investment, Export Performance and Dutch Disease in Low Income Countries," Department of Economics Discussion Paper No. 201 (Oxford: University of Oxford).

Agénor, Pierre-Richard, and Peter J. Montiel, 1999, *Development Macroeconomics* (Princeton, New Jersey: Princeton University Press, 2d ed.).

Arellano, Cristina, Aleš Bulíř, Timothy Lane, and Leslie Lipschitz, 2005, "The Dynamic Implications of Foreign Aid and Its Variability," IMF Working Paper 05/119 (Washington: International Monetary Fund).

Arrow, Kenneth, 1962, "The Economic Implications of Learning by Doing," *Review of Economic Studies*, Vol. 29 (June), pp. 155–73.

Basu, Kaushik, 2003, *Analytical Development Economics: The Less Developed Economy Revisited* (Cambridge, Massachusetts: MIT Press, 2d ed.).

Bulíř, Aleš, and Timothy Lane, 2002, "Aid and Fiscal Management," paper presented at IMF conference on Macroeconomics and Poverty, Washington, March 14–15. Available via the Internet: http://www.imf.org/external/np/res/seminars/2002/poverty/abtl.pdf

Burnside, Craig, and David Dollar, 2000, "Aid, Policies, and Growth," *American Economic Review*, Vol. 90 (September), pp. 847–68.

Clemens, Michael, Steven Radelet, and Rikhil Bhavnani, 2004, "Counting Chickens When They Hatch: The Short-Term Effect of Aid on Growth," Working Paper No. 44 (Washington: Center for Global Development).

Clements, Benedict, Sanjeev Gupta, Alexander Pivovarsky, and Erwin R. Tiongson, 2004, "Foreign Aid: Grants versus Loans," *Finance and Development*, Vol. 41 (September), pp. 46–9.

Corden, Max, 1984, "Booming Sector and Dutch Disease Economics: Survey and Consolidation," *Oxford Economic Papers*, Vol. 36 (November), pp. 359–80.

Department for International Development, 2005, "Partnerships for poverty reduction: rethinking conditionality—A UK policy paper" (March). Available via the Internet: http://www.dfid.gov.uk/pubs/files/conditionality.pdf

Dixit, Avinash, 2003, "Some Lessons from Transaction-Cost Politics for Less-Developed Countries," *Economics and Politics*, Vol. 15 (July), pp. 107–33.

———, Gene M. Grossman, and Elhanan Helpman, 1997, "Common Agency and Coordination: General Theory and Application to Government Policy Making," *Journal of Political Economy*, Vol. 105 (August), pp. 752–69.

Dornbusch, Rudiger, 1976, "Expectations and Exchange Rate Dynamics," *Journal of Political Economy*, Vol. 84 (December), pp. 1161–76.

Easterly, William, 2001, *The Elusive Quest for Growth: Economists' Adventures and Misadventures in the Tropics* (Cambridge, Massachusetts: MIT Press).

Galor, Oded, and Joseph Zeira, 1993, "Income Distribution and Macroeconomics," *Review of Economic Studies*, Vol. 60 (January), pp. 35–52.

Gelb, Alan, and Associates, 1988, *Oil Windfalls: Blessing or Curse?* (New York: Oxford University Press for the World Bank).

Gelb, Alan, and Benn Eifert, 2005, "Improving the Dynamics of Aid: Towards More Predictable Budget Support," paper presented at the Practitioner's Forum on Budget

Support, Cape Town, May 5–6. Available via the Internet: http://siteresources.worldbank.org/PROJECTS/Resources/AgendaBudgetSupportDraft.pdf

Heller, Peter S., 2005, "Pity the Finance Minister: Managing a Substantial Scaling-Up of Aid Flows," paper prepared for discussion at seminar at the Overseas Development Institute, London, June.

İmrohoroğlu, Ayse, 1989, "Cost of Business Cycles with Indivisibilities and Liquidity Constraints," *Journal of Political Economy*, Vol. 97 (December), pp. 1364–83.

International Monetary Fund, 2005, "Review of PRGF Program Design—Overview" (September 16). Available via the Internet: www.imf.org/external/np/pp/eng/2005/080805r.htm

———, and International Development Association, 2004, "Debt Sustainability in Low-Income Countries: Further Considerations on an Operational Framework and Policy Implications" (September 10). Available via the Internet: http://www.imf.org/external/np/pdr/sustain/2004/091004.pdf

———, 2005, "Operational Framework for Debt Sustainability Assessments in Low-Income Countries—Further Considerations" (March 28). Available via the Internet: http://www.imf.org/external/np/pp/eng/2005/032805.pdf

International Monetary Fund, Independent Evaluation Office, 2002, *Evaluation of the Prolonged Use of IMF Resources* (Washington: International Monetary Fund).

Lucas, Robert E., Jr., 1987, *Models of Business Cycles* (Cambridge, Massachusetts: Blackwell).

Matsuyama, Kiminori, 1992, "Agricultural Productivity, Comparative Advantage, and Economic Growth," *Journal of Economic Theory*, Vol. 58 (December), pp. 317–34.

North, Douglass C., 1990, *Institutions, Institutional Change, and Economic Performance* (New York: Cambridge University Press).

Olson, M., 1965, *The Logic of Collective Action: Public Goods and the Theory of Groups* (Cambridge, Massachusetts: Harvard University Press).

Organisation for Economic Co-operation and Development, 2005, "Paris Declaration on Aid Effectiveness," DCD/DAC/EFF(2005)1/REV3 (March 11).

Radelet, Steven, and Hanley Chiang, 2003, "Providing New Financing to Low-Income Countries with High Levels of Debt: Some Considerations," Issue Paper on Debt Sustainability No. 2 (Washington: Center for Global Development).

Rajan, Raghuram, and Arvind Subramanian, 2005, "What Undermines Aid's Impact on Growth?" IMF Working Paper 05/126 (Washington: International Monetary Fund). Available via the Internet: http://www.imf.org/external/pubs/ft/wp/2005/wp05126.pdf

Sachs, Jeffrey, John W. McArthur, Guido Schmidt-Traub, Margaret Kruk, Chandrika Bahadur, Michael Faye, and Gordon McCord, 2004, "Ending Africa's Poverty Trap," *Brookings Papers on Economic Activity: 1*, Brookings Institution, pp. 117–216.

United Nations, 2003, "Indicators for Monitoring the Millennium Development Goals: Definitions, Rationale, Concepts and Sources." Available via the Internet: http://ddp-ext.worldbank.org/ext/MDG/content/pdf/document_final.pdf

SESSION I

Aid, Growth, and Poverty Reduction

What Should Aid Be Trying to Achieve? How Good Is the Record?

2

Aid and Growth

The Current Debate and Some New Evidence

STEVEN RADELET, MICHAEL CLEMENS, AND RIKHIL BHAVNANI*

Controversies about the effectiveness of foreign aid go back decades. Milton Friedman (1958), Peter Bauer (1972), William Easterly (2001), and other economists have leveled stinging critiques at aid, charging that it has enlarged government bureaucracies, perpetuated bad governments, enriched the elite in poor countries, or just been wasted. They cite the widespread poverty in Africa and South Asia despite three decades of aid, and point to countries that have received significant amounts of aid and have had disastrous growth records, including the Central African Republic, the Democratic Republic of the Congo, Haiti, Papua New Guinea, and Somalia. Critics call for aid programs to be dramatically reformed, substantially curtailed, or eliminated altogether.

Supporters counter that these arguments, while partially correct, are overstated. Jeffrey Sachs (2004), Joseph Stiglitz (2002), Nicholas Stern (2002), and others have argued that although aid has sometimes failed, it has supported poverty reduction and growth in some countries and prevented even worse performance in others. Advocates argue that many of the weaknesses of aid have more to do with donors than recipients, especially since much aid is given to political allies rather than to support development. They point to a range of successful aid recipients such as Botswana, Korea, Taiwan Province of China, Indonesia, and (more recently) Uganda and Mozambique, along with broader aid-financed initiatives such as the Green Revolution, the campaign against

---

*Steven Radelet, Michael Clemens, and Rikhil Bhavnani are Senior Fellow, Research Fellow, and Research Assistant, respectively, at the Center for Global Development. This paper was completed in June 2005.

river blindness, and the introduction of oral rehydration therapy. They note that in the 40 years since aid became widespread in the 1960s, poverty indicators have fallen in many countries around the world, and health and education indicators have risen faster than any other 40-year period in human history.

This paper explores the current debates on aid and growth. It begins by providing an overview of three prominent and different views of the aid-growth relationship: that there is (1) no relationship (or a negative one); (2) a positive relationship, usually with diminishing returns; or (3) a conditional relationship in which aid works in some circumstances but not others, depending on the characteristics of the recipient country or donors' practices and procedures. It then explores in depth one of the newer contributions to the debate–evidence that different types of aid have different relationships with growth. Specifically, aid that is actually aimed directly at growth (e.g., for infrastructure and agriculture) has had a strong and positive impact on growth, on average.

I. Three Broad Views on Aid Effectiveness

Most of the academic debate on aid effectiveness has centered on the relationship between aid and growth (even though a substantial portion of aid is not primarily aimed at growth). Three broad strands have emerged in the empirical literature.[1]

1. Aid has no affect on growth, and may actually undermine growth. Peter Bauer was perhaps the most outspoken proponent of this view (e.g., Bauer, 1972), arguing that aid created disincentive effects on investment, undermined the private sector, and otherwise inhibited development. However, while influential, he never provided systematic empirical research to support his argument. Griffen and Enos (1970) were among the first to publish quantitative empirical research questioning aid effectiveness, finding negative simple correlations between aid and growth in 27 countries. Many other studies followed showing little or no relationship (Mosley, 1980; Mosley and others, 1987; Dowling and Hiemenz, 1982; Singh, 1985; Boone, 1994; Rajan and Subramanian, 2005).

Researchers have suggested a variety of reasons why aid might not support growth. First, it simply could be wasted on limousines or presidential palaces. Second, it could encourage corruption, not just in aid programs but more broadly. Third, it could undermine private sector incentives for investment or to improve productivity. Aid can cause the currency to appreciate, undermining the profitability of the production of all tradable goods (known as the Dutch disease). Food aid, if not managed appropriately, can reduce farm prices and hurt farmer income. Fourth, aid flows can reduce saving, both private sav-

[1] This summary draws heavily from the review in Clemens, Radelet, and Bhavnani (2004).

ing (through its impact on interest rates) and government saving (through its impact on government revenue). Fifth, it can help keep bad governments in power, thus helping to perpetuate poor economic policies and postpone reform.

While these empirical studies have been influential, many use questionable techniques and methodologies, leaving the results less than convincing. For example, one of the most widely cited studies is Boone (1994), which concludes that there is no relationship between aid and growth. However, his aid-growth results were never published, and were based on a simple linear relationship that ruled out by assumption the possibility of diminishing returns between aid and growth, which would have been much more consistent with both theory and evidence. His specification also ignored potential endogeneity between aid and growth, and used an unconventional set of other explanatory variables for growth. Rajan and Subramanian's new study (2005) also assumes a simple linear relationship for most of its results. They find a weak relationship not just between aid and growth, but between almost all of their other explanatory variables for growth, including institutions, health, and policies.

2. Aid has a positive relationship with growth on average across countries (although not in every country), but with diminishing returns as the volume of aid increases. Early analysts assumed that aid would increase growth by augmenting saving, financing investment, and adding to the capital stock. Aid might also help increase worker productivity (e.g., through investments in health or education) or provide a conduit for the transfer of technology or knowledge from rich countries to poor countries (by paying for capital goods imports or through technical assistance). Several early studies found a positive relationship between aid and growth (e.g., Papenek, 1973; Levy, 1988), sparking a lively debate between researchers that found a positive relationship and those that did not.

This strand of the literature took a significant turn in the mid-1990s, when researchers began to investigate whether aid might spur growth with diminishing returns. Oddly—given Solow's response to the Harrod-Domar model in the 1950s—research on aid and growth until the mid-1990s only tested a linear relationship, a specification which persists in some studies even today. A large group of studies that allow for diminishing returns have found a positive relationship (Hadjimichael and others, 1995; Durbarry and others, 1998; Dalgaard and Hansen, 2000; Hansen and Tarp, 2000 and 2001; Lensink and White, 2001; and Dalgaard and Tarp, 2004). Most of these studies do not conclude that aid has always worked, but rather that *on average*, higher aid flows have been associated with more rapid growth. These studies have received much less public attention than those that have found a zero or conditional relationship, even though several have been published in peer-reviewed journals. Roodman (2004) conducts comprehensive sensitivity analyses on three of these studies, and finds two of the three (Dalgaard and Tarp, 2004; and the GMM results of Hansen and Tarp, 2001) to be fairly robust.

3. Aid has a conditional relationship with growth, only helping to accelerate growth under certain circumstances. This view is based on the idea that aid has supported growth in some circumstances but not others, and searches for key characteristics associated with the difference. This "conditional" strand of the literature has two subcategories, with the effectiveness of aid depending on either the characteristics of the recipient country or the practices and procedures of the donors.

Recipient country characteristics. Isham, Kaufmann, and Pritchett (1995) found that World Bank projects had higher rates of returns in countries with stronger civil liberties. Burnside and Dollar (2000), in a very influential study, concluded that aid stimulated growth in countries with good policies, but not otherwise. Other researchers have proposed different country characteristics that might affect the aid-growth relationship, including export price shocks (Collier and Dehn, 2001), climatic shocks and the terms of trade (Guillaumont and Chauvet, 2001; Chauvet and Guillaumont, 2002), policy and institutional quality (Collier and Dollar, 2002), institutional quality alone (Burnside and Dollar, 2004), policy and warfare (Collier and Hoeffler, 2002), "totalitarian" government (Islam, 2003), and location in the tropics (Dalgaard and Tarp, 2004).

All of these studies rely on an interaction term between aid and the variable in question, and (not surprisingly) many of the interaction terms are fragile. Easterly, Levine, and Roodman (2004) find that the original Burnside and Dollar results do not hold up to modest robustness checks. Roodman (2004) tests several other "conditional" studies and finds most of them to be relatively fragile, although the conclusions of Dalgaard and Tarp (2004) are more robust.

Nevertheless, the view that aid works best (or in a stronger version, aid works *only*) in countries with good policies and institutions has become the conventional wisdom among donors, partly based on this research and partly due to development practitioners that believe this to be the case based on their own experience. The appeal of this approach is that it can explain why aid seems to have supported growth in countries such as Botswana, Indonesia, and Korea, and more recently in Mozambique and Uganda, while at the same time not stimulating growth in countries such as Haiti, Liberia, the Philippines, and Zaïre (now the Democratic Republic of the Congo). These findings have had an enormous impact on donors (World Bank, 2000). The concept feeds directly into the World Bank's Performance Based Allocation (PBA) system for distributing concessional International Development Association (IDA) funds, and was the foundation for the United States' new Millennium Challenge Account (Radelet, 2003).

Donor practices. Many analysts have argued that donor practices strongly influence aid effectiveness. For example, multilateral aid might be more effective than bilateral aid, and untied aid is thought to have higher returns than tied aid (where donors require that certain aid funds be used to purchase goods and services from the donor country). Many observers argue that donors that have large bureaucracies do not coordinate or harmonize with other donors, or have ineffective monitoring, and evaluation systems undermine the effectiveness of their own programs. Two influential and overlapping views argue that aid would be more effective if there were greater "country ownership" or broader "participation" among government and community groups in recipient countries in setting priorities and designing programs. There has been substantial debate about these issues which in some cases has begun to lead to changes in donor practices, but to date there has been little systematic research connecting specific donor practices to aid effectiveness.

II. New Directions in Aid-Growth Research: Not All Aid Is Alike

One new strand of research has begun to explore the idea that not all aid is alike in its impact on growth. According to this view, most research on aid and growth is flawed, for two reasons: substance and timing. On substance, almost all studies look at the relationship between total aid and growth, when large portions of aid are not directed at growth. Food aid, for example, is directed at supporting consumption, not growth. The same is true for the provision of medicines, bed nets, and school books. Aid to support democracy or for humanitarian relief efforts is not primarily aimed at stimulating growth. Since growth is not the objective, it would not be surprising if much of this aid had no relationship with growth. By contrast, aid to build roads, bridges, telecommunications facilities or to support agriculture and industry should be expected to accelerate growth. But research that combines these different kinds of aid is likely to get mixed results, and to show an overall weak relationship between aid and growth.

With respect to timing, most cross-country studies of economic growth (whether they are examining aid or some other factor that might influence growth) use panel data with each observation (usually) corresponding to four years, but include aid flows that cannot possibly affect growth in that period. Aid to support education and health, for example, may stimulate growth, but the impact is likely to take decades, not years. One option for researchers is to use a longer time period, ideally (to be consistent with theory) as long as possible. But there is a trade-off: the longer the time period, the harder it is to isolate the impact of aid (or any other variable) on growth from other influences. Shorter periods allow for more observations per country, and permit using "fixed effects" estimators that can remove the bias which might be created by leaving out country-specific traits that do not change or change very slowly over time. However, most research that uses shorter time periods includes all aid flows rather than the subset of aid that is most appropriate for the time period in question.

Only a few studies have explored this line of reasoning, and most focus on specific countries. Owens and Hoddinott (1999) find that household welfare in Zimbabwe is increased by "development aid" (infrastructure, agricultural extension, etc.) far more than by "humanitarian aid" (food aid, emergency transfers, etc.). In Uganda, Mavrotas (2003) finds a positive effect from program and project aid, but negative impacts from technical cooperation and food aid. However, in India, Mavrotas (2002) finds a negative correlation between growth and three categories of aid.

Growth and Growth-Oriented Aid: Some New Results

In a new study (Clemens, Radelet, and Bhavnani, 2004), we examine the relationship between growth-oriented aid and growth across 67 countries between 1974 and 2001. Here we summarize our key results and their policy implications.

We begin by dividing aid into three categories.[2] To illustrate, some of the major types of aid in each of the three categories are shown in Table 2.1. The first group is aid for disasters, emergencies, and humanitarian relief efforts, including food aid. We expect that this kind of aid would have a *negative* simple relationship with growth, since a disaster would simultaneously cause growth to fall and aid to increase. For example, Hurricane Mitch caused extensive damage and undermined economic growth in Central America, and donors responded with substantial increases in aid. In a simple cross-country growth regression, these cases would appear to have high aid and low or negative growth, making it appear that aid had a poor relationship with growth. But this is misleading, since both the high aid and the low growth are being caused by something else—the disaster—which in most studies is left out of the analysis. In theory, more sophisticated modeling techniques could correct for this effect, but it would be difficult to do so effectively, and almost no growth regressions attempt to do so. We simply recognize that the aid-growth relationship here is different from other kinds of aid, and exclude this category of aid from our main analysis.

[2] All the data come from the OECD, which reports aid *commitments* disaggregated into 233 distinct purposes back to 1973, and aid *disbursements* by purpose back to the early 1990s. We assign each of the 233 purposes into either "humanitarian," "early-impact," or "late-impact" aid, as described in the text. We then estimate disbursements of each category data back to the 1970s based on the relationship between commitments and disbursements in the 1990s for each category. For a full description of the data and methodology, see Clemens, Radelet, and Bhavnani (2004).

Table 2.1. Three Categories of Aid

Humanitarian Aid	"Early-Impact" Aid	"Late-Impact" Aid
Disaster relief	Transport and storage	Government and civil society
Emergency aid	Communications	General environmental protection
Humanitarian relief	Energy generation and supply	Women in development
Food aid	Most banking and financial services	Health
	Business and other services	Education
	Agriculture, forestry, and fishing	Populations policies
	Industry, mineral resources, and mining	Water supply and sanitation
	Construction	Policy and administrative management
	Structural adjustment assistance	Support to NGOs
	Budget support	Other social infrastructure and services
	Debt relief	

Source: Clemens, Radelet, and Bhavnani (2004).

The second category is aid that might affect growth, but if so, only indirectly and over a long period of time. No one should expect that aid to halt environmental degradation or to support democratic or judicial reform will affect economic growth quickly, and certainly not over a four-year period. Similarly, aid to strengthen health and education is likely to affect labor productivity over many years, but not immediately (with some exceptions). In a standard cross-country growth regression, these observations are likely to appear as high aid and zero or very little growth.

The third category is aid that might reasonably be expected to affect economic growth in the four-year period standard in most cross-country growth regressions. Aid to build infrastructure—roads, irrigation systems, electricity generators, and ports—should affect growth rates fairly quickly, as should aid to support directly productive sectors, such as agriculture, industry, trade, and services. Aid that comes as cash, such as budget or balance of payments support, also should be expected to positively affect growth fairly immediately if it is to do so at all. In our disaggregation, this kind of aid accounts for slightly more than one-half of all aid flows. For these kinds of aid flows, it is perfectly reasonable for policymakers to expect and for researchers to test for a positive relationship with growth over a four-year period.

Most research lumps all three of these kinds of aid together, even though the impact of each on growth is likely to be quite different. Thus it is not surprising that some research on aid and growth has shown a weak relationship. Indeed, it would be astonishing if these mixed inputs gave any clear results at all. Instead, when we disaggregate aid and concentrate on aid flows that are aimed at affecting growth relatively quickly, a much clearer picture emerges. We find a strong, positive, and causal effect between this "early-impact" aid, as we call it,[3] and economic growth over a four-year period. The results exhibit diminishing returns, with larger amounts of aid having a progressively smaller impact on growth. The estimated impact is large—conservatively more than double the magnitude found in other studies. The results are also very robust, remaining firm across a variety of specifications and estimation techniques. They do not depend on the choice of other regressors or instrumentation strategy. We find the impact of aid on growth is somewhat larger in countries with stronger institutions, but controlling for institutions is not necessary to establish the result. The results do not imply that aid has worked everywhere—it most definitely has not—but rather that on average, this type of aid has had a positive and significant impact on growth.

Core Results

Table 2.2 shows some of the basic results. Column 1 shows the relationship between aggregate aid (net of debt repayments) and growth, controlling for a wide variety of other factors that might influence growth such as geography, policy, and health endowments. In this example, we use a two-stage least squares (2SLS) estimation technique to control for possible endogeneity.[4] We include terms for both aid and aid squared to allow for diminishing returns. The coefficient on aid is positive and statistically significantly different from zero at the 5 percent level, but it is fairly small. These results are in accord with the studies cited above that have found a positive relationship with growth when allowing for diminishing returns, such as Dalgaard and Tarp (2004). But in our view, these results, while positive, are misleading.

Column 2 shows the results including all three of our subcategories of aid separately but simultaneously, with debt repayments as a separate term. The coefficient on early-impact aid is more than three times the coefficient on gross aid and is significant at the 10 percent level. As expected, the coefficient on late-impact aid is small and insignificant, while the coefficient on humanitarian aid

[3] In earlier versions of this paper, we referred to our three categories of aid as "short-impact," "long-impact," and "humanitarian." However, this terminology led to some confusion that our findings suggested that the influence of "short-impact" aid only lasted for a short period of time and then dissipated (which we do not find), rather than the intended meaning that this aid required a shorter length of time to register its impact. Thus, in later versions we changed "short-impact" and "long-impact" to "early-impact" and "late-impact," respectively. The methodology and categorization of these aid flows remains the same.

[4] The instruments, here and in later regressions using 2SLS, are all the independent variables, supplemented by the instruments in Hansen and Tarp (2000), including a dummy for Egypt, arms imports, a lagged policy index and its square, population interacted with policy, GDP and its square interacted with policy, and each of the lagged variables and the lagged variables interacted with policy. As we show later, the results do not depend on instrumentation.

Table 2.2. Core Results

Dependent variable: GDP per capita growth	1 2SLS	2 2SLS	3 2SLS	4 GMM
Net ODA	0.248 (0.105)**			
Net ODA squared	−0.00660 (0.00358)*			
Early-impact aid		0.793 (0.413)*	0.960 (0.328)***	0.930 (0.251)***
Early-impact aid squared		−0.0556 (0.0285)*	−0.0588 (0.0264)**	−0.0507 (0.0190)***
Late-impact aid		0.146 (0.266)		
Late-impact aid squared		0.0000762 (0.012)		
Humanitarian aid		−0.407 (1.29)		
Humanitarian aid squared		0.146 (0.317)		
Log repayments		−0.404 (0.189)**	−0.384 (0.188)**	−0.508 (0.159)***
Log initial GDP per capita	0.018 (0.402)	0.0223 (0.496)	−0.0593 (0.493)	−0.253 (0.439)
East Asia	2.333 (0.630)***	2.33 (0.635)***	2.39 (0.648)***	2.62 (0.601)***
Institutional quality	0.301 (0.107)***	0.299 (0.121)**	0.333 (0.114)***	0.323 (0.106)***
Inflation	−1.80 (0.541)***	−1.83 (0.530)***	−1.60 (0.558)***	−1.30 (0.403)***
Budget balance	8.29 (5.30)	6.90 (5.18)	8.28 (5.47)	6.22 (4.24)
Openness Sachs-Warner	1.16 (0.435)***	1.32 (0.460)***	1.41 (0.456)***	1.47 (0.388)***
Tropics	−2.11 (0.374)***	−2.23 (0.423)***	−2.13 (0.398)***	−2.28 (0.290)***
Log initial life expectancy	3.37 (1.710)**	3.12 (2.12)	3.49 (1.85)*	4.06 (1.54)***
Civil war	−1.90 (0.726)***	−1.75 (0.767)**	−2.19 (0.891)**	−1.82 (0.813)**
Lagged civil war	1.78 (0.494)***	1.27 (0.617)**	1.86 (0.730)**	1.56 (0.644)**
Observations	368	366	368	368
R-squared	0.444	0.398	0.388	0.383

Source: Clemens, Radelet, and Bhavnani (2004).

Note: Dependent variable is four-year average GDP per capita growth. Robust and clustered standard errors in parentheses. * significant at 10%; ** significant at 5%; *** significant at 1%. All regressions include period dummies and a constant term. Aid, aid squared, and repayments are instrumented.

is negative. These results show that these three categories and debt repayments of aid have dramatically different relationships with growth. Note that our results do not necessarily mean that late-impact and humanitarian aid have no impact on growth—we believe that standard cross-country regressions with four-year panels are the wrong technique to use in measuring these other impacts. Examining these relationships appropriately would require different models and estimation techniques, which we leave to future work.

The results also suggest that aid is not fully fungible, at least in the sense that all aid is the same, and aid for any purpose is the same as cash. If all aid were the same, or all aid were fully fungible, different subcategories of aid would show similar (or identical) relationships with growth. Instead, our results show that aid intended for different purposes has dramatically different relationships with growth. It is more likely that aid is partially but not fully fungible.

Column 3 shows the results using exclusively early-impact aid. The estimated coefficient is now more than four times larger than for aggregate aid and is significant at the 1 percent level. Column 4 shows the results for the same specification, but this time estimating the results using the more efficient generalized method of moments (GMM) estimator.

Figure 2.1 shows these estimated relationships between aid and growth in graphical form. The bold curve shows the relationship between aggregate aid and growth, while the other three curves show the estimated relationship for the three subcategories of aid.[5] Early-impact aid has a much stronger relationship with growth than the other subcategories, and combining the three together, as is done in most research, masks these differential effects and shows a much weaker relationship.

Since the instrumentation used in the 2SLS estimation technique raises some difficult issues, Table 2.3 shows the results using some alternative estimation techniques. Column 1 shows the results using ordinary least squares (OLS). To control for possible endogeneity, we used early-impact aid (and early-impact aid squared) lagged one four-year period. In this case, the estimated coefficient (not surprisingly) is smaller, although it remains significant at the 1 percent level. Since this is the smallest coefficient among our results, to be conservative, we use it in interpreting the results in the next section. Columns 2–4 run the same regression in differences to eliminate country-fixed effects that may bias the coefficients. Differencing introduces endogeneity bias for differenced log initial GDP per capita, which is instrumented in the results shown in column 3. Column 4 reintroduces late-impact aid and shows that its effect differs

[5] Note that the curve for "long-impact aid" is nonlinear (estimated using both aid and aid squared), although the curve is small enough that the figure appears to be linear. For humanitarian aid we show the curve only to 2 percent of GDP since there are no observations beyond that point, and to show an upward-sloping curve thereafter would be misleading.

Figure 2.1. The Relationship Between Aid and Growth

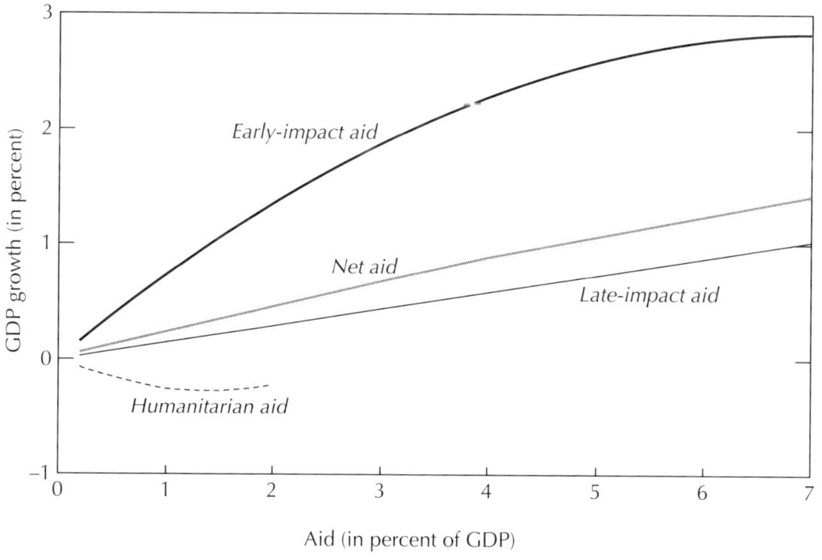

Source: Clemens, Radelet, and Bhavnani (2004), based on the estimated coefficients shown in column 2 of Table 2.1.
Note: As we emphasize in the text, the weaker relationship for "late-impact" and "humanitarian" aid does not necessarily mean these flows have no impact on growth. In our view, a different modeling technique is required to explore these relationships, which we leave for future research.

from that of early-impact aid using the OLS estimator as well. The basic results stand throughout, with the coefficient slightly larger than in column 1 and still significantly different from zero.

What about the claim that aid works best in countries with good policies and institutions? Our results show that early-impact aid has a positive impact on growth, on average. This does not mean that aid works equally well everywhere. Some of the observations fall above the line, suggesting a stronger than average aid-growth relationship, while others fall below the line, suggesting a weaker relationship. We examined each of the independent variables as possible explanations of a stronger or weaker relationship: level of income, policy, geography, etc. Only two variables stood out as showing some explanatory power in distinguishing countries with stronger or weaker relationships: institutional quality and life expectancy, as shown in Table 2.4. The results are suggestive that in countries with better institutions, the relationship between early-impact aid and growth is stronger than otherwise (but we emphasize that results do not depend on strong institutions). Similarly, in countries with higher life expectancy (that is, better health), the relationship is stronger than

Table 2.3. Robustness Tests

	1 OLS	2 OLS	3 2SLS	4 GMM
		Difference equations (boldface coefficients correspond to instrumented variables)		
Early-impact aid lagged	0.484 (0.162)***	0.679 (0.251)***	0.590 (0.297)**	0.525 (0.256)**
Early-impact aid squared lagged	−0.0275 (0.0110)**	−0.0403 (0.0147)***	−0.0362 (0.0202)*	−0.0289 (0.0166)*
Late-impact aid lagged				0.000864 (0.163)
Late-impact aid squared lagged				−0.00789 (0.00549)
Log repayments lagged	−0.307 (0.133)**	−0.307 (0.277)	−0.244 (0.316)	−0.179 (0.325)
Log initial GDP per capita	−0.370 (0.351)	−6.34 (1.38)***	**−10.0** **(4.65)****	**−10.8** **(4.59)****
East Asia	2.10 (0.479)***			
Tropics	−1.94 (0.342)***			
Log initial life expectancy	3.23 (1.41)**	−5.66 (7.24)	−2.80 (5.56)	−1.70 (5.18)
Civil war	−2.22 (0.580)***	−2.17 (0.774)***	−2.10 (0.715)***	−2.26 (0.818)***
Lagged civil war	1.95 (0.584)***	1.38 (0.748)*	0.906 (1.14)	0.645 (1.07)
Institutional quality	0.341 (0.100)***	0.344 (0.299)	0.343 (0.226)	0.334 (0.238)
Inflation	−1.97 (0.377)***	−1.84 (0.567)***	−1.91 (0.517)***	−2.05 (0.513)***
Budget balance	7.74 (3.59)**	11.2 (5.26)**	10.5 (8.36)	10.0 (8.36)
Openness Sachs-Warner	1.38 (0.389)***	1.40 (0.735)*	1.20 (0.536)**	1.24 (0.551)**
Observations	367	297	297	298
Adjusted *R*-squared	0.430	0.263	0.280	0.280

Source: Clemens, Radelet, and Bhavnani (2004).
Note: Dependent variable is (differenced, in regressions 2–4) four-year average GDP per capita growth. Robust and clustered standard errors in parentheses. * significant at 10%; ** significant at 5%; *** significant at 1%. All regressions include period dummies and a constant term.

Table 2.4. Aid Interaction Effects

Dependent variable: GDP per capita growth	1 2SLS	2 GMM	3 2SLS	4 GMM
Early-impact aid	−3.47 (1.98)*	−2.32 (1.45)	0.424 (0.341)	0.356 (0.273)
Early-impact aid squared	−0.0416 (0.0118)***	−0.0379 (0.0081)***	−0.0519 (0.0211)**	−0.0651 (0.0131)***
Log repayments	−0.450 (0.173)***	−0.535 (0.160)***	−0.460 (0.178)***	−0.568 (0.161)***
Log initial GDP per capita	0.010 (0.517)	−0.404 (0.414)	−0.138 (0.591)	−0.153 (0.479)
East Asia	2.44 (0.607)***	2.70 (0.564)***	2.51 (0.688)***	2.96 (0.624)***
Tropics	−2.27 (0.372)***	−2.35 (0.290)***	−2.13 (0.507)***	−2.36 (0.353)***
Log initial life expectancy	−2.05 (3.31)	0.15 (2.46)	3.52 (1.90)*	3.80 (1.61)**
Civil war	−1.32 (0.771)*	−1.70 (0.721)**	−2.23 (0.901)**	−1.57 (0.827)*
Lagged civil war	1.39 (0.625)**	1.38 (0.582)**	2.01 (0.698)***	1.56 (0.621)**
Institutional quality	0.419 (0.118)***	0.398 (0.108)***	0.103 (0.272)	0.008 (0.196)
Inflation	−1.86 (0.658)***	−1.68 (0.534)***	−1.63 (0.558)***	−1.06 (0.354)***
Budget balance	6.89 (4.86)	5.90 (4.22)	7.78 (5.34)	4.64 (4.58)
Openness Sachs-Warner	1.52 (0.431)***	1.43 (0.371)***	1.52 (0.468)***	1.50 (0.383)***
Early-impact aid × log inital life expectancy	1.04 (0.485)**	0.748 (0.352)**		
Early-impact aid × institutional quality			0.104 (0.122)	0.162 (0.086)*
Observations	363	363	370	370
R-squared	0.374	0.386	0.350	0.278

Source: Clemens, Radelet, and Bhavnani (2004).

Note: Dependent variable is four-year average GDP per capita growth. Robust and clustered standard errors in parentheses. * significant at 10%; ** significant at 5%; *** significant at 1%. All regressions include period dummies and a constant term. Aid, aid squared, repayments and the interaction terms are instrumented.

in countries with low life expectancy (controlling for other variables, including income levels).

Interpreting the Results

To interpret the results, we use the smallest and most conservative of the estimated relationship between early-impact aid and growth, as found with the OLS estimation in Table 2.3, column 1. Our results show diminishing returns to aid, so the marginal impact on growth is largest with smaller amounts of aid, and falls as the amount of aid climbs. To give some sense of the magnitude, we focus on the mean observation, where early-impact aid is 2.7 percent of GDP. Since early-impact aid is about one-half of total aid, this is equivalent to total aid of about 5.4 percent of GDP for the representative country. At this point, we find that a 1 percentage point of GDP increase in aid produces an additional 0.31 percentage points of annual growth over the four-year period. Since the increment to GDP will be maintained to some extent over time, we find a high payoff for early-impact aid on average using plausible assumptions (a discount rate and depreciation rate summing to 35 percent). Under these assumptions, each $1 in early-impact aid yields $1.64 in increased income in the recipient country in net present value terms. Under reasonable assumptions, this corresponds to a project-level rate of return of about 13 percent—a quite plausible result. From a different perspective, we find that higher-than-average early-impact aid to sub-Saharan Africa raised per capita growth rates there by about 1 percentage point over the growth that would have been achieved by average aid flows.

Our results with diminishing returns suggest some limits on the ability of typical recipient countries to absorb very large amounts of early-impact aid. However, the point at which the marginal impact of aid reaches zero is well above the amount of aid that most countries receive. Whereas the average country receives early-impact aid flows of about 2.7 percent of GDP, our estimates indicate that the maximum total growth rate (where the marginal impact of additional aid reaches zero) occurs on average when early-impact aid represents 8–9 percent of GDP. Note that since early-impact aid is slightly more than one-half of total aid on average, this implies that the maximum growth rate occurs when total aid reaches about 16–18 percent of GDP in the typical country.

These results do not mean that in any particular country, early-impact aid flows greater than 8–9 percent of GDP are a bad idea. Instead, they represent the typical pattern over the last 30 years. Absorptive capacity can be expanded over time, and some countries undoubtedly can absorb more aid flows than others. Indeed we find that in the presence of strong institutions and better health, the maximum point occurs with larger amounts of aid, suggesting that efforts to strengthen institutions and build human capital can increase returns to aid and help countries effectively absorb larger amounts of aid.

Moreover, we stress that although the quadratic term implies a region in which large amounts of aid could have a negative marginal impact on growth, the data do not support such a conclusion. There are no observations in the sample with early-impact aid exceeding 9 percent of GDP, therefore the data do not show negative returns to aid. The quadratic simply represents a good approximation of the relationship as early-impact aid increases from 0 to 9 percent of GDP, but not thereafter.[6]

Policy Implications and Conclusions

In recent years, scholars have tried to explain the weak relationship between aid and growth in terms of differences in recipient countries. While that explanation retains merit, these results suggest that differences in types of aid are a very strong part of the explanation. Since significant amounts of aid are not directly aimed at supporting growth, it makes little sense for researchers or policymakers to gauge aid effectiveness for those types of aid by their impact on growth. Thus the strong pessimism on aid effectiveness expressed by some analysts is too strong and based on faulty analysis: there is a strong positive and casual relationship between growth-oriented aid and growth.

At the same time, no one should conclude that aid has always worked or that it cannot be made more effective. There are many countries that have received substantial amounts of aid that have stagnated or worse, and much aid has been wasted, stolen, or otherwise used to support poor governments. The results reviewed here suggest, however, that on average, aid that has been aimed at growth in fact has had a positive impact on growth. There is little doubt that aid can be made even more effective by reducing bureaucracy, harmonizing donor procedures to reduce the cost on recipients, making aid flows more predictable, reducing tied aid, and allocating aid based on ability to achieve results (Birdsall, 2004; Radelet, 2004; World Bank, 1998).

The relationship between early-impact aid and growth seems to be stronger in countries with good institutions and better health. Thus, those that argue that aid works *only* in countries with good institutions overstate their case. It would be more accurate to say that aid works better in countries with good institutions, but can be effective in other situations as well. While it is easy to think of countries with weak institutions that have failed, there are some that have had some success as well. Aid helped support growth in Mozambique and Uganda in the early years after their civil conflict ended even through policies and institutions were far from ideal. Most observers believe that aid has played an important role in stabilizing Sierra Leone since the end of its civil war. Aid helped to support sustained growth and poverty reduction in Indonesia during

[6] We achieve almost the same results using the log of aid rather than a quadratic term, in which there is no region in which the growth rate falls as aid increases.

the Suharto regime, even in the 1970s and 1980s, when institutions were weak, corruption was problematic, and policies were less than ideal.

We hasten to add that the weak relationship between late-impact and humanitarian aid and growth over a four-year period should not be interpreted to mean that they are ineffective. Different modeling techniques are required to explore those relationships, which we leave for future research. There is other evidence that at least some aid for health and education has been effective. For example, recent work has shown the role that aid has played in supporting large-scale successful health interventions, such as eradicating small pox, significantly reducing the prevalence of polio and river blindness, and reducing the incidence of diarrheal diseases (Levine and others, 2004).

Finally, the evidence (from the study reviewed here and from other research on aid and growth) suggests that absorptive capacity constraints are real, but should not be seen as an immutable barrier to growth. The impact of aid on growth appears to diminish as aid volumes increase. But the impact can be enhanced by improving health and by strengthening institutions. In other words, absorptive capacity can be expanded by strengthening human and institutional capacity. This suggests that policy discussions should not focus exclusively on determining the limits of aid on growth, but rather on how those limits can be expanded, and how aid can be made even more effective in supporting growth and development in the future.

References

Bauer, Péter, 1972, *Dissent on Development* (Cambridge, Massachusetts: Harvard University Press).

Birdsall, Nancy, 2004, "Seven Deadly Sins: Reflections on Donor Failings," Working Paper No. 50 (Washington: Center for Global Development).

Boone, Peter, 1994, "The Impact of Foreign Aid on Savings and Growth," Centre for Economic Performance Working Paper No. 677 (London: London School of Economics).

Burnside, Craig, and David Dollar, 2000, "Aid, Policies, and Growth," *American Economic Review*, Vol. 90 (September), pp. 847–68.

Clemens, Michael, Steven Radelet, and Rikhil Bhavnani, 2004, "Counting Chickens When They Hatch: The Short-Term Effect of Aid on Growth," Working Paper No. 44 (Washington: Center for Global Development).

Collier, Paul, and David Dollar, 2002, "Aid Allocation and Poverty Reduction," *European Economic Review*, Vol. 46 (September), pp. 1475–500.

Dalgaard, Carl-Johan, and Henrik Hansen, 2000, "On Aid, Growth, and Good Policies," CREDIT Research Paper No. 00/17 (Nottingham, United Kingdom: Centre for Research in Economic Development and International Trade, University of Nottingham).

———, and Finn Tarp, 2004, "On the Empirics of Foreign Aid and Growth," *Economic Journal*, Vol. 114 (June), pp. F191–216.

Dowling, J. Malcolm, and Ulrich Hiemenz, 1982, "Aid, Savings, and Growth in the Asian Region," Report No. 3 (Manila: Economic Office, Asian Development Bank).

Durbarry, Ramesh, Norman Gemmell, and David Greenaway, 1998, "New Evidence on the Impact of Foreign Aid on Economic Growth," CREDIT Research Paper No. 98/8 (Nottingham, United Kingdom: Centre for Research in Economic Development and International Trade, University of Nottingham).

Easterly, William, 2001, *The Elusive Quest for Growth: Economists' Adventures and Misadventures in the Tropics* (Cambridge, Massachusetts: MIT Press).

———, Ross Levine, and David Roodman, 2004, "New Data, New Doubts: A Comment on Burnside and Dollar's 'Aid, Policies, and Growth,' " *American Economic Review*, Vol. 94 (June), pp. 774–780(7).

Friedman, Milton, 1958, "Foreign Economic Aid: Means and Objectives," *Yale Review*, Vol. 47, No. 4, p. 500.

Hadjimichael, Michael T., Dhaneshwar Ghura, Martin Mühleisen, Roger Nord, and E. Murat Ucer, 1995, *Sub-Saharan Africa: Growth, Savings, and Investment*, 1986–93, IMF Occasional Paper No. 118 (Washington: International Monetary Fund).

Hansen, Henrik, and Finn Tarp, 2000, "Aid Effectiveness Disputed," *Journal of International Development*, Vol. 12 (April), pp. 375–98.

———, 2001, "Aid and Growth Regressions," *Journal of Development Economics*, Vol. 64 (April), pp. 547–70.

Isham, Jonathan, Daniel Kaufmann, and Lant Pritchett, 1995, "Governance and Returns on Investment: An Empirical Investigation," Policy Research Working Paper No. 1550 (Washington: World Bank).

Lensink, Robert, and Howard White, 2001, "Are There Negative Returns to Aid?" *Journal of Development Studies*, Vol. 37 (August), pp. 42–65.

Levine, Ruth, and the "What Works" Working Group, with Molly Kinder, 2004, *Millions Saved: Proven Successes in Global Health* (Washington: Center for Global Development).

Levy, Victor, 1988, "Aid and Growth in Sub-Saharan Africa: The Recent Experience," *European Economic Review*, Vol. 32 (November), pp. 1777–95.

Mavrotas, George, 2002, "Aid and Growth in India: Some Evidence from Disaggregated Aid Data," *South Asia Economic Journal*, Vol. 3, No. 1, pp. 19–49.

———, 2003, "Assessing Aid Effectiveness in Uganda: An Aid-Disaggregation Approach" (Oxford: Oxford Policy Management).

Mosley, Paul, 1980, "Aid, Savings, and Growth Revisited," *Oxford Bulletin of Economics and Statistics*, Vol. 42, No. 2, pp. 79–95.

———, John Hudson, and Sara Horrell, 1987, "Aid, the Public Sector and the Market in Less Developed Countries," *Economic Journal*, Vol. 97, No. 387, pp. 616–41.

Owens, Trudy, and John Hoddinott, 1999, "Investing in Development or Investing in Relief: Quantifying the Poverty Tradeoffs Using Zimbabwe Household Panel Data," Centre for the Study of African Economies, Department of Economics, Working Paper No. 99-4 (Oxford: University of Oxford).

Papanek, Gustav F., 1973, "Aid, Foreign Private Investment, Savings, and Growth in Less Developed Countries," *Journal of Political Economy*, Vol. 81, No. 1, pp. 120–30.

Radelet, Steven, 2003, *Challenging Foreign Aid: A Policymaker's Guide to the Millennium Challenge Account* (Washington: Center for Global Development).

———, 2004, "Aid Effectiveness and the Millennium Development Goals," Working Paper 39 (Washington: Center for Global Development).

Rajan, Raghuram, and Arvind Subramanian, 2005, "Aid and Growth: What Does the Cross-Country Evidence Really Show?" IMF Working Paper 05/127 (Washington: International Monetary Fund).

Singh, Ram D., 1985, "State Intervention, Foreign Economic Aid, Savings and Growth in LDCs: Some Recent Evidence," *Kyklos*, Vol. 38, No. 2, pp. 216–32.

Stern, Nicholas, 2002, "Making the Case for Aid," in *World Bank, A Case for Aid: Building a Consensus for Development Assistance* (Washington: World Bank).

Stiglitz, Joseph, 2002, "Overseas Aid Is Money Well Spent," *Financial Times* (London), April 14.

World Bank, 1998, *Assessing Aid: What Works, What Doesn't, and Why* (Washington: Oxford University Press).

3

Aid, Growth, and Poverty

AART KRAAY*

The organizers of this conference have asked me to speak about aid and poverty alleviation. We have already heard Steven Radelet provide a very thorough review of the state of the evidence on the effects of aid on growth.[1] I would like to use this presentation to make three broad points linking this evidence on aid and growth to poverty alleviation.

First, I would like to review the cross-country evidence on the links from growth to poverty reduction, in order to underscore a basic point that should not be too controversial: sustained poverty reduction is impossible without sustained growth. In fact, I would like to go a step beyond this and argue, based on cross-country empirical evidence, that the recent vogue among development practitioners for debating the extent to which growth is "pro-poor" may be somewhat misguided. As we shall see, cross-country differences in the extent to which growth is more or less pro-poor are dwarfed by cross-country differences in growth performance itself. This should focus our minds squarely on understanding the fundamentals of growth as a vehicle for poverty reduction.

Second, while I believe that there is plenty of evidence in support of the proposition that aid has a positive impact on growth (and through this, on poverty), I would like to put the magnitude of the growth benefits of aid in perspective. In particular, while several careful and sensible papers have been able to find positive and significant effects of aid on growth, it is important to note that the share of cross-country variation in growth performance that we can

*World Bank. I would like to thank, without implication, Alan Gelb and Steve Knack for helpful comments. This paper draws heavily on recent work of my own, as well as joint work with Claudio Raddatz, and Daniel Kaufmann and Massimo Mastruzzi.

[1] Clemens, Radelet, and Bhavnani (2004).

explain using aid is typically not that large. Measures of policies and institutions, as well as exogenous shocks, account for much more of cross-country variance in growth than does aid itself. And of course, as is common in the entire empirical growth literature, a substantial share of growth remains unexplained.

This brings me to my third broad point: gaining a better understanding of the nonaid determinants of growth, and the extent that foreign aid can help to improve them, seems important for thinking about the effectiveness of aid in the long term as an instrument for poverty reduction. This point is of course very broad, and potentially opens the door to a discussion of many issues. Since there is no way I can be comprehensive, I will instead be very selective and focus on two issues that I think are important and that I have been working on in my own research.

One of these issues is the link between good governance and economic performance. By now, we have a great deal of empirical evidence showing an important causal effect of better governance on economic outcomes. Against this background, the on-average poor performance of countries in sub-Saharan Africa on most measures of governance, and the absence of any clear evidence of improvements in recent years, is of great concern. Yet some of the recent discussion of scaling up of aid to Africa seeks to minimize governance issues in the region by pointing out that governance is no worse than would be expected given low income in the region. Claims like this are difficult to substantiate without a clear understanding of the directions of causation between income and governance, and vice versa. As I will argue in more detail below, I do not think that there is much compelling evidence to suggest that weak governance in sub-Saharan Africa can be attributed to low income, and so it think it is misleading to suggest that governance is not an issue in the region. And a better understanding of how aid should be allocated to recognize differences in governance that affect how well it can be used, as well as a better understanding of how aid can be used to improve governance, seems central to the growth and poverty reduction agenda in the region.

The other issue concerns the importance of poverty traps for understanding low-income levels and the slow pace of development in sub-Saharan Africa. Many observers have argued that a variety of self-reinforcing mechanisms, or poverty traps, are responsible for the region's stagnant income levels. To the extent that this argument is correct, it has important implications for aid and for development policy. Put simply, the existence of poverty traps lends support to the idea that a "big push" or a major scaling up of aid is required to break countries out of these poverty traps and launch them on sustainable growth paths. Given the significance of such a policy recommendation, it seems important to have a good empirical understanding of the importance of such poverty traps. But as I will discuss in more detail below, in my view, there is actually relatively little compelling evidence that such traps exist. This is not to say that substantial increases in aid to Africa are a bad idea—on the contrary, there probably are very many useful interventions and policies that foreign aid can support. But the absence of clear evidence supporting poverty traps should caution us against thinking that large increases in aid are a necessary condition for growth, or that large increases in aid will have proportionately much larger growth benefits than small increases in aid.

I. Growth and Poverty Reduction

Figure 3.1 shows the relationship between growth and poverty reduction, using household survey data from a sample of developing countries in the 1980s and 1990s. Each point in the figure corresponds to an episode or "spell" lasting at least five years and averaging 10 years in length, over which available data allow us to calculate the proportional change in the headcount measure of poverty and the proportional change in mean income or consumption. It is clear from this figure that there is a very strong negative relationship between growth and changes in poverty. Virtually all observations are clustered in the bottom-right quadrant (positive growth and declines in poverty) or the top-left quadrant (negative growth and increases in poverty).

Certainly there are also deviations from this average relationship. In Ghana, Mauritania, and Uganda, for example, growth was similar in the 1 percent to

Figure 3.1. Growth and Poverty Reduction

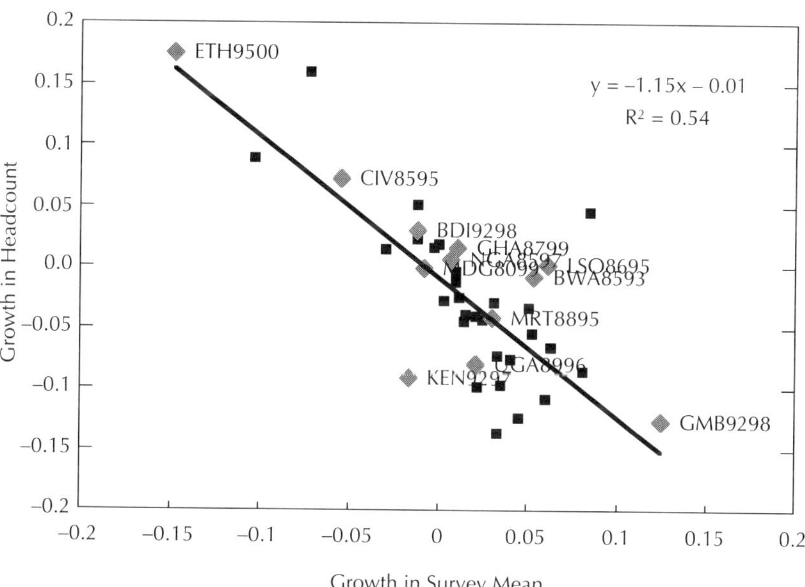

Source: Kraay (2005).

3 percent range over the indicated periods, but the rates of change in poverty ranged from about –8 percent to +2 percent a year. For Africa as a whole, it is telling that 8 of the 12 countries fall above the regression line, indicating a poverty reduction performance that was worse than what would be expected for a typical developing country with similar growth performance.

How should we think about deviations from this average relationship between growth and poverty reduction? To answer this, it is useful to decompose changes in poverty somewhat mechanically into three components:

$$\textit{Percent Change in Poverty} = \textit{Growth in Mean} \times \textit{Sensitivity of Poverty to Growth} + \textit{Changes in Relative Incomes}$$

The first two terms in this decomposition—growth times the sensitivity of poverty to growth—are referred to as the "growth component" of changes in poverty. This captures the extent to which poverty would have fallen had there been no changes in relative incomes, that is, no change in the distribution of income, over the period. The third term captures the part of the change in poverty that is attributable to changes in relative incomes.[2]

In a recent paper, I have empirically implemented this decomposition using a large cross-country dataset on growth and changes in poverty (Kraay, 2005). A useful way to summarize the relative importance of these components of poverty reduction is by using variance decompositions. Figure 3.2 provides a graphical depiction of this variance decomposition. It plots the total change in poverty on the horizontal axis, and the growth component of changes in poverty on the vertical axis. The slope of the line of best fit has a variance decomposition interpretation: it is the share of the cross-country variation in changes in poverty that can be accounted for by cross-country differences in the growth component of changes in poverty. The fact that this slope is 0.97 indicates that virtually all of the cross-country variation in changes in poverty is due to cross-country differences in the growth component. Conversely, virtually none of the variation in changes in poverty is due to changes in relative incomes. Put simply, the figure shows us that if poverty fell, it is by far most likely because the growth component of changes in poverty was large (in absolute value), and it is quite unlikely that poverty fell because income inequality fell in such a way as to reduce poverty.

We can also decompose the growth component of changes in poverty into growth itself, and cross-country differences in the sensitivity of poverty to growth. While it is more difficult to do a variance decomposition here (because we now have the product of two terms rather than the sum), it still is very informative to graph the growth component against growth itself, as is done in Figure 3.3. It is clear from this figure that if the growth component of poverty

[2] This decomposition was introduced by Datt and Ravallion (1992).

Figure 3.2. Decomposing Changes in Poverty: Growth vs. Distribution

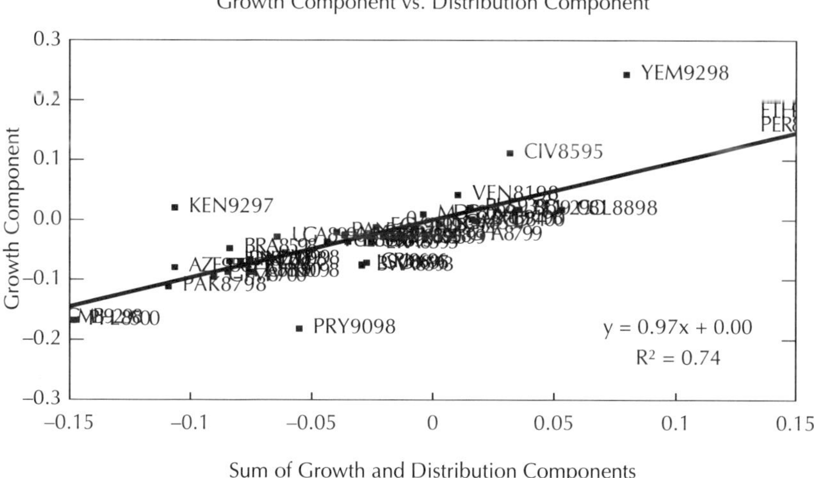

Source: Kraay (2005).

Figure 3.3. Decomposing Growth Component of Changes in Poverty

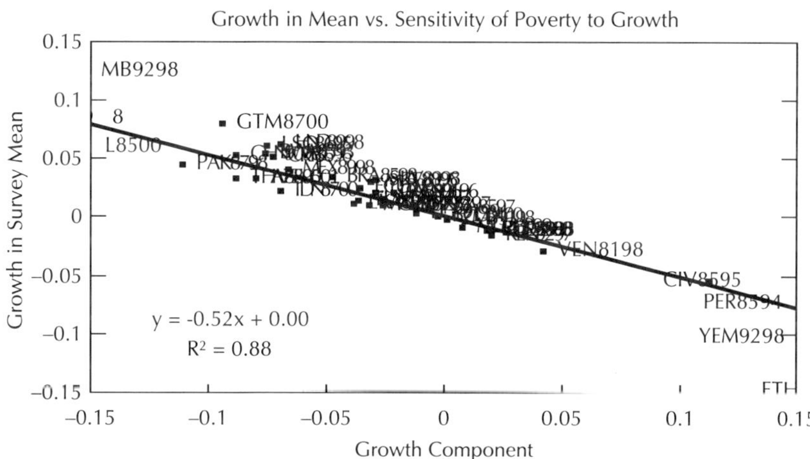

Source: Kraay (2005).

reduction is large, it is most likely that growth itself was large, rather than the sensitivity of poverty to growth that was large. This figure captures the fact that cross-country differences in the sensitivity of poverty to growth (holding constant relative incomes) are in fact relatively small.

The variance decompositions in the two previous figures refer only to the headcount measure of poverty, and also to a set of spells of poverty changes that cover fairly long periods of time, averaging about 10 years. I have also implemented these decompositions for different poverty measures, and for a much larger sample of short spells of changes in poverty averaging about three years in length. These results are summarized in Table 3.1. Briefly, I find that for more bottom-sensitive poverty measures, the share of poverty reduction due to growth is somewhat smaller than for the headcount. This evidence does not mean that the poorest of the poor are less likely to share in the benefits of growth. Rather it simply reflects the fact that more bottom-sensitive poverty measures place lower weight on growth in average incomes. It is also the case that over shorter periods, the share of growth is somewhat smaller than for the sample of long spells. This to a large extent reflects greater volatility of measured inequality within countries, which tends to average out considerably over time. Overall, however, these results are broadly consistent with results we have seen for the headcount measure of poverty: most of the variance in changes in poverty is due to growth itself, especially over the medium to long run.

This decomposition is also useful for thinking about why it is that countries in Africa have on average had slower poverty reduction for a given rate of growth, as seen in Figure 3.1. One possibility is that countries in the region were relatively more likely to see increases in inequality, which dampened the effect of growth on poverty. We have already seen that on average, these relative income changes account for very little of the changes in poverty. The top panel of Figure 3.4 plots this (typically small) component of poverty reduction

Table 3.1. Variance Decompositions of Changes in Poverty

	Share of variance in changes in poverty due to growth component	Share of variance of growth component due to growth
Long Spells (Average Length = 10 years)		
Headcount	0.97	0.89
Poverty Gap	0.79	0.92
Squared Poverty Gap	0.68	0.92
Watts	0.72	0.92
All Spells (Average Length = 3 years)		
Headcount	0.70	0.91
Poverty Gap	0.53	0.92
Squared Poverty Gap	0.43	0.92
Watts	0.46	0.92

Source: Kraay (2005).

Figure 3.4. Growth and Poverty Reduction in Sub-Saharan Africa

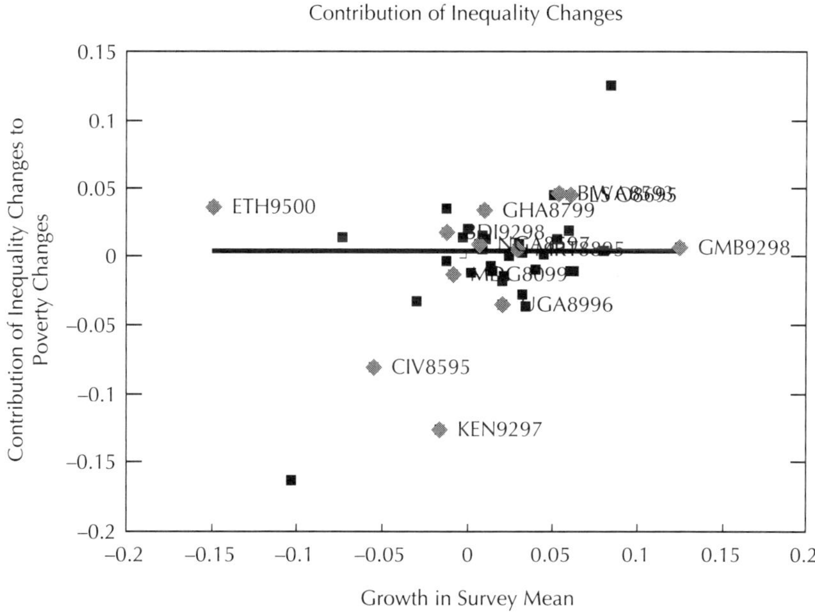

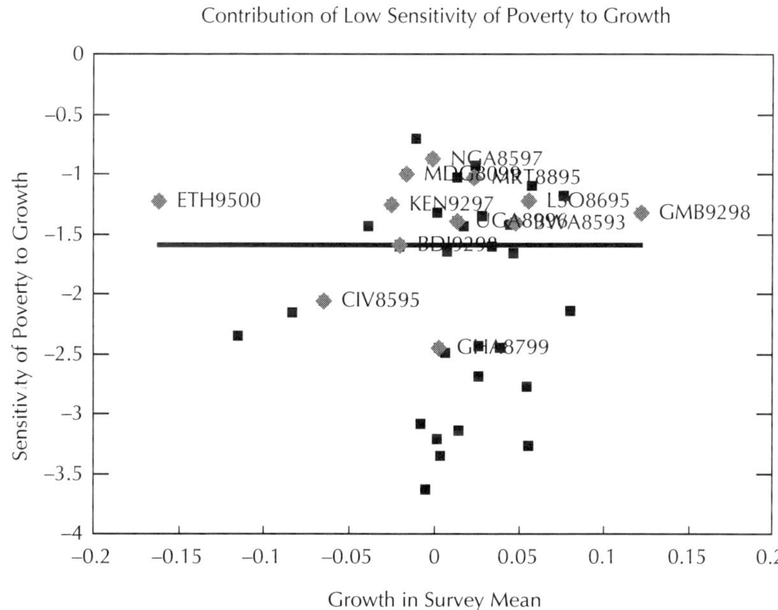

Source: Author's calculations based on Kraay (2005).

on the vertical axis, against growth itself on the horizontal axis. It is interesting to observe that the spells in countries in Africa are fairly evenly distributed above and below the horizontal heavy line corresponding to the median for all countries. What this tells us is that countries in this region were not especially likely to have increases in inequality offsetting the effects of growth on poverty reduction.

The other possible explanation for slower-than-expected poverty reduction given growth is that the sensitivity of poverty to growth has been lower in Africa. This is highlighted in the bottom panel of Figure 3.4, which plots the sensitivity of poverty to growth (holding constant relative incomes) on the vertical axis, and again has growth on the horizontal axis. Here the striking observation is that 10 out of the 12 spells occurring in Africa fall above the heavy line indicating the median value for all countries. This means that the sensitivity of poverty to growth in Africa was on average lower (in absolute value) than in the rest of the world. This lower-than-average sensitivity of poverty to growth in Africa can be traced back to Africa's low-income levels, and somewhat higher-than-average inequality, which together dampen the effect of growth on poverty. In my view, this lower-than-average sensitivity of poverty to growth in the region also underscores the importance of more rapid and sustained growth for poverty reduction.

Finally, this empirical evidence is useful for the broader discussion around the notion of "pro-poor growth" which has become widespread in recent years. While the term "pro-poor growth," has become quite popular, there is not yet much consensus as to its exact meaning. At one extreme is the view that growth is pro-poor only if relative incomes change in such a way as to reduce poverty (Kakwani, 2000). At the other extreme is the view that growth is pro-poor as long as poverty falls (Ravallion and Chen, 2003). It seems to me that the choice between these two definitions is fairly clear, and that the latter definition makes much more terminological sense. Consider the case of China's rapid growth, and also rising inequality, since 1980. This period has seen enormous reductions in the numbers of the absolutely poor in China, and it would seem quite odd to refer to this experience of massive poverty reduction as not being pro-poor simply because inequality also increased over this time. Conversely, there have been cases of countries with declining incomes, rising poverty, but also declining inequality—it would also seem peculiar to refer to such episodes as pro-poor.

There is, however, in my view a more substantive problem with this discussion of pro-poor growth. It seems to me that the value-added of the pro-poor prefix appended to the term growth depends greatly on (a) the extent to which there are differences between pro-poor growth and just plain growth, and (b) the extent to which policies can influence these differences. The variance decompositions that we have seen suggest that the distinctions between growth and pro-poor growth are actually quite small on average in historical data, relative to the overall variation in poverty reduction. If we adopt the purely relative definition of pro-poor growth, then discussions of the pro-poorness of growth concern just a small part of poverty reduction. And even if we take the second and more sensible definition of pro-poor growth, the fact that the growth component of changes in poverty is dominated by growth itself (particularly in the long run) again suggests that the gap between growth and pro-poor growth is relatively small. Finally, at the cross-country level of analysis, we do not yet have a great deal of empirical evidence as to the policy determinants of changes in relative incomes that might make growth more pro-poor. There are relatively few robust cross-country findings on the determinants of levels or changes in summary statistics of inequality.[3]

In summary, we have seen that reductions in poverty require sustained growth, and that historically most of the variation in countries' experience with poverty reduction can be traced back to cross-country differences in growth performance. This points to the centrality of growth for poverty reduction, which in turn underscores the importance of aid, and other factors, for growth. Before moving on to these issues, two final qualifications or caveats are in order. First, in this discussion, I have focused on income and/or consumption-based measures of poverty, which as we have seen move very strongly with changes in average incomes. However, we also care about nonincome dimensions of poverty, notably health and education outcomes. While these are also strongly correlated income levels across countries, within countries over time, the relationship between growth and improvements in health and education outcomes tends to be weaker.[4] There are many reasons for this, and their discussion would occupy an entire additional presentation. For now, however, I want simply to acknowledge that the links between growth and these nonincome dimensions of poverty reduction are not as strong as those we have seen with income poverty. Second, the fact that on average, changes in relative incomes matter little for poverty reduction, and the fact that we have few robust cross-country correlates of these relative income changes does not mean that policymakers in any country can be oblivious to the distributional consequences of macroeconomic policies. Any policy change in any given country will impact individuals differently, and careful country-specific analysis can shed light on likely impacts. But neither of these qualifications undermine the broader message of this section concerning the importance of growth for poverty reduction.

[3] See Dollar and Kraay (2002) for an example of the difficulty in finding statistically significant determinants of the first quintile share using cross-country data. In addition, in Kraay (2005), I also look at the precise measures of inequality change that matter for different poverty issues of interest, and I again find no strong patterns linking these to a variety of measures of policy.

[4] See, for example, Easterly (1999).

II. Growth and Poverty Reduction Depend on Much More Than Aid

In the previous section, we have seen that growth is central to poverty reduction. We also have a large body of evidence pointing to a significant impact of aid on growth. As has been nicely summarized by Steven Radelet, this impact of aid on growth may depend on the type of aid, how it is financed, the time horizon, and also on the policy and institutional environment of the recipient country. Putting these two observations together provides a direct link from aid to poverty reduction. But at the same time, I think it is important to put this channel from aid to poverty reduction in perspective, by noting the obvious: growth depends on much more than just aid.

This point can be seen most vividly by taking a representative growth regression from the aid and growth literature. I take one of the core specifications from Burnside and Dollar (2000), which is one of the most influential papers documenting the extent to which the effectiveness of aid depends on the quality of policies in the country.[5] This paper gives in my view a reasonable, and probably representative, estimate of the growth effects of aid. The empirical specification is based on a panel dataset of four-year average growth rates spanning a large sample of developing countries. I decompose the variance of the dependent variable—growth—into portions explained by different groups of explanatory variables in the regression. Figure 3.5 summarizes the results of this decomposition. The effect of aid on growth is captured by two variables, measuring the direct effect of aid, as well as the interaction of aid with their index of policy. While these terms are statistically significant, it is important to note that they account for just 4 percent of the variation in the dependent variable. By contrast, the direct effect of policies, as well as institutional quality, together account for about 17 percent of the variation in growth; and exogenous factors such as regional dummies and ethnic fractionalization account for another 18 percent. In total, this still leaves 61 percent of the variation in growth unaccounted for.

My objective here is not to criticize this regression in particular, nor is it to criticize cross-country growth empirics in general. As noted above, the Burnside-

[5] While the results in this paper have been criticized for their lack of econometric robustness, it is important to note that the argument that aid works better in good policy and institutional environments is built on much more than this one paper. Burnside and Dollar (2004) provide updated cross-country empirical evidence in support of this interaction. Several papers have also documented that aid projects tend to work better in countries with good institutions (Isham and Kaufmann, 1999; Dollar and Levin, 2005). And similar conclusions about the greater effectiveness of aid in good policy environments can be found in the case studies of aid and reform in Africa documented in Devarajan, Dollar, and Holmgrem (2001).

Figure 3.5. Estimated Contribution of Aid to Growth

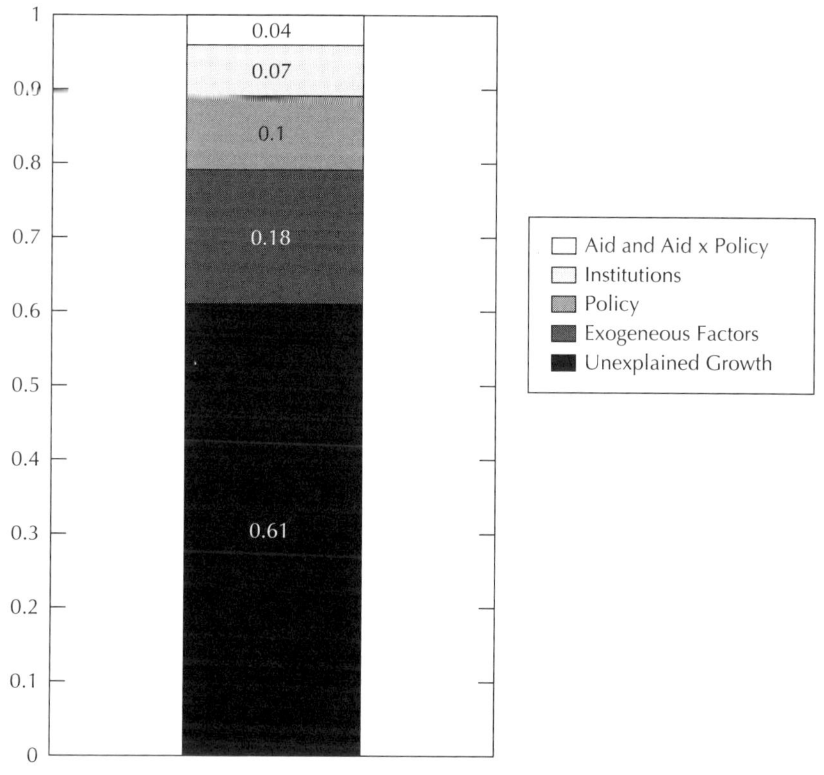

Source: Author's calculations based on Burnside and Dollar (2000).

Dollar (2000) paper is rightly one of the most influential papers on the effects of aid on growth. Rather, this simple variance decomposition underscores the observation that growth depends on much more than just aid. Thus while aid can contribute to poverty alleviation, over the medium to long term—where most of the changes in poverty depend on growth—factors other than aid will be important as well for determining the pace of poverty reduction.

Finally, it should also be noted that aid can also have direct effects on poverty independent of any effect on aggregate growth. In terms of direct effects on income-poverty, such a redistributive channel is likely to be small—after all, we have seen in the previous section that the contribution of relative income changes to poverty reduction has historically been small on average. But at the same time it is worth noting that a significant fraction of aid is—often very successfully—directed at attacking nonincome forms of poverty in ways that may not have any significant impact on growth in the medium run.

For example, a recent book from the Center for Global Development documents 17 very successful public health interventions in developing countries, often significantly financed by foreign aid.[6] These include campaigns against river blindness in Africa, tuberculosis in China, measles in Latin America, and many more. There are also many successful examples of aid financing improvements in education, particularly among those traditionally having less access to schooling. And a renewed emphasis on impact evaluation among aid donors is contributing to making these kinds of interventions increasingly effective. These types of human capital improvements vividly illustrate how aid can directly impact nonincome forms of poverty without necessarily affecting growth over the medium run, or possibly even the long run.

III. Governance, Poverty Traps, and Growth

We have seen that growth is central to poverty reduction, and that while there is evidence that aid can raise growth, the share of the variation in growth accounted for by aid is relatively modest. This emphasizes the importance of nonaid determinants of growth for poverty reduction. It also points to the question of how well aid can help to support these other determinants of growth. As noted earlier, this opens the door to a very large set of issues that could possibly be discussed. Since I cannot be comprehensive, I would like to instead discuss two broad issues that I have been working on in my recent research: governance and poverty traps.

Governance and Growth in Africa

Extensive literature over the past 10 years or so has provided compelling evidence that various dimensions of good governance—including the protection of property rights, the absence of corruption, and the existence of competent and effective governments—have important causal effects on economic development. There is also evidence in support of the eminently plausible proposition that aid is more effective in countries with good governance. Against this background, it is sobering to note that available data suggest that the quality of governance in Africa remains on average quite low, and that there is also no strong pattern of improvements in governance that would improve the situation.

Figure 3.6 gives a snapshot of African countries' standing on one cross-country measure of property rights protection or "rule of law" in 2004, taken from Kaufmann, Kraay, and Mastruzzi (2004). The governance measure is on the vertical axis, and countries are organized by per capita income on the horizontal axis. Note that the per capita income variable has been rescaled to have mean zero and standard deviation of 1, as does the governance indicator. Not surprisingly, countries in Africa are concentrated on the extreme left side of

[6] Center for Global Development (2004).

Figure 3.6. Governance and Growth in Sub-Saharan Africa

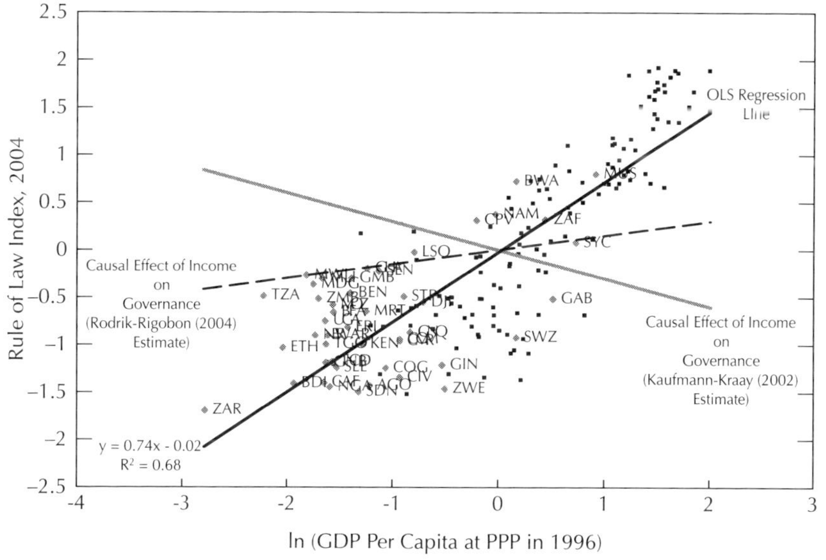

Source: Author's calculations, based on Kaufmann and Kraay (2002), and Rigobon and Rodrik (2004).

the figure, corresponding to very low-income levels. And all but a handful of the countries in the region fall below the median score of zero on the governance indicator. This figure shows clearly that countries in Africa in general are poor and have weak governance.

However, in a recent paper, Jeffrey Sachs has argued that weak governance is not a major factor in Africa's poor growth performance (Sachs and others, 2004). The argument is that once we control for per capita income, countries in sub-Saharan Africa do not have particularly poor governance indicators. A simple way to capture this argument is to put a line of best fit through the points in Figure 3.6 and ask where countries in sub-Saharan Africa fall relative to this line. A somewhat surprising observation from this figure is that more than one-half (27 out of 46) of the countries in the region actually fall above the line of best fit, shown in black. At first glance, this seems to suggest that if we take levels of development into account, governance in the region is roughly what might be expected given low incomes. This line of argument rapidly leads to two strong conclusions. First, it suggests that weak governance in the region may not be a major obstacle to aid effectiveness. And second, by implicitly arguing that Africa's weak governance is the causal outcome of low-income levels, it suggests that increases in income will automatically lead to improvements in governance and that direct interventions to improve governance may not be a great priority.

I do not think that either of these conclusions are appropriate, because they flow from an overly simplistic interpretation of the evidence in Figure 3.6. This interpretation of the figure is valid only to the extent that the line of best fit captures a causal relationship from higher income to better governance. But there is a large body of research which indicates that there is substantial causation in the other direction as well—better governance leads to higher incomes. This means that the simple correlation represented by the black line in Figure 3.6 will exaggerate the positive effects of income on governance because it also reflects the strong effect in the opposite direction, from governance to incomes. In order to compare governance in sub-Saharan Africa to what might be expected given income levels, we therefore need to first isolate these two directions of causation.

The broken and bold lines in Figure 3.6 show two alternative estimates of the causal effect of income on governance. The upward-sloping line comes from Rigobon and Rodrik (2004). They study the causal relationships between per capita income, democracy, rule of law, openness to international trade, and geography using identification through heteroskedasticity to isolate the causal effects.[7] As expected, the broken line is substantially flatter than the ordinary least-squares regression line, consistent with the intuition that the latter relationship overstates the true causal effect of incomes on governance. This flattening has important consequences for our conclusions about the quality of governance in Africa controlling for income levels. Once we isolate this much weaker effect of income on governance, we find that only 7 out of 46 countries in the region fall above the regression line: Botswana, Cape Verde, Ghana, Lesotho, Mauritius, Namibia, and South Africa. In contrast, the vast majority of countries in Africa have governance that is worse than their income levels would predict.

The downward-sloping bold line presents another estimate of the effect of income on governance, coming from Kaufmann and Kraay (2002). They use a different approach to identification and find a zero or even negative impact of income on governance. While this finding is somewhat extreme, it leads to the same conclusions regarding the quality of governance in Africa—now only 6 out

[7] We use their specification excluding democracy, which implies that a 1 standard deviation increase in log per capita GDP improves rule of law by 0.14 standard deviation. They use a different measure of rule of law for the mid-1990s taken from Knack and Keefer (1995). However, its correlation with our rule of law indicator is above 0.8, so we can reasonably use the estimated coefficient from this paper with our governance indicator, suitably standardized. Note also that in the system of equations estimated by Rigobon and Rodrik (2004), the conditional expectation of governance given per capita income also reflects the indirect effects of income on openness, which in turn affects the rule of law. However, these estimated indirect effects are so small that our conclusions are essentially unaffected by ignoring them.

of 46 countries in the region fall above the regression line, indicating governance levels better than what per capita incomes would predict. Overall this evidence suggests that we cannot conclude that governance is not a problem in sub-Saharan Africa, even after taking into account the region's low per capita income levels. If anything, the evidence suggests that, even after controlling for incomes, governance in the region is worse than one might expect.

In order to isolate the causal effects of income on governance in Figure 3.6, we also had to identify the opposite direction of causation, from governance to per capita incomes. Figure 3.7 shows estimates of the causal relationship in this direction, with the two alternative estimates based on the same two papers discussed above. Both papers find a statistically significant causal impact of governance on per capita incomes, although the magnitudes of the estimated effects differ substantially. From this figure, it should be clear that while governance matters, it surely is not the only thing that matters, as there is substantial dispersion around the fitted relationships. And for Africa in particular, it is again striking that the majority of countries in the region fall below the regression lines capturing the effects of governance on income. For the Rigobon and Rodrik (2004) estimate, 40 out of 46 countries fall below the line, and for the Kaufmann and Kraay (2002) estimate, 30 out of 46 countries fall below the line. This observation emphasizes the fact that low-income levels in Africa are not solely attributable to on-average weak governance performance, and that other factors such as Africa's difficult geography, its dependence on natural resources, the prevalence of civil conflict, and many other factors play a role. In short, I do not want to conclude from these figures that governance is the

Figure 3.7. Effects of Governance on Income

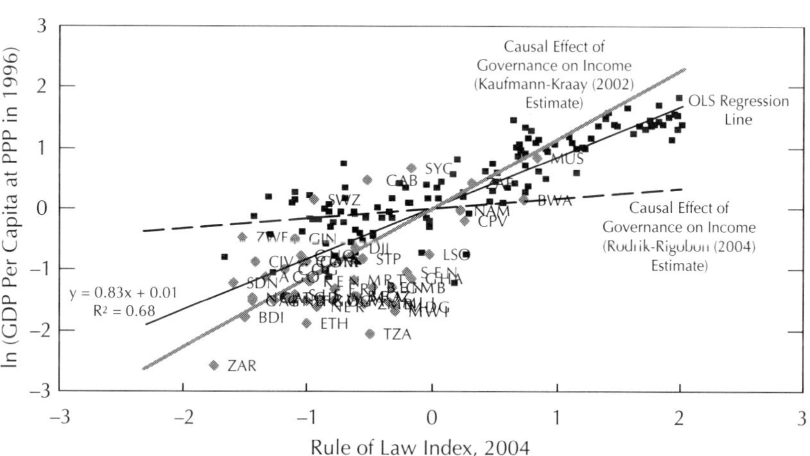

Source: Author's calculations, based on Kaufmann and Kraay (2002), and Rigobon and Rodrik (2004).

Figure 3.8. Improvements in Democratic Accountability Worldwide
(Proportion of countries with competitive elections)

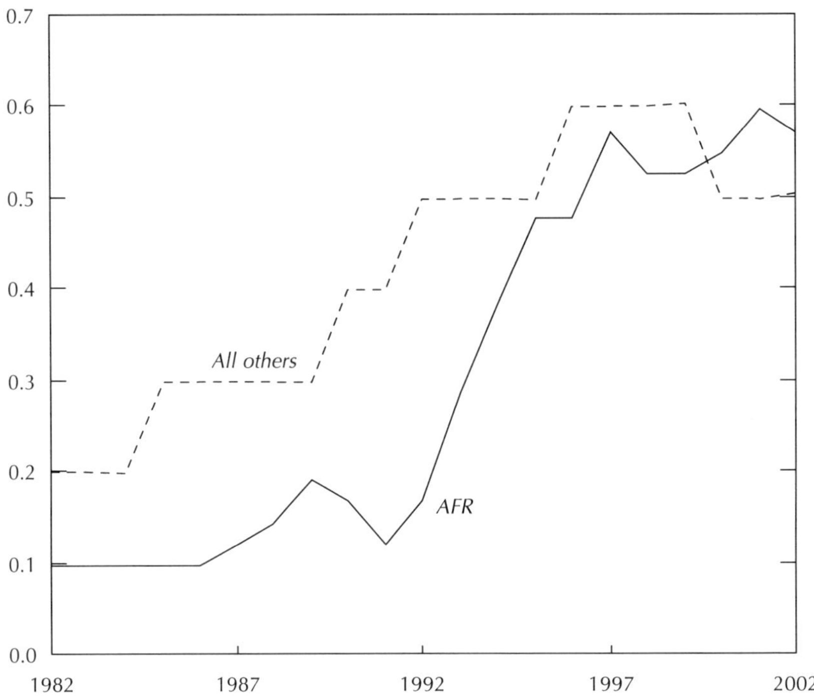

Source: Author's calculations based on Beck and others (2001).

only thing that matters. Rather, I want to emphasize that governance does matter for development, and the causal effect of incomes on governance is sufficiently modest that it does not seem appropriate to "discount" the governance performance of the region simply because it is poor.

Finally, it is useful to briefly examine available evidence on trends in governance in Africa. It is worth noting at the outset that by some measures, notably democratic accountability, there have been substantial improvements over the past 25 years. Figure 3.8 shows that there have been sharp increases in the proportion of countries with competitive elections, and this increase has been more dramatic in Africa than elsewhere, albeit from a lower base.[8] Currently more than one-half of the countries in Africa have chief executives installed as a consequence of competitive elections, a proportion similar to that in the rest of the developing world.

[8] In this figure, elections are deemed to be "competitive" if the winner obtained less than 75 percent of the vote. The data originate from Beck and others (2001).

Figure 3.9. Trends in Governance in Sub-Saharan Africa
(Regional average (2004))

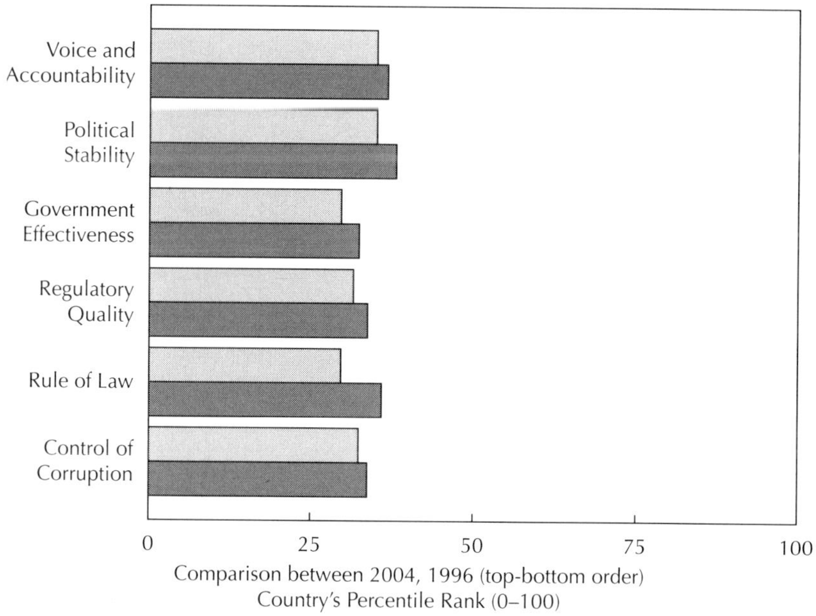

Source: D. Kaufmann, A. Kraay and M. Mastruzzi, 2003: Governance Matters III: Governance Indicators for 1996–2002 (http://www.worldbank.org/wbi/governance/pubs/govmatters3.html)

There is, however, less evidence of clear-cut improvements of governance in the region over the more recent period for which we have more data. Figure 3.9 reports a comparison of six different dimensions of governance between 1996 and 2004. Governance indicators are part of an ongoing project at the World Bank to measure governance and capture perceptions of "voice and accountability," "political instability," "government effectiveness," "regulatory quality," "rule of law," and "control of corruption." Governance measures are composite indicators that combine data from a large number of sources of data on perceptions of the quality of governance.[9] The figure reports the average (across all countries in the region) of the percentile rank of countries on each of the six indicators, in the two periods. The top bar for each indicator corresponds to 2004, while the bottom bar corresponds to 1996. All of the bars are just above 0.25, indicating that the typical country in Africa has a governance score just above the bottom quartile for the world as a whole. It is clear from this figure that there is no obvious trend toward better governance in the region. In fact, the averages show very slight declines in all six dimensions, although one should be

[9] See Kaufmann, Kraay, and Mastruzzi (2004) for a description of governance indicators.

Figure 3.10. Trends in Rule of Law, 1996–2004

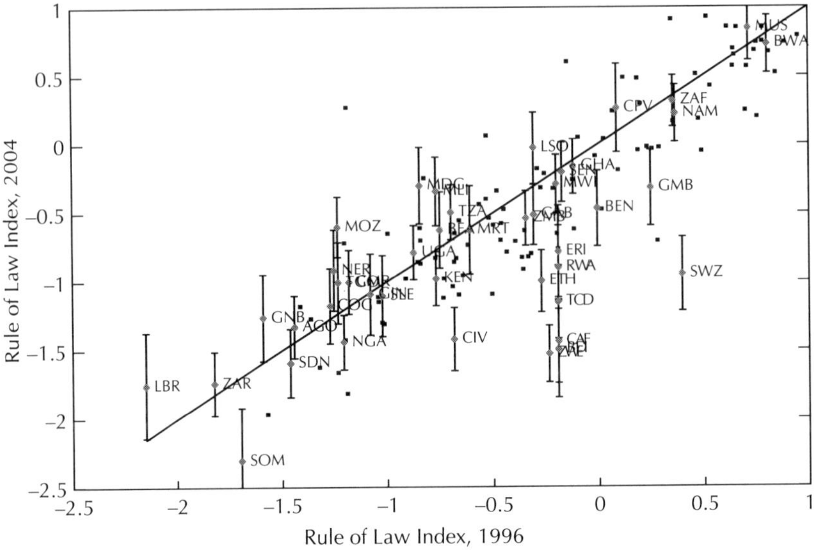

Source: Kaufmann, Kraay, and Mastruzzi (2004).

careful not to conclude too much from these changes because of the non-trivial margins of error associated with governance estimates.

Figure 3.10 goes below these regional averages to show trends in one dimension of governance, the rule of law or property rights protection that we saw earlier. The 2004 score is on the vertical axis, while the 1996 score is on the horizontal axis; therefore countries falling below the 45-degree line correspond to countries where perceptions of this dimension of governance have deteriorated since 1996.[10] Countries in Africa are again labeled, and the vertical line shows the margin of error (technically a 90 percent confidence interval) associated with the governance estimate for each country. For many countries, this vertical line crosses the 45-degree line, suggesting that the change in governance since 1996 is small relative to the unavoidable margins of error that arise when measuring governance. But there are also countries that have registered non-trivial improvements (such as Madagascar, Mali, and Mozambique), while there are quite a few others where there have been non-trivial declines (such

[10] Note that the figure has been truncated at the high end in both dimensions in order to make it more legible. Countries in roughly the top quarter of governance in both periods are not shown as a result.

as Côte d'Ivoire, Somalia, and Zimbabwe). The point of this figure is to show that even over relatively short periods, such as the eight years shown here, there are movements in governance in both directions underlying the fairly stable regional averages shown in Figure 3.9.

I have argued above that good governance has important direct impacts on growth, and also is an important determinant of the effectiveness of foreign aid. In light of Africa's on-average poor performance in various dimensions of governance, and in the absence of compelling evidence of an upward trend for the region as a whole, it seems important for the purpose of this conference to ask what role aid can play in improving governance or institutional quality. It is difficult to do justice to such an important question in the limited time available. And it is all the more difficult given how little we as yet know from an academic and policymaking perspective about the dynamics of institutional change. It does seem useful to at least mention a few specific interventions that are promising. The World Bank Institute, at the request of several governments around the world, has carried out in-depth governance diagnostic surveys in countries that have been useful in sparking a process of debate and discussion over the specifics of institutional strength and weakness. Another example is the Extractive Industries Transparency Initiative proposed by the British government in 2002, developing a set of standards of conduct in the management of natural resource revenues. As argued by Collier (2004), this could be part of a larger set of standards or codes of conduct that could usefully be deployed to improve policymaking and accountability in developing countries, just as a different set of standards has been useful among rich countries (such as standards applying to European Union member states by mutual agreement).

Poverty Traps, Aid, and Growth

Poverty traps have captured the imagination of academics and development practitioners for many years. It is not hard to see why—there are many plausible self-reinforcing mechanisms whereby countries, or individuals, that start out poor might remain poor. If saving rates, or technology, or other positive forces for growth are low precisely because countries are poor, then countries may find themselves trapped at low levels of development. The poverty trap view of Africa's underdevelopment has also been made forcefully in Sachs and others (2004).

Despite both the popularity and plausibility of poverty traps, there is relatively little empirical work testing for poverty traps, and much of this tends not to be too supportive of the poverty trap hypothesis. Some of this work is at the very reduced-form level. A number of papers have documented that the distribution of per capita incomes across countries is gradually becoming bimodal over the past 50 years, with a group of countries clustering around a quite low-income level.[11] Another type of reduced-form evidence comes from looking at the dynamics of individual incomes. Many models of poverty traps suggest that individuals receiving large negative income shocks may take a very long time to recover, and if incomes fall below a certain threshold, they may never recover. However, Lokshin and Ravallion (2004) carefully examine household data from Hungary and Russia, and conclude that there is no evidence of the kind of "threshold effects" associated with models of poverty traps.

The difficulty with this kind of reduced-form evidence is that it provides no guidance as to what underlying mechanism is generating the poverty trap. Without this information, it is difficult to formulate an appropriate policy response. Several recent studies have looked for evidence of particular mechanisms generating poverty traps. One such mechanism has to do with financial market imperfections. If the up-front cost of starting a small business is large, and poor individuals cannot borrow to finance this investment, then they will be unable to reap the benefits of self-employment. McKenzie and Woodruff (2004) use detailed data on microenterprises in Mexico and document that the costs of starting such a small business are surprisingly small, averaging just two weeks' income of a typical low-wage Mexican worker. This casts doubt on the idea that fixed costs combined with financial frictions are responsible for poverty traps.

Another possible mechanism is that productivity is low at low levels of development. This may be because it is difficult to reach minimum efficient scales of production, or because complementary investments in public goods such as infrastructure are inadequate in poor countries. Once these thresholds are crossed, it is possible that productivity increases sharply, allowing countries to reach much higher income levels. Kraay and Raddatz (2005) embed this mechanism in a standard growth model and show that for this mechanism to generate a poverty trap, it must be the case that productivity increases implausibly sharply with the level of development. In particular, they show that if this mechanism is at work, we should expect to see increasing returns to scale that are substantially larger than is ever seen in the large empirical literature on estimating production functions. And somewhat more directly, McKenzie and Woodruff (2004) find in their Mexican data that returns to investment are quite high even for very small enterprises.

Poverty traps might also arise because saving rates are low in poor countries. If many households live at the margins of subsistence, they will be unable to save very much. Public saving might also be low at low-income levels because governments of extremely poor countries have difficulty with tax collection. These low saving rates may translate into sufficiently low investment rates that

---

[11] See Azariadis and Stachurski (2004) for links between models of poverty traps and this kind of empirical evidence; Quah (1993a, 1993b, 1996, and 1997) for evidence; and Kremer, Stock, and Onatski (2001) for a critique. Bloom, Canning, and Sevilla (2003) also provide closely related cross-country evidence.

countries are unable to accumulate very large stocks of productive assets per capita. And if saving rates only begin to increase at much higher levels of development, then countries that start out poor may be stuck in a poverty trap. Kraay and Raddatz (2004) take this hypothesis seriously but find little evidence to support it. From an empirical perspective, they find no evidence that saving rates increase sufficiently quickly with the level of development to generate a poverty trap in a standard growth model with exogenous saving. They also calibrate a growth model with subsistence consumption and find that the impact on saving and growth is substantial only for countries that start out very close to subsistence levels. The significant dispersion in per capita incomes even within a poor region such as sub-Saharan Africa therefore implies that the role of subsistence consumption can only explain low saving and growth in just a few of the poorest countries in the region.

There are also potential poverty traps based on self-reinforcing dynamics in the area of governance. There is, for example, evidence that civil wars are both a consequence and a cause of low income, creating the possibility of a conflict trap (Collier and others, 2003). There are also reasons to believe that high levels of corruption create self-perpetuating expectations of future corruption. The role of such mechanisms in generating stable poverty traps in growth models is not yet fully studied. But these mechanisms are arguably more plausible than some of the others discussed here.

What does all this imply for foreign aid? If saving or technological poverty traps were important, it would be likely that large-scale increases in aid would be necessary in order to get countries across the relevant thresholds and set them on sustained growth paths. But there are at least two reasons to be skeptical of such an argument. First, we have seen that the direct evidence for such traps is not very compelling. Second, most of the empirical evidence on growth impacts of aid suggests that there are diminishing, not increasing, returns to aid. The implications for aid also depend on the mechanisms generating poverty traps in Africa. If, for example, civil conflict or corruption-related poverty traps are important, then large increases in financial assistance might actually be counterproductive, increasing incentives and opportunities for corruption and conflict. As argued in Collier (2004), tackling these underlying dysfunctions directly must be done in parallel with any large increases in aid. Overall, however, the state of the empirical evidence should discourage us from any strong expectation that sufficiently large amounts of aid are likely to trigger sustainable growth booms as countries escape from poverty traps.

IV. Conclusions

My task in this presentation was to discuss the links between aid and poverty reduction. As I have discussed in some detail, there is an abundance of evidence in support of the proposition that growth is central to poverty reduction.

In light of this, the direct growth effects of aid create potentially a strong channel from aid to poverty reduction. But at the same time it should be remembered that cross-country differences in aid account for only a small share of the cross-country differences in growth performance, and for good reason. As Steven Radelet has discussed, not all types of aid should be expected to raise growth. And of course, growth depends on much more than just aid; therefore, a better understanding of how aid can support these other drivers of growth seems important to the discussion of aid and poverty reduction.

I have tried to argue that tackling governance problems in Africa must be part of the growth and poverty reduction agenda, and while we as yet know less than we should about the process of improving governance, there are interventions where aid can play a role. At the same time, I have cautioned against the argument that large-scale increases in aid are essential to breaking the poverty trap in Africa. We do not have sufficient empirical evidence to conclude that such a large scaling up of aid will have disproportionate effects on economic growth. This is not to say that Africa does not need, or cannot effectively use, more development assistance. Rather, we should not be appropriately cautious in our expectations of what the long-term growth effects of such aid may be.

References

Azariadis, Costas, and John Stachurski, 2005, "Poverty Traps," in *Handbook of Economic Growth*, ed. by P. Aghion and S. Durlauf (Amsterdam: North-Holland, forthcoming).

Beck, Thorsten, and others, 2001, "New Tools in Comparative Political Economy: The Database of Political Institutions," *World Bank Economic Review*, Vol. 15, No. 1, pp. 165–76.

Bloom, David E., David Canning, and Jaypee Sevilla, 2003, "Geography and Poverty Traps," *Journal of Economic Growth*, Vol. 8 (December), pp. 355–78.

Burnside, Craig, and David Dollar, 2000, "Aid, Policies, and Growth," *American Economic Review*, Vol. 90 (September), pp. 847–68.

———, 2004, "Aid, Policies, and Growth: Revisiting the Evidence," Policy Research Working Paper No. 3251 (Washington: World Bank).

Clemens, Michael, Steven Radelet, and Rikhil Bhavnani, 2004, "Counting Chickens When They Hatch: The Short-Term Effect of Aid on Growth," Working Paper No. 44 (Washington: Center for Global Development).

Collier, Paul, 2003, *Breaking the Conflict Trap: Civil War and Development Policy* (Oxford: Oxford University Press).

———, 2004, "African Growth, Why a Big Push?" (unpublished; Oxford: University of Oxford).

Datt, Gaurav, and Martin Ravallion, 1992, "Growth and Redistribution Components of Changes in Poverty Measures: A Decomposition with Applications to Brazil and India in the 1980s," *Journal of Development Economics*, Vol. 38 (April), pp. 275–95.

Dollar, David, Shantayanan Devarajan, and Torgny Holmgren, eds., 2001, *Aid and Reform in Africa* (Washington: World Bank).

Dollar, David, and Aart Kraay, 2002, "Growth Is Good for the Poor," *Journal of Economic Growth*, Vol. 7 (September), pp. 195–225.

———, and Victoria Levin, 2005, "Sowing and Reaping" (unpublished; Washington: World Bank).

Easterly, William, 1999, "Life During Growth," *Journal of Economic Growth*, Vol. 4 (September), pp. 239–76.

Isham, Jonathan, and Daniel Kaufmann, 1999, "The Forgotten Rationale for Policy Reform: The Productivity of Investment Projects," *Quarterly Journal of Economics*, Vol. 114 (February), pp. 149–84.

Kakwani, Nanak, and Ernesto M. Pernia, 2000, "What Is Pro-Poor Growth?" *Asian Development Review*, Vol. 18, No. 1, pp. 1–16.

Kaufmann, Daniel, and Aart Kraay, 2002, "Growth Without Governance," *Economia*, Vol. 3, No. 1, pp. 169–215.

———, and Massimo Mastruzzi, 2004, "Governance Matters III: Governance Indicators for 1996, 1998, 2000, and 2002," *World Bank Economic Review*, Vol. 18, No. 2, pp. 253–87.

Kraay, Aart, 2006, "When Is Growth Pro-Poor? Cross-Country Evidence from a Panel of Countries," *Journal of Development Economics* (forthcoming).

———, and Claudio Raddatz, 2005, "Poverty Traps, Aid, and Growth," Policy Research Working Paper No. 3631, background paper for *Global Monitoring Report 2005* (Washington: World Bank).

Levine, Ruth, and the "What Works" Working Group, with Molly Kinder, 2004, *Millions Saved: Proven Successes in Global Health* (Washington: Center for Global Development).

Lokshin, Michael, and Martin Ravallion, 2004, "Household Income Dynamics in Two Transition Economies," *Studies in Nonlinear Dynamics and Econometrics*, Vol. 8 (September), Article 4.

McKenzie, David, and Christopher Woodruff, 2004, "Is There an Empirical Basis for Poverty Traps in Developing Countries?" (unpublished; Stanford, California: Stanford University; San Diego, California: University of California, San Diego).

Quah, Danny T., 1993a, "Empirical Cross-Section Dynamics in Economic Growth," *European Economic Review*, Vol. 37 (April), pp. 426–34.

———, 1993b, "Galton's Fallacy and Tests of the Convergence Hypothesis," *The Scandinavian Journal of Economics*, Vol. 95, No. 4, pp. 427–43.

———, 1996, "Twin Peaks: Growth and Convergence in Models of Distribution Dynamics," *Economic Journal*, Vol. 106, No. 437, pp. 1045–55.

———, 1997, "Empirics for Growth and Distribution: Stratification, Polarization, and Convergence Clubs," *Journal of Economic Growth*, Vol. 2 (March), pp. 27–59.

Ravallion, Martin, and Shaohua Chen, 2003, "Measuring Pro-Poor Growth," *Economics Letters*, Vol. 78 (January), pp. 93–99.

Rigobon, Roberto, and Dani Rodrik, 2004, "Rule of Law, Democracy, Openness, and Income: Estimating the Interrelationships," NBER Working Paper No. 10750 (Cambridge, Massachusetts: National Bureau of Economic Research).

Sachs, Jeffrey, and others, 2004, "Ending Africa's Poverty Trap," *Brookings Papers on Economic Activity: 1*, Brookings Institution, pp. 117–240.

SESSION II

Aid Absorption

Recognizing and Avoiding Macroeconomic Hazards

4

An Analytical Overview of Aid Absorption

Recognizing and Avoiding Macroeconomic Hazards

DAVID L. BEVAN*

I. Introduction

In recent years, aid flows have tended to become more concentrated on a subset of developing countries. [1] In consequence, they have sometimes become large relative to the recipient economy. Present efforts directed at radically increasing the total aid flow, if successful, will tend to reinforce this effect.[2] Current concerns about aid absorption partly reflect the recognition that aid has often been poorly managed and ineffective in the past, but they also reflect the worry that aid may become problematic when it is large relative to the economy it is intended to assist, even if it is well managed.

This paper is concerned primarily with the second of these issues. This is a large subject, and it will be helpful to start by categorizing the types of impact that need to be considered. Most important, we need to distinguish between a narrow and a broad interpretation of macroeconomic hazards. The narrow interpretation focuses on macroeconomic issues *given* the institutional and political

*The author is at the Department of Economics, Oxford University.

[1] Given the purpose of the paper and the extent of the ground it covers, it would be neither feasible nor desirable to attempt to include a full set of references. However, some representative examples, which include extensive references of their own, are provided. These footnotes are largely dedicated to signalling these representative references.

[2] Sachs and others (2004).

framework in the country. The wider interpretation includes possibly adverse impacts on this framework, which may in turn lead to macroeconomic problems. It is important to acknowledge this wider interpretation here, precisely because many of the most prevalent anxieties about aid impact are of this type.

Section II accordingly reviews concerns about the danger of institutional damage, and what may be done to reduce this. The remainder of the paper then considers the narrower set of questions that arise when the institutional framework is taken as independent of the aid flows. Section III examines absorptive capacity constraints, and how to reduce the costs of recognizing them and responding to them. Section IV then looks at the related concern that high aid inflows may appreciate the real exchange rate and undercut the expansion of exports, putting a brake on growth. Section V looks briefly at government operations in the long run, both as regards spending and resources. This section is to prepare the ground for the longer Section VI, which discusses the problem of the inconstancy of aid flows in both the long and short run. Section VII examines debt sustainability and the grant/loan issue, and Section VIII concludes.

It may be felt that this paper ranges rather widely given its brief to look at macroeconomic hazards. However, there are few macroeconomic problems that are not, at least partially, rooted in microeconomic frictions or political processes. It may also be felt that the paper devotes far too little attention to each of the many issues considered. In mitigation, its role is largely to provide an introductory overview of issues that will be considered in more depth in later sessions of the seminar.

II. The Institutional and Political Framework

Impact on the Institutional and Political Framework

There are two related concerns that high aid inflows may damage this framework. One concern is that they will induce aid dependency, weakening a government's capacity to generate domestic resources, and undermining the democratic process. This view is encapsulated in a phrase that inverts the rallying cry of the American War of Independence, to read "no representation without taxation." The argument is that it is only when citizens pay substantial taxes that they begin closely to monitor the government's actions and to enforce accountability.[3] This creates a pressure for institutional evolution of a kind that appears to be growth enhancing. Conversely, if a government has access to substantial external resources, this reduces the pressure to mobilize domestic taxes, weakening this beneficial institutional evolution.

The other concern is that plentiful aid may induce corruption and other rent-seeking activities in much the same way that resource rents have fre-

[3] For example, see Moore (1998).

quently done.[4] This may have been especially true of aid driven by geopolitical concerns; developmental aid has typically been accompanied by devices to increase the probability that it is spent as intended. Even here, however, the fungibility of government resources means that diversion of funds remains possible.

For both these reasons, there is concern that high aid inflows may weaken the political, social, and legal institutions that constrain political elites and interest groups, restrain corruption, and permit the effective enforcement of property rights. This impact need not necessarily involve an absolute institutional deterioration; there would also be a problem if it simply involved a reduction in what would otherwise have been the rate of institutional improvement.

Implications if There Are Such Adverse Impacts

There is evidence that countries with weak institutions have poorer macroeconomic policies, and experience lower growth and greater instability. Indeed, it has been argued that poor macroeconomic policies are a *symptom* of poor institutions, so that institutional reforms are a prerequisite for improved policies.[5] It has also been argued that sustained growth requires not only sustained investment but also sustained institutional improvement. If it were true that increased aid led to institutional damage, then it might be self-defeating even if efficiently deployed.

The evidence that aid is often correlated with higher growth suggests that there is no inevitability about this perverse link. However, it seems wise to try to associate increased aid inflows with attempts at institutional reforms, and this has indeed become common practice.[6] An example is the initiative to make production of a Poverty Reduction Strategy Paper a prerequisite for HIPC (Heavily Indebted Poor Countries) debt relief. These have typically included a program of institutional reforms; moreover, the consultative process that is part of their preparation is intended to strengthen civil society and increase the domestic constituency in support of these reforms.

There is a danger in all this. Donors' ostensible intention is to provide support that will pump prime or accelerate a process of domestic political and institutional evolution, given the view that the existing structure is inadequate. However, the distinction between this attempt at support and an unwarranted intrusion in a country's domestic affairs is not so much a fine line as a fuzzy one. Even at its most altruistic, it may involve an attempt by donors to substitute outside pressure for inadequate domestic representation.

---

[4] Auty (2001).

[5] For example, see Acemoglu and others (2003).

[6] A major shift in thinking toward acceptance of the need for explicit attention to institutional reform was marked by the World Bank (1997).

I do not think there is any easy resolution to this danger. Our current understanding of the factors underpinning sustained growth, let alone sustained pro-poor growth, is incomplete, but few would now accept that they are narrowly economic in scope. It would be irresponsible to ignore the role of political and institutional factors, and these need to be included in the dialogue between donors and recipient countries. However, this does raise sensitive issues of legitimacy.

III. Absorptive Capacity Constraints

Absorptive capacity constraints are likely to be quite sector-specific. Specific constraints are more likely to be encountered where there is a generalized lack of capacity. However, while the absorptive capacity of a whole economy may be low, it is most unlikely to be uniformly so everywhere. In an economy where capacity is a problem, this has two implications. First, good management of the composition of government spending cannot be based simply on straightforward prioritization. There is little point in routing a large increase in funds into a high priority sector if it is already unable to deploy its existing resources to good effect. Hence the composition of spending may need to be revised from what would otherwise have been chosen. Second, it will be necessary to develop a strategy to relax the existing constraints in priority sectors. This will typically also involve some form of expenditure, and is likely further to alter the chosen composition. For example, suppose the initial prioritization favored expansion of primary social services, at the expense of provision at higher levels. If there are inadequate human resources for this expansion, priorities will have to be revisited, with expansion of the associated training programs, and increased spending at the higher levels.

There is a related question. How are capacity constraints to be recognized? In the illustration in the previous paragraph, a simple headcount of nurses or teachers might give sufficient indication of problems in store. More generally, the symptom that a problem has been encountered will be a deterioration in the relation between expenditure and some measure of output or, more difficult, of outcomes. This requires that appropriate measures have been agreed to and are monitored. Even so, this procedure is essentially ex post and will only identify the severity of a problem some time after it has been encountered. This is inefficient, both because the problem is only identified by the waste of real resources, and because corrective action is delayed.

The alternative is demanding, however, particularly where capacity is generally weak. It requires forward-looking diagnostic measures, including, for example, activity-based budgeting, so that problems can be identified in advance. In all this, the old adage must be kept in mind—that the best may be the enemy of the good. One of the encouraging elements in discussions of public expenditure management in recent years has been the increased recognition that recommendations should respect "good enough" rather than "best" practice.[7] This may mean that capacity constraints cannot always be well identified in advance.

Three other complications are worth noting. First, there is a time dimension. Since attempts will be made to alleviate capacity constraints, the pattern will not be static, and they will shift over time; this needs to be taken into account in planning expenditures. The time required to relax different constraints may also differ significantly. It is also the case that capacity is not static, even in the absence of organized attempts to improve it. Capacity may well evolve in response to increased demands, as a consequence of "learning by doing."

The second complication arises from the uncoordinated nature of much activity in aid-receiving countries, particularly as regards social service provision. Those involved in service delivery typically include government, bilateral donors, as well as international and domestic NGOs. If the sector suffers capacity constraints, there is competition for these scarce resources, and no expectation that the rationed allocation resulting from this bidding process will be efficient.

The third complication arises from the manifold market inefficiencies in many developing countries. One consequence of these is that there may be serious bottlenecks in some sectors simultaneously with spare capacity in others. Indeed the bottlenecks may largely explain the inability to utilize the spare capacity. Since one function of aid is to help remove the bottlenecks, it may well act to remove capacity constraints and permit utilization of existing spare capacity. An example would be an aided road program unlocking increased agricultural supply, which might in turn increase the capacity of the economy to absorb agricultural inputs. The main conclusion of this discussion is that while absorptive capacity constraints may have important macroeconomic implications, they are largely microeconomic phenomena, and need to be analyzed and addressed as such.

IV. The Potential Problem of Real Exchange Rate Appreciation

The Usual Diagnosis

There is a common concern that increased aid will translate into appreciation of the exchange rate and that this will damage the economy. This concern is rooted in three sets of observations. The first observation concerns the role of growing exports in underpinning growth more generally; the second, the mechanics of aid absorption; and the third, a possible negative feedback from the second to the first.

[7] World Bank (1997).

A central feature in successful economic development is a process of growth and diversification in exports. The openness of an economy (the relative importance of trade to GDP) tends to rise as per capita income grows, and the causality runs at least in part from exports to growth. This is because the increase in export earnings provides the foreign exchange to pay for the increased imports required to support the growth process. More strongly, however, it is often argued that diversifying into nontraditional exports plays a crucial role in raising domestic productivity; having to meet the exacting standards of export markets forces domestic producers to raise their standards and acquire new skills, possibly in conjunction with international partners. What is more, this process is claimed to exhibit cumulative properties through "learning by doing." In consequence, any sustained interruption to export growth may have consequences that cannot be quickly reversed.[8]

Unless they are kept offshore and unspent, increased aid flows will tend to put upward pressure on the real exchange rate, and may lead it to appreciate. This will happen irrespective of whether the funds are spent through the government budget, or by NGOs, or by private citizens (if a means of distributing the aid direct to them were installed), provided that they are not spent entirely on imported goods. The reason is that any spending on domestic output requires production to be switched from exports or from import substitutes to nontradables. To induce producers to make this switch, the price of nontradables must rise relative to tradables, and this means an appreciation in the exchange rate. While the presence of unemployed resources may reduce this effect, it will not, in itself, eliminate it.

However, the implication of this scenario is that exporting becomes less profitable and the development of more diversified, nontraditional exports may be inhibited and delayed. If this damage could be factored into the cost-benefit calculations, the level of aid to GDP, which could be successfully absorbed, might be substantially reduced. It is often argued that there is some maximum level of aid that can usefully be absorbed before the marginal returns become negative. If there is a negative impact on export performance, and if this has long-term adverse growth consequences, this maximum usable level of aid may be reduced.

Some Qualifications to this Diagnosis

Despite this rather pessimistic diagnosis, we have the practical observation, noted earlier, that even high rates of aid absorption do not seem in general to have been growth reducing. So the evidence, over the aid levels so far attained, suggests that this anxiety may not be justified. And there are indeed several rea-

[8] More recently, the primacy of exports as opposed to imports as a channel for technology transfer has been increasingly challenged. For example, see Lawrence and Weinstein (2001).

sons, derived from economic analysis, which offer some explanation for this practical observation, and suggest that the pessimism may be overdone.[9]

First, while some aid may be intended to relieve constraints on current consumption, much of it is intended to permit higher investment and higher growth. But this must mean an expansion in the supply side of the economy. The usual diagnosis, summarized above, takes account only of demand-side consequences of the aid inflow—the available domestic productive resources are fixed. However, if the aid is successfully designed to increase these resources, the story is more complicated. If aid is particularly successful in raising productivity of nontradables, this may be sufficient to fully offset the appreciation of the exchange rate. The increased supply of nontradables may more than match the increase in demand. In this case, the adverse price effects on exporters do not materialize, or do so only briefly. At the other extreme, if aid is particularly successful in raising productivity of exportables, this may make the real appreciation even larger, but this does not necessarily reduce the incentive to export, since profitability rises sufficiently to match the fall in export prices. The distributional consequences of these different productivity biases may, however, be different.[10] In either case, all these relations are likely to evolve in complex ways over time, and may be susceptible to intelligent policy design.

Second, even when aid is not designed to raise the economy's full capacity productive potential, it may still enable it to work closer to its existing potential, by relieving bottlenecks and reducing unutilized capacity, as noted in the previous section. In developed economies, this type of waste is usually cyclical in character; the remedy is to attempt to smooth short-run deviations from full employment. In developing countries, the problem is not so much one of smoothing a fairly regular cycle. It is more that market inefficiencies permit there to be sustained pockets of reduced activity, and also that there are large shocks that induce extended periods of disequilibrium. To the extent that aid can reduce these sources of waste, it is much less likely to set off the perverse chain of events in the usual story.

These arguments share a common feature. They stress that the extent to which real exchange rate appreciation is likely to be a problematic feature of aid absorption depends largely on the balance between the aid's relative impact on supply and demand. However, even where the demand effects dominate (as in the usual diagnosis), the extent of the appreciation depends on how difficult it is to shift resources within the economy toward the production of nontradables. If this is difficult, the appreciation will be correspondingly greater. But shifting resources is likely to be more costly if a large shift is attempted rapidly. This means that we might expect the problem to be worse if a rapid increase in aid

[9] Adam and Bevan (2004).

[10] Ibid.

is attempted, as opposed to a more gradual increase, for an equivalent total transfer over some extended horizon.

Implications

This scenario has rather complex and difficult implications for aid policy. It suggests that the likelihood of problems arising through real exchange rate appreciation, and of the severity of any such problems, is not a given, but is contingent on policy design. However, it makes the problem of designing policy to use aid productively even more difficult than it used to be. Economic payoffs always involve some mixture of direct effects and the indirect effects discussed above. The latter type, often called "external effects", are always more difficult to measure and assess than direct effects. The present case is no different.

This may suggest that the best practical approach would often be to ignore these effects in the design of spending programs except where there is (unusually) specific information on their magnitudes. This strategy relies on two presumptions. First, that, on average, the supply response is adequate to keep pressures on exporters to manageable levels. Second, that these indirect effects can be presumed to average out reasonably reliably across different expenditure categories.

There are, however, two general cases where this neutral approach may be harder to justify. The first is the argument that gradualist changes in aid flows may be more easily absorbed than rapid ones, given a similar total increase in transfer over time. The second also reflects the time dimension, though in a rather different way. While the supply payoff to social sector spending may be great, it will often be slow in coming. The supply payoff to physical infrastructure spending and to income-generating projects may be much more rapid. Given the dangers noted earlier of repressing nontraditional export growth for an extended period, this suggests that the massive concentration of increased aid into the social sectors in many countries may need to be reviewed.

V. The Long-Run Spending/Revenue Mobilization Program

This section provides a fairly extended discussion of problems arising from the inconstancy of aid flows. However, this inconstancy has a wide range of time dimensions, running from within-year fluctuations right through to a perspective extending over several decades. To place these matters in context, it is helpful to precede this discussion by considering some long-run issues facing the governments of developing countries, particularly low-income countries. The central issue concerns the scale of government operations, and the way these are intended to evolve over time. It is convenient to think of these in proportion to GDP, though there are some dangers to this. There are four principal components to these operations: domestic revenue mobilization; net aid inflows; net domestic borrowing; and expenditures. The key fact is that the arithmetic of the budget identity requires that the first three (sources of finance) cover the fourth (uses of finance). Hence a change in any one requires accommodation in one or more of the other three.

In principle, all of these could remain constant as shares of GDP, and government operations be maintained in a relative "steady state." Among others, there are two important reasons why this will not occur.

First, for a highly aided country, it is not conceivable that the net aid inflow should remain a constant share of GDP indefinitely. Eventually, the share will fall, whether the inflow does so absolutely, or simply fails to keep pace with growth in GDP. This relative fall in financing cannot be replaced in the long run (or, typically, even in the short run) by an increase in domestic financing. Hence the budget identity requires that it be accommodated either by an increase in the revenue share or by a reduction in the spending share or some mixture of the two.

Second, as countries achieve higher per capita incomes, the relative size of government has tended to rise. This could reflect greater ease in mobilizing revenue, a greater demand for public services in richer countries, or simply an outcome of changing political processes. Here, we suppose that at least in part, the first of these explanations applies.

One simple way of putting these two observations together in a forward-looking low-income country would be to suppose that enhanced revenue capability would match the relative erosion of aid, so that expenditure would remain constant as a share of GDP. But there is no inevitability about this balance; it might not be feasible, and it might not be desirable even if feasible.

In particular, there is much evidence that raising the share of domestic revenue in GDP is a difficult and slow business. It appears, for example, hard to raise this share by as much as one-half of 1 percent of GDP a year. Even at this (highly optimistic) rate, a country now receiving aid at the rate of 10 percent of GDP, which would expect this to continue for 10 years and then drop to 5 percent, would need to begin maximum attempts to raise domestic revue immediately if it did not wish to be faced with expenditure reductions in 10 years' time.

To project these matters forward over several decades may seem fantastical; but some type of forward view over the long run needs to be taken, however crudely, for current decisions to be prudent. Also, this process has become necessary if strategies to achieve the Millennium Development Goals are to be more than mere statements of aspiration. Given reasonable assumptions about the future paths of aid and domestic revenue mobilization, a variety of spending paths is feasible. The link between different feasible paths is their alternative related debt profiles. For example, having an expenditure path that is "front-loaded" will involve an early buildup of debt which is subsequently wound down (relative to GDP), when compared to a path with a stable share of spending. However, as a cautionary note, front-loaded paths are more vulnerable to adverse changes in projected growth or interest rates, which may render them unsustainable. In essence, the planned relation between government operations and GDP is more likely to be disrupted in these cases.

VI. Inconstancy of Aid Flows

Recipient countries know that aid flows are not to be relied on, and in several different ways. First, they are most unlikely to be constant relative to GDP in the long run. Paradoxically, they may fall relatively faster in more successful economies, even if donors remain keen to support them, since GDP will be growing rapidly in these cases. Second, they may show major fluctuations in the medium run. This will reflect shifts both in donors' priorities and in the extent to which a country continues to be seen as "on course," given these priorities. A related issue is that donors are usually unable to commit much in advance of the current budget year, so projections based on aid commitments usually show fairly sharp falls in the medium term, even when a reasonable judgment would be to expect medium-term stability in these flows. Third, even within a stable medium-term framework, aid flows may be unstable and volatile in the short run (within the budget year). Closely related to this is the cyclicality of aid, and its consequences. Each of these groups of issues is considered in turn, though evidently they overlap to a marked extent. All of them pose problems not only for the improved allocation of aid, but also for macroeconomic policy management.

Long-Run Trends in the Aid-to-GDP Ratio

Until fairly recently, discussions of the future path for this ratio centered on the notion that it was likely to fall—this being both the experience and the expectation for the average relation across all developing countries. Experience had been quite different in a select group of low-income countries, some of which had experienced substantial jumps in the ratio; even for these countries, however, the general expectation was that these enhanced inflows would not be long sustained, let alone further increased.

Recent initiatives have raised the possibility that, even for countries already receiving substantial aid, there may be further sustained increases. If this situation does indeed transpire, it highlights even more sharply that there must ultimately be a correspondingly large exit from aid.

This scenario would be problematic even if two ideal circumstances held. One would be that the actual future long-run pattern was guaranteed from the outset. The other would be that donors allow the recipient government complete freedom to separate the timing of the aid flows from the timing of the use of resources within the country. This would mean freedom to invest the aid on international markets and to draw on these foreign assets only when better domestic opportunities became available.

The reason why this type of long-run "pulse" in aid would still be problematic, even in these idealized circumstances, is that it would present government with a severe management problem. There is now much experience of booms in government-owned resources where the transitory nature of the income flow is often well understood, and where there are no constraints on using foreign assets to smooth absorption. This experience is not encouraging as regards a government's usual capacity to handle this type of intertemporal management challenge.

In respect of aid flows, over the long run, there is no such freedom to separate the timing of receipts from expenditures; if aid takes the form of an extended pulse, it must, at least approximately, be spent simultaneously. This means that these long swings in external resources must either be matched by offsetting swings in domestic mobilization, or require equivalent swings in expenditures. The first may be extremely difficult to achieve, and may possibly be excessively costly even if it can be achieved. The second may also be costly in terms of wasted resources, both in the expenditure upswing, and in the subsequent downswing.

Ideally, there would be some way of addressing this problem within the context of the current scaling-up discussions. Since this seems unlikely to be achieved in practice, it is probable that—in respect of this long-run timing issue—it will be a matter of taking the pattern that is on offer, or refusing it. It seems probable that even though there may be a substantial waste of resources in the actual pattern on offer, there will still be a real gain, so that accepting it is the better course.

Medium-Term Fluctuations and Falling Commitments

The previous subsection discussed the problem of handling substantial long-run pulses in aid flows, even if these are reasonably predictable. Another problem in practice is that donors are unable to make long-run commitments, so that recipient countries typically have only reasonably firm expectations in the short or medium term. Since donors differ in the horizons over which they will commit funds, even in the medium term, these projected commitments often fall over time. Likewise, pledges do not always lead to commitments, and commitments do not always lead to disbursements.

This poses a continuing problem for governments. For good reason, they are encouraged to adopt a medium-term expenditure framework that permits coherent planning of expenditure programs over (typically) a three-year horizon. To do this, they need to plan expenditures on the basis of a "resource envelope," which includes projections of aid inflows over that horizon. However, there will usually be some considerable uncertainty surrounding these projections.

Views differ as to what a prudent course of action would look like under these circumstances. One view, often associated with IMF missions, but also commonly held within budget offices, is based on the notion of "a bird in the hand." The argument is that it is costly to be forced to downsize a program once it has been undertaken, so that programs should be designed that rely only on securely committed funds. If, as will often transpire, more resources become available than this projected lower bound, they can either be used to reduce domestic public debt, or to supplement ongoing expenditure programs.

This view presumes that it is always prudent to be cautious. That would be correct if there is an asymmetry of losses from getting things wrong, specifically if it is wasteful to cut planned programs back during implementation in light of shortfalls, but not wasteful to boost spending above the program in light of additional resources above the anticipated lower bound. That there should be such an asymmetry is not self-evident, particularly when there is a systematic bias to underpredict inflows, so that upward revision is commonplace.

The above suggests that there is no robust general conclusion on how these medium-term problems should be handled. The solution is likely to be country-specific. A country will have its own past experience, as to the relation between (a) pledges and commitments, (b) forward commitments and subsequent budget year commitments, and (c) commitments and disbursements. This experience should provide some basis for improving on central projections, though this will be vulnerable to major shifts in the aid environment.

How conservative a view government should take relative to this central estimate also depends partly on past experience. However, this could be supplemented by looking carefully, within sectoral programs, at what the scope is for reducing or increasing the program at relatively short notice, and the associated costs of doing so. This would provide some concrete evidence on whether, and where, there is the sort of asymmetry mentioned above.

Matters are even more difficult when there is a substantive change in relations between donors and the recipient government. If, for example, a large increase in the net aid flow materializes, it will be difficult to decide how persistent this change is likely to be. In the language often used to describe macroeconomic shocks, is the change "permanent" (persistent) or "temporary" (transient)? It is remarkably difficult to decide between the two. Of course, if a conservative view is taken, positive shocks will be treated as being temporary, and negative shocks as being permanent. This form of extreme prudence would have the merit of ensuring policies that were sustainable, at least in the technical sense. However, in a volatile world, they might be unnecessarily costly (there would be little smoothing of spending in the medium term), and it is hard to believe that they represent the best option. By inflicting high transition costs on the population, they might also prove not to be sustainable in the political sense.

Short-Term Volatility and Cyclicality

Volatility

Even when medium-term flows are reasonably stable, there may also be a problem of short-run volatility. Aid promised for the first quarter of the fiscal year may, for example, be delayed to the second or third quarter. For the moment it is supposed that this aid volatility is uncorrelated with any volatility in domestic revenues; this assumption is relaxed later. The volatility in receipts would matter little if the economy exhibited financial depth, so that the government could easily finance temporary mismatches between receipts and expenditures. However, this is not the case in many low-income countries. A particularly severe example is that of governments operating a monthly cash budget, where use of accommodating domestic finance within-year is ruled out in an attempt to run a tight fiscal regime, because a lack of credibility prevents use of a more discretionary policy.

In these circumstances, short-run volatility of aid inflows translates directly into short-run volatility of expenditures. Since some categories of spending (for example, interest payments and wages) are less compressible than others (for example, operations and maintenance), the more discretionary items are likely to suffer exaggerated volatility relative to the volatility of receipts. This results in an uneven and erratic pattern of spending that is inefficient and inequitable.

The obvious solution to this problem would be for donors (individually) to be more careful to disburse aid according to the previously agreed timetable, and to have (collectively) agreed a disbursement schedule that was relatively smooth and/or well correlated with the likely pattern of spending. Of course, disbursement delays are sometimes the fault of recipient governments, "acts of God," as well as donors. Sometimes they reflect coordination failures between the parties. In any case, experience suggests that this problem is difficult to eradicate, though that does not excuse the various actors from increasing their efforts to resolve it.

The increased use of budget support for aid delivery, while in many respects an admirable development, may also make this difficulty harder to fix. Shortfalls in external project finance are to a large extent self-sterilizing; if the finance does not materialize, the project gets delayed in a fairly automatic fashion. Traditionally, this has often occurred "off budget." With budget support, this direct link is broken, and explicit decisions must be made over how to accommodate the shortfall; it becomes a problem in budget management. In an ideal world, this would be fine; but these problems should be handled in a consistent manner, and the budget is the right mechanism for doing so. However, if there are severe capacity constraints within government, this extra challenge, and the increased volatility within the budget, may be hard to handle.

Given that these short-run timing problems are severe and that they are unlikely to be eradicated at the source, there remains the question of how best to handle them. There are only three options. The first option is to use domestic financing to smooth spending given the erratic arrival of resources; as already noted, this mechanism may be quite destabilizing in financially shallow economies. The second option is to force spending to follow this erratic pattern; as also noted, this is damaging to the delivery of public services. The third option is to use foreign financing as a smoothing device. In the discussion of long-run mismatches, it was stated that using foreign assets as a matching device was more or less ruled out in the aid context. However, this is not the case for short-run mismatches. Governments can use their foreign exchange reserves for this purpose.

Holding substantial foreign exchange reserves has always been seen as a device to combat volatility. In the usual story, the government wishes to insulate the country's capacity to maintain an efficient flow of imports from the erratic behavior of exports. These reserves permit imports to be maintained when there is a temporary shortfall in export receipts, without forcing sharp movements in the exchange rate. However, foreign exchange reserves held by the government can also be used in precisely the same way to permit its spending to be maintained when there is a temporary shortfall in aid receipts, without creating a domestic financing problem. Countries facing more volatile exporting conditions have needed to hold larger foreign exchange reserves. The same is true for countries facing large and volatile aid inflows.

Cyclicality

The discussion so far has concentrated on volatility in aid inflow. However, one characteristic of developing countries, accentuated in low-income countries, is that domestic revenues are also unstable. This raises the question of whether the two sets of volatility might tend to reinforce each other (are procyclical) or to offset each other (are countercyclical). If short-run movements in aid are negatively correlated with those in domestic revenue, might they not reduce overall volatility, so that aid volatility is a blessing in disguise? There has been some dispute about this, but the best evidence suggests that the relation is weakly procyclical.[11] This means that the costs of aid volatility are not mitigated by offsetting movements in domestic revenue; to the contrary, aid instability makes the originally unstable position even worse.

This is another area which policy improvements might address. However, this may prove difficult. One circumstance in which aid might be procyclical is where it is tied to policy performance, but it would be inappropriate to invert this relation. Also, previous attempts to make aid countercyclical—for example, through

[11] Bulíř and Hamann (2001).

stabilization funds—have usually failed to do so, or even made matters worse because of disbursement delays. In consequence, it may be better to concentrate on reducing volatility and postpone any attempt at reducing procyclicality.

Macroeconomic Policy in the Face of Aid Inconstancy

There is a substantial literature on the difficulties of macroeconomic policy design even in industrialized countries that are highly stable and diversified, and where instability usually takes the form of a fairly mild cycle. The difficulties for most developing countries are much greater; they inhabit a world of much greater relative shocks, and they are less diversified and hence more vulnerable to these. This is particularly true for small economies.[12] Aid inconstancy is only part of this picture, but it is an important part.

Apart from the large relative size of the shocks, their other major characteristic, evident from the discussion above, is that it is usually difficult to distinguish whether they are persistent or transitory. The appropriate policy response to each is quite different—smooth a temporary shock, accommodate to a permanent one. Hence the difficulty of diagnosis presents real problems in the design of fiscal, monetary, and exchange rate policy, though it obviously places a premium on flexibility. This is being increasingly studied, but we cannot yet have much confidence in our ability to design a robust policy in these circumstances.[13] Apart from posing problems for macroeconomic policy, macroeconomic shocks may also impact differentially on particular groups, not least the poor, and ways must be found to at least partly offset these effects.[14]

VII. Debt Sustainability and the Grant/Loan Issue

External and domestic government debt have different properties and consequences. There is insufficient space here to cover both, so attention is limited to external debt, since aid is the present focus.[15] Debt sustainability is a slippery concept, and may not be the appropriate one, especially for low-income countries.

To place this last proposition in context, consider briefly the idea of optimal debt, in the case where this is nonconcessional, and where neither repudiation nor forgiveness is an issue. Then, in principle, there will be some path for debt which will be optimal given international interest rates and domestic investment

[12] Commonwealth Secretariat/World Bank (2000).

[13] For some implications in respect of monetary and exchange rate policy, see O'Connell and others (2004); for some implications in respect of fiscal policy, see Basci and others (2004), Chapters 2–4 in Addison and Roe (2004), and Gupta and others (2004).

[14] For example, see Ferreira and others (1999).

[15] However, it is worth noting that domestic debt is an important and neglected issue, even in the aid context.

opportunities. It would not be worth incurring more debt than this, because the additional investment that could be financed would not have a sufficiently high return to finance the additional cost. Even so, it *would* be possible to incur more debt and still service it; it would be sustainable even if above the optimal level. If borrowing were raised sufficiently further (assuming willing and presumably short-sighted creditors), it would eventually become unsustainable, in the sense that a default would become inevitable. Between the two will be a range of debt levels which are sustainable though undesirable. A key difference needs to be noted between the concepts of optimality and sustainability, and the level of debt that can be carried under each. Optimality involves the relation between the domestic rate of return and the international interest rate; sustainability involves that between the growth rate (of GDP, or possibly of exports) and this interest rate.

Now consider the consequences of starting with a given level of debt in these circumstances. A larger debt imposes larger debt service obligations, and reduces the productive expenditure that the government can make in the future, given its expected future tax revenues. What level of external debt would a government choose to inherit on acceding to power, if it had the choice? The answer, clearly, is none at all, or better still, an indefinitely large volume of foreign assets (negative debt).

How does this relate to the current and prospective circumstances of a low-income country which has been highly indebted, has received debt forgiveness under HIPC, and is eligible for concessional finance? Concessional finance has three characteristics which distinguish it from nonconcessional finance, apart from the obvious one of being cheaper. First, its access is rationed in the present. Second, its access will be withdrawn at some point in the future. Hence it will not be possible to roll it over indefinitely. Third, the actual degree of concessionality is unclear, since there could be future debt forgiveness in certain circumstances. Furthermore, these characteristics are not independent. For example, a rapidly growing country would tend to lose access and be unlikely to obtain forgiveness in the future compared to a country that remains in a low-income trap. All this makes the concessional case quite different from the conventional one.

From this analysis, four propositions for low-income countries arise. The first proposition is that there is no clear way of assessing sustainable limits for external debt. What now seems easily sustainable might prove not to be so if *future* access to concessional finance were quickly withdrawn. What now seems unsustainable might prove unproblematic if there were further debt forgiveness in the future. Second, there may be a complete divorce between a country's capacity to absorb aid and its capacity to accept more concessional indebtedness according to any arbitrary rule concerning sustainability, such as the HIPC criteria.[16]

Third, if the real purpose of aid is to assist development, then the criterion should be to allocate available aid resources between countries according to their

[16] This is not to deny the operational importance of the HIPC criteria in mobilizing necessary debt forgiveness by giving concrete rules on which to act.

need and capacity to use and absorb these resources. It does not seem helpful to interpose an additional constraint reflecting some alleged limit on debt sustainability as a subsidiary rationing mechanism.[17] Of course, it would be possible in principle to continually vary the grant element in loans so that a level of resource transfer determined by donor willingness and the capacity of the recipient country could be kept consistent with an NPV (net present value) of debt that obeyed some HIPC-type rule. But this would be onerous to compute and virtually impossible to implement, as well as seeming to serve no useful purpose.

Hence and fourth, if this argument is accepted, there is little merit in persevering with concessional loans to low-income countries, as opposed to moving comprehensively to a grant mechanism for delivering aid. There are, of course, counterarguments.

One of the arguments for retaining concessional loans is that they provide a disciplinary mechanism that would be absent under a pure grant regime. However, this is arguable. With concessional finance of the International Development Association (IDA) type, for example, the "discipline" is deferred for so long that a different government is likely to be in power before it (weakly) binds. Indeed, it is likely to be perverse, with governments being called to account for the actions of their predecessors, but not for their own. No serious incentive mechanism design would have these properties. A related argument is that, despite this mismatch in time, at least loans—whoever incurred them—act to discipline the current government because of the need to cover the associated debt service. But this is a two-edged sword, since the donor community shrinks from enforcing a default on itself. Hence large gross donor flows may provide an illusory degree of discipline. In many respects, it is the net flow that constitutes the real discipline, and that would remain under a straight grant system.

Another argument in favor of persevering with loans is that it would require some reengineering of the international financial institutions (IFIs) to permit them to operate on a grant basis instead of on a loan basis. However, while this may be an important difficulty as a matter of practical operations, it is hard to accept that it could not be circumvented if the will was there.

VIII. Conclusions

This paper has reviewed an extensive list of macroeconomic issues that may arise in connection with a substantial increase in aid inflows. By and large, the conclusion is that while there are indeed complications to be handled, there is no general case for believing that enhanced resources cannot be used effectively. More light will be shed by the case studies in this session, by papers in subsequent sessions, and by the general discussion in this seminar. Rather than summarizing what is already a summary, we end with a hypothetical, and perhaps politically

[17] This is becoming increasingly recognized, also by the IMF. For example, see Fedelino and Kudina (2003).

incorrect, question. Suppose that a low-income country was annexed by a rich neighbor, becoming a new region of this richer country. Does it really seem believable that it would be beyond the capacity of this rich country to deploy substantial resources into its new disadvantaged region and succeed in engendering highly accelerated development?

References

Acemoglu, D., S. Johnson, J. Robinson, and Y. Thaicharoen, 2003, "Institutional Causes, Macroeconomic Symptoms: Volatility, Crises and Growth," *Journal of Monetary Economics*, Vol. 50 (January), pp. 49–123.

Adam, C., and D. Bevan, 2004, "Aid and the Supply Side: Public Investment, Export Performance, and Dutch Disease in Low Income Countries," Department of Economics Discussion Paper No. 201 (Oxford: University of Oxford).

Addison, T., and A. Roe, eds., 2004, *Fiscal Policy for Development: Poverty, Reconstruction, and Growth* (New York: Palgrave Macmillan).

Auty, R., ed., 2001, *Resource Abundance and Economic Development*, WIDER Studies in Development Economics (Oxford: Oxford University Press).

Basci, E., M. Fatih Ekinci, and M. Yülek, 2004, "On Fixed and Variable Fiscal Surplus Rules," IMF Working Paper 04/117 (Washington: International Monetary Fund).

Bulíř, A., and A. Hamann, 2001, "How Volatile and Unpredictable Are Aid Flows, and What Are the Policy Implications?" IMF Working Paper 01/167 (Washington: International Monetary Fund).

Commonwealth Secretariat/World Bank Task Force, 2000, "Small States: Meeting Challenges in the Global Economy" (Washington: World Bank).

Fedelino, A., and A. Kudina, 2003, "Fiscal Sustainability in African HIPC Countries: A Policy Dilemma?" IMF Working Paper 03/187 (Washington: International Monetary Fund).

Ferreira, F., G. Prennushi, and M. Ravallion, 1999, "Protecting the Poor from Macroeconomic Shocks," Policy Research Working Paper No. 2160 (Washington: World Bank).

Gupta, S., B. Clements, G. Inchauste, 2004, *Helping Countries Develop: The Role of Fiscal Policy* (Washington: International Monetary Fund).

Lawrence, R., and D. Weinstein, 2001; "Trade and Growth: Import-Led or Export-Led?: Evidence from Japan and Korea," in *Rethinking the East Asian Miracle*, ed. by J. Stiglitz and S. Yusuf (Washington: World Bank and Oxford: Oxford University Press).

Moore, M., 1998, "Death Without Taxes: Democracy, State Capacity, and Aid Dependence in the Fourth World," in *The Democratic Developmental State: Political and Institutional Design*, ed. by M. Robinson and G. White (Oxford: Oxford University Press).

O'Connell, S., C. Adam, E. Buffie, and C. Pattillo, 2005, "Managing External Volatility: Central Bank Options in Low-Income Countries," paper presented at the annual meeting of the American Economic Association, Philadelphia, January.

UN Millennium Project, 2005, *Investing in Development: A Practical Plan to Achieve the Millennium Development Goals* (New York).

World Bank, 1997, *World Development Review for 1997: The State in a Changing World* (Washington).

5

High Aid Inflows
The Case of Ghana

SHEKHAR AIYAR, ANDREW BERG, MUMTAZ HUSSAIN,
AMBER MAHONE, AND SHAUN ROACHE*

I. Introduction

Increases in foreign aid inflows allow recipient countries to increase consumption and investment. Aid offers an opportunity to raise the standard of living, reduce poverty, and generate sustained growth. But to achieve these results, the increased aid must be used effectively. Aid recipients must find and manage good projects and must agree on the conditions for budgetary support. The imperative to use aid funds well can strain the administrative capacity of recipient governments. Aid flows can also weaken ownership, fragment and impair budgetary procedures, encourage rent-seeking behavior, and undermine the accountability of domestic institutions.

Related to, yet distinct from, these microeconomic and institutional issues are the macroeconomic challenges of managing aid inflows. Aid inflows can cause upward pressure on the real exchange rate to the detriment of the exporting industries that may be critical to long-run growth. This is fundamentally rooted in the real effects of aid; in other words, microeconomic in nature. Macroeconomic policies, however, can determine how aid is absorbed in the domestic economy. Aid inflows can also create problems of fiscal management

*This paper is part of a larger study, whose authors are Shekhar Aiyar, Andrew Berg, Mumtaz Hussain, Amber Mahone, and Shaun Roache. Shaun Roache is the principal author of this Ghana case study.

and debt sustainability, particularly when they are volatile and when they take the form of debt.

Aid flows to low-income countries have increased somewhat over the past 10 years. In a few relatively well-performing low-income countries, inflows have expanded substantially from already significant levels. Larger and more widespread increases in aid inflows are seen as critical to achieving the Millennium Development Goals (MDGs).[1] A scaling-up of aid will amplify the macroeconomic policy challenges arising from the management of aid inflows. The IMF also needs to confront these challenges squarely in its capacity as a key provider of advice on macroeconomic policies. Helping countries to manage effectively increased aid inflows would be one of the IMF's main contributions to the achievement of the MDGs.

Like the other papers in this volume, this study draws lessons from recent country experience about key issues in the macroeconomic management of high aid inflows. Some of the questions we seek to answer are as follows. Do we observe macroeconomic absorptive capacity constraints? Is Dutch disease a concern? Are aid inflows inflationary, and what is the appropriate monetary and exchange rate policy response? Is there a role for sterilization? Did the Poverty Reduction on Growth Facility (PRGF)-supported program adequately manage the macroeconomic impact of surging aid inflows? While the benefits of higher aid and challenges of scaling up are frequently discussed, limited systematic analysis of country experiences has been done on these issues. This paper examines the experience of one low-income country—Ghana—that has grappled with these questions over the past decade or so.

The approach taken in this study limits the range of topics that can be covered. In particular, it is difficult in this framework to address the equally important long-run implications of increases in aid flows. To understand long-run implications for resource allocation, policies, institutions, and growth, it would be necessary to pursue either much longer-run cases or a broader cross-country analysis.

II. A Macroeconomic Framework for the Analysis of Increases in Aid Inflows

The macroeconomic impact of aid depends critically on the policy responses to aid. In particular, it is the interaction of fiscal policy with monetary and exchange rate policy that is important. In order to highlight this interaction, it is useful to introduce two related but distinct concepts: *absorption* and *spending*.

---

[1] A key recommendation of the United Nations Millennium Project Task Force is to increase official development assistance rapidly—at least for a dozen or so fast-track countries—to support the MDGs. The World Bank and IMF (2005) also advocate a substantial increase in aid to low-income countries.

Absorption is defined in this paper as the extent to which the nonaid current account deficit widens in response to an increase in aid inflows.[2] This measure captures the quantity of net imports financed by an increment in aid, which represents the real transfer of resources enabled by aid. Absorption captures both the direct and indirect increase in imports financed by aid, that is, direct purchases of imports by the government, as well as second-round increases in net imports resulting from aid-driven increases in government or private expenditures. Absorption reflects the aggregate impact of the macroeconomic policy response to higher aid inflows, encompassing monetary, exchange rate, and fiscal policies.

Absorption can be defined and understood in terms of the balance of payments identity:

$$\textit{Current Account} + \textit{Capital Account} = \Delta \textit{Reserves}.$$

Breaking the current and capital accounts into their aid and nonaid components, and rearranging items, the following identity is produced:

$$\begin{aligned}\textit{Aid Inflows} = \Delta\textit{Reserves} - (&\textit{Nonaid Current Account}\\ &+ \textit{Nonaid Capital Account}).^{3}\end{aligned}$$

Thus, an *increase* in aid can serve some combination of three purposes: an increase in the rate of reserve accumulation; an increase in nonaid capital outflows; or an increase in the nonaid current account deficit. The rate of absorption of an increase in aid is then defined as the change in the nonaid current account deficit as a share of the change in aid inflows:[4]

$$\textit{Absorption} = \Delta(\textit{Nonaid Current Account Deficit})/\Delta \textit{Aid}$$

---

[2] This usage of absorption should not be confused with the related concept of "absorptive capacity," which, in addition, involves questions about the rate of return on investments financed by aid.

[3] The nonaid current account balance is the current account balance excluding official grants and interest on external public debt. The nonaid capital account balance is the capital account net of aid-related capital flows, such as loan disbursements and amortization.

[4] With this definition, aid that finances capital outflows is not absorbed. This makes sense insofar as aid that flows back out of the country does not transfer real resources to the country. However, there are instances in which aid that finances capital outflows can be seen as allowing an increase in absorption relative to a particular counterfactual—that is, relative to what might have happened without the aid. Suppose, for example, that an increase in political uncertainty causes residents suddenly to desire to move capital abroad. The authorities use a large aid inflow to accommodate this capital outflow. Now suppose also that without the aid the authorities would not have accommodated this desire with reserve sales but rather would have allowed an exchange rate depreciation. This depreciation might have resulted in a reduced trade deficit. Compared to this counterfactual, the aid has allowed a larger trade deficit and hence more absorption. This is an unusual set of circumstances, but it may prevail when reserve levels are very low.

For a given fiscal policy, absorption is controlled by the central bank, through its decision about how much of the foreign exchange associated with aid to sell, and through its interest rate policy, which influences the demand for private imports via aggregate demand.[5] The mechanism will depend on the exchange rate regime, but under any regime, the monetary authority can choose to accumulate reserves or to make them available for importers.[6] In the extreme case where the central bank uses the full increment in aid to bolster international reserves and does not increase net sales of foreign exchange, none of the extra aid will be absorbed.

Spending is defined as the widening in the government fiscal deficit net of aid that accompanies an increment in aid:[7]

$$Spending = \Delta(G - T)/\Delta Aid$$

Spending captures the extent to which the government uses aid to finance an increase in expenditures or a reduction in taxation. Even if the aid comes tied to particular expenditures, governments can choose whether or not to increase the overall fiscal deficit as aid increases. The aid-related increases in expenditures could be on imports or domestically produced goods and services. Analyzing spending is important because of the natural focus on the budget as a policy variable, and also because of the importance of tensions between the fiscal policy response to aid and broader macroeconomic objectives with respect to the exchange rate and inflation.

These definitions of absorption and spending take into account, by construction, the *fungibility* of aid. For example, if the foreign exchange associated with a particular grant is sold by the central bank, but overall net sales of foreign exchange do not increase, this does not constitute an increase in absorption,

[5] Aid that is used directly to finance imports by the government (e.g., a grant in kind, a grant of foreign exchange that the government immediately uses to purchase imports, or aid that goes directly to nongovernmental organizations, or NGOs, to finance imports) effectively bypasses the central bank and leads directly to absorption.

[6] This point may require further elaboration. Consider, for example, the case where the central bank wishes to ensure full absorption. Assume, for simplicity, that the capital account is closed except for aid. Under a float, the central bank sells all the aid-related dollars on the market and the agents who buy the dollars spend them on imports. The real exchange rate appreciates through nominal exchange rate appreciation. Under a fixed exchange rate regime, the central bank must loosen monetary policy to allow real exchange rate appreciation through an increase in inflation. Some level of the real exchange rate will yield an increase in import demand sufficient to ensure full absorption of the aid dollars at the fixed nominal exchange rate.

[7] The deficit net of aid is equal to total expenditures (G) less domestic revenue (T) and is financed by a combination of net aid and domestic financing: $G - T = Nonaid\ fiscal\ deficit = Net\ aid + Domestic\ financing$.

because no extra foreign exchange is available to finance an increase in net imports. Similarly, if the government allocates a new grant to financing a domestic project that was earlier financed from different sources, this does not constitute an increase in spending, since the nonaid fiscal deficit remains unchanged.

Absorption and spending are distinct though related concepts and policy choices.[8] If aid comes in kind, or if the government spends aid dollars directly on imports, spending and absorption are equivalent, and there is no impact on macroeconomic variables like the exchange rate, the price level, and the interest rate.[9] This paper concentrates on the more difficult and empirically relevant case where aid dollars are gifted to the government, which immediately sells them to the central bank. Subsequently, the government decides how much of the local currency counterpart to spend on domestic projects, while the central bank decides how much of the aid-related foreign exchange to sell on the market. Spending differs, in general, from absorption.[10]

Taken together, different combinations of absorption and spending out of incremental aid define the policy response to a surge in aid inflows. Below are described the four basic combinations of absorption and spending, together with a discussion of the macroeconomic implications of each. Box 5.1 provides a numerical example showing how the central bank and fiscal accounting works in each of these four cases.

Aid Absorbed and Spent

This is the textbook case, in that this is the situation assumed (explicitly or implicitly) in most discussions of the macroeconomic implications of aid

[8] The distinction between absorption and spending, in the terminology used in this paper, is one of the central issues associated with the "transfer problem" and discussed in Keynes (1929). Keynes was concerned with Germany's problems in generating current account *surpluses* to pay reparations after World War I. He argued that for the fiscal authorities to accumulate the local currency counterpart to the required transfers was only part of the transfer problem—the other part being generating the net exports and therefore the required foreign exchange. See Milesi-Ferreti and Lane (2004) for a recent general discussion of the transfer problem and the real exchange rate.

[9] Strictly speaking, this is true only if the gifted or directly imported good is one for which there was no existing effective demand. If the good transferred was already demanded domestically, then increasing the good's supply would depress the price of tradables relative to nontradables, leading to real appreciation.

[10] Prati and Tressel (2005) find that monetary policy can determine the timing of absorption. Aid could also go to the private sector directly. Here, too, if the private sector uses the dollars to directly finance imports, there is unlikely to be much macroeconomic impact. Where the private sector sells the dollars to the central bank and uses the local currency proceeds to finance domestic expenditures, similar issues will arise as in the case of government spending.

Box 5.1. Absorption, Spending, and Central Bank and Fiscal Accounting

In this numerical example, the government sells the aid dollars to the central bank and receives a local currency deposit at the central bank in return. Net international reserves (NIR) increase by 100 and net domestic assets of the central bank (NDA) fall by 100 (because government deposits with the central bank are a negative NDA item). This places the economy in the lower-right box of the matrix. What happens next depends on whether the central bank sells the foreign exchange and on whether the government increases the deficit; each case is discussed in the text. The example below assumes a floating exchange rate regime. The accounting story would be the same, but the numbers and details different, with a peg.

Central Bank and Fiscal Accounts
Example With Aid Inflow of 100

	Spend				Do Not Spend			
Absorb	Central Bank Balance Sheet				Central Bank Balance Sheet			
	NIR	0	M	0	NIR	0	M	−100
	NDA	0			NDA	−100		
	Fiscal Accounts				Fiscal Accounts			
	Ext. Fin.	+100	Deficit	+100	Ext. Fin.	+100	Deficit	0
	Dom. Fin.	0			Dom. Fin.	−100		
Do Not Absorb	Central Bank Balance Sheet				Central Bank Balance Sheet			
	NIR	+100	M	+100	NIR	+100	M	0
	NDA	0			NDA	−100		
	Fiscal Accounts				Fiscal Accounts			
	Ext. Fin.	+100	Deficit	+100	Ext. Fin.	+100	Deficit	0
	Dom. Fin.	0			Dom. Fin.	−100		

Notes:
NIR is net international reserves and M is reserve money.
NDA is net domestic assets.
Ext. Fin is external financing, and Dom. Fin is domestic financing of the deficit.

inflows.[11] The government spends the aid increment and foreign exchange is sold by the central bank and absorbed by the economy via a widening of the current account deficit. The fiscal deficit is larger but financed by higher aid. Spending and absorption allows an increase in government spending by redeploying resources that had been devoted to the traded goods sector. In terms of the familiar national income identity $Y = C + I + G + (X{-}M)$, for a given output, a fall in $(X{-}M)$ allows a rise in G.

[11] See Bevan (2005).

Of course, output may not be fixed. Government expenditures may well increase output, both in the short run through the effects of associated spending on aggregate demand and in the long run through the increase in the capital stock permitted by the associated investment. To the extent that output can rise without a deterioration in the nonaid current account, however, these increases in aggregate demand and investment could have been undertaken without the aid flows. Aid absorption refers to the use of aid to finance the nonaid current account deficit associated with these aid-related increases in aggregate demand, investment, and output in general.

Some real exchange rate appreciation may be necessary and indeed appropriate in response to a sustained higher level of aid. This is because some combination of exchange rate appreciation and (if there is excess capacity) increased aggregate demand is necessary to generate the increased net imports that aid allows.[12]

The degree of exchange rate appreciation required to absorb the aid will in general depend on the structural response of the economy and the extent to which aid *directly* finances imports. For example, real appreciation would be higher to the extent that aid inflows finance expenditures on nontradable goods rather than directly financing imports.[13] On the other hand, if higher incomes feed strongly into higher import demand and if the supply of nontraded goods responds strongly to the increase in their relative price, the real appreciation would be limited. In economies with significant unemployment and the potential for a quick supply response, the additional demand for nontradable goods could induce additional employment and production, with little increase in the price level and limited real appreciation. In the longer run, investments that increase productivity in the nontradable sector could also reduce or even eliminate the real exchange rate appreciation.

The mechanism for real appreciation would vary depending on the exchange rate regime. In a pure float, the central bank would sell the foreign exchange associated with the aid, causing a nominal (and real) exchange rate appreciation. In a peg, the real appreciation would take place through a period of inflation, with the increase in government expenditure being accommodated

[12] The real exchange rate is generally understood in this paper to refer to the relative price of nontraded to traded goods, as a conceptual matter. When it comes to measurement, the case studies unfortunately tend to follow the common practice of measuring the real exchange rate as a function of the nominal exchange rate and changes in consumer price indices. It turns out for the cases under consideration that this is unlikely to make a major difference, but further work on the correct measurement of the real exchange rate would appear justified.

[13] One category of nontradable goods that might be important in this process is skilled labor; if aid raises the wages of skilled professionals, this could translate into real appreciation.

by the central bank. The increase in aggregate demand and the real appreciation would again increase net import demand, leading the central bank to sell foreign exchange in defense of the peg.

Aid Neither Absorbed Nor Spent

The authorities could choose to respond to the aid inflow by building international reserves, and neither increasing government expenditures nor lowering taxes. In this case there is no expansionary impact on aggregate demand, and no pressure on the exchange rate or prices.[14]

Aid Absorbed but Not Spent

Increased aid inflows can be used to reduce inflation in those countries that have not yet achieved stabilization. In such a case, the authorities can sell the foreign exchange associated with increased aid inflows to sterilize the monetary impact of domestically financed fiscal deficits. The result would typically be slower monetary growth, a more appreciated real exchange rate, and lower inflation. Aggregate demand may increase as the inflation tax declines, with a corresponding increase in private consumption and investment. The deterioration of the trade balance that often accompanies such a stabilization program is financed by the aid inflow.[15]

In countries that have already achieved inflation stabilization but have large domestic public debt, the government could use the proceeds from aid to reduce the stock of local currency government bonds outstanding. This would tend to result in increased private consumption and investment, which would raise net imports through the indirect effect of higher private after-tax income on import demand. The extra foreign exchange sold by the central bank would finance this increased demand for net imports. Again, some real exchange rate appreciation is likely to be necessary to mediate the increase in net imports.

Whether a strategy of absorbing but not spending aid is feasible in a particular situation depends on whether a monetary relaxation would translate into higher domestic investment or consumption. If there are no good private investment opportunities, for example, an increase in credit to the private sector could result in private capital outflows or a buildup of excess commercial bank reserves at the central bank.[16]

---

[14] There may be second-order effects, for example, expectations may change as a result of the central bank's higher international reserve position.

[15] This is the case emphasized by Buffie and others (2004).

[16] The IMF Independent Evaluation Office (2004) argues that assumptions under the Poverty Reduction and Growth Facility (PRGF) that crowding in will ensue from an increase in availability of credit to the private sector are often left unexamined and often prove not to be correct.

Aid Spent but Not Absorbed

A fourth possibility is that the fiscal deficit, net of aid, increases with the jump in aid, but the authorities do not sell the foreign exchange required to finance additional net imports. The macroeconomic effects of this fiscal expansion are similar to increasing government expenditures in the *absence* of aid, except that international reserves are higher. The increased deficits inject money into the economy.

In this case, the aid does not serve to support the fiscal expansion. This point is central and deserves elaboration. A transfer of real resources to the recipient country occurs only if aid finances additional net imports. Aid also serves as a way for the government to finance its domestic expenditures, as an alternative to domestic tax revenue or borrowing, either from the public or from the central bank. It may seem, therefore, that the financing of domestic expenditures, such as the hiring of nurses, is an *alternative* use for aid, in addition to imports. But this approach to the function of aid is misleading; after all, the government could always simply borrow from the central bank (i.e., print money) to finance increased domestic expenditures. Rather, the purpose of the aid is to provide the foreign exchange required to satisfy the increased demand for foreign currency resulting from the higher import demand.[17]

Consider a thought experiment in which, for a given level of aid, the government first decides on the appropriate level of government expenditure and its financing. This set of decisions, in principle, takes into account the scope for seigniorage, the supply response to increased fiscal expenditures, the productivity of the resulting public investment and the generation of higher exports that may result, and other such factors. Then, aid increases. The thing that has changed is *not* that the government could now productively hire, say, more nurses to fight HIV/AIDS. They could have done that before. The difference is that, whereas before such additional expenditures would have caused too much inflation or an un-financable deterioration of the current account

[17] Related to this point is an accounting issue: "domestic financing" as usually defined in the budgetary accounts is misleading as an indicator of aid usage. Consider the following example: Aid is saved entirely in the form of gross international reserves, the government builds up deposits at the central bank, and the fiscal deficit excluding aid remains unchanged. By construction, the fiscal accounts will show a shift in financing from domestic financing (which will fall owing a reduction in net central bank credit to the government) to external financing. But the aid has no macroeconomic effects in this no-absorption-and-no-spending scenario—the money supply, fiscal stance, interest rates, and so on are unaffected (except insofar as interest earnings of the central bank are higher). More generally, aid that is not absorbed does not contribute to financing the government deficit in an economic sense. Thus, it would be misleading to conclude from a perusal of below-the-line financing items in the budget that aid inflows were actually financing the deficit to a greater extent than before.

through second-round increases in import demand, now the incremental aid increases international reserves, which could be sold to pay for the higher imports. But this is the definition of aid absorption; aid that is not absorbed cannot fulfill this function.

There are several possible monetary policy responses to a situation in which aid is being spent by the government but not absorbed in the economy. Absent foreign exchange sales to mop up the additional liquidity, the monetary policy options are the same as in the case of any domestically financed fiscal expansion. One could be to allow the larger fiscal deficits to lead to money supply increases. This is essentially monetizing the fiscal expansion and would tend to be inflationary. In the absence of a willingness to sell foreign exchange, the nominal exchange rate will tend to depreciate as well, with a larger supply of domestic currency pushing up the price of foreign exchange. The resulting inflation tax helps contain absorption by transferring resources from the private sector. Another response is to sterilize the fiscally driven monetary expansion through the issuance of treasury bills. This strategy would tend to crowd out private investment. In effect, there is a switch from private investment to government consumption or investment.[18]

There are opposing effects on the real exchange rate in the spend-but-do-not-absorb case. In a given situation the net effect will depend on specific factors, including the strength of contrasting policy choices and other influences, such as the terms of trade. The fiscal expansion tends to raise demand for non-traded goods, causing an appreciation; on the other hand, it increases import demand and lowers export supply, pushing the exchange rate toward depreciation. The net effect depends, among other things, on the price and income elasticity of the country's export supply and import demand. In addition, the central bank's resistance to absorption creates pressures for real depreciation. In a float, aid-related liquidity injections will tend to depreciate the nominal and, in the short run, the real exchange rate. Over time, higher inflation and the associated inflation tax will reduce private demand and lower the real exchange rate and absorption. Alternatively, sterilization through the sale of treasury bills will also depress private demand and hence the real exchange rate and absorption. In a peg, only the sterilization channel operates.

Which of these combinations is best in the face of extra aid depends on many factors, including the level of official reserves, the existing debt burden,

---

[18] Private investment and government expenditure could have different import intensities, which would modify the details of the argument but not alter the main point. Similarly, the fiscal expansion may increase aggregate output, so it is not the case that there need be a one-for-one trade-off between government spending and private investment. But such an aggregate output expansion could have been engineered without the aid.

the current level of inflation, and the degree of aid volatility. For specific situations, some responses are more promising than others.[19]

- To *absorb and spend* the aid would appear to be the most appropriate response under "normal" circumstances. In this case there is a real resource transfer through an aid-financed increase in net imports, and a corresponding increase in public expenditures.
- To *absorb but not spend* the aid might be an appropriate response if inflation is too high (possibly owing to a very expansionary fiscal policy), resources are scarce for private investment, or the rate of return on public expenditure is relatively low. Sustained non-spending of aid may be infeasible, however, given donor objectives, unless the budget is very fungible.
- To *neither absorb nor spend* may be an appropriate short-run strategy where aid inflows are volatile or international reserves are precariously low.[20] Accumulating international reserves while avoiding an injection of domestic liquidity through fiscal expansion could help smooth the path of the real exchange rate if aid inflows are temporarily high but expected to fall. However, it is not an appropriate response to a permanent increase in the level of aid, unless it is felt that Dutch disease concerns fully outweigh the benefits from the absorption of aid inflows (Appendix I).
- To *spend and not absorb* would appear to be the least attractive option. The use of aid to build reserves while financing the increased deficit domestically is generally unwise. Inflation can only finance a small amount of expenditure; attempts to go further tend to raise little finance while damaging the economy.[21] The use of domestic sterilization is also unlikely to be a sensible medium-run strategy—it tends to shift resources from the private to the public sector and does not allow the country to benefit from a real transfer of resources financed by aid.

---

[19] In general, debt sustainability is an important consideration for low-income countries. However, once the decision has been made to borrow internationally, all of the combinations of absorption and spending described in this paper imply a similar rise in public external debt and in future debt service. Of course, any response that restricts absorption and channels the dollars into international reserves thereby makes resources available for future debt service. But this is equivalent to borrowing money in order to service debt and cannot therefore be regarded as an appropriate medium-term use of aid.

[20] Recent cross-country evidence (e.g., Bulíř and Hamann, 2005) indicates that aid continues to be volatile, that aid commitments consistently exceed disbursements, and that aid disbursements are generally procyclical—thereby increasing the volatility of public expenditures rather than lowering it. Prati and Tressel (2005) construct a theoretical model to consider the optimal pattern of absorption. Implicitly, they compare absorbing and spending to neither absorbing nor spending in the terminology used here.

[21] See IMF (2005).

Table 5.1. Net Aid Inflows and Selected Economic Indicators
(In percent of GDP)

	1997	1998	1999	2000	2001	2002	2003	2004
Gross aid inflows	8.8	8.7	7.5	8.8	14.9	5.9	9.5	7.4
Project aid	7.8	6.9	5.6	5.0	9.3	3.4	4.4	3.3
Program aid	1.0	1.8	1.9	3.8	5.6	2.5	5.1	4.1
Debt service[1]	5.3	5.6	4.7	9.0	4.2	3.4	2.4	–0.6
Net aid inflows	3.5	3.2	2.8	–0.3	10.6	2.5	7.1	8.0
Private inflows[2]	14.0	6.5	12.9	14.8	12.7	13.9	13.7	8.5
Memorandum items								
GDP (real percent change)	4.2	4.7	4.4	3.7	4.2	4.5	5.2	5.2
Inflation (percent change)	18.4	16.3	13.1	39.3	23.5	14.1	24.0	. . .
Cedi per U.S. dollar (average)	2,050	2,314	2,669	5,455	7,170	7,932	8,677	9,004
percent change	–20.1	–11.4	–13.3	–51.1	–23.9	–9.6	–8.6	–3.6
RER vs U.S. dollar (percent change)	–7.6	1.5	–4.1	–34.0	–8.6	1.5	10.8	
REER (percent change)	6.0	8.2	0.5	–35.5	0.6	–0.6	1.4	0.0

[1] Net of arrears and debt relief, including HIPC.
[2] Includes private transfers (largely remittances) reported in the current account.

III. Aid Inflows to Ghana: 1996–2003

Overview

Ghana's economy has performed relatively strongly in recent years compared with its regional peers. Per capita GDP growth averaged 1.6 percent annually in the 1990s. After a period of economic volatility around the turn of the century, Ghana has pursued economic policies that have delivered a degree of fiscal consolidation, lower inflation, and steadily increasing real GDP growth. Together with its granting of debt relief in 2002—by reaching the "decision point" under the Heavily Indebted Poor Countries Initiative (HIPC Initiative)[22]—international support jumped by the equivalent of several percentage points of GDP. Net aid averaged 7.3 percent of GDP during 2001–03 relative to 2.8 percent during 1996–2000 (Table 5.1).

The Ghanaian authorities have therefore had to cope with managing the huge jump in aid inflows, as well as with their volatility. This case study looks at Ghana's experience during 1996–2003, a period in which the country was almost continuously engaged in economic adjustment programs supported by

[22] The point at which a country has made sufficient progress toward meeting the criteria to qualify for debt relief under the HIPC Initiative.

the IMF's Enhanced Structural Adjustment Facility (ESAF) and its successor, the Poverty Reduction and Growth Facility (PRGF). The key features of Ghana's experience are the following:

1. Ghana cumulatively saved *all* of the increase in aid during 2001–03, relative to 1996–2000—where we define the increase in aid as the actual aid flow during 2001–03 less the amount of aid that would have been received had flows continued at their 1996–2000 rate. The aid inflow was saved, from the point of view of the country as a whole, insofar as gross reserve accumulation over the period ($1.2 billion) was almost equal to the incremental aid inflow ($1.3 billion). The inflow saving can be viewed from another perspective: that the nonaid current account deficit (investment less nonaid savings) did not grow at all with the higher aid inflows. On the contrary, the nonaid current account deficit averaged about 3½ percent of GDP during 2001–03, down from some 11 percent over the preceding three-year period.
2. Just as Ghana saved the aid inflows from a national point of view, the government also saved the aid inflows to the budget. The fiscal deficit (before grants) averaged 10 percent of GDP during 2001–03, almost equal to the average for the preceding five years.
3. Ghana avoided Dutch disease, or real effective exchange rate appreciation during 2001–03; the real effective exchange rate (REER) changed by less than 1 percent.
4. This is a tale of three policy responses, reflecting the pattern of aid flows.
   - In 2001, the aid surge was largely sold into the foreign exchange market, to stabilize the currency (and inflation) after a negative terms-of-trade shock; it was partly spent by the government in the sense that the fiscal deficit before grants widened, although by somewhat less than the increase in aid.
   - In 2002, a planned fiscal consolidation, aimed at reducing domestic public debt outstanding, fell short of compensating for an even larger negative aid shock. Despite the aid shortfall, however, reserves were accumulated.
   - In 2003, aid surged again and this time the authorities responded cautiously. All of the aid (and more) was accumulated as reserves. The fiscal deficit before grants did not widen.

The Pattern of Aid Inflows

The pattern of aid inflows is critical to understanding Ghana's policy response to, and economic outcomes of, the aid during 2000–03. Net aid jumped in 2001, collapsed in 2002, and jumped again in 2003. Most of these

Table 5.2. Aid Shocks in Ghana
(In percent of GDP)

	1998[1]	1999[2]	2000[3]	2001[4]	2002[5]	2003[6]
Project grants	–0.1	–0.5	–0.7	1.8	–1.0	–0.2
Program grants	0.3	0.2	–0.6	2.0	–0.1	0.3
HIPC assistance	0.0	0.0	0.0	0.0	0.0	0.2
Project loans	1.9	1.1	–0.7	–0.1	–1.8	0.2
Program loans	0.2	–0.3	–3.9	1.0	–1.2	0.6
Gross aid shock	2.3	0.6	–6.0	4.7	–4.1	1.8
Net aid shock	0.5	0.0	–6.1	4.9	–4.5	1.3

[1] Program as detailed in April, 1999 staff report EBS/99/57.
[2] Ibid.
[3] Program as detailed in August, 2000 staff report EBS/00/160.
[4] Ibid.
[5] Program as detailed in March, 2002 staff report No. 02/38.
[6] Program as detailed in May, 2003 staff report no. 03/133.

changes were driven by changes in gross aid flows.[23] This volatility was unexpected and thus required large and rapid policy adjustments (Table 5.2). HIPC debt relief was also a contributing factor; the value of HIPC assistance was about half that of loans and grants in 2002–03. Private flows, mostly transfers but also including unidentified items, also rose sharply, amplifying the effects of aid shocks.

The policy response to, and the economic outcomes of, recent aid inflows in Ghana was probably strongly influenced by the volatile pattern of aid. This volatility was largely unexpected and demanded substantial policy adjustments. To illustrate this, Table 5.2 shows aid actually received less aid programmed around the start of that year (as reported in the closest IMF staff report). A positive number implies a surprisingly large amount of aid.[24]

The Use of Aid Inflows

Ghana's macroeconomic response to the increased aid flows may be usefully studied using the analytical framework outlined in Section II.

[23] Net aid flows are calculated as the sum of gross aid, less debt service adjusted for debt relief and changes in arrears. Gross aid flows are calculated as the sum of project and IMF-supported program loans, and grants.

[24] The source of most of these aid shocks is not clear. Almost half of the 2002 negative shock, however, reflected nondisbursement of a World Bank loan tranche owing to a delay in the divestiture of Ghana Commercial Bank.

Absorption

During the entire 2001–03 period in which aid soared, Ghana's nonaid current account deficit narrowed. In other words, the aid was not used to increase net imports, or more generally to raise investment relative to domestic savings. Rather, inflows were fully accumulated as reserves.[25] The narrower nonaid current account deficit reflected stable or declining import volumes (Table 5.3).

Consistent with Ghana's saving the aid as higher reserves, there was little evidence of Dutch disease. The real effective exchange rate changed by less than 1 percent during the period and exhibited little volatility.[26] In view of the absence of real appreciation, it would seem unnecessary to examine the performance of exports for Dutch disease symptoms. Nonetheless, the decline in nontraditional export volumes during the period of higher aid is puzzling (Table 5.3).

This picture for 2001–03 masks three distinct episodes, which mirrored the fluctuations in aid:

- About half of the 2001 aid jump (equivalent to 5.1 percent of GDP) remained in reserves, while the rest financed a deterioration in the capital account (indeed more than the rest, as the nonaid current account strengthened).
- The 2002 aid collapse of 5.9 percent of GDP was more than outweighed by a strengthening of the nonaid current account.[27] This and some capital inflows permitted a further reserve accumulation equivalent to 3.3 percent of GDP.
- Finally, the 2003 aid jump (equal to 6.5 percent of GDP) and a further strengthening of the nonaid current account (of 1 percent of GDP) fed a further reserve buildup (to 7.3 percent of GDP).[28]

---

[25] IMF support is generally intended to augment reserves. In our definition of net aid, IMF support is included. However, IMF disbursements were a small part of aid flows to Ghana; for example, they averaged 1.1 percent of GDP (net of repayments to the IMF) during 2001–03.

[26] The real exchange rate versus the U.S. dollar appreciated by roughly 10 percent, mainly when the dollar began to broadly depreciate.

[27] This was driven by a $307 million narrowing in the trade balance, plus an $80 million rise in private transfers, largely made up of remittances.

[28] In one sense, some of the aid could be said to have been absorbed, with the terms-of-trade-related increase in export proceeds going into reserves. However, the terms-of-trade effect simply means that it would have taken a larger real exchange rate appreciation to absorb the aid than otherwise.

Table 5.3. Ghana's Balance of Payments
(In percent of GDP)

	1997	1998	1999	2000	2001	2002	2003
Levels							
Aid and reserves	6.4	6.2	4.9	4.4	6.9	−2.2	−2.5
Net aid[1]	5.1	6.2	2.4	3.3	8.4	2.4	7.5
Δ gross reserves (+ = increase)	1.3	0.0	2.5	1.1	−1.5	−4.6	−10.0
Nonaid balance of payments	−6.4	−6.2	−4.9	−4.4	−6.9	2.2	2.7
Nonaid current account	−15.2	−8.4	−11.7	−9.3	−8.3	−1.1	−1.0
Nonaid capital account[2]	8.8	2.2	6.8	4.9	1.4	3.2	3.6
Changes							
Aid and reserves (changes)		−0.2	−1.3	−0.5	2.5	−9.1	−0.3
Δ net aid[1]		1.2	−3.8	0.9	5.1	−6.0	5.1
ΔΔ gross reserves (+ = increase)		−1.3	2.5	−1.4	−2.6	−3.1	−5.4
Nonaid balance of payments (changes)		0.2	1.3	0.5	−2.5	9.1	0.5
Δ nonaid current account		6.8	−3.4	2.5	1.0	7.3	0.1
Δ nonaid capital account[2]		−6.6	4.7	−2.0	−3.5	1.8	0.4
Memorandum items (percent change)							
GDP (millions of U.S. dollars)	6,884	7,474	7,774	5,000	5,298	6,354	7,952
Real GDP growth	4.2	4.7	4.4	3.7	4.2	4.5	5.2
Gross reserves (millions of U.S. dollars)	508	508	317	264	344	635	1,427
Cedi per U.S. dollar (average)	−20.1	−11.4	−13.3	−51.1	−23.9	−9.6	−8.6
RER vs U.S. dollar (average)	−7.6	1.5	−4.1	−34.0	−8.6	1.5	10.8
REER (average)	6.0	8.2	0.5	−35.5	0.6	−0.6	1.4
Trade balance (percent of GDP)	−17.9	−10.8	−16.0	−16.5	−18.2	−10.8	−12.0
Exports fob	0.0	15.6	−4.1	−3.5	−3.6	10.2	20.1
Export volume	−0.6	16.3	−2.8	2.2	−1.3	−2.1	−6.8
Nontraditional export volumes	2.6	−1.3	−18.2	5.8	6.3	−2.4	−32.9
Imports fob	32.4	−4.7	12.3	−15.2	2.6	−4.1	20.1
Import volumes	14.4	24.5	10.4	−24.9	10.0	−6.8	6.9
Nonoil import volumes	15.8	23.6	10.3	−30.3	8.6	−7.6	9.0
Terms of trade	−0.7	13.7	−8.7	−16.6	4.8	9.4	14.8
Import cover (months)	2.1	1.9	1.9	1.1	1.5	2.3	4.7

[1] This definition of net aid is taken from the balance of payments and may differ from the net aid inflows reported in the government's accounts and reported in Table 5.1.
[2] Includes unidentified capital flows and errors and omissions.

GDP growth and the real exchange rate, on an average year-on-year basis, were remarkably steady through the entire period. The cedi nominal exchange rate depreciated by nearly 50 percent in 2000, but the use of aid in 2001 helped arrest the decline. Reserve accumulation after 2001 contributed to ongoing nominal depreciation (Table 5.2), a policy choice discussed below.

Table 5.4. Ghana: Net Aid Flows and the Fiscal Response
(In percent of GDP)

Net aid shock

	1997	1998	1999	2000	2001	2002	2003
Δ Financing	−0.7	−0.5	0.7	−0.8	4.5	−5.6	1.3
Δ net aid	−1.4	−0.4	−0.3	−3.1	10.9	−8.1	6.1
Of which: unexpected		0.5	0.0	−6.1	4.9	−4.4	2.3
Δ domestic financing[1]	0.7	−0.1	1.0	2.3	−6.4	2.5	−4.8
Δ Balance (before grants)	1.0	0.9	0.4	−0.2	−4.6	6.5	−0.1
Δ expenditure	−1.3	0.2	−2.4	1.5	5.0	−6.6	2.9
Δ revenue ex-grants	−0.3	1.1	−2.0	1.3	0.4	−0.1	2.8
Memorandum items							
Revenue and grants	19.2	20.5	18.0	19.8	25.0	21.1	25.5
Revenue	17.3	18.4	16.4	17.7	18.1	18.0	20.8
Grants	1.9	2.2	1.7	2.1	6.9	3.1	4.7
Expenditure	28.4	28.6	26.2	27.7	32.7	26.1	29.0
Recurrent exp. (excl. interest)[2]	10.3	10.3	10.8	11.1	12.1	13.8	13.8
Wages and salaries	5.3	5.5	5.6	5.2	6.1	8.5	8.4
Capital expenditure	11.6	11.3	9.8	9.2	12.8	6.1	8.9
Poverty expenditure	. . .	. . .	. . .	. . .	4.5	4.8	6.5
Overall balance	−9.2	−8.1	−8.2	−7.9	−7.7	−5.0	−3.5
excl. grants	−11.1	−10.2	−9.8	−10.0	−14.6	−8.1	−8.2
Debt service (% of rev. excl. grants)	37.6	38.0	34.1	42.4	43.1	33.9	29.8
Debt service (% exports)[3]	24.7	25.0	21.7	19.4	22.1	19.9	19.8
Interest payments	6.5	7.0	5.6	7.5	7.8	6.1	6.2

[1] Net domestic financing, given by the period's change in the domestic net credit to government.
[2] From 2001, on a cash basis.
[3] Includes subventions in separate line items from 2002 onward.

Spending

Recall that we have defined "spending" as the increase in the government's fiscal deficit (before grants) accompanying an increase in aid inflows. On a cumulative basis, none of the aid Ghana received was spent. As noted above, this does not mean that aid money itself was not spent, but that if it was, other spending was reduced correspondingly.

Aid going to the budget followed the same pattern as aid measured through the balance of payments (Table 5.4). During 2001–02, fiscal policy was sensitive to aid flows. In 2001, the fiscal deficit widened by half the increase in aid. The next year's large and unexpected aid shortfall triggered a large fiscal consolidation but not enough to close the shortfall. However, fiscal policymakers responded cautiously to the aid surge in 2003; the fiscal balance did not react at all. Although spending rose, it was fully financed by higher non-

Figure 5.1. Ghana: Aid Flows and Public Expenditure Patterns

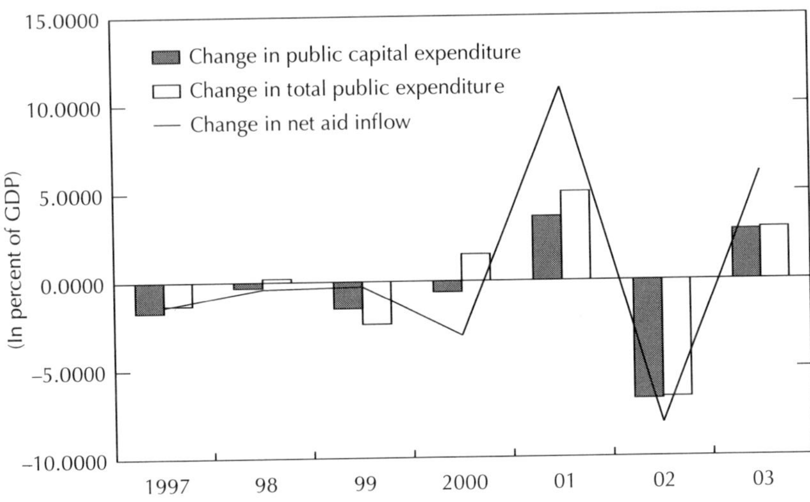

grant revenues. On a cumulative basis, aid had little fiscal impact during 2001–03.

The surprise volatility of the aid flows seems to have complicated expenditure management and perhaps undermined the efficiency of spending (Figure 5.1). The increase in spending associated with the 2001 aid jump came mainly in the form of higher public capital expenditure, but also recurrent expenditure (Table 5.4). When aid declined by more than 8 percent of GDP in 2002, capital expenditure fell by nearly 7 percentage points of GDP, as current expenditures continued to rise. In 2003, capital expenditures rose with higher domestic revenues, but to levels well below the average of the four pre-aid boom years.

The volatile, but increasing, trend in net aid did not lead to any apparent reduction in Ghana's fiscal consolidation efforts. Revenues excluding grants have increased steadily as a share of GDP since 1999.

Why did Ghana not spend the aid on a cumulative basis? Three motivations seem to have been at work:

- a desire to resolve underlying fiscal problems and achieve disinflation,
- IMF conditionality on fiscal policy and its interaction with volatility; and
- an underlying concern for the implications of aid volatility.

Throughout 2001–03, the IMF-supported program targets implied that a large part of the aid increment—between 2 to 4 percentage points of GDP—not be spent, in order to reduce the large stock of domestic public debt, high domestic interest rates, and the resulting large share of interest payments in expenditures.

Given the (unpredicted) volatility of aid to Ghana, the interaction between the surprise component of aid flows and the fiscal performance criteria is an important part of the story. The criteria were subject to "adjustors" to account for deviations between expected and realized aid flows. These adjustors were not symmetric. Positive aid shocks were to be saved and were not to be used to increase spending. Negative aid shocks were to be partially dealt with through a reduction in spending and, hence, a narrower deficit (before grants). Some cushion was built in, so that the adjustment was some fraction of the aid shortfall, but this cushion was limited because of the program's focus on the domestic financing restraint. If the criteria were binding, shortfalls still implied a tightening of policy.[29] (See Appendix III for more details on the adjustor mechanism.)

As noted earlier, roughly half of each aid jump during 2001–03 was unexpected. In 2001, the increase in domestic credit roughly matched the expected component of the aid inflow. Correspondingly, the actual size of the primary deficit and domestic financing of the budget were close to, though somewhat below, the adjusted program targets. This small degree of outperformance implies that the program was almost binding; there was little scope to boost spending, and this led the authorities to save almost all of the aid surprise. Figure 5.2 illustrates this point for domestic financing, which implies the same constraints applied to the fiscal deficit.

In 2002, Ghana's IMF-supported program again called for a large reduction in domestic financing. This was because of the need to begin reducing the large stock of domestic debt—which had reached 20 percent of GDP—and because of high real interest rates (Figure 5.4). In the event, the substantial fiscal consolidation (equivalent to 6.5 percent of GDP) did not fully compensate for the huge aid shortfall. The adjustors allowed for some rise in domestic financing, but the program's targets were still breached. As a result of these fiscal slippages, the final IMF Executive Board review under the 1999–2002 PRGF-supported program could not be completed and the program was essentially suspended. In May 2003, Ghana began another PRGF-supported economic program.

In 2003, however, even the expected component of the surge was not spent. In this case, the targets were clearly not a binding constraint on fiscal policy. This is illustrated by the large degree of outperformance against the domestic borrowing criteria in Figure 5.2, indicating that the authorities had room to

[29] Initially, from 1999 to mid-2001, this fraction was set at one half; the remainder of the deficit-financing shortfall was to be met by domestic borrowing. In later program reviews, this fractional approach was replaced by a U.S. dollar cap on additional domestic borrowing.

Figure 5.2. Ghana: Performance Against Domestic Financing Targets

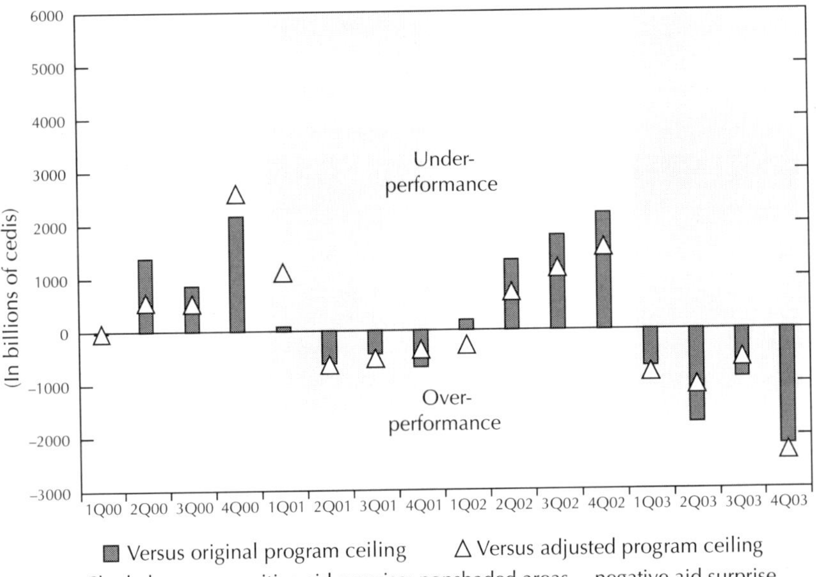

increase spending under the program. Increases in spending were largely financed by terms-of-trade-related increases in tax revenues.

Ghana's choice not to spend the aid surge of 2003 requires further explanation. One obvious inference is that the largely unexpected aid volatility of the previous few years dictated caution, particularly in view of the impact of aid and, hence, fiscal volatility on capital expenditures.

Ghana's fiscal caution in 2003 is consistent with its policy on reserve accumulation. The authorities saved the entire 2003 aid jump (and more) in reserves. Spending the aid in the face of reserve accumulation would have been equivalent to a domestically financed fiscal expansion, as discussed earlier. Thus, the reserve accumulation policy made the fiscal savings more advisable. The reserve accumulation itself may have been driven partly by fiscal policymakers' desire to save the aid jump. In either case, the two policies were both designed to save the aid inflows.

Finally, the lack of fiscal expansion in 2003, despite the surge in aid, afforded the authorities scope to use the aid inflows to stabilize the exchange rate and inflation, which had increased sharply in late 2002 and in early 2003. In order to understand this better, we now turn to Ghana's monetary policy response to the aid inflows.

Table 5.5. Ghana in a Regional Context: Classification by Aid Absorption and Spending

	Not Spent[2]	Partly Spent	Mostly Spent	Fully Spent
Not Absorbed[1]	Ghana (0, 7)		Tanzania (0, 92)	
Partly Absorbed	Ethiopia (22, 0)		Uganda (27, 78)	
Mostly Absorbed				Mozambique (64, 100)
Fully Absorbed				

[1] "Absorb" variable = Nonaid Current Account Deterioration as percent of Incremental Aid Inflow; truncated at 0 and 100.

[2] "Spend" variable = Nonaid Fiscal Balance Deterioration as percent of Incremental Aid Inflow; truncated at 0 and 100.

Monetary Policy Response

The monetary policy response to aid surges is conditioned by whether it is absorbed and spent (as discussed in Section II). Table 5.5 summarizes where Ghana stands in this context, along with four other countries in Africa that recorded large increases in aid inflows over roughly the same period. Taking the sample period (2001–2003) as a whole, Ghana's aid surge was neither used nor spent.[30]

This pattern of absorption and spending implies that the aid inflows in and of themselves had no overall impact on Ghana's monetary policy. In effect, the aid left the country in the form of higher reserves, and the government compensated for any aid-related expenditure increase by cutting spending elsewhere. This contrasts with the strategy outlined in Ghana's PRGF-supported program, which was to mostly absorb and partly spend the expected aid increments in order to reduce the burden of domestic debt on the economy.

Again, this big picture masks some interesting year-by-year variations. Ghana experienced two major surges of inflation during the period—in 2000–01 and again in 2002–03. Each followed sharp and unexpected aid declines, and in the first case a major terms-of-trade decline as well. Each was also accompanied by a loosening of domestic monetary and fiscal policy. In the first case, the authorities used aid to help stabilize the economy; in the second, they did not.

The first aid surge came when the Ghanaian economy was still reeling from a terms-of-trade decline of 25 percent during 1999–2000 (Appendix II).[31] In response to this shock, and with foreign reserves equal to one month of imports

[30] Again, it is important to caveat that accumulating reserves may have been the appropriate response, given the potential value of reserves for buffering shocks, including to aid.

[31] Compounding the effect of the terms-of-trade shock was a decline in net aid inflows of 0.3 percent of GDP, as against IMF staff expectations of a 5.8 percent-of-GDP *increase* in aid flows in 2000 (Table 5.1).

Figure 5.3. Ghana: Exchange Rates, Inflation, and Aid Inflows

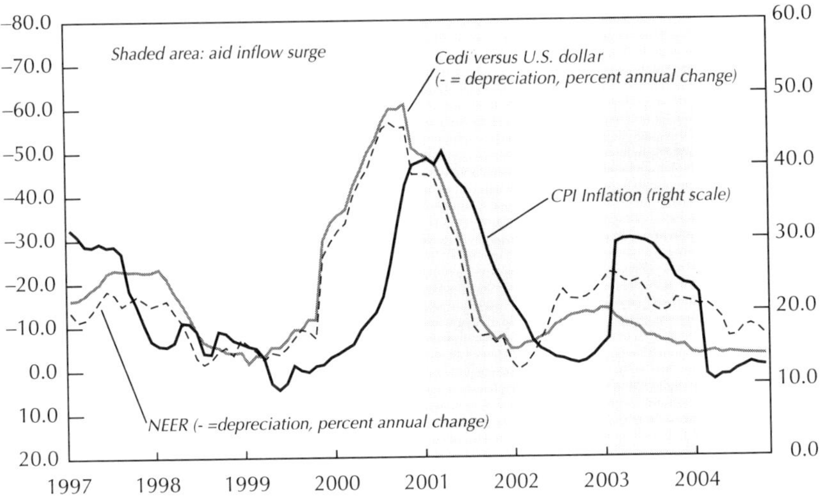

at the end of 2000, the authorities failed to tighten fiscal policy sufficiently; rather, they increased domestic borrowing and ran up domestic arrears to plug the shortfall. Reserve money growth took off and the result was a 50 percent loss in the currency's nominal effective value and a sharp rise in inflation, which rose to an annual average of about 40 percent.

The aid surge in 2001 was partly sold into the foreign exchange market, strengthening the cedi and helping reduce money growth. Given the worsening capital account, it is likely that in the absence of the aid surge the nominal exchange rate declines in 2001 would have been much larger than the modest 5 percent experienced.

In 2001, IMF staff supported the Ghanaian monetary authorities' strategy, effectively advising that aid flows be used to support the currency as a way to curb inflation.[32] The IMF-supported program specified a floor for the accumulation of net international reserves (NIR) and a ceiling for central bank net domestic assets (NDA). Both targets were generally met in 2001; NDA targets were waived as money demand increased more than forecast while inflation eased.

[32] "Ghana: 2001 Article IV Consultation and Third Review Under the PRGF Facility and Request for Waiver of Performance Criteria: Staff Report" EBS 01/141. Paragraph 33 notes that "the [May 2001] mission emphasized the need for significantly positive real interest rates, to reduce credit demand, strengthen the incentive to save, and support the exchange rate". Paragraph 70 notes that 'the staff encourages the authorities to allow the value of the cedi to be market determined, with intervention being limited to achieve the government's target for foreign reserves.'

As the aid shortfall hit in 2002, monetary policy was eased. The fiscal contraction was less than the aid decline, and the government borrowed directly from the central bank to partly cover the resulting financing gap. There was little sterilization of these liquidity injections during this period, either domestically or in terms of foreign exchange, as reserves continued to be accumulated.[33] In part, reserve accumulation was programmed, because import cover at the start of 2002 remained fairly low (at just 2.3 months). The nominal exchange rate depreciation accelerated and inflation began to pick up by the end of 2002.[34]

The monetary and fiscal targets under the IMF-supported program were overshot by the end of 2002. While adjustors in the program allowed for some loosening in response to the surprise aid decline, and there was a substantial contraction, it was not as sharp as called for by the program, given the aid decline. Despite a reasonably large increase in the NIR floor for 2002, the program left substantial room to sell reserves; indeed, reserves ended the year $80 million above the adjusted program floor. This would have reduced monetary expansion without requiring further contraction of domestic credit by the central bank.[35] These slippages prevented the IMF's Executive Board from completing the final review of the 2002 PRGF-supported program.[36]

In 2003, the authorities had to stabilize. One approach might have been to sell some reserves to reduce money growth and stabilize the exchange rate. The authorities in fact steadily reduced the rate of nominal exchange rate depreciation, contributing to the inflation stabilization. However, the authorities could have made more aggressive use of foreign exchange sales. Instead, as discussed above, the authorities continued to accumulate more reserves. One motivation, emphasized earlier, was the need to create a buffer for volatile aid flows. A desire to keep the real exchange rate from appreciating may have also played a role, however, as the authorities actually bought reserves in the foreign exchange market and accumulated more than would be implied by the aid jump.

To reduce inflation, the authorities conducted policy through domestic monetary operations, selling Treasury bills for local currency and increasing reserve requirements for domestic banks to reduce money supply growth and raise interest rates. In the event, inflation fell to less than 5 percent on a six-month annualized basis by the end of 2003.

---

[33] In effect, the policy response in 2002 corresponded to the case in which aid inflows are spent and partly absorbed. The fiscal deficit was larger than the decline in aid flows would imply had the deficit moved one-for-one with aid, while reserves did not fall with the decline in aid.

[34] In early 2003, inflation pressures were exacerbated by one-off petroleum price hikes linked to the removal of subsidies.

[35] The monetary performance criterion was changed from reserve money to net domestic assets in June 2001. Reserve money became an indicative target.

[36] It would seem unlikely that this event contributed much to the shortfall in aid, which had already mostly emerged by then.

IMF staff urged the authorities to avoid further reserve accumulation and once again use the aid to allow the currency to adjust, in order to slow the pace of monetary expansion, restrain inflation expectations, and avoid the crowding-out effects of domestic sterilization.[37] Reserve accumulation exceeded the program floor by $310 million, approximately $200 million more than the positive aid surprise. Despite this, high-powered money was just 7 percent above its indicative target as a result of the aggressive domestic monetary tightening.

The potential costs of domestic sterilization were twofold: the possible effect on private investment and the quasi-fiscal costs of the higher domestic debt level. Excluding the early part of the year, when petrol prices affected inflation, real interest rates in Ghana tended to rise from already high levels in 2003 (Figure 5.3). Private investment remained stable, at about 14 percent of GDP. Meanwhile, domestic debt remained high, at 20 percent of GDP, and with interest rates high, domestic debt service continued to absorb 5 percent of GDP, or 17 percent of total public expenditure.

One aim of policy over this period was to reduce the domestic debt burden, in order to lower real rates, stimulate private investment, and reduce the burden of domestic interest payments on the budget. A number of factors supported higher private investment after 2001, including improving terms of trade, recovering GDP growth, and fiscal consolidation. It is thus possible that the domestic sterilization policy may have kept real interest rates higher, the domestic debt burden higher, and private investment lower than otherwise would have been the case (Table 5.6). While this was appropriate in view of the need to reduce inflation, a more aggressive use of aid—via sales of foreign exchange—may have mitigated some of these problems.

IV. Conclusions

Ghana avoided real exchange rate appreciation and Dutch disease during a three year period in which aid flows were 4.4 percentage points of GDP higher than during the previous five years. This cannot be attributed to offsetting forces as Ghana's terms of trade improved and private inflows rose significantly during the same period. Rather, the fact that Ghana effectively saved all of the aid and prevented it from having a cumulative impact on the economy explains the lack of a real exchange rate effect.

[37] See "Ghana: 2003 Article IV Consultation and Requests for a Three-Year Arrangement Under the Poverty Reduction and Growth Facility and for Additional Interim Assistance under the Enhanced HIPC Initiative: Staff Report" EBS 03/133. Paragraph 52 notes that, "given the positive terms of trade outlook, the market may seek a strengthening of the exchange rate this year. The staff believes that this could be accommodated in the interests of helping to bring down inflation without unduly affecting external competitiveness."

Table 5.6. Monetary Conditions
(In millions of cedis, except where indicated)

	1997	1998	1999	2000	2001	2002	2003
Δ Reserve money	301	315	584	1,145	1,333	2,116	1,882
Δ NFA	111	294	–550	–930	1,405	1,752	6,115
Δ NDA	189	21	1,133	2,076	–72	364	–4,233
Memorandum items							
Net aid flows (millions of U.S. dollars)	243	236	221	–13	563	157	566
Δ gross reserves (millions of U.S. dollars)	–91	0	–62	–182	80	291	792
Δ NEER percent change (average)	–16	–5	–21	–49	–5	–18	–16
Δ REER percent change (average)	6	8	1	–36	1	–1	1
Inflation percent change (average)	18	16	13	39	23	14	24
Treasury bills (average nominal rate)	43	27	30	41	33	26	22
Treasury bills (average real rate)	25	11	17	2	10	12	2
Reserve money (percent change)	33	26	38	55	41	46	28
Broad money (percent change)	44	17	25	54	32	49	34
Velocity	4.9	4.2	4.4	4.2	3.6	3.8	3.1
Private investment (percent of GDP)	12	12	13	15	14	14	14
Private investment (percent of inv.)	49	52	58	62	52	69	60

Figure 5.4. Real Treasury Bill Rates Using Annualized Quarterly Inflation

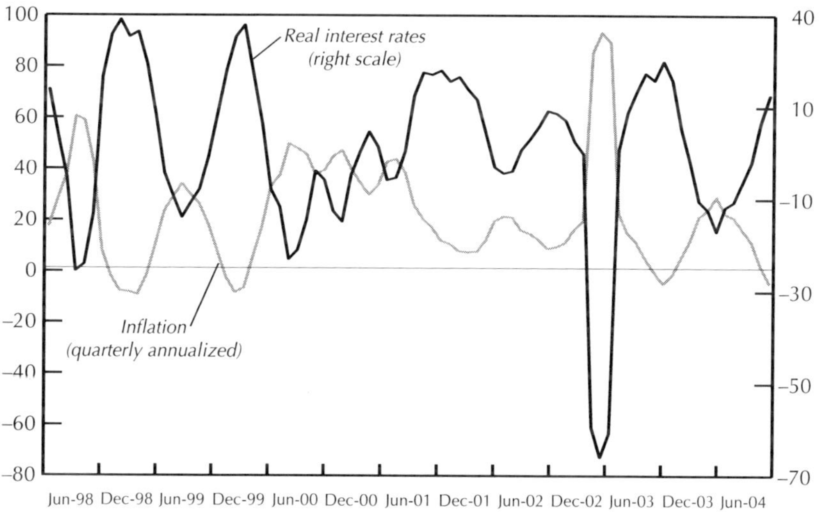

The aid inflows and Ghana's policy response differed in each of the three years:

- In 2001, aid inflows jumped unexpectedly. Fiscal policy was restrained, in keeping with the IMF-supported program, which did not allow spending of aid surprises. Much of the extra aid was absorbed in that it was sold in the foreign exchange market, putting this episode in the category of aid *mostly absorbed but not spent*. The sale of foreign exchange and associated policies allowed the exchange rate to stabilize and inflation to fall.
- In 2002, aid inflows fell just as unexpectedly. Fiscal policy contracted but not proportionally, leaving a net increase in domestic financing of the deficit. Reserves were further accumulated, in excess of the actual aid flows. The combined impact of the less-than-full fiscal adjustment and the accumulation of reserves was a loose monetary policy that contributed to an increase in inflation by the end of 2002.
- In 2003, aid again surged unexpectedly. This time, the authorities more than accumulated the jump in reserves and avoided any increase in the fiscal deficit before grants. Aid was *neither absorbed nor spent*. Inflation was stabilized, in part through the sale of government paper that contracted the money supply, which contributed to high interest rates and a large stock of domestic public debt. The authorities did not take the opportunity to stabilize through more aggressive foreign exchange sales, a more appreciated real exchange rate, and a reduction in the level of domestic public debt.

A number of questions emerge:

First, why did policymakers limit the impact of aid on the economy? The answer does not seem to lie in the strictures of the IMF-supported program. Most notably, the lack of fiscal and exchange rate reaction to the 2003 aid inflow expansion cannot be ascribed to program fiscal and reserve accumulation targets.

Part of the reason for the reserve accumulation was presumably Ghana's desire to rebuild reserves from low levels. And part of the reason for the lack of proportionate increase in the fiscal deficit was a desire to "crowd in," that is, to reduce the large stock of domestic public debt that had led to high real interest rates and incurred large interest costs for the budget.

However, these explanations are perhaps not the full story. The clearest indication of this is that IMF floors for reserve accumulation and ceilings on domestic financing of the deficit were substantially exceeded in 2003. In addition to the above motivations, the policy may have reflected a desire to avoid real exchange rate appreciations. In this sense, perhaps we are observing Dutch disease in the same way that one may observe the effects of crime, even in the absence of a break-in, in the form of armed guards and barbed wire on top of walls. However, there is little direct evidence on this point.

Clearly, aid volatility—particularly unexpected and large swings—has contributed to Ghana's policy difficulties and, most likely, to the authorities' caution in spending the 2003 aid surge. The volatility of aid carried other costs as well. It is surely more difficult to revert back to a given level of expenditure after an increase than to simply maintain the current level of spending. In this sense, the volatility in 2001–02 surely contributed to the fiscal, and then monetary, policy relaxation, and high inflation, in 2002. Moreover, recurrent expenditures appear to have been harder to restrain than capital spending during the 2002 downturn. This implies that spending the aid as it arrives could help reduce the share of capital expenditures over time. Recent improvements in donor coordination in Ghana should help limit the volatility of aid flows in the future.[38]

IMF-supported program targets, with their asymmetric adjustors, may significantly affect how aid surprises are absorbed. The system of adjustors in Ghana was, in part, designed to reduce the risks of excessive public domestic borrowing and facilitate "crowding in." With these objectives in mind, although the asymmetric adjustors may have appeared excessively tight ex ante, in the event, they turned out to be useful. Had the aid jump of 2001 been fully spent, the collapse of 2002 would have been even harder to manage.[39] Had the aid collapse effect on policy been fully smoothed by domestic borrowing, the public debt stock would have risen from already high levels, while the emerging inflation problem of 2003 would have been worse.

There is no universally optimal approach to managing high aid inflows. Unless Dutch disease is a major concern or the return to public expenditure low, to *absorb and spend* the aid would appear to be the most appropriate response. However, if resources are scarce for private investment, the rate of return on public expenditure is low, or fiscal policy is already too loose, *to absorb and not spend* may be the most appropriate short-run response. *To neither absorb nor spend* the aid may be useful temporarily when international reserves are precariously low or when aid volatility is a major concern. *To not absorb but spend* the aid would appear to be the least attractive option, particularly when domestic sterilization is used to avoid pressure on inflation and for exchange rate appreciation. This cannot be a sensible long-run strategy for an aid recipient as it combines crowding out the private sector with a zero real resource transfer to the aid recipient.

---

[38] The government takes the overall lead in coordinating external assistance and has introduced a "mini-Consultative Group" process, in which it meets with external partners on a quarterly basis. The World Bank has stepped back from its traditional role to leave scope for the government to lead external partner coordination.

[39] The maintained assumption is that the aid collapse of 2002 was not a result of donor or recipient dissatisfaction with the partial failure to spend the aid in 2001.

The lack of consensus in the theoretical and empirical literature indicates that there is no easy "cookie cutter" response to high aid inflows. In each economy the response should be dictated by the particular circumstances. In the case of Ghana, the volatility of the aid inflows was clearly a central factor.

Appendix I. Dutch Disease: Theory and Evidence

Dutch disease is related to the idea that productivity growth is particularly high when resources are devoted to exports, particularly of nontraditional products, because of learning-by-doing or other dynamic externalities in these relatively competitive and technologically advanced industries. The decline of the export sector, mediated by an increase in the demand for and price of nontradables, may lower the attainable growth path of the economy. For this argument to hold, dynamic externalities in the export sector would have to outweigh the benefits of capital accumulation associated with aid-financed investment (as well as any related productivity growth). A slightly different argument is premised on imperfect capital markets and hysteresis: if aid is temporarily high and crowds out export firms through real appreciation, it may not be possible to resuscitate these firms once aid falls and the real exchange rate depreciates.

The theoretical case for Dutch disease is ambiguous. For example, when learning-by-doing externalities can take place also in the nontradable sector, the long-run damage will be limited, even if the real exchange rate appreciates in the short term.[40]

Over the longer run, the investments in physical and human capital—both in the government and in the private sector—begin to bear fruit, and productivity increases not only in the tradable sector but also in the nontradable sector, potentially offsetting the initial loss of competitiveness.[41]

The effects of Dutch disease would be enhanced if the aid-recipient economy had weak financial markets. For example, in thin foreign exchange markets, volatile and lumpy aid disbursements can cause overshooting in the exchange rate or interest rate. Similarly, in the short run, when the real exchange rate appreciation attributable to excess demand for nontradables is not yet compensated by the increase in productivity, firms may be forced out of business if they do not have access to adequate credit to smooth out the shock. Temporary overshooting of the actual real exchange rate after an increase in aid may therefore be more damaging than the longer-term shift in the equilibrium real exchange rate.

---

40 Torvik (2001).

41 Nkusu (2004a) discusses the theoretical determinants of Dutch disease and emphasizes the mitigating role of excess domestic capacity. Adams and Bevan (2003) describe a nonmonetary theoretical model, and calibrate it for Uganda.

Despite a substantial body of theoretical literature on the implications of Dutch disease from aid inflows, empirical work is limited—particularly in low-income countries. Recent cross-country studies find some evidence for the real appreciation effect. For example, Elbadawi (1999) finds that a 10 percent increase in the aid-to-GDP ratio appreciates the real exchange rate by about 1 percent. Individual country studies, however, offer mixed results. Some (such as Malawi and Sri Lanka) find that aid inflows cause real appreciation, but others (such as Ghana, Nigeria, and Tanzania) find that aid flows are related to real depreciations.[42]

In a related literature, some papers find evidence of a significant detrimental impact of real appreciation on exports, particularly nontraditional exports.[43] Empirical evidence also suggests that real appreciation has contributed to wider trade deficits in four African economies.[44]

A recent approach is to look directly at the impact of aid on exports without attempting to trace through the real exchange rate channel. Rajan and Subramanian (2005b) examine the effects of aid in a sample of 33 countries during the 1980s and 15 countries in the 1990s. They find that export and labor-intensive manufacturing industries grew significantly slower in those countries that received the most aid, and that a 1-percentage-point increase in the ratio of aid to GDP is roughly equivalent to a 4-percentage-point overvaluation of the exchange rate. Arellan and others (2005) find that aid significantly depresses the export sector in a sample of developing countries.

The risks of Dutch disease need to be balanced against the potential benefits from the investment that aid can finance. Here, the evidence is also mixed. The benefits of public investment are not clearly established empirically, as a general rule.[45] Of course, the rate of return will depend on the particular investment and on a variety of country-specific circumstances. A strong case can nonetheless be made for a higher level in poor countries.[46] While the systematic evidence for a positive growth impact of private investment is stronger, it is less clear that aid can be effectively channeled into higher private investment.

More broadly, a huge literature asks directly whether aid affects growth, and the conclusions are somewhat mixed.[47] Substantial cross-country evidence, however, suggests that exchange rate overvaluations are one of the few policy

42 White and Wignaraja (1992, Sri Lanka), Ogun (1995, Nigeria), Nyoni (1998, Tanzania), Sackey (2001, Ghana), and Ouattara and Strobl (2004, CFA countries), Fanizza (2001, Malawi).

43 Sekkat and Varoudakis (2000) and Elbadawi (2002).

44 Adenauer and Vagassky (1998).

45 Leite and Tsangarides (2005).

46 United Nations Millennium Project Report (2005).

47 See Clements and Radelet (2004) for results showing a positive correlation between aid and growth, as well as Rajan and Subramanian (2005a) and Easterly, Levin, and Roodman (2003) for more skeptical views.

variables that matter for growth after controlling for institutions. There is also substantial micro-based evidence on the benefits of trade and, to some extent, learning-by-doing associated with exports. Weak exchange rates may also help predict the incidence of episodes of growth acceleration.[48] Case studies that examine the entire chain from aid through export performance to final outcomes include Nkusu (2004b), who finds little sign of Dutch disease in Uganda.

On balance, the evidence on Dutch disease is mixed. Presumably, the seriousness of the problem and the benefits of aid-financed investments depend on each country's circumstances. A country with strong dynamic externalities in the tradable goods sector may wish to consider carefully the level of aid it can absorb without triggering too much real appreciation. It may also wish to seek aid in forms that are less likely to induce real appreciation.[49] It can safely be concluded, however, that the risk of Dutch disease raises the stakes: if aid-financed investments have poor rates of return, not only is the aid wasted but overall growth may be impaired.

Appendix II. Terms-of-Trade Shocks and Aid Flows

Table A5.1 illustrates the relative importance of net aid flows, private flows, and the trade balance for overall foreign exchange flows to Ghana between 1998 and 2003. The existence of significant terms of trade volatility is the most difficult complicating factor in analyzing aid flows. Three commodities dominate the terms of trade: gold and cocoa exports, and oil imports.[50] Price volatil-

[48] Acemoglu and others (2003) present important evidence on overvaluation and growth, while Easterly, Levine and Roodman (2003) summarize the literature. Hausmann and others (2004) discuss the role of depreciated real exchange rates in sparking growth accelerations. Berg and Krueger (2003) summarize some of the literature on learning-by-doing and exports.

[49] This is harder than it seems. It is sometimes argued that aid-in-kind has no impact on the real exchange rate. This is true, however, only if the transferred good is one for which there was no existing effective demand. If the good transferred was already demanded domestically, then increasing the good's supply would depress the price of tradables relative to nontradables, leading to real appreciation. On the other hand, the transfer of a good for which there is no pre-existing demand is clearly of limited utility in general (although not always: for example, one could imagine aid taking the form of expensive drugs or treatments for which there is no effective pre-existing demand).

[50] In 1996, two commodities—gold and cocoa—accounted for roughly equal shares of 74 percent of exports; by 2003, this had declined modestly to roughly equal shares of 64 percent (i.e., one-third each). Price independence provides some diversification (the correlation of annual prices since 1996 is not statistically significant from zero), but overall exposure to prices remains high. Between 10–20 percent of imports are accounted for by oil.

Table A5.1. Net Aid and Terms-of-Trade Effects, 1998–2003
(In millions of U.S. dollars)

	1998	1999	2000	2001	2002	2003
Exports (+ve = higher export values)	282	−86	−70	−69	190	414
Of which: price effects	−11	−28	−112	−44	234	594
Imports (+ve = lower import values)	144	−355	493	−72	117	−545
Of which: price effects	714	−49	−422	185	−81	−335
Trade balance (+ve = narrower deficit)	426	−441	423	−141	307	−131
Of which: terms-of-trade effect	703	−77	−534	141	153	259
Net aid (+ve = higher net aid flows)	−7	−15	−233	576	−406	409
Private capital (+ve = higher inflows)	−350	405	−305	132	10	285
Total	**69**	**−51**	**−115**	**567**	**−89**	**563**
Memorandum items						
Change in gross reserves (°ßmillions of U.S. dollars)	−62	−62	−182	80	291	792
Terms of trade (annual percent change)	14	−9	−17	5	9	15

[1] Positive (negative) numbers refer to an inflow (outflow) of foreign currency relative to the previous year in all cases.
[2] These items correct the approximations made in the individual price and volume effects.

ity in these commodities can greatly influence the flow of foreign exchange into the economy and either worsen, or ameliorate, the potential for net aid flows to induce real exchange rate appreciation. A summary of the approximate effect of the terms of trade and net aid on Ghana's foreign exchange flows is presented in Table A5.2.

In 2000, Ghana suffered a large negative terms-of-trade shock that amplified the impact of the aid decline. During 2001–03, terms-of-trade effects were not as large as aid movements but were still important: in 2002, they offset some of the decline and in 2003, they moved in the same direction as the large jump in aid, driven largely by export price increases.

Appendix III. Program Adjustors for Aid Surprises

The criteria set out in the PRGF-supported program for Ghana were subject to asymmetric "adjustors" to account for deviations between expected and realized aid flows. Positive aid shocks were to be saved in higher net international reserves (NIR) and lower net domestic assets (NDA), while negative aid shocks were to be partially dealt with through a reduction in NIR and some increase in NDA. Some cushion was built in, so that the adjustment was some proportion of the aid shortfall, but if the criteria were binding, shortfalls still implied a tightening of policy.

Table A5.2. IMF-Supported Program Aid-Flow Relevant Performance Criteria

	Positive aid shock (actual higher than programmed)	Negative aid shock (actual lower than programmed)
Performance criteria		
Net domestic financing of government (ceiling)[1]	Lowered by full amount of the aid shock	Raised by some proportion of the aid shock
Net domestic assets of the central bank (ceiling)[1,2]	Lowered by full amount of the aid shock	Raised by some proportion of the aid shock
Net international reserves (floor)[3]	Raised by full amount of the aid shock	Lowered by some proportion of the aid shock
Indicative targets		
Domestic primary fiscal balance (floor)[4]	No effect	Implicitly raised by some proportion of the aid shock
Reserve money (stock)[2]	No effect	Implicitly lowered by some proportion of the aid shock

[1] The adjustor allowing for a higher ceiling to account for unexpected aid shortfalls changed from 50 percent of the shortfall to a fixed $50 million cap in June 2001. This cap was raised to $75 million in March 2002.

[2] The performance criteria were changed from reserve money to net domestic assets in June 2001. Reserve money became an indicative target.

[3] The adjustor allowing for a lower floor to account for unexpected aid shortfalls changed from 50 percent of the shortfall to a fixed $50 million in June 2001. This limit was raised to $75 million in March 2002. Aid shortfalls could therefore only be partly financed by drawing down reserves.

[4] Excludes grants and foreign-financed capital expenditure.

References

Acemoglu, D., S. Johnson, J. Robinson, and Y. Thaicharoen, 2003, "Institutional Causes, Macroeconomic Symptoms: Volatility, Crises and Growth," *Journal of Monetary Economics*, Vol. 50 (January), pp. 49–123.

Adam, C. S., and D. L. Bevan, 2003, "Aid, Public Expenditure and Dutch Disease," CSAE Working Paper No. 2003–02 (Oxford: Centre for the Study of African Economies, University of Oxford).

Adenauer, I., and L. Vagassky, 1998, "Aid and the Real Exchange Rate: Dutch Disease Effects in African Countries," *Intereconomics*, Vol. 33 (July/August), pp. 177–85.

Adler, J. H., 1965, "Absorptive Capacity: The Concept and Its Determinants," Brookings Institution Staff Paper (Washington: Brookings Institution).

Agénor, P.-R., N. Bayraktar, and K. El Aynaoui, 2005, "Roads Out of Poverty? Assessing the Links Between Aid, Public Investment, Growth and Poverty Reduction," Policy Research Working Paper No. 3490 (Washington: World Bank).

Arellano, C., A. Bulíř, T. Lane, and L. Lipschitz, 2005, "The Dynamic Implications of Foreign Aid and Its Variability," IMF Working Paper 05/119 (Washington: International Monetary Fund).

Auty, R., 1993, *Sustaining Development in Mineral Economies: The Resource Curse Thesis* (London: Routledge).

———, ed., 2001, *Resource Abundance and Economic Development*, WIDER Studies in Development Economics (Oxford: Oxford University Press).

Berg, A., and A. Krueger, 2003, "Trade, Growth, and Poverty: A Selective Study," IMF Working Paper 03/30 (Washington: International Monetary Fund).

Berg, F., 1983, "Absorptive Capacity in the Sahel Countries," *Report to the Club Du Sahel* (Paris: Organisation for Economic Co-operation and Development).

Bevan, D. L., 2005, "An Analytic Overview of Aid Absorption: Recognizing and Avoiding Macroeconomic Hazards," paper presented at the IMF Seminar on Foreign Aid and Macroeconomic Management, Maputo, Mozambique, March 14–15.

Bourguignon, F., H. Lofgren, M. Bussolo, H. Timmer, and D. van der Mensbrugghe, 2006, "Building Absorptive Capacity to Meet the MDGs" (Washington: World Bank, forthcoming).

Bräutigam, D., and K. Botchwey, 1998, "The Impact of Aid Dependence on Governance and Institutions in Africa" (unpublished; Washington: American University).

Buffie, E., C. S. Adam, S. O'Connell, and C. Pattillo, 2004, "Exchange Rate Policy and the Management of Official and Private Capital Flows in Africa," *IMF Staff Papers*, Vol. 51 (June), pp. 126–60.

Bulíř, A., and J. Hamann, 2006, "Volatility of Development Aid: From the Frying Pan into the Fire?" IMF Working Paper (Washington: International Monetary Fund, forthcoming).

Calvo, G. A., C. M. Reinhart, and C. A. Végh, 1995, "Targeting the Real Exchange Rate: Theory and Evidence," *Journal of Development Economics*, Vol. 46, pp. 357–78.

Clemens, M., S. Radelet, and R. Bhavnani, 2004, "Counting Chickens When They Hatch: The Short-Term Effect of Aid on Growth," Working Paper No. 44 (Washington: Center for Global Development).

Clément, J., 2005, *Postconflict Economics in Sub-Saharan Africa: Lessons from the Democratic Republic of the Congo* (Washington: International Monetary Fund).

Corden, W. M., and J. P. Neary, 1982, "Booming Sector and De-Industrialization in a Small Open Economy," *Economic Journal*, Vol. 92 (December), pp. 825–48.

Devarajan, S, and D. R. Dollar, 1998, *Aid and Policies* (Washington: World Bank).

Easterly, W., and R. Levine, 2003, "Tropics, Germs, and Crops: How Endowments Influence Economic Development," *Journal of Monetary Economics*, Vol. 50 (January), pp. 3–39.

———, and D. Roodman, 2003, "New Data, New Doubts: A Comment on Burnside's and Dollar's 'Aid, Policies and Growth,' (2000)" NBER Working Paper No. 9846 (Cambridge, Massachusetts: National Bureau of Economic Research).

Elbadawi, I. A., 1999, "External Aid: Help or Hindrance to Export Orientation in Africa?" *Journal of African Economies*, Vol. 8 (December), pp. 578–616.

———, 2002, "Real Exchange Rate Policy and Non-Traditional Exports in Developing Countries," in *Non-Traditional Export Promotion in Africa: Experience and Issues*, ed. by G. Helleiner (London: Palgrave Macmillan).

Gali, J., and T. Monacelli, 2002, "Monetary Policy and Exchange Rate Volatility in a Small Open Economy," NBER Working Paper No. 8905 (Cambridge, Massachusetts: National Bureau of Economic Research).

Gomanee, K., S. Girma, and O. Morrissey, 2002, "Aid and Growth in Sub-Saharan Africa: Accounting for Transmission Mechanisms," CREDIT Research Paper

No. 02/05 (Nottingham, United Kingdom: Centre for Research in Economic Development and International Trade, University of Nottingham).

Guillaumont, P., 1971, *L'absorption du capital* (Paris: Cujas).

———, and L. Chauvet, 2001, "Aid and Performance: A Reassessment," *Journal of Development Studies*, Vol. 37 (August), pp. 66–92.

Gupta, S., B. Clements, A. Pivovarsky, E. R. Tiongson, 2003, "Foreign Aid and Revenue Response: Does the Composition of Aid Matter?" IMF Working Paper 03/176 (Washington: International Monetary Fund).

Hausmann, R., L. Pritchett, and D. Rodrik, 2004, "Growth Accelerations," NBER Working Paper No. 10566 (Cambridge, Massachusetts: National Bureau of Economic Research).

Heller, P., 2005, "Pity the Finance Minister: Managing a Substantial Scaling-Up of Aid Flows," paper presented at seminar for the Overseas Development Institute, London, June.

———, and S. Gupta, 2002, "Challenges in Expanding Development Assistance," IMF Policy Discussion Paper No. 02/5 (Washington: International Monetary Fund).

International Monetary Fund, 2003, "Fund Assistance for Countries Facing Exogenous Shocks," SM/03/288 (Washington).

_____, 2004, "Macroeconomic and Structural Policies in Fund-Supported Programs—Review of Experience," SM/04/406 (Washington).

_____, 2005, "Can PRGF Policy Levers Improve Institutions and Lead to Sustained Growth? SM/05/307 (Washington).

_____, 2005a, "The Macroeconomics of Managing Increased Aid Inflows—Experiences of Low-Income Countries and Policy Implications," SM/05/306 (Washington).

_____, 2005b, "Monetary and Fiscal Policy Design Issues in Low-Income Countries," SM/05/305 (Washington).

———, 2006, "Review of Recent IMF Experience in Post-Conflict Countries," IMF Occasional Paper (Washington, forthcoming).

———, Independent Evaluation Office, 2004, "Evaluation of the IMF's Role in Poverty Reduction Strategy Papers and the Poverty Reduction and Growth Facility" (Washington).

Issa, H., and B. Ouattara, 2004, "Foreign Aid Flows and Real Exchange Rate: Evidence from Syria," School of Economics Discussion Paper No. 0408 (Manchester, United Kingdom: University of Manchester).

Keynes, J. M., 1929, "The German Transfer Problem," *Economic Journal*, Vol. 39 (March), pp. 1–7.

Klein, M., and T. Harford, 2005, *The Market for Aid* (Washington: World Bank).

Knack, S., 2000, "Aid Dependence and the Quality of Governance: A Cross-Country Empirical Analysis," Policy Research Paper No. 2396 (Washington: World Bank).

Krugman, P., 1987, "The Narrow Moving Band, the Dutch Disease, and the Competitive Consequences of Mrs. Thatcher: Notes on Trade in the Presence of Dynamic Scale Economies," *Journal of Development Economics*, Vol. 27 (October), pp. 41–55.

Lal, D., and H. Myint, 1996, *The Political Economy of Poverty, Equity, and Growth: A Comparative Study* (Oxford: Oxford University Press).

Lane, P. R., and G. M. Milesi-Ferreti, 2004, "The Transfer Problem Revisited: Net Foreign Assets and Real Exchange Rates," *Review of Economics and Statistics*, Vol. 86 (November), pp. 841–57.

Leite, C., and C. Tsangarides, 2006, "Infrastructure for Developing Countries: The Growth Pill?" IMF Working Paper (Washington: International Monetary Fund, forthcoming).

McGillivray, M., and O. Morrissey, 2001, "Fiscal Effects of Aid," WIDER Discussion Paper No. 2001/61 (Helsinki: World Institute for Development Economics Research, United Nations University).

McMohan, G., 1997, "The Natural Resource Curse: Myth or Reality?" Economic Development Institute (Washington: World Bank).

Nyoni, T. S., 1998, "Foreign Aid and Economic Performance in Tanzania," *World Development*, Vol. 26 (July), pp. 1235–40.

Obstfeld, M., 1986, "Capital Flows, the Current Account, and the Real Exchange Rate: The Consequences of Stabilization and Liberalization," in *Economic Adjustment and Exchange Rates in Developing Countries*, ed. by S. Edwards and L. Ahamed (Chicago: University of Chicago Press).

Ogun, O., 1995, "Real Exchange Rate Movements and Export Growth: Nigeria, 1960–1990" (unpublished; Nairobi: African Economic Research Consortium).

Ouattara, B., and E. Strobl, 2003, "Do Aid Inflows Cause Dutch Disease? A Case Study of the CFA Franc Countries Using Dynamic Panel Analysis," School of Economics Discussion Paper No. 0303 (Manchester, United Kingdom: University of Manchester).

Pallage, S., and M. Robe, 2001, "Foreign Aid and the Business Cycle," *Review of International Economics*, Vol. 9 (November), pp. 641–72.

Prati, A., R. Sahay, and T. Tressel, 2003, "Is There a Case for Sterilizing Foreign Aid Inflows?" (unpublished; Washington: International Monetary Fund).

———, 2005, "Can Monetary Policy Make Foreign Aid More Effective?" paper presented at DESAA Development Forum on "Integrating Economic and Social Policies to Achieve the United Nations Development Agenda," United Nations, New York, March 14–15.

Rajan, R., and A. Subramanian, 2005a, "Aid and Growth: What Does the Cross-Country Evidence Really Show?" IMF Working Paper 05/127 (Washington: International Monetary Fund).

———, 2005b, "What Undermines Aid's Impact on Growth?" IMF Working Paper 05/126 (Washington: International Monetary Fund).

Sachs, J. D., and A. M. Warner, 1995, "Natural Resource Abundance and Economic Growth," NBER Working Paper No. 5398 (Cambridge, Massachusetts: National Bureau of Economic Research).

Sackey, H. A., 2001, "External Aid Inflows and the Real Exchange Rate in Ghana" AERC Research Paper No. 110 (Nairobi: African Economic Research Consortium).

Sala-i-Martin, X., and A. Subramanian, 2003, "Addressing the Natural Resource Curse: An Illustration From Nigeria," NBER Working Paper No. 9804 (Cambridge, Massachusetts: National Bureau of Economic Research).

Sekkat, K., and A. Varoudakis, 2000, "Exchange Rate Management and Manufactured Exports in Sub-Saharan Africa," *Journal of Development Economics*, Vol. 61 (February), pp. 237–53.

Spatafora, N., and A. Warner, 1999, "Macroeconomic and Sectoral Effects of Terms-of-Trade Shocks: The Experience of the Oil-Exporting Developing Countries," IMF Working Paper 99/134 (Washington: International Monetary Fund).

Torvik, R., 2001, "Learning by Doing and the Dutch Disease," *European Economic Review*, Vol. 45 (February), pp. 285–306.

UN Millennium Project, 2005, *Investing in Development: A Practical Plan to Achieve the Millennium Development Goals* (New York).

Van Wijnbergen, S., 1994, "The 'Dutch Disease': A Disease After All?" *The Economic Journal*, Vol. 94 (March), pp. 41–55.

White, H., and G. Wignaraja, 1992, "Exchange Rates, Trade Liberalization and Aid: The Sri Lankan Experience," *World Development*, Vol. 20 (October), pp. 1471–80.

World Bank, 2005, *Global Monitoring Report—Millennium Development Goals: From Consensus to Momentum* (Washington).

6

Absorptive Capacity and Achieving the MDGs

The Case of Ethiopia

MARK SUNDBERG AND HANS LOFGREN*

I. Introduction

The issues of effectiveness and absorptive capacity have attracted increasing attention in view of growing efforts to raise new and large-scale financial resources—beyond the 2000 Monterrey commitments—to help developing countries achieve the Millennium Development Goals (MDGs). The estimated annual cost of achieving the MDGs range from about $50 billion to $66 billion initially, rising to $126 billion by 2015, in incremental MDG spending requirements, on top of current aid flows.[1] This represents a major increase in official development assistance (ODA) flows to developing countries as a share of OECD-Development Assistance Committee (DAC) country gross national income. At the individual country level, this implies a large increase in ODA, in some cases a tripling or quadrupling of current flows to countries already receiving high levels of aid.

*World Bank. This work is part of a larger effort in the Development Economics Department of the World Bank (DECVP) to examine the financing requirements and economic impact of aid flows to support MDG-based poverty reduction strategies. See Bourguignon and others (2004, 2005) and Lofgren and Diaz-Bonilla (2005).

[1] Lower estimates are from the World Bank and various Development Committee papers (see *Global Monitoring Report*, 2004) and higher estimates from the *Millennium Project Report*, 2005.

Can low-income countries implement MDG programs and effectively absorb much higher levels of aid and efficiently use them to achieve the MDGs? Some have argued that the MDG targets are overly ambitious "stretch targets," whose achievement has no historical precedent (Clemens and others, 2004). Others argue (e.g., the Millennium Project Report 2005) that given the right environment and level of external support, the MDGs are well within reach. All agree, however, that recipient countries must build adequate absorptive capacity. In this paper, we consider the case of Ethiopia and examine several important constraints to its absorption of aid in pursuit of the MDGs.

Ethiopia is a good case study of the impact of increased aid flows since considerable work has been done to assess its needs, limitations, and capacity. A 2003 report by the Development Committee (the Joint Ministerial Committee of the Boards of Governors of the Bank and Fund on the Transfer of Real Resources to Developing Countries) for the 2003 Annual Meetings of the World Bank and IMF included a case study of Ethiopia that examined its capacity to absorb significantly higher aid flows in pursuit of the MDGs. The report concluded that a 60–100 percent increase in aid could be effectively absorbed if capacity-building efforts and accelerated structural reforms were put in place. This would allow Ethiopia to attain most of the core MDG targets (Development Committee, 2003). Ethiopia was also one of the pilot countries for work on Harmonization and Alignment of donor practices, and has made significant progress toward coordinating assistance and harmonizing ODA flows.[2] A study by Foster and Keith (2003) for the British Overseas Development Institute on Ethiopia and other African countries argues that a doubling of aid flows to Ethiopia over the next five years is realistic. The *Commission for Africa Report*, released in March 2005 by the British government, also examines the potential for Ethiopia to scale up spending for the MDGs and argues that a doubling of aid flows over the coming three to five years is feasible. An MDG "needs assessment" has been prepared for the Ethiopian government (Geda and others, 2005) and is being integrated into the government's Poverty Reduction Strategy under the World Bank's Sustainable Development and Poverty Reduction Program (SDPRP). World Bank team and Millennium Project teams have both been helping the Ethiopian government develop the methodology and provide a consistency framework for the country's medium-term MDG-focused forecasts. The World Bank's "Maquette for MDG Simulations" (MAMS) has been one of the modeling frameworks used for this purpose.[3]

Large increases in aid clearly pose important macroeconomic risks and raise questions about the underlying ability of the economy to effectively absorb

[2] Harmonization and Alignment of donors refers to the efforts by bilateral and multilateral donors to harmonize their aid processing requirements with recipient country practices and align their support with the strategic priorities of recipient countries.

[3] See Bourguignon and others (2004) and Lofgren (2004).

much higher resource flows. In this paper, we examine these issues for Ethiopia in a way that distinguishes between the implications of: directing aid at investments in basic infrastructure (roads, energy, and irrigation) to help generate rapid growth and reduce the headcount poverty rate (consistent with pursuing MDG 1); and spending aid on social sectors to achieve the "social MDGs"—those for education, reduced mortality rates, and access to safe water and basic sanitation. We draw on simulations with the World Bank's economy-wide MAMS model to address the issue of "Dutch disease"—whereby heavy aid inflows appreciate the exchange rate and hurt domestic demand and relative prices. We explore the implications of different scenarios for real exchange rates and exports as a share of GDP. We then analyze the trade-offs between front-loading aid disbursements and waiting until more absorptive capacity is in place, and we also look at the implications of a hypothetical increase in the rate of efficiency gain in public services achieved by "improved governance." We provide a brief overview of Ethiopia's macroeconomic performance and its main challenges. And then we briefly present an overview of the MAMS approach, which we use to present the main MDG simulation results for the period 2005–15.

II. Ethiopia's Economy and MDG Challenges

Ethiopia faces macroeconomic challenges characteristic of several low-income sub-Saharan African economies. Historically, it has experienced low growth rates, is deeply indebted (it participates in the Heavily Indebted Poor Countries "HIPC" Initiative), is highly dependent on the agricultural sector and agricultural exports (coffee), and has experienced volatile growth owing to frequent external shocks (mainly from drought and terms of trade shocks).

GDP growth in the 1980s was very low under Ethiopia's socialist Derg regime. The overthrow of the regime in 1991, however, ushered in multiparty elections in 1995 as well as a period of transition to market mechanisms, with reforms that significantly boosted growth. In fact, growth accelerated during the 1990s, reaching 4.7 percent a year for the period from 1993 to 2003 (Table 6.1). Growth remained highly volatile throughout this period, however, and in 2003 growth fell by nearly 4 percent as the result of a drought that badly damaged agriculture output. Preliminary estimates for 2004 indicate that the economy expanded at a rate of nearly 11 percent. Following years of extremely weak performance during the 1980s and early 1990s, per capita incomes are today roughly where they were in the early 1970s.

The Ethiopian economy remains highly dependent on agriculture. The agricultural sector accounts for more than 40 percent of GDP and more than 85 percent of the population still depends on agriculture for its livelihood. This leaves a large part of the population at risk of famine owing to low yields and vulnerability to frequent drought, which is compounded by the weak rural infrastructure. The national infrastructure overall is very poor, with far lower road density

Table 6.1. Ethiopia: Main Economic Indicators, 1983–2003

Average annual growth rate	1983–93	1993–2003	2002	2003
GDP	0.9	4.7	2.7	−3.7
Agriculture	1.8	1.6	−2.3	−12.6
Industry	−3.0	4.8	5.8	4.6
Services	1.6	7.4	4.6	2.3
Exports of goods and services	−0.8	11.4	13.1	18.9
Imports of goods and services	1.2	7.8	10.0	17.1
ODA flows	24.5	3.4	17.1	15.1
Key ratios and indicators	1983	1993	2002	2003
Current government revenue (percent of GDP, includes current grants)	18.6	12.7	22.6	25.4
Overall surplus/deficit (percent of GDP, includes current grants)	−11.6	−6.9	−11.3	−10.5
Exports of goods and services (percent of GDP)	9.1	8.1	16.2	17.1
Imports of goods and services (percent of GDP)	15.9	20.2	34.2	36.5
Trade (goods and services) balance (percent of GDP)	−6.8	−12.1	−18.0	−19.4
Total debt (percent of GDP)	63.5	155.3	107.6	98.5
Total debt service (percent of exports)	18.3	17.9	10.3	9.9
Reserves including gold as months imports	2.5	3.9	3.8	4.6
Consumer price (percent change)	3.8	10.0	−7.2	15.1
Terms of trade (1995=100)	79.0	70.0	47.0	42.0

Source: "Ethiopia at a glance," The World Bank.

than the average for sub-Saharan Africa, and with relatively little of the country's arable land under irrigation. While poverty rates fell during 1995–2000—by between 1 and 5 percent—they still exceeded 40 percent.

Ethiopia's current debt-to-GDP ratio is about 100 percent, with debt service equal to about 10 percent of total exports. The country was one of the early HIPC countries and has been a beneficiary of debt reduction. In 2004, Ethiopia reached its HIPC "completion point" (the point at which it has demonstrated sufficient progress to qualify for debt relief) and has exited from the enhanced HIPC program on a stronger footing. Still, it remains highly vulnerable to export shocks and has an extremely limited capacity to undertake new borrowing. Stress tests using the IMF Debt Sustainability Assessment scenarios suggest that debt service indicators are highly sensitive to the terms of new borrowing and negative export shocks (IMF, 2004).

Despite these challenges, fiscal policy has been well managed since the early 1990s: Ethiopia has relied little on domestic financing of the deficit and monetary and exchange rate policies have kept inflation moderate. In addition, domestic tax and nontax revenues have been relatively high, mobilizing about

Table 6.2. Government Finance, 1998/99–2003/04
(In percent of GDP)

	1998/99	1999/00	2000/01	2001/02	2002/03 Est.	2003/04 Proj.
Revenue	18.0	17.9	18.8	20.0	19.5	18.6
Tax revenue	11.3	12.2	13.7	15.3	14.4	14.8
Nontax revenue	6.6	5.7	5.0	4.8	5.1	3.7
External grants	3.6	3.2	4.8	4.7	8.0	7.8
Expenditure and net lending	31.7	32.3	28.4	32.1	34.8	30.3
Fiscal balance, including grants (cash basis)	–10.1	–11.2	–4.8	–9.3	–9.7	–4.8
	1998	1999	2000	2001	2002	2003
ODA total	10.1	9.9	10.6	17.1	21.6	22.7
Multilateral	5.6	5.0	5.8	5.6	8.1	15.6
DAC	4.3	4.7	4.6	11.1	12.9	6.6

Sources: IMF Staff Report (2004a); OECD Development Assistance Committee, 2004.
Note: ODA data and fiscal data are not on comparable basis.

20 percent of GDP in recent years (Table 6.2). The real exchange rate has been relatively stable since the early 1990s, under a "tightly managed float;" the rate has held close to the U.S. dollar in recent years and depreciated against the euro (IMF, 2005). The Ethiopian authorities have maintained export competitiveness; they have built up reserves and kept them at prudent levels. Aid has been an increasingly important source of financing; it rose as a share of GDP from the mid-1990s, declined as the conflict with Eritrea erupted, and then rose again after the conflict ended. While aid is fairly high as a share of GDP,[4] per capita—between $15 and $20 per capita in recent years—aid levels are much lower than many sub-Saharan African countries.

Ethiopia is far from achieving many of the MDG targets and will need to accelerate progress rapidly if it is to reach them (Table 6.3 shows the historic trends between 1995 and 2000). Depending on how poverty is measured, the rate of reduction in the head count index will need to accelerate substantially. Gross primary enrollment rates increased rapidly during 1995–2000 and appear relatively on track. By contrast, success in reducing the under-five mortality

[4] OECD Development Assistance Committee data on ODA to Ethiopia shows total ODA rising to nearly 23 percent of GDP in 2003, which is not consistent with Ethiopian fiscal accounts. It is difficult to reconcile ODA data since there are many items, such as administrative costs, technical assistance, and aid channeled through NGOS, which DAC countries report but do not pass through the recipient government's budget.

Table 6.3. Historic and Required Rates of Change in Key MDG Indicators

	Recent trend, 1995–2000 (percent p.a.)	Required rate of change to reach MDG (percent p.a.)
Poverty head count rate	−0.73	−3.8
Food poverty head count index	−2.40	−3.2
Gross primary enrollment rates	12.40	3.8
Under five child mortality	−1.00	−7.0
Access to clean water	1.00	6.5

Source: World Bank Country Assistance Strategy Progress Report, 2004.

rate and increasing access to clean water has been far less impressive and will have to accelerate dramatically to achieve the MDGs.

These conditions underscore Ethiopia's need for international efforts to help it speed up the achievement of the MDGs under its Sustainable Development and Poverty Reduction Program. At the same time, however, Ethiopia may also face significant macroeconomic and microeconomic risks attributable to sharp increases in aid flows.[5] Aid flows have been volatile and have shown large swings mainly because of political regime changes and periods of conflict. There appears to be little evidence, however, that high aid flows have led to Dutch disease problems. Recent empirical analysis by the IMF finds that the relationship between aid and the real exchange rate is inconclusive. However, after the 1991 regime change and after structural reforms were initiated, foreign aid had a *positive* impact both on Ethiopia's noncoffee exports (which are driven by international prices and are less sensitive to exchange rate movements) and on their share in total exports (IMF, 2005b). This may have been the result of the positive impact of foreign aid on infrastructure and capital investment, and of the reduction in logistical and transactions costs associated with these investments. This in turn suggests that the impact of aid flows on underlying infrastructure and economic productivity are important determinants of whether large aid flows are associated with Dutch disease effects, a point we return to below.

III. Absorptive Capacity and the MAMS Approach

We now turn to the impact of MDG-targeted aid flows on Ethiopia's absorptive capacity, using a modeling framework developed in the World Bank to address macroeconomic and microeconomic linkages and aid flows. Absorptive

[5]Heller and Gupta (2002) provide a useful overview of macroeconomic risks—inflation, exchange rate appreciation, and a weakening trade balance (Dutch disease), crowding out of private investment, disincentives to revenue collection, fiscal uncertainty and aid volatility. They also review the microeconomic risks—strained capacity, aid-dependence, weakening of accountability, and rent-seeking.

capacity is a dynamic process linked to underlying forces of economic, social, and institutional development. The approach used here focuses on aid requirements to reach the MDGs in Ethiopia. It abstracts from several elements of absorptive capacity seen as instrumental to development, including governance, institutional capacity, ownership, and social and political stability. The approach also abstracts from several very real constraints facing Ethiopia today: severe financing constraints, frequent exogenous shocks (particularly adverse climate and the terms of trade shocks), and unpredictable and volatile levels of foreign aid.

A Brief Overview of the MAMS Model

The MAMS model is a dynamic computable general equilibrium (CGE) model that has been extended to include a module that covers MDGs related to poverty, health, education, and water and sanitation. As noted earlier, the rationale for using a model of this type is that the pursuit of MDG strategies has strong effects throughout the economy—via markets for foreign exchange, factors (especially labor), and goods and services—with feedback effects that may significantly alter the findings of more narrow sectoral analyses. For example, the amount of real health or education services that a dollar in aid can buy may change significantly in light of changes in exchange rates, prices, and wages. In addition, existing relationships between different MDGs (e.g., health and education) may influence the expansion in real services required—for example, improvements in water and sanitation may reduce the expansion in health services required to achieve the health MDGs.

In the application described here, the model is applied to an Ethiopian database and solved for the period 2002–15.[6] More specifically, building on the recent literature and sector studies on health and education outcomes, MAMS considers the following MDGs:

- MDG 1: halving, between 1990 and 2015, the headcount poverty rate;
- MDG 2: achieving universal primary education (100 percent completion rate by 2015);
- MDG 4: reducing by two thirds the under-five child mortality rate by 2015;
- MDG 5. reducing by three fourths the maternal mortality rate; and
- MDG 7: cutting by half the number of people without a) access to safe water, and b) basic sanitation.

[6] The model is presented in detail in Bourguignon and others (2004) and in Lofgren (2004). Preliminary applications to Ethiopia are discussed in Lofgren and Diaz-Bonilla (2005) and in Bourguignon and others (2005). The MAMS modeling remains a work in progress.

The model gives relatively detailed treatment to MDG-related government activities. Government consumption, investment, and capital stocks are disaggregated by function into four education sectors, three health sectors, sectors for water and sanitation, public infrastructure, and other government activities. The major government revenue sources are taxes (direct and indirect), foreign borrowing, and foreign grants. The nongovernment economy is represented by a single activity. The primary factors of production are divided into public capital, private capital, and three types of labor (unskilled, skilled, and highly-skilled). GDP growth is a function of growth in the stock of labor and capital and productivity growth. The composition and overall growth of the labor force depends on the evolution of the education sector whereas capital stock growth depends on investments. Productivity growth is also endogenous, depending on growth in the stock of public capital in infrastructure.

The core MDG module specifies how changes in the different MDG indicators are determined. To the extent possible, it is parameterized on the basis of detailed sector studies on Ethiopia. In the education module, the government has an annual primary education budget covering teacher salaries, recurrent operations and maintenance costs, and capital investment (for example, in new classrooms). Recurrent expenditures and the capital stock in primary education together determine the supply side.[7] Demand for primary schooling and student behavior—the population share that enrolls in the first grade, graduation shares among the enrolled, and the share of graduates that choose to continue to the next grade—depend on six variables: the quality of education (student-teacher and student-capital ratios), income incentives (using current wages as a proxy, the expected relative income gain from climbing one step on the salary ladder), the under-five mortality rate (a proxy for the health status of the school population), household consumption per capita, and the level of public infrastructure services.

This specification of sector demand and supply captures lags between investment and outcomes, which is one strength of the approach. Based on sector studies, the lags between increased enrollments and outcomes at different education levels are related to the number of years required for completion and on actual completion rates.

The specification of health services draws on a World Bank health sector strategy report for Ethiopia. Improvement in under-five and maternal mortality rates (MDGs 4 and 5) are determined by the level of health services per capita (public and private services), per-capita consumption, and the population shares with access to improved water and sanitation services (MDG 7). The package of health services that achieves MDGs 4 and 5 also includes HIV/AIDS prevention services sufficient to halt the spread of the disease (part

[7] Private supply of education services has not been separately included since it is relatively small in Ethiopia, but this could be elaborated for countries where it is important.

of MDG 6). For water and sanitation, the population share with access to improved services is specified as a function of per capita household consumption and per capita provision of government water and sanitation services.

The provision of the additional government services needed to reach the MDGs clearly requires additional resources—capital, labor, and intermediate inputs—that then are unavailable to the rest of the economy. The effects of a program depend on how it is financed—from foreign sources, domestic taxes (which reduce consumption), or domestic borrowing (which crowds out private investment). Even with 100 percent foreign grant financing for additional services, which minimizes domestic resource costs, the rest of the economy is affected through two main channels—labor markets and relative prices. Expanding the provision of health or education services increases demand for teachers and doctors, reducing the number of skilled workers available in other sectors. Increased school enrollment also reduces the size of the overall labor force (since it removes a larger part of the school-age population from the labor force), although in the medium run it adds to the share of skilled labor in the labor force. Two forces drive changes in relative commodity prices. First, domestic demand switches toward MDG-related government services with effects on production costs and prices throughout the economy. Second, increased aid flows lead to an appreciation of the real exchange rate, manifested in increased prices of nontraded relative to traded outputs. These manifestations of Dutch disease can bring about long-lasting changes in the structure of production, which is diverted from exports and competition with imports.

The limitations on absorptive capacity are captured through three main channels—the two channels just mentioned, in the labor market and in changes in the real exchange rate), as well as through potential infrastructure bottlenecks, particularly in transport and energy infrastructure. Large investments in education services, for example, will tend to reduce further absorptive capacity as skilled labor is diverted to education as the relative price of nontradables rises (e.g., real wages are bid up reflecting the Dutch disease effect), and if infrastructure bottlenecks reduce the efficiency of public service delivery. Moreover, the impact will not be limited to the education sector; it also affects costs throughout the economy, including other public services and costs in the private sector.

Policymakers thus face important trade-offs: increased investment in public service delivery is essential for improved MDG outcomes but beyond some point the unit costs begin rising, along with indirect costs to other sectors. The challenge is to keep costs down while targeting social outcomes over time. Building absorptive capacity is clearly a central element of this process.

There are also important complementarities in spending across different MDGs—in our modeling framework represented by cross-elasticities—where progress toward one MDG may contribute to progress toward others. For example, progress in providing improved water and sanitation services has a positive impact on heath outcomes. Another example is education: provision of primary and secondary education helps expand the skilled workforce needed to increase productivity both in the private sector and with respect to work in publicly funded schools and clinics.

IV. Simulation Results from the Ethiopia MAMS Model

These simulation results build on work under way at the World Bank, in coordination with the Ethiopian authorities, to provide analytic inputs for Ethiopia's development strategy framework (the SDPRP). The model used for this purpose has been calibrated around an Ethiopian country database for 2002 and a basic Social Accounting Matrix prepared for Ethiopia, and supplemented by more detailed sector studies relevant to the MDGs, as described above. The simulations help to identify ODA magnitudes required to scale up public service delivery to achieve the MDGs, illustrate some of the major macro-economic impacts under different financing and sequencing scenarios, and help quantify some of the key trade-offs facing policymakers. The following basic simulations draw heavily on Lofgren and Diaz-Bonilla (2005). We first examine the base case and variants on it and then discuss the issue of Dutch disease and its relevance for Ethiopia, frontloading and the implications of frontloading for costs and outcomes. We then briefly address the key role of governance and institutional reform in capacity building.

The reference point used to compare results is a "business-as-usual" *base case*, under which Ethiopia continues to receive external assistance and to perform along current trends. As a result of increased grant financing (annual foreign borrowing does not increase over time), external aid as grant financing is assumed to expand at an average rate of 1.5 percent a year from its level in 2002—to $19 per capita in 2015—while foreign loans remain at their 2002 level.[8] The different areas of government services as well as GDP all grow at an annual rate of about 4 percent. This performance is similar to the long-run growth trend for Ethiopia's economy.

This *base-case scenario* is contrasted with three other scenarios that include additional ODA levels directed toward: (1) strengthening Ethiopia's basic national infrastructure and "connectivity" (Base + Infrastructure); (2) additional ODA flows targeted to reach each of the five education, health, water and sanitation MDGs in the model; and (3) ODA flows targeted to meet these social MDGs, but without the underlying infrastructure financing. Using these four scenarios allows comparison across different levels ODA inflows with different objectives and economic impact. Figure 6.1 shows the different foreign grant financing paths underlying each scenario. In each of these scenarios, the

[8] ODA here refers to official development assistance *to government* only, excluding flows to "other official entities," and thus differs from data on total ODA.

Figure 6.1. Foreign Grant Financing (US$ per capita)

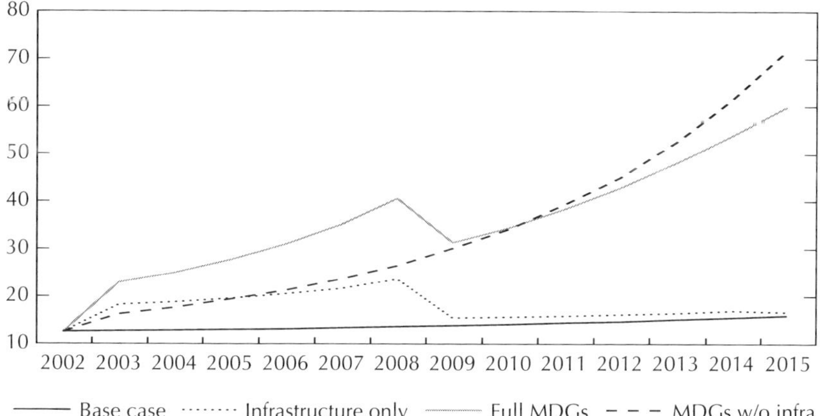

financing gap (arising from government spending more to reach the MDGs) is covered through foreign grants.

Ethiopia's basic infrastructure requirements have been separated out from investments necessary to reach the key social MDG targets since these investment streams are quite distinct, and raising infrastructure spending is considered particularly critical to improving growth performance. Growth in household incomes and consumption is essential to achieving MDG 1—to reduce national poverty to half of its 1990 level by 2015. The importance of infrastructure to national growth prospects is discussed in detail in a recently completed Country Economic Memorandum on Ethiopia.[9] Improving the basic transport system and expanding power generation and distribution to link the urban, peri-urban, and rural economies, while investing in large-scale water management and irrigation systems to improve agricultural productivity, are all considered core elements of Ethiopia's national growth strategy.

Under *the second scenario*, *Base-Infrastructure*, the government embarks on a major effort to improve Ethiopia's infrastructure (roads, energy, and irrigation), thereby linking producers and consumer to national and international markets to capture important network effects and enhance growth. Another avenue is through infrastructure investments helping reduce the indirect

[9] World Bank (2005a). The three priorities for growth identified are: (1) to focus public investment on infrastructure to support urban rural linkages; (2) to reduce risks to agricultural producers by investing in improved water management, social safety nets, and security of land tenure; and (3) to improve the investment climate and reduce risk facing private producers and investors.

costs (affected by such factors as the reliability of power and transport logistics and timing) and business-related losses that depress firm productivity, as highlighted in recent work on African economies by Eiffert and others (2005). Higher infrastructure spending (both recurrent and investment) is assumed to be financed through additional foreign grants. Under this scenario, provision of infrastructure services grows at an annual rate of 10 percent between 2003 and 2009 and decelerates to an annual rate of 5 percent thereafter.[10] This requires an increase in grant financing relative to the base case of about $10 per capita to $24 per capita at its peak in 2008. The productivity response of the private sector to the larger public capital stock in infrastructure is raised beginning in 2009, reflecting the impact of network effects when the capital stock exceeds a critical threshold.[11] As a result, annual real GDP growth rises by about 1.3 percent above the base-case trend to 5 percent.

The *third scenario (MDG)*, examines the level and impact of investments calibrated to expand delivery of MDG-related public services to just meet each of the targets (MDGs 2, 4, 5, 7A, 7B), as discussed above, but *without* the underlying investment in infrastructure. Hence, this scenario does not support the productivity gains from improvements in basic economic infrastructure. The expansion of public spending includes capital investment in service-specific infrastructure (schools, clinics, water, and sanitation) as well as recurrent costs to deliver and maintain the higher service levels. This requires a much larger increase in public spending—rising to more than $70 per capita, or nearly half of GDP, by 2015. The higher financing requirement is fully met through external grants.

The *final scenario (Full MDG)* combines external financing on both the infrastructure and MDG services. This scenario most clearly illustrates the impact of full external grant financing in achieving achieve both the required growth improvements to reduce poverty to MDG 1 levels and to achieve the social MDGs. The combined external financing requirements rise to some $60 per capita by the end of the period, or approximately 40 percent of GDP compared with current levels of just below 20 percent. Note that the cost of the Full-MDG scenario is less than where MDGs are met without infrastructure financing ($60 versus $70 per capita). This is attributable mainly to the additional growth and productivity generated by basic infrastructure investment, less erosion of trade competitiveness, and the additional boost to government revenues that accompanies higher growth. Together these reduce overall aid requirements.

---

[10] Note the sudden drop in financing is a result of both lower growth in infrastructure services and of the increase in growth, which raises government revenues and reduces external grant financing needs.

[11] The underlying rationale for this is described in greater detail in Lofgren and Diaz-Bonilla (2005) and more generally in World Bank (2005a).

Figure 6.2. MDG1: Share of Population Living on $1 (PPP) Per Day or Less (percent)

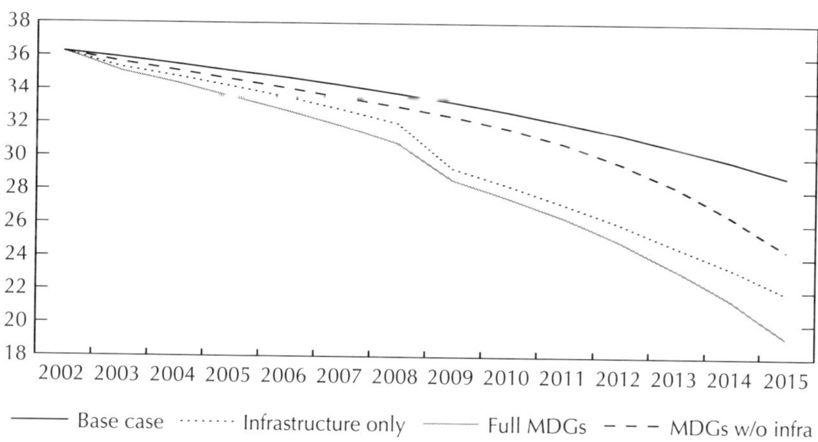

Meeting the MDGs

The simulation results suggest that, under a set of specific conditions, *it is possible to achieve the MDGs by 2015*. One condition is that a predictable flow of external grant aid is available as needed in each simulation. The progress toward selected MDGs is shown in Figures 6.2–6.4, which illustrate the different contributions made by these investments in basic infrastructure and direct investment in the MDGs. The contribution of investment in basic infrastructure, which helps accelerate the growth rate relative to the base case by about

Figure 6.3. MDG2: Net Primary School Completion Rate (percent)

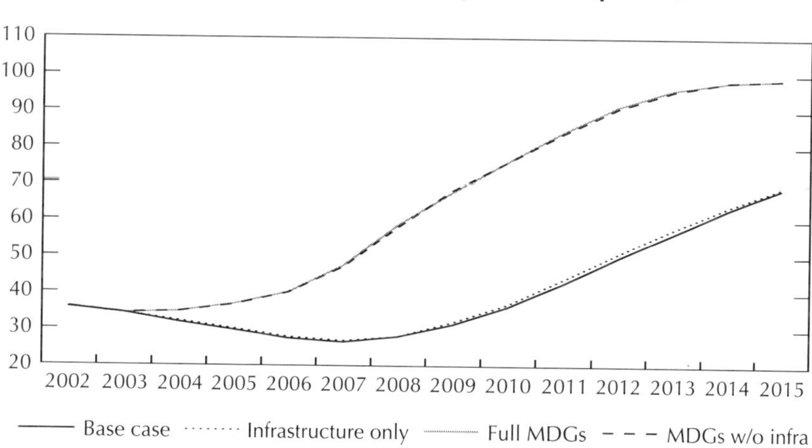

Figure 6.4. MDG4: Under-Five Mortality per 1,000 Live Births

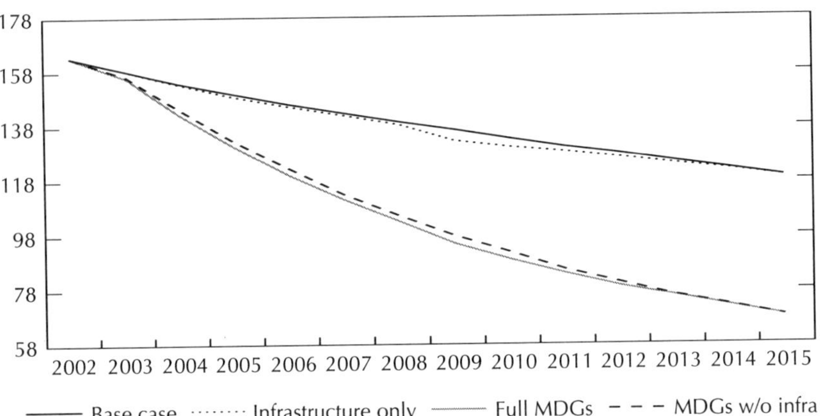

1.5 percent annually, is critical for achieving MDG 1—that is, halving the incidence of poverty from its 1990 level of 36 percent of the population. Growth in household consumption[12] helps drive poverty down to about 22 percent by 2015 (using a poverty elasticity of −1 with respect to mean household consumption per capita). Spending on MDG-related sectors also helps boost growth and household consumption, mainly by raising the supply of skilled labor and through increased employment generated by higher public investment.[13] Relative to the investment share, however, the contribution from basic infrastructure is much greater. In the Full-MDG scenario, where both investments are taken together, the MDG 1 target (to halve the incidence of extreme poverty to about 19 percent) is just met.

Raising the underlying GDP growth rate of the economy is clearly critical to meeting MDG 1. However, a lack of employment opportunities may prevent the economy from generating higher growth rates, despite substantial spending on human-capital MDGs and significant improvements in health and education standards. Capacity is raised, but opportunity is withheld. Put another way, as some argue (Millennium Project, 2005, and World Bank, 2005a), failing to raise growth, generate higher household and public savings, and reduce risk-averse behaviors associated with agrarian poverty will fail to lift Ethiopia out of the poverty traps that currently preclude more rapid growth.

[12] Income growth is assumed to be distributionally neutral across household income groups. Ongoing work with MAMS disaggregates the economy by major sectors—agriculture, services, and manufacturing—allowing greater refinement in the treatment of sector growth rates, intersectoral migration, and more differentiated returns to labor.

[13] Also contributing to higher growth and consumption is the exchange rate effect of the currency's appreciation, which helps raise average real purchasing power.

The converse of this is that growth alone will not achieve the human development MDGs unless accompanied by massive investments to expand public services. Figures 6.3 and 6.4 show the progress made toward meeting the primary school completion target of 100 percent and reducing the under-five child mortality rate by two thirds. The drop seen in the first five years for primary school completion reflects the rapid expansion in out-of-cohort enrollment, reducing educational quality and enrollment for within-cohort children. After this initial period, growth in primary school services is sufficiently rapid to improve quality while absorbing growing shares of within-cohort children.

Without targeted investment to achieve the MDGs, little progress will be achieved beyond the business-as-usual base case. Investment in building up basic infrastructure is important for raising income and consumption growth rates, but the MDG outcomes differ only slightly from the base case. The small differences in completion rates induced by infrastructure investment and higher growth (in Base+Infrastructure) arise mainly from higher government revenues, a portion of which is then directed to the MDGs and to demand-side factors.

Dutch Disease

A major concern across the MDG scenarios relates to the risk that large aid inflows will negatively affect domestic demand, relative prices, and the real exchange rate. Aid flows permit a much larger trade deficit, draw resources to nontraded sectors, and place upward pressure on the real exchange rate, reducing competitiveness and resources flowing to traded goods and services. These concerns are well recognized.[14] As Bevan (2005) emphasizes, the extent to which aid flows are associated with the problem of real exchange rate appreciation depends largely on the relative impact on demand and supply. The supply response, depending on the effects of aid on productivity across sectors, largely determines the depth and duration of adverse effects following the surge in aid.

Under all of the scenarios, there is evidence of exchange rate appreciation, rising real wage rates, and a deterioration in the trade balance as imports surge and export performance deteriorates. Differences in the level of external financing and how it is invested determine the impact on the exchange rate, real wages, and trade performance (Figures 6.5-6.8). The effects are more pronounced for the Full-MDG case through the first half of the period, and for the case of the MDGs without infrastructure financing in the second half since it requires much larger ODA flows.

The pressure on real wages is greatest in the first half of the period, before investment in expanding education and the skilled labor base begins to show results (with a lag of several years). Wages of workers with a secondary edu-

[14] Heller and Gupta (2004) provide a clear overview of the issues, citing several country studies.

Figure 6.5. Real Exchange Rate

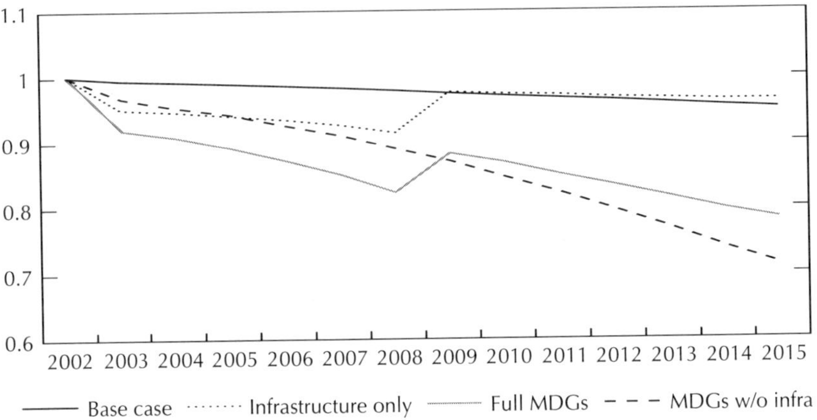

cation grow most rapidly until 2009 and thereafter stabilize as the number of graduates entering the labor market increases, mitigating wage pressures. Wages for workers with less than a high school education, by contrast, continue to rise through 2015 as supply is outpaced by demand from the growing economy.

Dutch disease effects are clearly a serious concern. Aid-induced appreciation of the exchange rate and the drop in exports are severe. Under the Full-MDG scenario, exports fall from about 14 percent of GDP to 8 percent by 2015, and the real exchange rate appreciates by close to 20 percent. The impact on

Figure 6.6. Real Wage for Workers with High School Completed

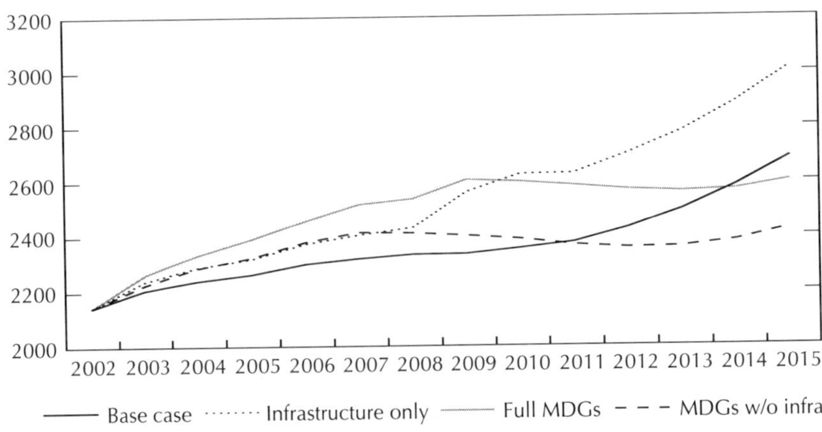

Figure 6.7. Trade Balance as a Share of GDP

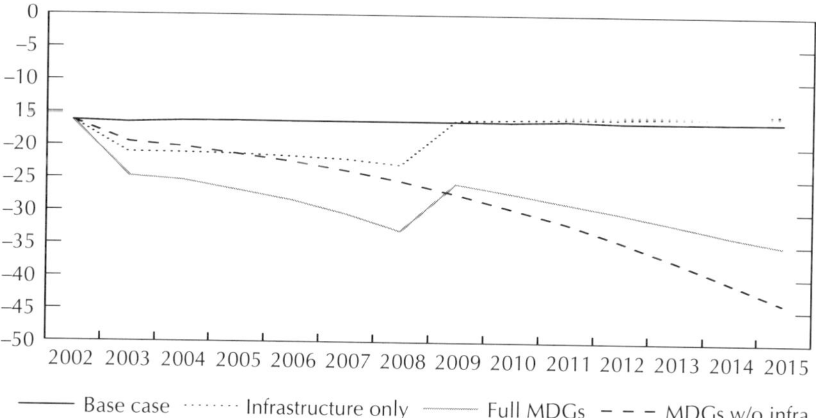

real GDP growth, which is driven by factor supplies and productivity, is quite limited however.

Public spending on infrastructure and MDG services differ in their effects on the supply side and in their import intensities. Infrastructure spending has a positive but lagged effect on productivity, whereas spending on MDG services has only a very modest impact on productivity in the short run, but affects supply by adding to the stock of skilled labor. Infrastructure spending initially causes some exchange rate appreciation, until productivity improvements raise GDP growth, incomes, and demand, with a significant import component. In

Figure 6.8. Export as a Share of GDP

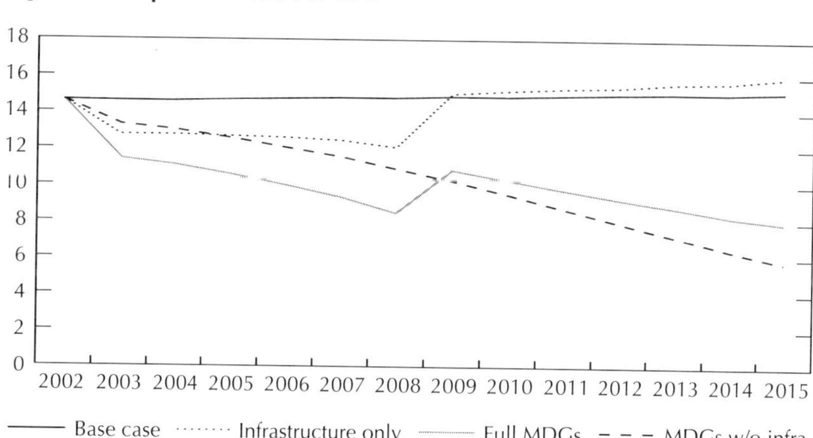

the process, government revenues also improve. The import intensity of basic infrastructure in a country with limited domestic capacity is also high, which reduces the adverse price and resource switching effects of Dutch disease, as opposed to public social services, which have a far higher nontraded content, primarily labor.

By contrast, investment in social services takes much longer to affect productivity, placing greater pressure on the exchange rate. In the case of ODA support for the MDGs without basic infrastructure investments, the real exchange rate will appreciate by about 30 percent and exports will fall to less than half their initial share of GDP by 2015. Note that the appreciation of the real exchange rate (the change in relative prices of the domestic good) also reduces the purchasing power of foreign grants, requiring larger flows to drive the MDG investments.

The simulations suggest that while the large surge in aid required for investment in the MDGs will help sharply reduce the incidence of income poverty and dramatically raise human development outcomes, it also poses serious risks to future capacity for growth after 2015. Ethiopia will still be highly dependent on aid flows to maintain the MDG levels of public services, although considerably less dependent on aid than when aid inflows were at their peak level. Moreover, production capacity for exports and import-competing goods may have been significantly eroded and the country may not be prepared to rapidly adapt to less foreign aid and lower trade deficits. This points to the importance of only a gradual reduction in aid after 2015, which will give the country sufficient time to improve international trade access, reduce behind-the-border barriers to trade, and pursue other reforms to attract investment and improve competitiveness of traded goods and services.[15] Aid and trade can be key complements.

Frontloading Aid to Meet the MDGs

An issue that arises regarding accelerating aid disbursements for the MDGs is how much aid should be frontloaded—that is, disbursed up front[16]—and how much disbursements should await the availability of greater absorptive capacity. Discussion of "fast-tracking" countries with a demonstrated commitment to poverty reduction and a "good" policy environment poses these questions of how much aid and how fast. The simulation results shed light on this. Consider the case where aid disbursements climb sharply in the first two years, effectively increasing growth in service provision 10 times as fast as in subsequent years. Underlying infrastructure investment remains unchanged. This is

[15] IMF (2005) also stresses the importance of further trade liberalization and opening up the Ethiopian economy in response to likely real exchange rate pressure rate from higher ODA inflows.

[16] Frontloading, as the term is used here, should not be confused with frontloading of ODA *commitments*.

Figure 6.9. MDG2: Net Primary School Completion Rate (percent)

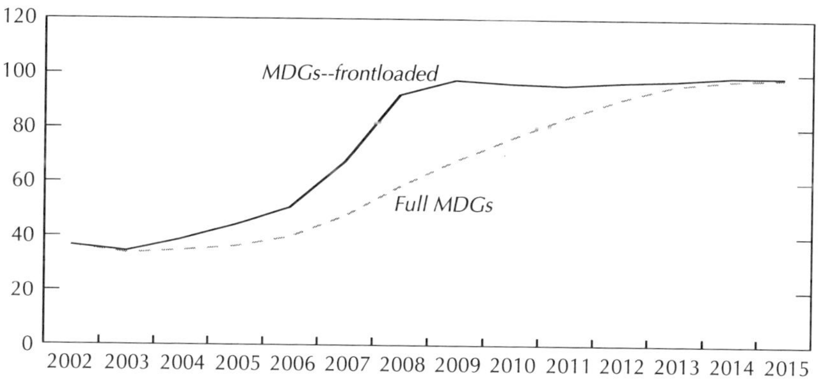

an extreme case that more clearly illustrates the trade-offs from frontloading disbursements. Aid per capita quickly climbs to $55 per capita, and thereafter falls to an average of $40 through 2015.

The impact of frontloading on the time profile of net primary education completion rates and access to potable (improved) water (two of the MDGs), is shown in Figures 6.9 and 6.10. Relative to the Full-MDG case, supply initially increases more rapidly and then stays at a higher level throughout the simulation period. As a result of the surge in aid, the exchange rate appreciates sharply early on, real wages rise strongly as skilled labor is pulled from the private sector, and the trade balance deteriorates sharply. With lower subsequent aid flows in the remaining years to 2015, these changes are mitigated, leaving the economy in a more favorable position.

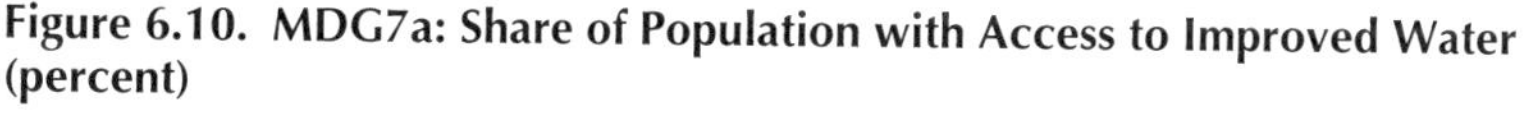

Figure 6.10. MDG7a: Share of Population with Access to Improved Water (percent)

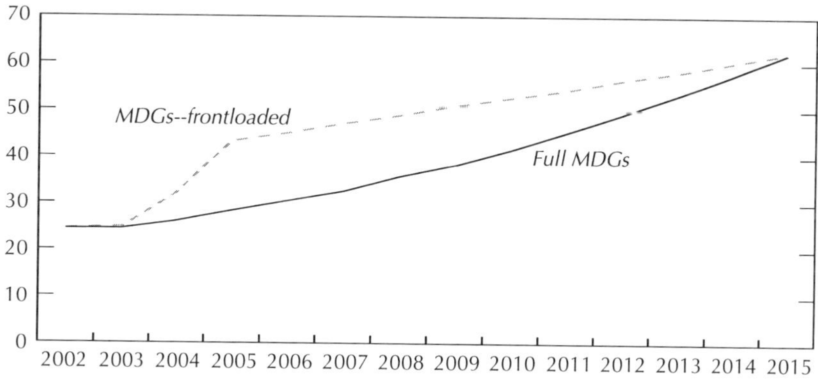

Note that the extent of real wage pressure and rising costs for skilled labor is a function of the sector parameters of the model, and alternative specifications can help to further illuminate policy choices. The model uses a 40:1 student-teacher objective (current rates are about 75:1) taken from the Education-for-All global fund targets as a quality standard to strive for and requires teachers to have 10 years of schooling plus three more years of teacher training. Some argue that relaxing these standards—allowing, for example, higher student teacher ratios and requiring just eight years of schooling for primary school teachers—could take advantage of more abundant local labor resources and lower wage costs, and free up resources to be used elsewhere. More innovative solutions where resources are scarce can clearly help get around absorptive capacity constraints.[17]

Frontloading aid sharply increases total foreign grant financing required to achieve the MDGs by 2015. In present value terms, grant financing requirements above the baseline (discounted at a rate of 5 percent) increase by nearly one fifth. As absorptive capacity constraints become more binding, unit costs for services rise. Although the more gradual acceleration in disbursements lowers costs while capacity is built up over time, this is not necessarily better since the path of service delivery is clearly quite different. With frontloading, fewer mothers and children will die and the labor force will be better educated by the time the full MDGs are reached in 2015. A comparison of these outcomes therefore requires a welfare function to weigh outcomes across the MDGs, including income poverty. A simple approximation to help illustrate this can be obtained with an index of "welfare" based on a weighted sum of the share of the required change for each MDG since 1990 that has been accomplished, with equal weights for each covered MDG (1, 2, 4, 5, 7a, and 7b). This index suggests that welfare in the frontloaded case is significantly higher, by roughly one fourth. Although it is hard to use this as a metric to guide optimal frontloading, it suggests that some level of frontloading may be desirable (if foreign resources are available in the amounts indicated in the simulations).

In this example of frontloading, underlying infrastructure investment was unchanged. Infrastructure expenditures have, however, already been frontloaded, as seen from the higher growth rate over the initial five years. This was done because the achievement of network effects and higher productivity growth requires a certain threshold of infrastructure services. For example, until a basic railway network is completed it cannot have a major impact on reducing transport and logistical costs across markets.

This illustrates the importance of *sequencing* investments to minimize costs and maximize efficiency over time. Frontloading of infrastructure investment is a case in point, which is specified to recognize a threshold level of national

[17] Discussion of alternative approaches to overcoming labor constraints in education are elaborated in *Education in Ethiopia* (World Bank, 2005).

Figure 6.11. Costs of Frontloading Different Shares of Total Aid for MDG Services
(Ratio of spending period 2003–09 over 2009–15)

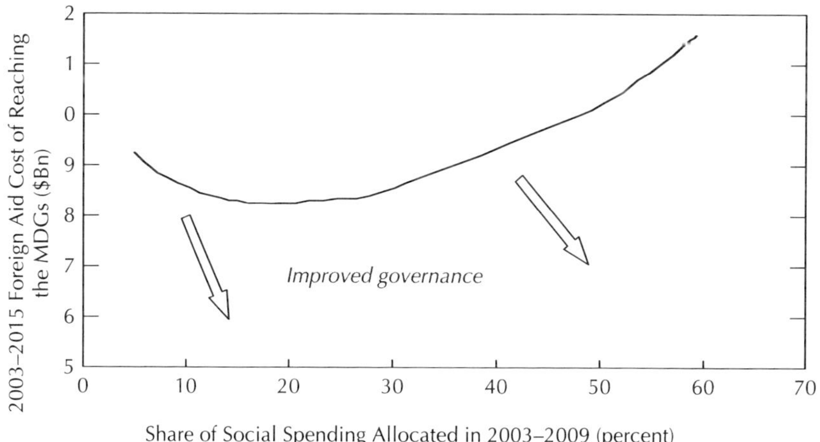

infrastructure that must be met before productivity gains can be realized. The threshold level should ideally be estimated based on detailed infrastructure sector studies.

Among the MDG services, investment in education services must be given priority, since skilled labor can only be produced with a lag, and since skilled labor is a key input to expanding the supply of all the MDG services. In addition, sequencing priority should be accorded to investment in public services that generate positive externalities and thereby help lower the investment cost of other MDGs. If access to improved water is a key element of reducing under-five mortality, then investment in developing and maintaining potable water supplies must precede or accompany other child-health-related investments. If this order of sequencing is reversed (i.e., the other MDGs are expanded before investment in water, education, and basic infrastructure services), total costs would rise and the likelihood of meeting the MDGs by 2015 would be reduced.

To explore the question of frontloading in more detail, Figure 6.11 shows how the total value of additional grants required to reach the MDGs (i.e., grants in excess of those received under the scenario Base+Infrastructure) varies as the proportion of spending in the first half of the forecast period (share spent in 2003–09 versus 2010–15). Frontloading expenditure increases this ratio as more funds are spent in the first half of the period.[18] The resulting "U-curve" shows how the present value of total costs falls as the share of frontloaded

[18] The model has been parameterized around 2002 and hence the actual simulation periods correspond to the two six-year periods, 2003–09 and 2009–15.

expenditures increases from very low shares. Costs are minimized when about 20 percent of resources are disbursed in the first period. Higher shares frontloaded lead to rising costs as constraints become more binding—labor costs rise, exchange rate appreciation reduces the purchasing value of aid, and congestion costs from infrastructure bottlenecks increase. At the extreme, some point above 70 percent of resources frontloaded, costs become effectively infinite and preclude reaching the MDGs.

We urge caution in interpreting this result, however. First, while this suggests that total present value costs are minimized at about 20 percent of outlays, different points along the curve show very different welfare outcomes. As more resources are frontloaded, MDG outcomes are also frontloaded and welfare, measured by the simple MDG index, clearly improves. Second, underlying exchange rate and wage dynamics are very different along the curve, with consequences for competitiveness of traded goods and sharp wage differentials. Our point is not to suggest an optimum, but rather to illustrate the real consequences of frontloading that merit consideration when countries plan aid-financed, long-term public investment programs.

Governance and Institutional Reforms

The model does not address the critical question of how to improve the underlying institutional capacity and governance in Ethiopia. The broad range of issues related to institutional capacity and governance are at the heart of most adjustment programs and poverty reduction strategies. These include improving expenditure management, strengthening accountability mechanisms, reducing leakages through "capture" and corruption, deregulating excessive government controls often associated with rent-seeking, and privatization and strengthening the environment for private business. In Ethiopia, particular importance has been placed on decentralization in the government's reform program, with selective devolution of resources and responsibilities—including important responsibilities over public service delivery[19]—to Ethiopia's nine regions. Successful implementation of the decentralization program is recognized as a key element of the country's poverty reduction strategy (SDPRP).

Taken together, governance and institutional reforms can be thought of as measures to improve the efficiency of public resource use. In terms of the model, they affect the underlying productivity of public activities and reduce the unit costs of achieving the MDGs—falling teacher absenteeism; reduced waiting times for processing legal cases, licensing, and regulatory issues; and less leak-

[19] As Heller and Gupta (2002) note, decentralization to channel resources through local governments in particular runs the risk of administrative constraints and deficiencies in expenditure management.

age in the use of central government resources for delivery of services to end-users. Sometimes simple reforms can have major consequences.[20]

To reflect further on this, we consider the effect of introducing governance and institutional reforms in the form of improvement in the underlying efficiency of public services at the rate of 2 percent, compounded annually, and independent of the rate of public investment. Introducing this to the model and recalculating the U-curve in Figure 6.11 suggests two results:

- The productivity gain in public services significantly reduces the cost of achieving the MDGs along all points of the curve and "flattens" the curve, reducing the total variation in costs. The total cost of achieving the MDGs by 2015 in present value terms falls by about one third.
- The new point of cost minimization leans slightly toward greater front-loading contrary to the expectation that it would shift to the left (less front-loading as productivity levels are higher and unit costs are lower during the second period). The ambiguity in this outcome arises from two underlying effects that push in opposite directions. Behavioral effects would tend to push toward delaying investment and reduce frontloading since it is more efficient to wait and take advantage of productivity gains. On the other hand, there is a change in relative prices between periods with no behavioral shift since the present value of expenditures in period one falls by less than the present value of expenditures in the second period.

One implication of this analysis is that anticipated incremental gains in underlying governance or productivity should not be a reason to delay public expenditures in capacity building and service delivery. Even with underlying efficiency gains that reduce costs over time, there is no reason to delay investment in the MDGs. Rather, the same constraints to absorptive capacity—labor costs, macroeconomic constraints, and infrastructure congestion—should guide the investment path.

V. Conclusions

One of the major concerns of governments over disbursing aid to help low-income countries achieve the MDGs is whether the large levels of aid required can be effectively absorbed. There are both macroeconomic and microeconomic constraints to aid absorption that are well recognized in the literature. In this paper, we have focused on selective aspects of this question related to the level,

[20] One frequently cited example is the Ugandan newspaper campaign to boost schools' and parents' ability to monitor local officials' handling of school grants. Through greater public awareness, "capture" or leakage of budget resources fell from 80 percent to 20 percent between 1995 and 2001 (Reinikka and Svensson, 2003).

sequencing, and frontloading of aid necessary to fulfill the MDGs. If external financing is not the constraint, we have posed the question of what major absorptive capacity constraints will guide identification of a cost-minimizing path to reach the targets. In particular, we looked at labor market, macroeconomic (Dutch disease), and basic infrastructure constraints. To address these questions, we have used a modeling approach that combines a relatively standard and highly aggregated computable general equilibrium model with an MDG module that links MDG performance to the provision of different public services (health, education, and water and sanitation), public infrastructure, per-capita income, and other economic indicators. The MDG module draws on detailed sector studies undertaken by the Ethiopian government and the World Bank.

We have used model simulations to examine a set of alternative scenarios for expanding public infrastructure and MDG-related services, with external grants covering the financing gap. Meeting the first MDG—reducing by half the incidence of income poverty in 2015 from 1990 levels—will require higher economic growth. We argue that one key to raising growth is substantial investment in basic infrastructure, particularly roads, energy, and water control. Reaching the other human development MDGs will require spending to boost the quality and quantity of publicly-supplied services related to MDGs. According to model simulations, for the main scenario—which achieves the different MDGs through a combination of frontloaded expansion in infrastructure spending and growth in MDG services at a constant rate—foreign grant financing requirements will rise from about $16 per capita at present to some $60 per capita in 2015, or nearly 40 percent of annual GDP in foreign grants. This is roughly twice the average level of ODA per capita reached in sub-Saharan Africa during the early 1990s.

On the basis of our analysis of the simulation results, we draw four other main conclusions from the simulations presented.

1. Careful sequencing of public investment is important for minimizing the total cost of reaching the MDGs. From the outset priority investment is needed in basic infrastructure to generate the basis for higher productivity growth and network effects improving linkages across and within regions and sectors. Among the MDG services, accelerating education spending is a priority since skilled labor only results with a lag and is a binding constraint on absorptive capacity. Priority in sequencing should be accorded to public investment in services that generate important positive externalities, and in doing so lower investment costs of other MDGs.
2. The macroeconomic impact of large aid flows on the tradable sector, through pulling resources into nontradables and exchange rate appreciation (Dutch disease), is a serious concern. The danger is that the MDGs may be met but at the cost of a severely diminished export sector—a sector that is a potentially vital source for future growth. This poses a potentially serious trade-off for MDG-oriented poverty reduction strate-

gies. More important, it underscores the need to push further trade liberalization, press for market access in OECD countries, and address behind-the-border barriers to trade.

3. Large-scale frontloading of aid disbursements (other than infrastructure) is costly as it pushes up against absorptive capacity constraints, increases the premium on skilled wages, bids labor away from the private sector (depressing growth), and incurs more serious Dutch disease effects. Comparing the present value of additional MDG grants while varying the share of total aid disbursed in the first five years suggests that costs are minimized when about one fifth of additional resources are used in the first five years. On the other hand, frontloading also has different welfare implications: greater frontloading secures earlier success of social outcomes, whose marginal benefits may outweigh rising costs.
4. Improvements in underlying governance and institutional structures may secure broad productivity improvements in public service delivery. Whether such gains suggest more or less frontloading of expenditures depends on the relative weight of behavior and price effects on supply. This, however, does not constitute a reason to delay public investment pending efficiency gains. Rather, it suggests that the same constraints to absorptive capacity—labor costs, macroeconomic constraints, infrastructure congestion—help guide the investment path.

We are not suggesting that simply tripling or quadrupling aid can achieve the MDGs in Ethiopia. Several other conditions, which may be even more important, must also be met. These include improvements in governance, strengthening institutions, and improving the business climate. At the same time, donor countries and the international financial institutions must take serious steps to improve the quality of assistance through better alignment of aid with national strategic priorities, and harmonization of their administrative procedures with country standards.

References

Adam, Christopher, and David Bevan, 2003, *Aid, Public Expenditure and the Dutch Disease*, CSAE Working Paper No. 2003–02 (Oxford: Centre for the Study of African Economies, University of Oxford).

Bevan, David, 2005, "An Analytical Overview of Aid Absorption: Recognizing and Avoiding Macroeconomic Hazards," paper for the Seminar on Foreign Aid and Macroeconomic Management, Maputo, Mozambique, March 14–15.

Birdsall, Nancy, Stijn Claessens, and Ishac Diwan, 2003, "Policy Selectivity Forgone: Debt and Donor Behavior in Africa," Working Paper No. 17 (Washington: Center for Global Development).

Bourguignon, François, 2004, "*A Framework to Monitor Country-Based Aid Effectiveness*" (unpublished; Washington: World Bank).

———, and others, 2006, *Building Absorptive Capacity to Meet the MDGs* (Washington: World Bank, forthcoming).

Bourguignon, François, Maurizio Bussolo, Luiz Pereira da Silva, Hans Timmer, and Dominique van der Mensbrugghe, 2004, MAMS. *Maquette for MDG Simulations* (unpublished; Washington: World Bank).

Bourguignon, François, Maurizio Bussolo, Hans Lofgren, Hans Timmer, Dominique van der Mensbrugghe, 2004, *Towards Achieving the MDGs in Ethiopia: An Economy-wide Analysis of Alternative Scenarios* (Washington: World Bank).

Bulíř, Aleš, and Timothy Lane, 2002, "Aid and Fiscal Management," paper presented at IMF Conference on Macroeconomics and Poverty, Washington, March 14–15.

Clemens, Michael A., Charles J. Kenny, and Todd J. Moss, 2004, "The Trouble with the MDGs: Confronting Expectations of Aid and Development Success," Working Paper No. 40 (Washington: Center for Global Development).

Development Committee, 2003, "Supporting Sound Policies with Adequate and Appropriate Financing," report prepared for the Annual Meetings of the World Bank and the International Monetary Fund, Dubai, September.

———, 2004, "Aid Effectiveness and Financing Modalities," report prepared for the Annual Meetings of the World Bank and the International Monetary Fund, Washington, September.

Eifert, Benn, Alan Gelb, and Vijaya Ramachandran, 2005, "Business Environment and Comparative Advantage in Africa: Evidence from the Investment Climate Data," Working Paper No. 56 (Washington: Center for Global Development).

FDRE (Federal Democratic Republic of Ethiopia), 2002, "Ethiopia: Sustainable Development and Poverty Reduction Program" (Addis Ababa: Ministry of Finance and Economic Development).

Foster, Mick, and others, 2003, *The Case for Increased Aid: Final Report to the Department for International Development*, Vols. 1 and 2 (Essex, United Kingdom: Mick Foster Economics Ltd.).

Geda, Alemayehu, Adbeb Shimlesse, Demse Chanyalewu, and Oladele Arowolo, 2004, "A Synthesis of Millennium Development Goals (MDGs) Need Assessment for Ethiopia," background paper for UNDP-MOFED, January.

Heller, Peter, and Sanjeev Gupta, 2002, "Challenges in Expanding Development Assistance," IMF Policy Discussion Paper No. 02/5 (Washington: International Monetary Fund).

International Monetary Fund, 2004, *Ethiopia: Article IV Staff Report—Selected Issues* (Washington).

———, 2005, *The Federal Democratic Republic of Ethiopia: 2004 Article IV Consultation and Sixth Review Under the Three-Year Arrangement Under the Poverty Reduction and Growth Facility*, IMF Country Report No. 05/25 (Washington).

———, 2005a, *The Federal Democratic Republic of Ethiopia: Debt Sustainability Analysis*, IMF Country Report No. 05/27 (Washington).

———, 2005b, *The Federal Democratic Republic of Ethiopia: Ex Post Assessment of Long-Term Fund Engagement*, IMF Country Report No. 05/26 (Washington).

———, 2005c, *The Federal Democratic Republic of Ethiopia: Selected Issues and Statistical Appendix*, IMF Country Report No. 05/28 (Washington).

Lofgren, Hans, 2004, "MAMS: An Economywide Model for Analysis of MDG Country Strategies—Technical Documentation" (unpublished; Washington: World Bank).

———, and Carolina Diaz-Bonilla, 2005, "An Ethiopian Strategy for Achieving the Millennium Development Goals: Simulations with the MAMS Model" (unpublished; Washington: World Bank).

Prati, Alessandro, Ratna Sahay, and Thierry Tressel, 2003, "Is There a Case for Sterilizing Foreign Aid Inflows?" paper presented at the IMF Research Workshop, "Macroeconomic Challenges in Low Income Countries," Washington, October 23–24.

Radelet, Steven, 2003, *Challenging Foreign Aid: A Policymaker's Guide to the Millennium Challenge Account* (Washington: Center for Global Development).

———, Michael A. Clemens, and Rikhil Bhavnani, 2004, "Counting Chickens When They Hatch: The Short-Term of Aid on Growth," Working Paper No. 44 (Washington: Center for Global Development).

Reinikka, Ritva, and Jakob Svensson, 2004, "The Power of Information: Evidence from a Newspaper Campaign to Reduce Capture," Policy Research Working Paper No. 3239 (Washington: World Bank).

UN Millennium Project, 2005, *Investing in Development: A Practical Plan to Achieve the Millennium Development Goals* (New York).

World Bank, 2004, "Ethiopia: Public Expenditure Review—The Emerging Challenge," Poverty Reduction and Economic Management 2 (AFTP2) (Washington).

———, 2005, "Education in Ethiopia: Strengthening the Foundation for Sustainable Progress," Human Development Department (AFTH3) (Washington).

———, 2005a, "Ethiopia: A Strategy to Balance and Stimulate Growth—A Country Economic Memorandum," Poverty Reduction and Economic Management 2 (AFTP2) (Washington).

SESSION III

Dutch Disease

Where Do We Stand?

7

Exogenous Inflows and Real Exchange Rates

Theoretical Quirk or Empirical Reality?

CHRISTOPHER ADAM*

There are "known knowns". These are things we know that we know. There are "known unknowns". That is to say, there are things that we know we don't know. But there are also "unknown unknowns". These are things we don't know we don't know.

—DONALD RUMSFELD
U.S. Secretary for Defense on the search for weapons of mass destruction in Iraq, February 2002

I. Introduction

Concerns that large aid inflows will induce a sharp and sustained appreciation of the real exchange rate, discourage the expansion of exports (particularly nontraditional exports), and thereby damage growth prospects in the recipient economy are rarely far from the center of contemporary debates on the macroeconomics of aid to low-income countries. These concerns have recently come to the fore in a number of well-managed low-income countries that have already participated in the debt relief Initiative for Heavily Indebted Poor Countries (HIPC Initiative)—and which are identified by the United Nations Millennium Project (2005) as potential "fast-track" candidates for rapid scaling-up of aid flows. These countries face the

*University of Oxford, United Kingdom.

prospect of significantly higher aid flows in the near future (and, arguably, strong pressure from donor nations to see these resources absorbed rapidly). Thus, many question whether this increased aid can generate sufficient returns, in terms of sustained growth, to outweigh the costs of absorbing it, or whether it will contribute to the unraveling of hard-won economic gains secured in recent years.

In his overview for this seminar, Bevan (2005) summarizes the key elements underpinning this anxiety but argues that this conventional diagnosis may be unnecessarily pessimistic, even when aid levels are already high. While acknowledging the risks associated with rising aid inflows, he suggests that these can be managed.

Many economists would probably concur with this assessment but they would also recognize that effective management requires evidence on the impact of aid against which policy interventions can be calibrated. One problem currently facing policymakers, and the international community more generally, however, is that even though much research has been undertaken on the topic, the evidence on the short- and medium-run macroeconomic effects of aid—the "empirical reality" referred to in the subtitle of this paper—is still partial, often contradictory, and generally ambiguous. Moreover, since most of the evidence on the impact of aid is drawn from an era when the political and economic circumstances were far different from those today, much of it is of questionable relevance to the contemporary policy debate on aid management. This has quite serious implications, both when a view is required on by how much aid flows to low-income countries could sensibly be increased, and also in thinking about how the supporting macroeconomic policy environment should be structured. Taking too sanguine a view, either on the limits of absorption, the rate at which aid flows can be increased, or on the degree of macroeconomic intervention required to manage a scale-up effectively runs obvious risks. But too conservative a stance is also costly, condemning the recipient to a lower level of consumption and growth than could otherwise be achieved.

This paper is concerned mainly with forms of evidence and it has two objectives: The first is to review the theoretical arguments concerning the macroeconomic transmission from aid inflows to the real exchange rate and export performance and to summarize the macroeconomic evidence on this link. This constitutes the "known knowns" from the quotation at the beginning of the paper. The second objective is to discuss how simulation methods, based on a blend of theory and partial empirical evidence, may be used to highlight some critical but typically hard-to-quantify factors that are likely to determine the macroeconomic response to increased aid flows. These, then, are the "known unknowns."

In Section II of this paper, I lay out the key theoretical arguments in the relationship between exogenous aid flows, the real exchange rate, and the structure of production in the recipient economy. In doing so, I address three specific issues: the role of dynamic growth effects from exporting; the problem of short-run real exchange rate overshooting; and the possibility that aid flows can generate a so-called "transfer paradox"—where a gift (e.g., an unrequited transfer of aid resources) may leave the recipient worse off than before the transfer. I argue that while the transfer paradox is, in some respects, a "theoretical quirk" and unlikely to materialize in the aggregate, elements of the paradox are germane to understanding certain distributional consequences of aid inflows. In Section III, I then review some of the empirical evidence and assess its relevance to the contemporary debate. Reflecting the rather pessimistic conclusions that emerge from this assessment, Section IV then presents some simulation-based evidence on the aid and real exchange rate link. I argue that this link helps sharpen the focus on the key variables shaping the macroeconomic response to aid inflows. Finally, Section V concludes with brief remarks about implications for policy.

II. Aid Flows, the Real Exchange Rate, and Export Performance

The Standard Argument

The standard analysis of the macroeconomics of aid flows to small open economies posits that foreign aid flows augment domestic resources, leaving the economy as a whole better off; how much so depends on how these increased resources are used. Two features of aid are important in considering the economy's response. The first is that aid accrues initially to the government. In this respect, it is similar to a resource windfall in state-owned natural resource sectors, as opposed to commodity price windfalls or remittance booms which tend to accrue in the first instance to the private sector. Consequently, parallels are often drawn between issues of aid management and the so-called "resource curse." The second feature is that while an aid inflow directly increases the economy's capacity to import (i.e., net imports must increase one-for-one with that part of the aid flow that is not saved), the expenditure supported by aid is often predominantly on domestic goods. The economic impact of aid flows therefore involves consideration of both the so-called transfer problem, that is, the process by which an inflow in the form of tradable goods is used to support increased consumption of nontradable (domestic) goods and the balance between the public and private sectors. The critical decision is, thus, how the authorities choose to respond to the aid inflow. The choices are straightforward. It could be saved, by adding to official reserves, passed to the private sector, either through tax cuts or some direct transfer or by substituting for domestic deficit financing, or it could be used to augment public expenditure (or some combination of all of the above).

If it is entirely saved, either by the public or private sectors, the real exchange rate will be unaffected, at least initially.[1] Similarly there is no impact on the real exchange rate (or the composition of domestic production) if the ultimate recipient of the aid, either in the public or private sectors, spends the entire increase on imports. In this case, the increase in net imports is met entirely by an increase in gross imports. However, it is much more likely that the aid inflow will boost total demand for both imports and domestically produced (i.e., nontradable) goods and services—including such public services as health and education. The real exchange rate response will therefore depend on the relative pattern of demand between the public and private sectors. Typically it is assumed that the public sector has a higher propensity to consume domestically produced goods and services; this component of demand is thus likely to be stronger if aid is used to finance increased public expenditure than if it finances direct transfers to households or tax cuts, or is used to reduce domestic deficit financing. But in either case the mechanism is the same, so that differences in outcomes are a matter of degree. For small economies, while imports can be acquired directly from the world market at fixed world prices, nontradables can, by definition, only be supplied by domestic producers. Unless there is considerable excess supply in the economy, this higher demand for domestic goods requires their prices to rise in order to induce the necessary supply response. In other words, the real exchange rate (i.e., the price of nontradable relative to tradable goods) must appreciate to entice resources, including labor, to switch from the production of exportable and import-substituting goods to the production of nontradable goods. In the process, then, as the real exchange rate appreciates, the tradable goods sector shrinks relative to the nontradable sector. The increase in net imports in this case is brought about partly by an increase in imports and partly by a reduction in the production of tradables (exports and/or import substitutes). This decline in export production is referred to as the "Dutch disease."[2]

[1] Even if donors were comfortable with the idea, this option is unlikely to be optimal for the recipient, particularly if the aid increase is permanent, or at least not expected to be reversed in the near future. Some reserve accumulation might be optimal if reserves are sufficiently far below the level required for sound macroeconomic management. In this case, however, the accumulation of reserves is best thought of as a temporary rather than permanent response.

[2] The term "Dutch disease" was first coined to describe the adverse effects on the Dutch manufacturing sector following the sharp appreciation in the real exchange rate induced by the discovery of natural gas off the coast of Holland in the 1960s. The Dutch disease framework has also been used to analyze the impact of gold inflows from the Americas to sixteenth century Spain and to the discovery of gold and other minerals in Australia in the 1850s. An early application of the framework to aid inflows is found in van Wijnbergen (1985).

Dutch disease effects involve a change in the balance between the tradable and nontradable sectors. Producers of tradables—both those currently in operation and potential producers—stand to lose: the purchasing power of export incomes declines and profit margins are squeezed as prices of domestic inputs, including labor, rise. On the other hand, producers of nontradable goods stand to gain as their income now purchases more imports and domestic tradables (i.e., import-substituting goods) than before. If the production of nontradable goods and services is relatively labor-intensive—as is often the case—then in the aggregate wage earners will also gain, either as a result of higher labor demand or through higher wages if there is close to full employment.

The magnitude of these short-run effects will depend on a number of things. As noted, they will be stronger the greater the share of nontradable goods in consumption, which is likely to be closely related to the proportion of the aid inflow directly spent by the public sector. They will be weaker the greater the capacity of consumers—in either the public or private sectors—to substitute between domestic and imported goods in response to changes in relative prices. Dutch-disease effects will also be weaker if there is substantial spare capacity in the economy; the larger the pool of unemployed labor, the easier it is to increase the supply of labor-intensive domestic goods without driving up prices, including the price of labor. Nkusu (2004) suggests that a failure to account for idle capacity may create a systematic expectation that Dutch-disease risks are higher than they truly are. How much genuine spare capacity really exists, however, is often unclear. Unemployed capital and labor are only relevant as excess capacity if they can be brought into productive use in response to increased demand. Hence, if critical inputs in short supply, such as specialist labor, cannot be substituted by more abundant factors, regardless of how far their price falls, "full capacity" can coexist with generalized unemployment of factors.

In the short run, the impact of aid on the economy is felt predominantly on the demand side. Over the medium term, however, the evolution of the economy depends equally on the nature of the supply side response to the aid inflow, in other words how, if at all, the productive capacity of the economy is augmented by aid inflows. This in turn will be determined by how aid is used and how the supply side of the economy responds to these different uses. As I will soon discuss, once appropriate consideration is taken of the supply side there is no presumption as to whether, over the medium term, aid inflows will be associated with an appreciation or depreciation of the real exchange rate, or, indeed, with an expansion or contraction in the tradable goods (exportables) sector of the economy. Before doing so, I consider three extensions to this basic argument.

The Costs of Temporary Exclusion from World Markets

Most economists believe that there are important growth-enhancing productivity gains to be obtained from producing for world markets. This belief appears to be borne out in empirical evidence, including for African manufacturing firms.[3] Hence, if the appreciation of the real exchange rate induces a protracted shift of resources away from the export sector and toward nontradable production, where latent productivity effects are typically assumed to be lower, an important engine of growth for the economy is jeopardized.[4] Although the evidence on the scale of these growth effects is contested, this argument is a serious one, particularly since because of past policy errors the exportable sector in many low-income countries is already too small. The policy challenge is thus to ensure that poor management of aid inflows does not leave the exportable sector *permanently* smaller than its growth-maximizing level. If productivity gains from aid-financed public investment can be secured, so that the exportable sector's share of total output expands over the medium term, the issue is simply an intertemporal one, at least in the aggregate; the temporary growth-retarding effects of a short-run real exchange rate appreciation are compensated for by future growth in the export sector, allowing higher export-led productivity gains to be accessed in the future.

Permanent Costs of Temporary Real Exchange Rate Overshooting

The interaction of the demand- and supply-side effects of aid means that the real exchange rate may overshoot its long-run value and may, in fact, move in the opposite direction so that a short-run appreciation is followed by medium-term depreciation. Temporary movements of this kind are often much more costly than conventional models suggest, even if they are anticipated. These costs are likely to be especially high when firms face high adjustment costs and when the domestic financial sector is relatively underdeveloped. If firms falsely believe temporary real exchange rate movements to be permanent, they incur costs as they first move into (what they think is) the booming sector and then out again when the temporary effects pass. These are one-off costs. More problematic, however, is the case where real exchange movements are known to be temporary, so that firms are not induced to reallocate resources in response to short-run relative price movements. If they are unable to access sufficient credit from underdeveloped financial markets to finance the short-run losses triggered by unfavorable temporary real exchange rate movements, the firms may run down their capital; lay off skilled workers; or at worst close down completely, even though the long-run prospects for the tradable sector may be highly favorable. Short-run movements in real exchange rates thus may again have *permanent* effects on the structure of production and growth. Given their lesser ability

[3] For example, see Ghei and Pritchett (1999) for a general discussion on this topic, Westphal (1990) and Kraay (1999) on evidence for East Asia and China, and Gautier (2002) and Bigsten and others (2004) for African exporting firms.

[4] See, for example, Adam and O'Connell (2004).

to access credit from the formal financial sector, small firms are likely to be disproportionately vulnerable to this kind of market imperfection.

It is important to distinguish here between the volatility of aid flows and the volatility of the real exchange rate itself. It is the real exchange rate volatility that matters for intersectoral resource allocation decisions. Whether the volatility of aid flows mitigates or worsens real exchange rate volatility depends on whether aid is pro- or countercyclical. Procyclical aid (i.e., flows that increase in "good" times as the real exchange rate is otherwise appreciating) may aggravate the problem, while countercyclical aid (which offsets other adverse shocks such as terms-of-trade shocks) may act to smooth both the current account and fiscal balances and the real exchange rate.

The Transfer Paradox

The original idea of a "transfer paradox" is that, as a result of distortions in the structure of trade, an aid transfer may move the terms of trade sufficiently far to its disadvantage that the recipient country is left worse off following the transfer. More recently, a number of economists have examined the possibility of a transfer paradox in the context of small-country aid recipients (where the terms of trade are independent of transfers), with attention switching to the role of the nontradable goods sector.[5] In this case, the risk to the recipient emerges not from the conventional Dutch-disease diagnosis (which is concerned with the switching of resources away from the dynamic tradable goods sector) but rather from its reverse. Specifically, when the transfer induces an expansion of the supply of nontradables that is strong enough relative to the growth in domestic demand, the relative price of nontradable goods may fall sufficiently far that real income falls too. While the models employed are highly specific (some might suggest contrived) and the empirical evidence marshaled in their support relatively weak, this analysis does highlight an important aspect of aid transfers not normally addressed in conventional macroeconomic analyses, namely, that the effects of potentially large relative price changes induced by responses to aid flows may be highly concentrated and therefore distributionally non-neutral. A particularly relevant example is in the market for basic food crops whose prices are determined by domestic market conditions. We frequently think of such goods as having a relatively low income elasticity of demand (i.e., above some subsistence level, the demand for food rises less than proportionally with income). In these circumstances shifts in supply arising, for example, from aid-funded public investment—and which are exogenous to the actions of producers themselves—can lead to a sharp fall in prices and hence a sharp decline in incomes for net sellers of basic foods, typically

[5]The small country "aid transfer paradox" problem was first introduced by Chichilinsky (1980) but the idea has recently been revived by Yano and Nugent (1999).

poor rural households. In reality, of course, households faced with this adverse movement in their terms of trade will tend to make some adjustment, either in, for example, their crop choice or their labor supply decision. The scope for adjustment may be very limited or take some time to take effect, however, so that the adverse distributional effects may be protracted.

III. The Absence of Reliable Macroeconometric Evidence

In principle, it should be a simple matter to answer the question of how aid flows affect the real exchange rate and the structure of domestic production, and how large these effects are. Attempts to measure this relationship date back to the early 1980s when parallels were first drawn with the natural resource curse and, hence, the possibility of Dutch-disease-like effects accompanying aid flows.[6] While a number of subsequent empirical studies have also found a tendency for aid inflows to be associated with an appreciation of the real exchange rate,[7] this evidence is not overwhelming. Econometric estimates of the impact of aid on the real exchange rate often show this effect to be small and statistically insignificant—what Bulíř and Lane (2002) refer to as "traces" of aid-induced real exchange rate appreciation. This tendency is echoed in more recent work by Prati, Sahay, and Tressel (2003), who, on the basis of a rather more sophisticated dynamic panel data model, suggest that for countries with net official development assistance (ODA) flows in exceeding 2 percent of GDP a year a doubling of aid would only appreciate the real exchange rate by at most approximately 4 percent in the short run, rising to about 18 percent over a five-year period, and to 30 percent over the decade. Time-series models describing the evolution of the real exchange rate also tend to find that it responds much less to variations in aid flows than to other exogenous foreign exchange flows, most notably commodity prices or terms-of-trade variations.[8] Moreover, a number of studies on African economies find that aid inflows appear to be associated with a depreciation rather than an appreciation of the real exchange rate.[9]

One possible reason why large real exchange rate movements are not widely observed in response to aid flows is that the required quantity adjustments

---

[6] For example, van Wijnbergen (1985).

[7] These include country-specific studies, for example, by Younger (1992) for Ghana, Atingi-Ego and Sebudde (2001) for Uganda, as well as cross-country analysis by Adenauer and Vagassky (1998) for a number of franc zone countries, and Prati and others (2003) for a range of low-income, aid-dependent economies.

[8] For example, Elbadawi (1994) for Ghana; Baffes and others (1999) for Côte d'Ivoire and Burkina Faso; Atingi-Ego and Sebudde (2001) for Uganda; and Cashin and others (2002).

[9] For example, Nyoni (1998); and Adam, Bevan, and Chambas (2001).

have actually occurred in conjunction with relatively weak real exchange rate effects.[10] A number of recent empirical studies from the IMF explore this more direct implication of the Dutch-disease argument and suggest that quantity adjustments to aid inflows have, in fact, been rather substantial. Bulíř and Lane (2002) present some striking evidence that suggests the tradable sector as a whole has declined by an average of 8 percent a year in a sample of aid-dependent economies. Arellano and others (2005), drawing on panel data regressions for 73 developing countries during 1981–2000, also find a strong and significant negative relationship between the level of aid a country receives and the share of manufactured exports in total exports. Their central estimates suggest that for the mean country in their sample, a rise in aid from 10 percent to 11 percent of GDP corresponds to an 8 percentage-point decline in the manufactured export share (from its mean of about 20 percent of total exports).[11] This effect is very large, but it is ultimately an association and does not control for the endogeneity of aid and the possibility that causality runs in the opposite direction—namely, that aid-dependent economies may receive high aid flows precisely because the tradable sector is declining.

Rajan and Subramanian (2005) approach the same question from a slightly different perspective. By exploiting within-country variations in sectoral growth rates, they test the hypothesis that in the presence of high aid inflows, relatively labor-intensive industries grow more slowly than relatively capital-intensive ones. Arguing that in developing countries firms producing tradable goods tend to be more labor-intensive than those producing nontradables, the authors conclude that high inflows have systematic adverse effects on competitiveness.[12]

Other evidence is less compelling. Yano and Nugent (1999), in their paper on the transfer paradox, also find rather mixed econometric evidence on the relationship between aid flows, real exchange rates, and the structure of production among a set of 44 aid-dependent economies during 1970–90. Aid dependence here means that a country receives more than 5 percent annually in aid. In 21 of these 44 countries, aid was associated with an appreciation in the real exchange rate; in only 2 cases, however, was the effect statistically significant, while in 23 cases the relationship was reversed (and was significant in 4 countries). In only 6 countries (Burkina Faso, Congo, Lesotho, Liberia, Senegal, and Yemen) did the authors find a negative and significant relationship between aid flows

[10] In other words, the intersectoral elasticity of substitution is relatively large, so that while incipient real exchange rate pressures may be strong, actual real exchange rate movements are more modest.

[11] Arellano and others (2005), Tables 4 and 7.

[12] Rajan and Subramanian (2005) also examine the relationship between aid flows and the growth of the manufacturing sector, finding results consistent with those of Arellano and others (2005).

and the symptoms of a transfer paradox (namely, an expansion of the nontradable sector, contraction of the tradable sector, and a decline in real GDP); only in the case of Liberia was there any evidence that the decline in real income was statistically significant.

Where there is an arguably stronger empirical consensus is on the costs of short-run temporary movements in real exchange rates. The generalized costs of real exchange rate volatility are extremely well documented, and an increasing body of firm-level evidence suggests that it is exactly this form of temporary misalignment—rather than anticipated medium-term movements in the equilibrium real exchange rate—that is particularly costly to sustained export growth in low-income countries.[13]

Making Sense of the Evidence

A first reading of this macroeconometric evidence would appear to suggest that while short-run real exchange rate volatility is costly, the case for strong Dutch-disease-like effects of aid is, at best, "not proven." At one level, this is consistent with the fact that it is impossible to think of any example in which surges in aid inflows have led to the kind of collapse in the tradable goods sector associated with conventional Dutch-disease episodes—such as, the collapse of export agriculture in Nigeria following the oil shocks of the 1970s. But equally it does not imply that these effects could not materialize nor that aid inflows have not choked off an incipient export-led growth. Moreover the evidence sits uncomfortably with well-articulated concerns about aid-induced real exchange rate movements emerging from policymakers in a number of African countries in recent years.[14] The problem would appear to lie with the evidence, particularly the aggregate macroeconomic evidence. There are at least four reasons why we might be cautious about accepting this evidence at face value.

First, all empirical work in this area is plagued by severe measurement problems, both of the real exchange rate itself and across alternative concepts of tradable and nontradable goods. Radelet (1996), for example, demonstrates that in Indonesia a conventional "IMF-style" real exchange rate measure of the kind used in most of the empirical work cited earlier (i.e., the ratio of consumer price indices expressed in a common currency) indicated a depreciation of the real exchange rate in the early 1990s while every other measure of the real exchange rate suggested an appreciation, the latter being more consistent with export trends. Bevan and others (2003) identify a similar phenomenon in Uganda in the late 1990s.

[13] See, for example, Servin (2003) and Bleaney and Greenaway (2001) on the general evidence; Elbadawi (1999) on country-level evidence for sub-Saharan Africa; and Bigsten and others (1999) and Sekkat and Vavoudakis (2000) on firm-level evidence.

[14] For example, the discussion in Buffie and others (2004).

It is equally difficult to derive accurate empirical proxies for tradable and nontradable goods. Not only do official statistics indicate that most goods and services are traded internationally between at least some countries, but the degree of tradability of different goods is often endogenous to trade and other policy factors and hence is likely to change over time. But the alternative of arguing that the degree of tradability can be proxied by the labor intensity of production, as suggested by Rajan and Subramanian (2005), seems equally debatable.[15]

Second, much of the empirical evidence cited above draws on periods in the recent past when underlying macroeconomic circumstances, and particularly those relating to the management of foreign aid inflows, were radically different from those prevailing at present. In some cases, aid transfers were driven by, and responded to, noneconomic factors (which might explain some of the high variation in the cross-country data such as that used by Yano and Nugent). In others, however, and especially throughout the 1980s and 1990s, aid was highly conditional on—or at least associated with—large macroeconomic reforms, particularly in the areas of exchange rate liberalization and unification and the removal of quantitative restrictions on trade. In these circumstances it becomes difficult to disentangle conventional aid and Dutch- disease effects—where aid inflows may be expected to appreciate the real exchange rate—from the associated (or at least contemporaneous) tendency for the real exchange rate to depreciate as a result of policy reforms aimed at removing macroeconomic distortions. Although considerable effort has been expended to address these issues, conventionally estimated effects of aid on the real exchange rate are highly likely to be biased downward so that, at best, only weak Dutch-disease effects are identified.

Similarly, over much of the period spanned by the econometric evidence, and especially when foreign exchange regimes were highly controlled, aid flows played a crucial role in financing critical imported inputs. This had the effect of making short-run supply responses (across the economy as a whole) sufficiently strong and rapid to shift the balance in favor of a depreciation in the real exchange rate as otherwise idle capacity was brought into use.

A third problem with most analyses of real exchange rate responses to aid is that the results are dominated by the average, either over time or across countries. One consequence of this is that such models rarely allow for the possibility that real exchange rates may first appreciate and then depreciate in response to aid (and, equally, that the exportable sector may contract and then expand). In principle, time-series analyses can allow for these effects to some degree but

[15] For example, while it is probably correct that tradable goods are produced in developing countries at a lower capital-labor ratio that they would be in industrial countries, it does not follow that their production is more labor-intensive than nontradables *in their own country*.

given the previous observations about relying too heavily on historical data, it is questionable how much weight can be put on this evidence.

Finally, as emphasized earlier, aid flows do not occur in isolation. Their impact is intimately linked not just with the fiscal response to the aid (i.e., how revenue mobilization, public expenditure, and the overall fiscal stance respond to aid flows), but also with the monetary and exchange rate policy response. Although some attempts have been made to develop sophisticated econometric "fiscal response" models,[16] it is highly debatable whether such models can ever successfully identify the underlying structural linkages of interest, especially given the severe data limitations they face.

IV. Using Simulation Approaches to Get Behind the Aggregate Data

In recent years, a second tradition has emerged to assess the quantitative significance of the macroeconomic effects of aid flows in circumstances where other direct forms of empirical evidence cannot be relied upon. This involves building simulation models that are informed by theory and calibrated by data and case study evidence where these exist, but which do not rely exclusively on actual history to provide quantitative insights on possible responses to aid. Simulation models differ greatly in terms of scale and structure, depending on the kinds of questions they seek to address.[17] Recently, however, a number of models have been constructed to focus specifically on the question of aid and public investment. These include work by the World Bank (2004), by researchers at the International Food Policy Research Institute (IFPRI), by Lofgren and Robinson (2004), and Adam and Bevan (2004). It is far beyond the scope of this paper to do justice to this research, but it is appropriate to illustrate how this approach can be used to understand the possible dynamic responses to aid inflows. Simulation models on their own are generally unable to "predict" the specific macroeconomic consequences of aid inflows. They can, however, in the spirit of the quotation at the beginning of this paper, focus attention on the key "known unknowns," those variables whose quantitative importance we need to know in order to gauge how a particular economy may respond to a scaling up of aid.

To give a sense of how this approach might contribute to the debate, this section reports on some simulations from a model built specifically to analyze possible short- and medium-term responses to alternative aid-financed public expenditure programs in low-income countries. The model, described in Adam and Bevan (2004), is designed to capture the salient features of a typical "post-

[16] For example, Mavrotas (2002).

[17] For example, there is a long tradition of using simulation models to analyze the likely impact of trade policy reforms. More recently these models have been promoted as a means of analyzing possible distributional effects of policy reforms.

stabilization" African country. Thus, it assumes that the economy produces basic food crops, an export cash crop, manufactured goods (including nontraditional exports), and services. This particular model does not assume any significant natural resource dependency. It embodies a standard characterization of consumption and saving behavior for a range of representative household groups, including rural households whose livelihoods depend overwhelmingly on the production and sale of cash- and food-crops. The government in the model undertakes the standard array of functions, taxing households' income and consumption and providing conventional government services, but also providing public infrastructure that can boost productivity in the private sector. The recent work by the World Bank (2004) on Ethiopia follows a similar strategy, but places more emphasis on the potential for productivity gains from investment in human capital, specifically through public expenditure on health and education.

The simulations reported here are designed to examine the sensitivity of possible macroeconomic responses to aid-funded public expenditure programs to assumptions about: the productivity of different forms of public expenditure; how this affects the private sector (on average and, for example, whether different forms of public infrastructure favors the production of the export sector over the domestic nontradable sector); how quickly public investment can be brought on line; the initial degree of capital scarcity in the economy; and the extent to which there are dynamic growth effects from nontraditional exporting. The simulations reported here represent only a fraction of the more extensive analysis carried out in Adam and Bevan (2004).

Figures 7.1 to 7.4 plot a set of simulated 10-year trajectories for the real exchange rate (Figure 7.1), export volumes (Figure 7.2), real GDP (Figure 7.3), and total income (Figure 7.4), in response to a scale-up of grant aid equivalent to slightly below 2 percent of GDP in an economy that is already operating with a relatively high aid-to-GDP ratio of 11 percent.[18] Since the aim is to focus exclusively on alternative public expenditure packages, other external factors such as terms-of-trade changes and other aspects of the potential fiscal response are assumed to be constant, although there is no requirement that this be the case.[19] The plots, which give a sense of the potential range of responses, are generated for only a small subset of the possible trajectories generated by the model.

Experiment 1 provides a reference benchmark. In this case public investment has no effect on private sector productivity: the economy's total capital

[18] This is similar to the top end of the scale of HIPC debt relief but somewhat smaller than some of the aid flows anticipated under the UNMP.

[19] In practice, of course, the government may decide to take all the adjustment on the side of expenditure, by increasing current expenditure or infrastructure investment, or to offset part of it by altering the rate of revenue mobilization. Some combination of both is likely to be optimal in many circumstances, especially if current tax structures are highly distortionary at the margin and the public sector's absorptive capacity is limited.

Figure 7.1. Trade Weighted Real Exchange Rate

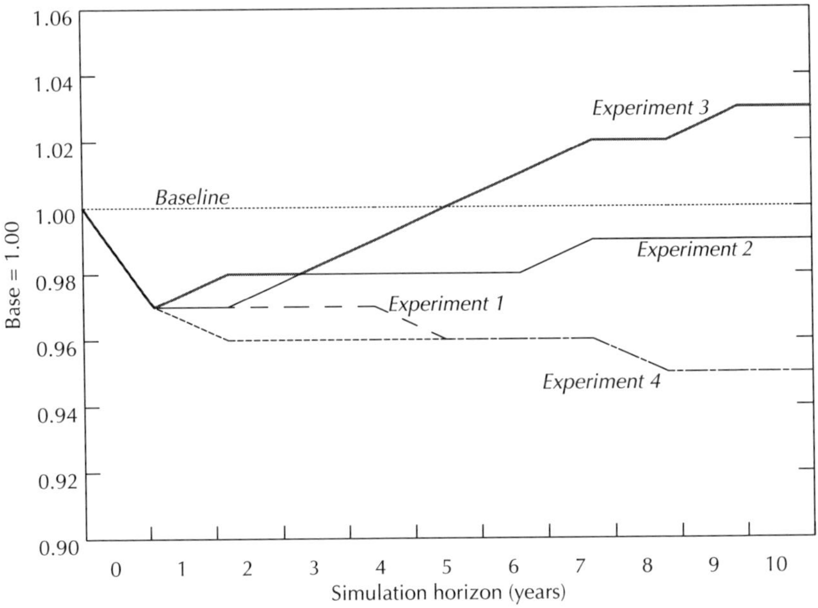

Source: Adam and Bevan (2004).
Notes: An increase in the index implies a depreciation of rate.
Experiment 1: Baseline: "non-productive" public investment; Experiment 2: "Productive" public investment–export biased; Experiment 3: "Productive" public investment–domestic goods biased; Experiment 4: "Productive" public investment–domestic biased but low returns.

stock is expanded but the increased public capital does not sustain higher private output. This allows us to isolate the pure demand-side effects of the aid flow. Experiment 2 examines the case where aid-financed public investment does enhance private sector productivity, but disproportionately in the nontraditional export sector (for example, by improving international market access). Experiments 3 and 4 consider the case where the productivity gains accrue overwhelmingly to producers of domestic nontradable goods (for example subsistence food). In Experiment 3, we assume this public investment has an immediate impact on productivity and occurs against a background or relative public- and private-capital scarcity so that the marginal returns to both kinds of capital are high. By contrast, Experiment 4 assumes a less favorable environment: the gestation lag for public investment is longer (it takes three years for investment to affect private productivity instead of one year, as assumed in Experiment 3); the economy is already working with somewhat higher levels of public and private capital (although the economy is still "capital scarce");

Figure 7.2. Total Exports

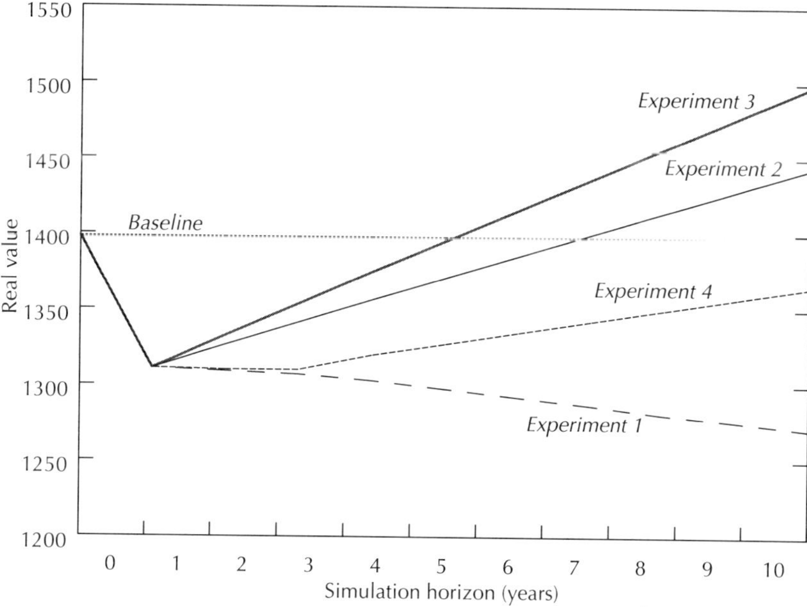

Source: Adam and Bevan (2004).
Note: Experiment 1: Baseline: "non-productive" public investment; Experiment 2: "Productive" public investment–export biased; Experiment 3: "Productive" public investment–domestic goods biased; Experiment 4: "Productive" public investment–domestic biased but low returns.

while the consequences of a temporary contraction of nontraditional export growth are more severe.

Experiment 1 highlights the classic Dutch-disease anxiety and reflects many of the features underpinning some of the econometric evidence discussed earlier. The aid flow obviously augments aggregate real income (Figure 7.4) but has little initial impact on GDP (Figure 7.3). The aid inflow does, however, lead to an appreciation of the export real exchange rate of about 3 percent, suggesting an elasticity somewhat larger than that estimated by Prati and others (2003), and a sizable contraction in exports (in favor of higher production of domestic goods). Moreover, the experiment suggests a progressive deterioration in overall economic performance that is, in fact, sufficiently large to reduce real disposable income below its initial level, despite the continued aid flow. This collapse reflects a decline in real private investment which, in turn, is underpinned by two features of the model. The first is the growth slowdown brought about by a squeeze on the nontraditional export sector. This is com-

Figure 7.3. Real GDP

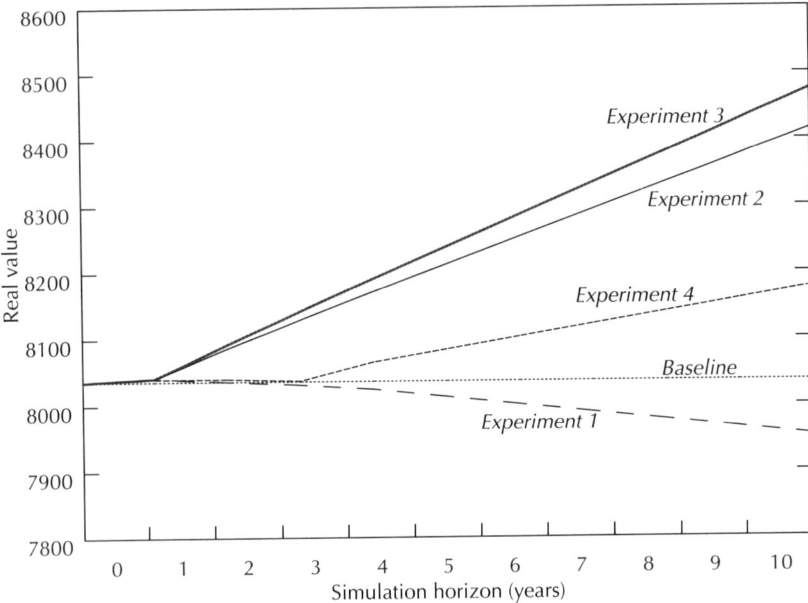

Source: Adam and Bevan (2004).
Note: Experiment 1: Baseline: "non-productive" public investment; Experiment 2: "Productive" public investment–export biased; Experiment 3: "Productive" public investment–domestic goods biased; Experiment 4: "Productive" public investment–domestic biased but low returns.

pounded, however, by the fact that the real exchange rate appreciation raises the cost of capital goods (since the model assumes, rather reasonably, that capital formation is intensive in nontradable services). This means that although the real exchange rate appreciation moderates over time, the deterioration of the capital stock ensures that the decline in export performance does not reverse and, hence, the initial welfare gains weaken over time. Over the medium term, therefore, aid that delivers no supply-side benefit does indeed act as a brake on economic growth.[20]

By contrast, in Experiments 2, 3, and 4 public infrastructure investment is assumed to raise the productivity of private factors of production. In Experiment 2, the gains from this infrastructure are biased in favor of the nontradi-

[20] These simulations are reported as deviations from a static baseline, represented by the horizontal line in each figure. In reality, of course, the no-aid increase baseline may reasonably exhibit some growth so that the contraction illustrated here represents a slowdown in the growth of output rather than an outright contraction.

Figure 7.4. Total Real Disposable Income

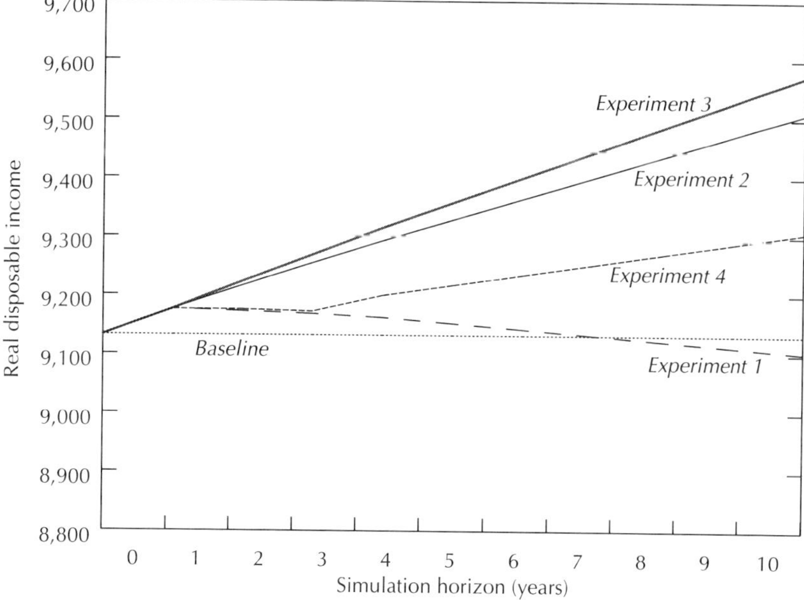

Source: Adam and Bevan (2004).
Note: Experiment 1: Baseline:"non-productive" public investment; Experiment 2: "Productive" public investment–export biased; Experiment 3: "Productive" public investment–domestic goods biased; Experiment 4: "Productive" public investment–domestic biased but low returns.

tional export sector. In this case, once the effects of the public investment begin to be felt, the now higher returns to producing nontraditional exports draw resources away from other sectors, including the nontradable sector, inducing a further appreciation of the real exchange rate (Figure 7.1). This real exchange rate appreciation has a deleterious effect on traditional exports (e.g., cash crops) in the short run. But as the supply-side effects feed in, nontraditional exports grow rapidly and this stimulates a fairly substantial cumulative growth in GDP and national income over the 10-year simulation horizon (Figures 7.3 and 7.4).

When the productivity gain is biased toward the production of domestic goods, however, as is shown in Experiments 3 and 4, outcomes are markedly different again. Here the productivity bias works to ease pressures in the nontradable sector and, in this case, is sufficiently strong to rapidly reverse the initial demand-side effects of the increased aid flows. The real exchange rate reverts to its initial value quite rapidly, despite the continued higher aid inflows. Indeed, it shows a depreciation over the medium term, which, as we shall see shortly, has important distributional implications.

As shown in this set of simulations, the domestic-biased supply response in Experiment 3 (when the external environment is relatively benign and identical to that assumed in Experiment 2) has a stronger impact on overall export performance and output growth than when infrastructure is specifically export-biased. This occurs because of the beneficial effects of the weaker real exchange rate appreciation in the short run, which helps suppress the overall cost structure for the export sector. This relative ranking is not guaranteed, however. In the case shown as Experiment 4, where longer gestation lags are associated with public investment, and where marginal returns to investment (both public and private) are somewhat lower, the export-biased case generates higher output growth over the medium term.

Finally, Figure 7.5 shows how aid inflows can worsen the income distribution, even when total national income is rising (as is shown in Figure 7.4 for Experiments 2 to 4). In this model, rural households are net producers of non-tradable food crops and urban households are net consumers. In cases where there is a strong export bias in the productivity gain induced by infrastructure spending, rural households enjoy a modest increase in real incomes (not shown here). This rise, however, is proportionally less than the rise in overall income, mainly because most of the positive demand-side effects of higher public investment expenditure are felt by the suppliers of goods and services to governments who tend to be found among urban households. The rural income share thus declines slightly. By contrast, when there is a strong domestic-goods bias in the supply response (which, as shown in Figures 7.3 and 7.4, generates higher aggregate income and output growth), this distributional effect is compounded by the fall in the relative price of food crops. This confers a direct benefit to net consumers of food (urban households) and a direct loss of real income to net producers. When the demand effects arising from the rise in overall national income are relatively weak (which may be the case if we consider basic foods), this disadvantageous shift in rural households' terms of trade may be sufficient to generate an absolute, as well as relative, loss of income and hence produce a variant of the "transfer paradox" noted above. This is the case here in Experiments 3 and 4.

V. Caveats, Summary, and Policy Implications

Although they only scratch the surface and are certainly not intended to be predictions for any specific country,[21] these simulations provide an interesting and informative perspective on what may lie behind the econometric evidence on the effect of aid flows presented earlier. But simulations are only

[21] Simulation models certainly can be used for country-specific predictions but to be effective in this role, much closer attention would need to be paid to the calibration of exogenous developments (and not just the aid shock) and the characterization of anticipated policy reactions to such changes.

Figure 7.5. Rural Share of Total Income

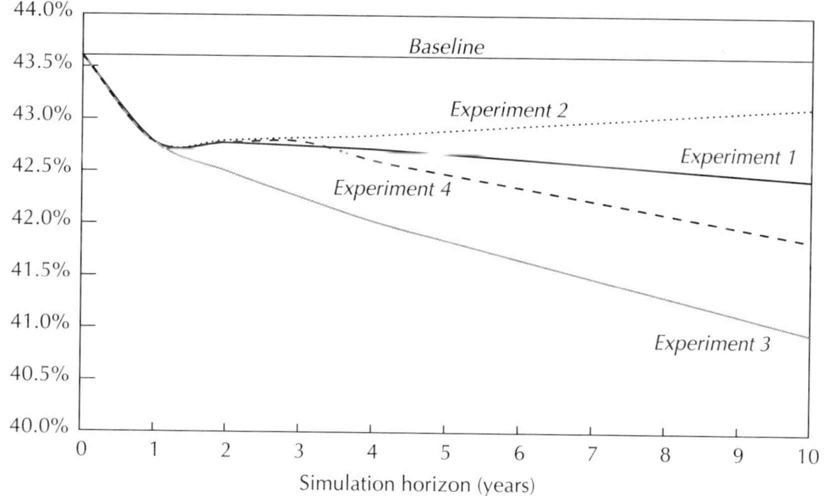

Source: Adam and Bevan (2004).
Note: Experiment 1: Baseline:"non-productive" public investment; Experiment 2: "Productive" public investment–export biased; Experiment 3: "Productive" public investment–domestic goods biased; Experiment 4: "Productive" public investment–domestic biased but low returns.

as good as the models generating them, and the model underpinning those presented in Figures 7.1 through 7.5 has many limitations. To name just a few: the initial calibration assumes no usable excess capacity in the economy; it assumes the evolution of the real exchange rate is not influenced by the nominal exchange rate regime (since domestic prices are assumed to be fully flexible) and there is no role for distortions arising from inflation. Moreover, the model does not allow for migration from rural to urban sectors in response to the shift in relative incomes nor provide for any form of human capital accumulation.

Listing the limitations is not really the point, though. The relevant issue here is that this analysis has moved beyond the econometric averages and has shifted attention onto some of the elements that determine the macroeconomic response to aid inflows and, in doing so, has helped identify some of the key "known unknowns."

For example, four central messages emerge from the simulations presented above:

1. When public infrastructure augments the productivity of private factors, and especially when there is an initial scarcity of public infrastructure,

there are potentially large medium-term welfare gains from aid-funded increases in public investment. These occur despite the presence of some short-run Dutch-disease effects and are compatible with growth in the export sector of the economy.

2. When supply-side responses to aid are important, however, real exchange rate overshooting may be a central feature of the economy's response to aid inflows.
3. The actual evolution of the economy will depend crucially on the form of public investment, how powerfully (and how quickly) it feeds back onto private production capabilities, and the costs of any short-run contraction of the export sector. Export promotion and growth, however, may be benefited as much, if not more, by public investment geared to improving the productivity of domestic nontradable goods production rather than directly to improving productivity in the export sector itself.
4. If aid flows do stimulate significant shifts in nontradable goods supply, this may aggravate underlying distributional tensions. In the case examined here, net suppliers of domestic goods will not share proportionately in the aggregate income gains to the economy, raising the possibility of a potential worsening in the income distribution.[22]

How does this discussion on forms of evidence contribute to the better management of aid?

I think two key implications emerge. The first is general, rather obvious, and does not necessarily imply specific macroeconomic policy actions. Just as the late Speaker of the U.S. House of Representatives, Tip O'Neil famously claimed that all politics is local, any serious analysis of the impact of aid relies on the dictum that "all macroeconomics is micro." More precisely, which of the wide range of simulated macroeconomic trajectories is relevant for a particular country and setting, depends intimately on the microeconomics underpinning public expenditure and its impact including:

- the demand-side characteristics of different forms of public investment, particularly their call on the nontradable goods sector, and the time taken for the effects of such investment to be realized;
- the extent of usable capacity and relevant unemployed (but employable) labor;

[22] How this effect is likely to translate into overall income distribution and poverty incidence will depend on the detailed structure of household activities (e.g., whether households are able to switch their production between subsistence and cash-crop production), patterns of off-farm employment, migration, and remittances, etc.

- the extent to which public expenditure alters private production capacities and how this varies across sectors; and
- how these constraints may vary with the rate at which public expenditure is scaled up.

An understanding of these microstructural features will clearly not emerge from macroeconomic data, but a burgeoning body of microeconomic and case-study evidence is increasingly able to provide some insight into the quantitative magnitudes of these features.

The second implication derives from the robust finding that there is a reasonable expectation that, in the short run, the real exchange rate will overshoot its medium-run value, particularly if aid inflows support productivity-enhancing public investment. This effect is likely to be larger and more protracted the more intensive is public investment in nontradables, the more attenuated the public investment process, and the stronger the productivity bias in favor of the export sector.

Thus while the medium-term profile for the economy clearly depends on the aid being spent, there may be a case for aid inflows to be accompanied by measures geared to smoothing the path of the real exchange rate in the short run. How this might be most efficiently achieved—given that the management of aid flows is only one of the issues competing for policymakers' attention—has been a major concern to central banks in a number of low-income African countries confronting surges in aid flows. While firm conclusions have yet to emerge, this is now an area of active debate.[23]

References

Adam, C., and D. Bevan, 2004, "Aid and the Supply Side: Public Investment, Export Performance and Dutch Disease in Low-Income Countries," Department of Economics Discussion Paper No. 201 (Oxford: University of Oxford). Available via the Internet: http://www.economics.ox.ac.uk/Research/wp/pdf/paper201.pdf

———, and G. Chambas, 2001, "Exchange Rate Regimes and Revenue Performance in Sub-Saharan Africa," *Journal of Development Economics*, Vol. 64 (February), pp. 173–213.

Adam, C., and S. O'Connell, 2004, "Aid versus Trade Revisited: Donor and Recipient Policies in the Presence of Learning-by-Doing," *Economic Journal*, Vol. 114 (January), pp. 150–73.

Adenauer, I., and L. Vagassky, 1998, "Aid and the Real Exchange Rate: Dutch Disease Effects in African Countries," *Intereconomics*, Vol. 33 (July/August), pp. 177–85.

[23] See, for example, Buffie and others (2004) for a discussion of alternative monetary and exchange rate rules in the face of persistent aid shocks (e.g., arising from debt relief).

Arellano, C., A. Bulíř, T. Lane, and L. Lipschitz, 2005, "The Dynamic Implications of Foreign Aid and Its Variability" IMF Working Paper 05/119 (Washington: International Monetary Fund).

Atingi-Ego, M., and R. Sebudde, 2001, "Uganda's Equilibrium Real Exchange Rate and Its Implications for Non-Traditional Exports," *Bank of Uganda Staff Papers*, Vol. 1, No. 1.

Baffes, J., I. Elbadawi, and S. O'Connell, 1999, "Single-Equation Estimation of the Equilibrium Real Exchange Rate," in *Exchange Rate Misalignment: Concepts and Measurement for Developing Countries*, by L. Hinkle and P. Montiel (Washington: Oxford University Press for the World Bank).

Bevan, D. L., 2005, "An Analytical Overview of Aid Absorption: Recognizing and Avoiding Macroeconomic Hazards," paper presented at the IMF Seminar on Foreign Aid and Macroeconomic Management, Maputo, Mozambique, March 14–15.

———, C. Adam, J. Okidi, and F. Muhumuza, 2003, "Economic Growth, Investment, and Export Promotion," Poverty Eradication Action Plan Revision 2002/03 Discussion Paper (Kampala, Uganda: Ministry of Finance, Planning and Economic Development).

Bigsten, A., and others, 1999, "Exports of African Manufactures: Macro Policy and Firm Behaviour," *Journal of International Trade and Economic Development*, Vol. 8, No. 1, pp. 53–71.

———, 2004, "Do African Manufacturing Firms Learn from Exporting?" *Journal of Development Studies*, Vol. 40 (February), pp. 115–41.

Bleaney, M., and D. Greenaway, 2001, "The Impact of Terms of Trade and Real Exchange Rate Volatility on Investment and Growth in Sub-Saharan Africa," *Journal of Development Economics*, Vol. 65 (August), pp. 491–500.

Buffie, E., C. Adam, S. O'Connell, and C. Pattillo, 2004, "Exchange Rate Policy and the Management of Official and Private Capital Flows in Africa," *IMF Staff Papers*, Vol. 51 (June), pp. 126–60.

Bulíř, A., and T. Lane, 2002, "Aid and Fiscal Management," IMF Working Paper 02/112 (Washington: International Monetary Fund).

Cashin, P., L. Céspedes, and R. Sahay, 2002, "Keynes, Cocoa, and Copper: In Search of Commodity Currencies," IMF Working Paper 02/223 (Washington: International Monetary Fund).

Chichilinsky, G., 1980, "Basic Goods, the Effects of Commodity Transfers and the International Economic Order," *Journal of Development Economics*, Vol. 7, No. 4, pp. 505–19.

Elbadawi, I., 1994, "Estimating Long-Run Equilibrium Exchange Rates," in *Estimating Equilibrium Exchange Rates*, ed. by J. Williamson (Washington: Institute for International Economics).

———, 1999, "External Aid: Help or Hindrance to Export Orientation in Africa?" *Journal of African Economies*, Vol. 8 (December), pp. 578–616.

Gautier, B., 2002, "Exchange Rate Impact on the Production and Productivity of Firms in Uganda" (unpublished).

Ghei, N., and L. Pritchett, 1999, "The Three Pessimisms: Real Exchange Rates and Trade Flows in Developing Countries," in *Exchange Rate Misalignment: Concepts and Measurement for Developing Countries*, by L. Hinkle and P. Montiel (Washington: Oxford University Press for the World Bank).

Gupta, S., B. Clements, and G. Inchauste, 2004, *Helping Countries Develop: The Role of Fiscal Policy* (Washington: International Monetary Fund).

Hinkle, L., and P. Montiel, 1999, *Exchange Rate Misalignment: Concepts and Measurement for Developing Countries* (Washington: Oxford University Press for the World Bank).

Kraay, A., 1999, "Exports and Economic Performance: Evidence from a Panel of Chinese Enterprises," *Revue d'Economie du Développement*, Vol. 1–2, pp. 183–207.

Lofgren, H., and S. Robinson, 2004, "Public Spending, Growth, and Poverty Alleviation in Sub-Saharan Africa: A Dynamic General Equilibrium Analysis," paper presented at the Centre for the Study of African Economies Conference, Oxford, March.

Mavrotas, G., 2002, "Foreign Aid and Fiscal Response: Does Aid Disaggregation Matter?" *Review of World Economics*, Vol. 138, No. 3, pp. 534–59.

Nkusu, M., 2004, "Aid and the Dutch Disease in Low-Income Countries: Informed Diagnoses for Prudent Prognoses," IMF Working Paper 04/49 (Washington: International Monetary Fund).

Nyoni, T., 1998, "Foreign Aid and Economic Performance in Tanzania," *World Development*, Vol. 26 (July), pp. 1235–40.

Prati, A., S. Ratna, and T. Tressel, 2003, "Is There a Case for Sterilizing Foreign Aid Inflows?" paper presented at the IMF Research Workshop, "Macroeconomic Challenges in Low Income Countries," Washington, October 23–24.

Radelet, S., 1996, "Measuring the Real Exchange Rate and Its Relationship to Exports: An Application to Indonesia," Discussion Paper No. 529 (Cambridge, Massachusetts: Harvard Institute of International Development).

Rajan, R., and A. Subramanian, 2005, "What Undermines Aid's Impact on Growth?" IMF Working Paper 05/126 (Washington: International Monetary Fund).

Sekkat, K., and A. Varoudakis, 2000, "Exchange Rate Management and Manufactured Exports in Sub-Saharan Africa," *Journal of Development Economics*, Vol. 61 (February), pp. 237–53.

Servén, L., 2003, "Real–Exchange-Rate Uncertainty and Private Investment in LDCs," *Review of Economics and Statistics*, Vol. 85 (February), pp. 212–17.

UN Millennium Project, 2005, *Investing in Development: A Practical Plan to Achieve the Millennium Development Goals* (New York).

Van Wijnbergen, S., 1985, "Aid, Export Promotion and the Real Exchange Rate: An African Dilemma," CEPR Discussion Paper No. 88 (London: Centre for Economic Policy Research).

Westphal, L., 1990, "Industrial Policy in an Export-Propelled Economy: Lessons from South Korea's Experience," *Journal of Economic Perspectives*, Vol. 4, No. 3, pp. 41–59.

Williamson, J., ed., 1994, *Estimating Equilibrium Exchange Rates* (Washington: Institute for International Economics).

World Bank, 2004, "Roads Out of Poverty: Assessing the Links Between Aid, Public Investment, Growth and Poverty Reduction," *Background Paper for Ethiopia Country Economic Memorandum* (Washington).

Yano, M., and J. B. Nugent, 1999, "Aid, Nontraded Goods, and the Transfer Paradox in Small Countries," *American Economic Review*, Vol. 89 (June), pp. 431–49.

Younger, S., 1992, "Aid and the Dutch Disease: Macroeconomic Management When Everybody Loves You," *World Development*, Vol. 20 (November), pp. 1587–97.

SESSION IV

Aid, Volatility, and Stabilization Policy. Does Aid Smooth Absorption or Exacerbate Shocks?

Reliability and Countercyclicality

8

Volatility of Development Aid

Unpleasant Bean Counting

ALEŠ BULÍŘ AND A. JAVIER HAMANN*

I. Introduction

The positive impact of foreign aid has been constrained by the lack of reliability in aid flows, which amplifies the already volatile macroeconomic environment of low-income countries. Donors and international financial institutions (IFIs) have begun to pay attention to this issue. Still, the recent changes in donor behavior and in the design of IMF-supported programs do not seem to have much impact on the way aid has been disbursed; aid disbursements remains volatile, unpredictable, and procyclical. The underlying causes of the volatility and unpredictability of aid appear not to have been addressed, which does not bode well for the success of the new initiatives and lending facilities being proposed by the Group of Seven (G-7) countries. In contrast, disbursing aid in a predictable manner, facilitated by recipients' compliance with program conditions, is likely to yield tangible economic gains.

Although the volatility and unpredictability of aid have long been recognized as a problem of macroeconomic management in low-income countries, the issue is receiving increasing attention in academia, as well as among bilateral donors and IFIs. Nancy Birdsall (2004) highlighted the problem in her typology of donor sins; her number 6 is called: "stingy and unreliable transfers."

---

*Aleš Bulíř is with the IMF's Policy Development and Review Department and A. Javier Hamann is with the Independent Evaluation Office. The authors are grateful to Tina Daseking, David Goldsbrough, Tim Lane, Mark Plant, Boriana Yontcheva, and participants at the Seminar on Foreign Aid and Macroeconomic Management (Maputo, March 14–15, 2005) for useful comments and suggestions.

A study by the OECD (2003) identified "uncoordinated donor practices" and "delays in disbursements" as two of the five most burdensome donor practices. In February 2005 G-7 finance ministers recommended that donor "deliver aid in a more predictable way" (HM Treasury, 2005). The United Kingdom proposed the International Finance Facility (IFF), a plan to increase aid flows with a goal of achieving the Millennium Development Goals, stating that the IFF would provide "for the first time, a predictable and stable flow of a critical mass of aid" (DFID, 2003). More generally, the international financial community has acknowledged the problem of macroeconomic volatility in low-income countries; it has called for the creation of new mechanisms aimed at reducing low-income countries' vulnerability to shocks.

Nonetheless, the problems of low-income countries do not seem to have been treated in a systematic manner (Lockhart, 2005). Specifically, the implicit goal of consumption smoothing, which could lead to sizable welfare gains in low-income countries, needs to be better integrated into the analysis. This will require greater recognition by donors and IFIs of the magnitude of the problem and also of their commitment to make reduced volatility an explicit goal of development assistance. The challenge for IFIs is to improve program design, particularly in the area of contingency planning. For bilateral donors, the challenge implies preventing aid from becoming a source of macroeconomic volatility and allowing a portion of aid to be used explicitly to neutralize other sources of volatility. For their part, aid-recipient countries need to commit to less erratic policy implementation.

In the remainder of this paper, we outline the problem, describe the data, and analyze in turn three alternative interpretations of aid volatility: relative volatility vis-à-vis fiscal revenue, unpredictability of aid disbursement relative to commitments, and failure of aid to smooth fluctuations in aggregate income. We then draw some policy implications.

II. Volatility and Predictability of Aid: What Exactly Is the Issue?

The issue of aid volatility did not feature prominently in the literature until fairly recently. Before the 1990s, the debate was centered on the effectiveness of the volume of aid and economists typically looked at aid committed and disbursed over long periods of time.[1] Subsequent research showed that aid was highly volatile, far exceeding that of other macroeconomic variables, such as GDP or fiscal revenue (Pallage and Robe, 2001; Bulíř and Hamann, 2003). Other key findings include the mild procyclicality of aid disbursements (i.e., aid tends to be disbursed mostly in periods when output or domestic revenue is high

[1] The neglect of volatility was not unique to development economics as the link between volatility and growth has been demonstrated only by Ramey and Ramey (1995).

and held back when domestic economic activity is contracting) and the fact that aid disbursements are difficult to predict, particularly on the basis of donor commitments (Bulíř and Hamann, 2003).

Aid-dependent countries are typically prone to large external shocks and are less able to cope with them, owing to their pervasive liquidity constraints and the lack of effective countercyclical policy tools. In this context, volatile, unpredictable, and procyclical aid can heighten overall macroeconomic instability, thus detracting from other beneficial effects of aid. Empirical estimates show that the consequences of aid volatility for aggregate growth and consumption are sizable (Lensink and Morrisey, 2000; Pallage and Robe, 2003; or Arellano and others, 2005). Not surprisingly, some of these models also illustrate the substantial potential gains, in terms of the stability of aggregate consumption, of disbursing aid in a stable and predictable manner.

Experience shows that the problematic characteristics of aid disbursements highlighted above are not easy to correct for various reasons. First, aid volatility reflects deeply-rooted problems with the way donor budgets are approved and administered.[2] Among other things, donor development agencies that make aid commitments are different from those that approve aid funding (parliaments) and disburse aid (ministries of finance). While the magnitude of this disconnect differs from country to country, it seems to be widespread.

A second source of aid volatility is conditionality—not only the conditions attached by bilateral donors, but frequently the requirement that aid recipients have the "seal of approval" associated with an on-track IMF-supported program. There are two sides to this issue. From the country's point of view, it means that complying with conditionality is important not only because of the merits of the policies to which conditions are attached but because it reduces volatility in aid inflows (Bulíř and Lane, 2004). But from the donor perspective, there is an obvious tension between the need to ensure that "good policies" are being implemented (an issue that goes beyond mere compliance with conditions but relates to the need for donors to be accountable to domestic constituencies for the aid funds they disburse) and the negative impact of disruptions in aid disbursements. Against this background, since the late 1990s the donor community and the IFIs have together developed a number of initiatives aimed at:

- improving domestic policymaking processes in aid-recipient countries,
- designing lending facilities better tailored to country-specific realities and based on improved modalities of conditionality,

[2] The United States exemplifies the vagaries of donor aid budgets: the U.S. administration announced that it would ask Congress for $1.7 billion in 2004 but it asked for $1.3 billion. In the end, only $1 billion was approved by Congress ("America's Promises," *New York Times*, January 28, 2005).

- providing debt relief, and
- harmonizing donor conditionality.

In this paper, we follow the methodology employed by Bulíř and Hamann (2003), with some minor modifications, and extend their data from 1997 to 2003. This longer period includes some years since the introduction of the various initiatives decribed above and allows us to assess whether they have led to a marked change in the behavior of aid flows.

The results are not encouraging. We continue to find that the volatility of aid is a multiple of that of domestic fiscal revenue. Furthermore, we find little evidence that the relative volatility of aid has decreased recently. Aid commitments are still poor predictors of disbursements, particularly in the poorest countries in our sample. As far as macroeconomic shocks are concerned, aid is still failing to compensate for negative GDP shocks. For example, during 1975–2003 countries hit by negative GDP shocks equivalent to 5 percent or more could have expect increased aid in only about one-fifth of all cases.

While we do not, in this paper, test directly how the various recent initiatives aimed at improving donor practices, domestic policy processes, program design, and so on have fared, we find no prima-facie evidence that they have had any meaningful impact on how aid is delivered. We take this to mean that the main underlying causes of aid volatility and unpredictability have not been confronted or addressed, or both. This does not bode well for the success of the new initiatives and lending facilities being proposed by the G-7 to tackle low-income countries' vulnerability to external shocks.

III. Data Issues

We now review our data and summarize the associated measurement problems. Compared with Bulíř and Hamann (2003), we extended the sample, added some countries, and filled some gaps in the coverage of domestic fiscal revenue.

The Dataset

Our database covers 76 countries from 1975 to 2003. The data on aid (disbursements and commitments) were taken from the World Bank's *World Development Indicators (WDI)*, which, in turn, are based on OECD data of Official Development Assistance (ODA). Fiscal data used in the paper—total domestic revenue in local currency—are drawn from the IMF's *International Financial Statistics (IFS)* and the IMF's regional databases, such as the WETA database for sub-Saharan Africa. All other series—nominal GDP in local currency and in purchasing power parity terms (PPP), market and PPP-based exchange rates vis-à-vis the U.S. dollar, and population—are drawn from the IMF's *World Economic Outlook (WEO)*. We have 29 annual observations for 50 countries and 24 annual observations for 18 countries in sub-Saharan Africa, where the revenue series do not begin until 1980 (Table A8.1). The remaining 8 countries are former communist states that started receiving aid only in the early 1990s and whose series are available for the last 9 to 12 years.

We applied the following filters to the universe of aid recipients:

1. All countries had to receive aid during the period under consideration (the minimum number of annual observation is 9 for Tajikistan).
2. To address the small-country bias, only countries with average population of more than 500,000 were included, eliminating most small island countries (World Bank, 2000).
3. To focus the analysis on countries where aid has some minimal macroeconomic impact, we included only countries where the sample aid-to-GDP ratio exceeds 1 percent. Thus, we excluded countries that receive either little aid or receive it only sporadically, such as the so-called capital account crisis countries.
4. To concentrate on development aid, we limited our sample to countries with average U.S. dollar GDP per capita below 3,000, eliminating such countries as Argentina or Brazil.

We found that both aid and revenue series are nonstationary, or, in a few cases, stationary around a deterministic trend, a result similar to that of Bulíř and Hamann (2003). Thus, we detrended our aid and revenue series using the Hodrick-Prescott filter (HP) and only then computed conventional measures of volatility.[3]

Common Denominator for Aid and Fiscal Revenue

The choice of a common denominator matters for the statistical measures of relative volatility. Typically, aid is denominated in U.S. dollars whereas domestic revenue is denominated in local currency units. Comparisons require first expressing both variables in the same currency. As a result, statistical measures of relative volatility are affected by the exchange rate. The impact of exchange rate volatility can be very large: on average, the coefficient of variation of the exchange rate is a multiple of that of domestic revenue.

[3] Following Pesaran and Pesaran (1997), we set the Hodrick-Prescott smoothing coefficient λ at 7. Changing the value of λ does not affect the estimated average relative volatility of aid and revenue, although it marginally affects sample variance of individual series.

To control for the impact of exchange rate volatility, we use three common denominators: percentages of nominal GDP, constant U.S. dollars in per capita terms, and percentages of purchasing power parity GDP. Arguably, denominating aid and revenue in per capita U.S. dollars is preferable if they both were to be spent on tradable goods, whose prices tend to be fixed in U.S. dollars (Bulíř and Lane, 2004). In reality, a significant portion of aid proceeds is spent on nontradable goods. More generally, if the objective is to assess the macroeconomic impact of aid, the relevant denominator is the aid-to-GDP ratio. Using PPP-based GDP and PPP-based exchange rates as opposed to nominal GDP and market exchange rates should, in principle, reduce the exchange rate volatility presented in the previous two calculations.

Why are we so concerned about the common denominator for aid and revenue? On the one hand, when expressing aid and revenue in U.S. dollars per capita, the volatility of domestic revenue becomes a composite measure of revenue volatility in local currency terms and exchange rate volatility. On the other hand, when expressing the variables in percent of GDP, the volatility of aid becomes a composite measure of aid volatility in U.S. dollars, exchange rate volatility, and the impact of those variables on GDP. Owing to the lack of a preferred denominator for aid and revenue, we use all three transformations and we keep in mind the biases that each of them are likely to introduce when we interpret our results.

IV. Measuring the Relative Variability of Aid and Revenue

As stated earlier, the aim of this paper is to re-examine the evidence on volatility and predictability of aid since our previous study. Years 1999–2000 provide a natural breaking point for the analysis as the introduction of the Poverty Reduction Strategy Papers (PRSP)[4] was expected to address some the inefficiencies in aid allocation, such as insufficient donor coordination or a lack of ownership by recipient countries. Specifically, we try to answer three questions:

- Does aid continue to be for the most part more volatile than domestic revenue?
- Has aid become more predictable (i.e., are aid disbursements better related to donor commitments)?
- Are aid inflows related to macroeconomic shocks in the recipient countries?

[4] PRSPs are required to be drafted for countries that seek debt relief under the Heavily Indebted Poor Countries (HIPC) Initiative.

Methodology

We follow closely the methods used in Bulíř and Hamann (2003). After downloading the raw data (aid in U.S. dollars and revenue in domestic currency) and expressing both series in common denominators (percentages of nominal GDP, percentages of PPP GDP, and constant per capita U.S. dollars), we take the natural logarithm in order to have both aid and revenue on the same scale.[5] Next, we de-trend aid and revenue series using the Hodrick-Prescott filter and calculate the sample variances of these series, θ^A and θ^R, respectively. We then define a measure of relative volatility as the average of the ratio of these variances, $\Phi = \theta^A/\theta^R$. In particular, we: (i) calculate Φ for each country; (ii) test the significance of sample averages and medians across countries;[6] (iii) calculate the correlation coefficient of de-trended aid and revenue, which amounts to a test of aid procyclicality as revenues are a strongly procyclical variable; and (iv) in order to check the robustness of our results, we arrange countries into three sub-groups according to their degree of aid dependency, and compare the results for the full sample with those obtained for the smaller samples.

Results

Building on a larger sample of aid and revenue data and a statistical methodology that focuses on pure volatility of aid and revenue, our findings are comparable with Bulíř and Hamann (2003). On this basis, we find no positive impact of recent aid initiatives on the relative volatility of aid.[7] More specifically, we find that aid:

- has been much more volatile than domestic revenue (with its volatility increasing recently),

---

[5] In Bulíř and Hamann (2003) we did not take logs, being focused primarily on the absolute size of aid and revenue shocks as relevant for the macroeconomic impact. As far as pure volatility is concerned, variables in logs are preferable because logs eliminate the scale problem. The scale difference remains a problem even after converting all variables into common denominators. For example, the aid-to-revenue ratio is about 0.37. Thus, when squared, the variances of domestic revenue are about ten times larger than those of aid.

[6] Given that Φ is a ratio of variances—estimated with a common number of observations per country in both the numerator and denominator—we checked the statistical significance of sample averages using an F-test.

[7] We hasten to say that this study does not present a counterfactual model of donor behavior in the absence of these initiatives; it could be that without these initiatives aid would be even more volatile than at present. Having said that, the available evidence makes us doubt this line of argument.

- has remained unpredictable, and
- has not acted as a buffer against GDP shocks.

Aid Volatility

We find that, first, the volatility of aid is much higher than that of revenue and, second, that the relative volatility of aid increased in the late 1990s and remained high in the early 2000s (Table 8.1). These results are statistically significant.

The average volatility of aid (**Φ**) is about 40 times higher than that of revenue when expressed in percent of GDP and 20 times higher when expressed in constant U.S. dollars per capita. Using medians, which are arguably better statistics in the presence of large outliers, the estimates of the relative volatility of aid are 23 times higher in percent of GDP and 6 times higher in constant U.S. dollars per capita. Furthermore, the relative volatility of aid is the highest in the subsamples of the least and most aid-dependent countries, defined as having aid-to-revenue ratios of less than 25 percent and more than 50 percent, respectively. Using medians, the result differs somewhat—**Φ** appears to decline with the increase of the aid-to-revenue ratio. Instances where aid is less volatile that revenue are rare: one in the GDP-based series and three in U.S. dollar per capita series.

On average, aid is delivered in a procyclical fashion—the average of individual-country correlation coefficient between aid and revenue is positive and statistically significant. Procyclicality is partly attributable to conditionality—when a country's policies go off-track, aid flows slow down.

The introduction of the PRSP in 1999 and related efforts at strengthening ownership, improving program design, and promoting donor coordination do not seem to have affected the relative volatility of aid. Indeed, aid has become more volatile in the late 1990s and early 2000s relative to the 1970s and 1980s, and there are a few ways of documenting it (Table 8.2). First, the average volatility of aid (**Φ**) was higher in the full sample (1975–2003) than in a subsample (1975–99). This result is robust across the three different common denominators used in this paper as well as across averages and medians. Second, during 2000–03 (the post-PRSP period), compared with 1995–98 (the pre-PRSP period),[8] the relative volatility of aid rose when measured by averages, and it roughly doubled when measured by medians.[9] Furthermore, the 1995–98 and 2000–03 **Φ** averages are much larger than the full sample average. This begs the question of when aid volatility increased.

We find that aid volatility increased sharply in the mid-1990s and remained relatively stable afterward (Figure 8.1). From 1975 to 1994, the **Φ**s have been relatively stable around a median of about 13 and 5 for the series in percentages

[8] We take 1999 as an interim period.

[9] The increases in relative volatility were large in several sub-Saharan African countries, such as Uganda, Tanzania, and Rwanda.

Table 8.1. Aid Is More Volatile than Revenue and Procyclical[1]
(Relative volatility of aid and revenue (Φ), correlation coefficient, and aid-to-revenue ratio)

	Full Sample	Subsample 1 *(A/R<25%)*	Subsample 2 *(25%<A/R<50%)*	Subsample 3 *(A/R>50%)*
	Variables expressed in percent of GDP			
Average	43.2***	65.8***	22.8***	87.8***
Median	12.5**	22.6***	11.1**	9.6**
Frequency indicators				
Sample size	76	15	47	14
Number of countries where Φ > 1	75	15	46	14
Number of countries where Φ < 1	1	0	1	0
Procyclicality of aid[2]	0.15***	0.07	0.20***	0.04
Number of countries where corr > 0	51	9	35	7
Aid-to-revenue ratio (in percent)	36.8	17.6	36.1	59.7
	Variables expressed in constant U.S. dollars per capita			
Average	17.9***	33.5***	10.7***	24.6***
Median	6.0*	6.3***	6.3**	4.4
Frequency indicators				
Sample size	76	15	46	15
Number of countries where Φ > 1	73	15	45	13
Number of countries where Φ < 1	3	0	1	2
Procyclicality of aid[2]	0.39***	0.30***	0.45***	0.28***
Number of countries where corr > 0	64	14	38	12
Aid-to-revenue ratio (in percent)	37.3	17.8	36.2	59.9
	Variables expressed in percent of PPP GDP			
Average	38.7***	26.3***	22.2***	–
Median	12.2**	11.7**	15.6***	–
Frequency indicators				
Sample size	76	67	8	1
Number of countries where Φ > 1	75	66	8	1
Number of countries where Φ < 1	1	1	0	0
Procyclicality of aid[2]	0.07	0.06	0.23	–
Number of countries where corr > 0	43	38	5	–
Aid-to-revenue ratio (in percent)	16.1	13.7	27.1	–

[1] All variables are in natural logs and filtered by the Hodrick-Precott procedure. Φ is a ratio of variances. '***, **, and *' denote significance at the 1, 5, and 10 percent level, respectively. The null hypothesis is Φ>1.

[2] Procyclicality is measured by a Pearson correlation coefficient between detrended aid and revenue; average of country-specific correlation coefficients. The null hypothesis is corr(A; R)>0.

Table 8.2. During 2000–2003 Aid Has Been More Volatile than Ever Before
(Relative volatility of aid and revenue (Φ))

	Full Period	1975–1998[1]	1995–1998	2000–2003
	Variables expressed in percent of GDP			
Average	43.2***	35.2***	244.0***	264.9***
Median	12.5**	11.0*	22.6**	46.8**
Frequency indicators				
Sample size	76	76	76	76
Number of countries where Φ > 1	75	73	72	76
Number of countries where Φ < 1	1	3	4	0
	Variables expressed in constant U.S. dollars per capita			
Average	17.9***	15.7***	81.1***	152.8***
Median	6.0*	5.2	9.9	16.3*
Frequency indicators				
Sample size	76	76	76	76
Number of countries where Φ > 1	73	73	66	70
Number of countries where Φ < 1	3	3	10	6
	Variables expressed in percent of PPP GDP			
Average	38.7***	31.1***	221.1***	243.3***
Median	12.2**	10.7*	23.4	40.7***
Frequency indicators				
Sample size	76	76	76	76
Number of countries where Φ > 1	75	73	69	76
Number of countries where Φ < 1	1	3	7	0

[1] '***, **, and *' denote significance at the 1, 5, and 10 percent level, respectively. The null hypothesis is Φ>1.

[2] For the exact starting year for each individual country see Table A8.1.

of GDP and U.S. dollars per capita, respectively. Starting in the mid-1990s, the median Φ doubled or trebled for all denominators. Except for the series in percentages of PPP-based GDP that recorded a small decline in 2000–03, all other results point to a further increase in the relative volatility of aid.

Aid Predictability

One could argue that aid volatility would be less of a problem if it were predictable.[10] An admittedly rudimentary assessment of predictability based on con-

[10] This would be is a weak argument, however, as all aid-dependent countries face serious liquidity constraints. They cannot borrow in capital markets to completely smooth out a volatile, but fully anticipated, pattern of aid disbursements.

Figure 8.1. Selected Countries: Relative Volatility of Aid and Revenue, Φ, 1975–2003[1]
(Sample median, N = 50)

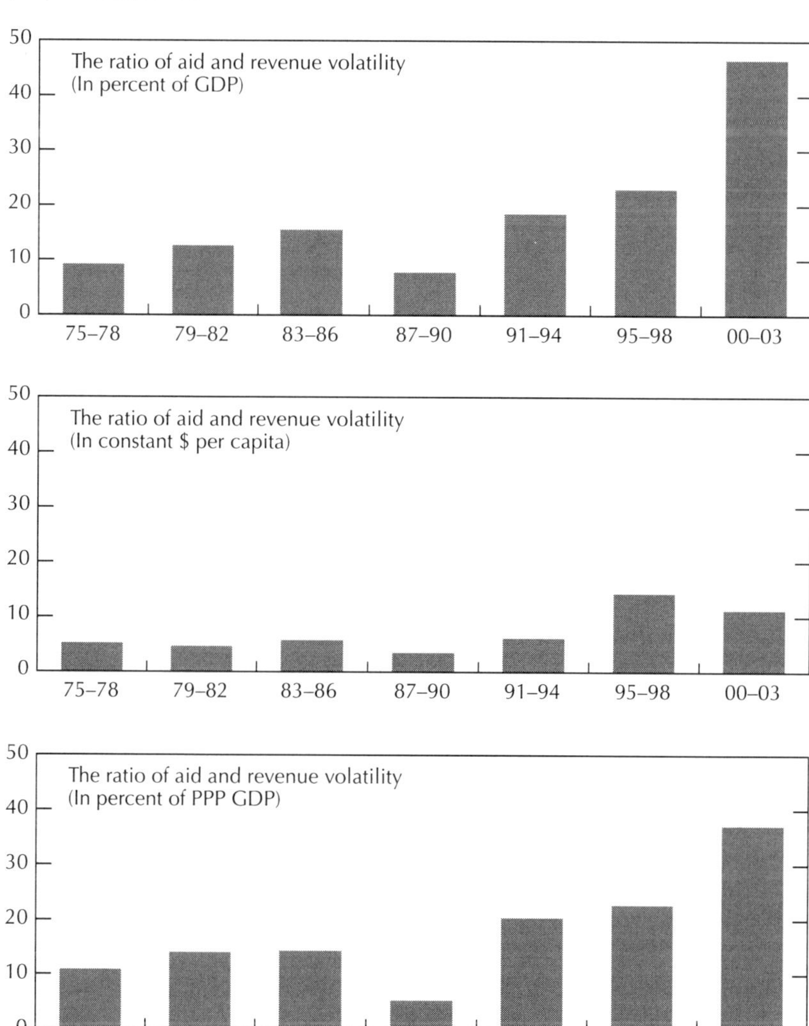

Sources: World Development Indicators; World Economic Outlook; authors' calculations.
[1]Only countries with complete series (1975–2003) are used in the calculation of the median.

trasting aid commitments and disbursements yields little evidence that aid predictability has improved recently.[11] Indeed, on average, actual aid delivery falls short of promises by more than 40 percent, in particular in the poorest countries.

While the excess of commitments over disbursements declined markedly in the late 1970s and 1980s, this trend ceased in the 1990s; indeed in 2000–03, disbursements fell short of commitments by almost 50 percent (Figure 8.2, upper panel). In other words, donors promised one-half more than they disbursed. The commitment-to-disbursement ratio was at one of its highest levels in 20 years. Moreover, we find evidence that the increase in the aid commitment-to-disbursement ratio was driven by larger commitments. During 2000–03, commitments grew by about 4 percent, relative to 1995–98, while disbursements fell by some 5 percent.

Even more disturbing is the finding that the unpredictability of aid (as measured by the ratio of commitments to disbursements) is negatively correlated with the level of development as measured by GDP per capita. While countries at the upper end of the income scale have on average received as much aid as promised, countries at the lower end of the income scale have received only about one-half of promised aid (Figure 8.2, bottom panel). These results provide little support for the argument that aid has recently been delivered predictably even if measured volatility has not declined. Of course, more sophisticated tests of predictability need to be carried out to reach a final conclusion on this issue.

Aid and Macroeconomic Shocks: Beyond Procyclicality of Aid

It could be even argued that donors may chose to ignore both aid volatility and procyclicality, as well as aid unpredictability, and focus on delivering aid when it is needed the most, that is, during periods of negative income shocks. Aid would therefore be countercyclical for large negative shocks only. This is the essence of "aid as an implicit insurance mechanism against shocks."[12] Low-income countries are more prone to shocks than other countries for various reasons: their economies are not diversified and are liquidity constrained or extreme weather fluctuation affects agricultural output, which employs the bulk of the population. It would seem logical that these countries would benefit from a fast and massive income-stabilizing mechanism. We argue that in the past this nexus

[11] Of course, high or erratic levels of commitments to disbursements may reflect a poor record of policy implementation in aid-recipient countries, and this is not being explicitly controlled for in this case. However, our earlier study (Bulíř and Hamann, 2003) showed that shortcomings in disbursements relative to commitments cannot be explained entirely in terms of compliance with conditionality under IMF-supported programs.

[12] Pallage, Robe, and Bérubé (2004) argue that the possibility of smoothing out the business cycle in low-income countries could be a major developmental contribution of aid.

Figure 8.2. Aid Commitments Are Poor Predictors of Disbursements, 1975–2003[1]

(Commitment-to-disbursement ratio)

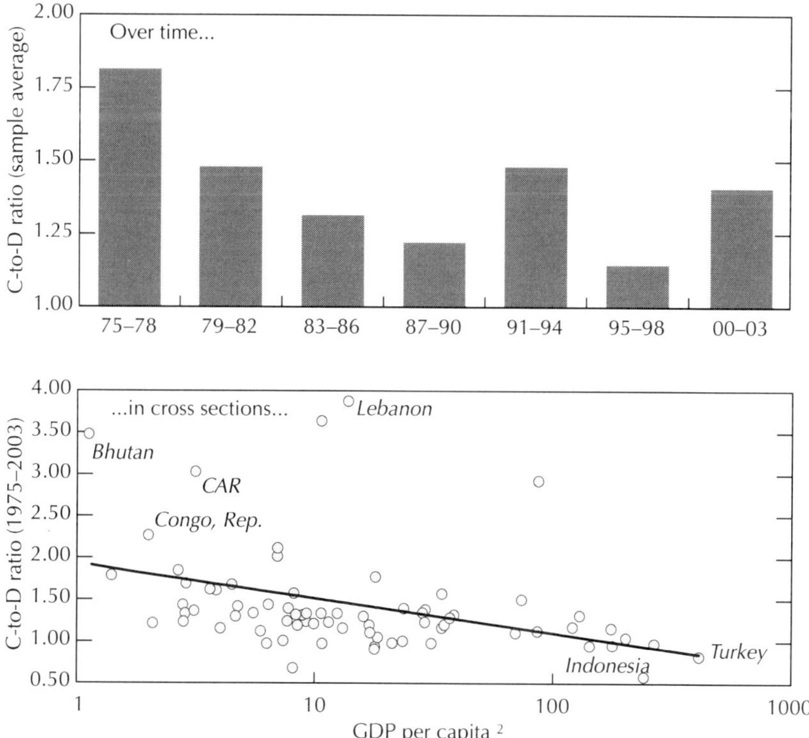

Sources: World Development Indicators; authors' calculations.
[1]Period sample average, N=76.
[2]In logs.

has not worked either: aid has failed to compensate for both large and medium-size GDP shortfalls. What kind of contemporaneous GDP and aid outcomes can be expected? Possible outcomes can be simplified in a two-by-two matrix, mapping income shocks (increases and decreases in GDP) and aid shocks (increases and decreases in aid disbursements in percent of GDP).[13] Under the implicit insurance mechanism, donors would step in with additional aid if the country is affected by a negative external shock, such as natural disaster, drought, or sudden

[13] A more precise exercise would be to ignore those cases of sharp negative income shocks when delivery of additional aid beyond humanitarian help is not feasible. Specifically, such shocks include war conflicts (e.g., Liberia, Rwanda or Sierra Leone), governments hostile to donors (e.g., Sudan and Zimbabwe).

terms-of-trade shock. Intuitively, for the insurance mechanism to work, additional aid would have to be disbursed very fast and in direct proportion to the loss of income. Of course, the insurance mechanism is implicit and it does not follow that the recipient countries should receive less aid in good times. The fact that aid increases or decreases under positive income shocks has no relation to the insurance mechanism. Indeed, aid can be mildly procyclical overall and it still can fulfill the role of the insurance mechanism, as long as it responds positively to large adverse shocks.

To test for the presence of an implicit insurance mechanism, we computed coincidence of a decline in per capita GDP and a contemporaneous increase in aid and found that substantial "additional" aid virtually never arrived when the country was hit by a sizable negative income shock, such as that equivalent to 10 or 20 percent of GDP (Table 8.3). We measured income by gross domestic product per capita in PPP terms because it reduces the impact of large exchange changes that were affecting other income measures.

In those cases where additional aid was disbursed, it typically fell far short of the initial GDP decline.[14] For example, in our sample of 2,010 annual observations, we have 27 occurrences of PPP GDP per capita falling by 10 percent or more. Although we have 31 occurrences of aid increasing by 10 percentage points of GDP, these increases did not coincide with the GDP shock. Looking at aid increases of 5 percentage points of GDP, these increases coincided with the output shocks in only three cases, or 11 percent of all 10-percent output shocks (Jordan 1989, Mozambique 1983, and Tajikistan 1994). These results are fairly similar for smaller GDP shocks (5 and 2½ percent): the chance of receiving additional aid in the wake of a GDP shock is between 10 and 20 percent for sizable aid increases (5 and 2½ percent of GDP) and 30 percent for small additional aid (1 percent of GDP or less). Furthermore, very few of those coincidences occurred in the 2000s to date.

Not only does additional aid not arrive on time, it often does not arrive at all. We tested also the possibility of aid arriving late—that is, the coincidence of a negative income shock at time *t* and a positive aid shock in time *t*+1—and found that on average the probabilities of delayed aid inflows were substantially smaller than for contemporaneous aid. Even when we considered jointly contemporaneous and lagged aid, the joint coincidence remained below one-third for additional aid equivalent to at least 2½ percentage points of GDP.[15]

We can also test the opposite relationship, that is, of rejecting the existence of an insurance mechanism. To this end, we computed the coincidence of negative

---

[14] We note that disbursements under IMF-supported programs are not counted as a part of aid. While some of the recent design changes in these programs, such as speedy augmentation of disbursements, could make an IMF-inclusive definition of aid more countercyclical, the amount of money involved is typically too small to contradict our findings.

[15] The detailed results are available from the authors on request.

Table 8.3. Aid Is Poor Insurance Against Negative GDP Shocks, 1975–2003[1]
(Coincidence of GDP declines and contemporaneous aid increases, in percent)

		GDP Decline in Percent (Number of GDP events)			
		20 (11)	10 (27)	5 (57)	2½ (95)
Aid increase[2] (Number of aid events)					
10 (31)	Coincidence[3]	0.0	0.0	1.8	2.1
5 (117)	Coincidence[3]	0.0	11.1	17.5	13.7
2½ (275)	Coincidence[3]	9.1	14.8	21.1	20.0
1 (532)	Coincidence[3]	36.4	33.3	29.8	28.4

Source: Authors' calculations.
Notes: The interpretation of the first cell is that out of 11 cases of annual GDP declines of 20 percent or more zero percent of them (none) coincided with an aid increase of 10 percent or more, of which there were 31 in the sample. Sample size is 2,010 observations.
[1] GDP per capita in constant U.S. dollars.
[2] Change in aid disbursements, in percentage points of GDP.
[3] Instances in which a given GDP shock (column) coincides with a given increase in aid (row). Expressed as a percent of total GDP decline events.

income shocks and aid declines and found that aid was just as likely to decrease as it was to increase in the wake of a negative GDP shock (Table 8.4). The income shocks in Tables 8.3 and 8.4 are identical and thus the coincidence of aid increases and decreases in the wake of negative income shocks can be assessed simply by comparing the respective cells in these two tables. For example, following a GDP decline of 10 percent, the coincidence of aid decreasing by 2½ and 1 percentage points were 19 percent and 30 percent, respectively. (For comparison, the coincidence of aid increasing by 2½ and 1 percentage points were 15 percent and 33 percent, respectively.) In sum, we find little evidence that during 1975–2003 aid served as an insurance scheme against large macroeconomic shocks.

V. Conclusions and Policy Implications

The discussion of aid effectiveness has been gradually moving away from narrowly defined measures of success, such as economic growth or poverty head count, to broader ones that encompass other aspects of the well being of aid recipients. The issue of the large economic costs associated with macroeconomic volatility in low-income countries and, in particular, the role played by an erratic stream of aid disbursements, is only now starting to be addressed in a systematic manner. Significant work remains to be done in order to understand the real extent of the problem and its key underlying causes.

In this paper, we have re-examined some of the issues taken up in Bulíř and Hamann (2003) on the volatility, predictability, and cyclicality of aid. The

Table 8.4. Negative Income Shocks Coincide with Negative Aid Shocks, 1975–2003[1]

(Coincidence of GDP declines and contemporaneous aid declines, in percent)

		GDP Decline in Percent (Number of GDP events)			
		20 (11)	10 (27)	5 (57)	2½ (95)
Aid decrease[2] (Number of aid events)					
10 (33)	Coincidence[3]	0.0	3.7	1.8	1.1
5 (117)	Coincidence[3]	0.0	3.7	3.5	3.2
2½ 309)	Coincidence[3]	18.2	18.5	17.5	15.8
1 (627)	Coincidence[3]	27.3	29.6	33.3	31.6

Source: Authors' calculations.

Notes: The interpretation of the first cell in the third row is that out of 11 cases of annual GDP declines of 20 percent or more 8.2 percent of them coincided with an aid decline of 2.5 percent or more, of which there were 309 in the sample. Sample size is 2,010 observations.

[1]GDP per capita in constant U.S. dollars.

[2]Change in aid disbursements, in percentage points of GDP.

[3]Instances in which a given GDP shock (column) coincides with a given decrease in aid (row). Expressed as a percent of total GDP decline events.

availability of six new years of data allowed us to look closely at whether the way in which aid is disbursed has improved since the late 1990s. We have assessed the impact of the introduction of various initiatives aimed at strengthening existing frameworks for granting debt relief; sharpening diagnoses of poverty and encouraging participatory processes; improving the design of macroeconomic programs; and enhancing cooperation among donors. All this was expected to lead to better compliance with IMF conditionality and a more predictable and less erratic stream of aid flows into low-income countries. Better compliance with conditionality, along with improved donor practices, should have also have led to aid being less procyclical.

The results of our study, however, are not encouraging. A retrospective analysis shows that aid has been more volatile than domestic fiscal revenues by a large margin. Looking more closely at recent developments, we find little evidence that aid volatility has decreased. Aid commitments continue to be poor predictors of disbursements, a problem that is particularly serious among countries with the lowest per capita incomes. The results are equally disappointing for the cyclical behavior of aid. We found disbursements to be procyclical on average and, worse, we found strong evidence that aid has failed to play any meaningful role in assisting countries to cope with large negative income shocks. For example, of all countries hit by negative GDP shocks of at least 5 percent, only one-fifth benefited from a concomitant increase in aid, and the ratio declined to one-seventh during 2000–03.

Although the paper does not test directly the impact of the above-mentioned recent initiatives, the results lead us to conclude that the main underlying causes of aid volatility and unpredictability have not been addressed.

This leaves us to ask: What next? In our view, ongoing work on strengthening the role of donors in helping low-income countries should:

- Give macroeconomic stability the prominence it deserves and make it an explicit goal of development assistance; and
- Discuss the various mechanisms through which aid can help achieve this goal. The most obvious way in which donors can foster a more stable environment is for them to disburse aid in a more stable and predictable manner. Donors also need to recognize the benefits of disbursing aid in a countercyclical manner: they should strive to find ways to respond more quickly and more efficiently to large adverse shocks.

But the potential for aid to reduce volatility in low-income countries is not confined to changing the time series properties of aid flows from the donor side. More ambitious targets for reserve accumulation in IMF-supported programs could be formulated, taking into account the extent to which low-income countries are vulnerable to various sources of external volatility, and aid could be used to fund this accumulation. Rules determining the circumstances under which these resources could be used and when they need to be replenished should, of course, also be part of IMF-supported programs. Critical for this to work is, of course, an acknowledgment by donor countries (not just donor agencies) of the tangible and meaningful economic gains associated with the use of aid to help poor countries dampen the destabilizing effects of external shocks.

In closing, we see a strong case for addressing the problems associated with macroeconomic instability in low-income countries in a systematic manner and, in this context, a specific role for aid. We doubt that recently proposed piecemeal proposals aimed at addressing specific sources of volatility will have a meaningful impact. What can be done until the donor community comes to terms with the use of aid as an explicit "insurance mechanism"? Aid-dependent countries need to adopt highly conservative fiscal policies and these should be supported by the international financial institutions. Building in a cushion of international reserves that could be drawn down to compensate for shortfalls in aid or other sources of budgetary revenue is an essential part of this approach. Obviously, a delicate balance needs to be struck as the opportunity cost of resources being used for reserve accumulation is likely to be high.

Table A8.1. List of Countries and Sample Periods

Country	Years	Country	Years
Albania	1992–2003	Kyrgyz Republic	1993–2003
Algeria	1975–2003	Lao People's Dem.Rep	1975–2003
Angola	1981–2003	Lebanon	1975–2003
Armenia	1994–2003	Lesotho	1975–2003
Bangladesh	1975–2003	Madagascar	1978–2003
Benin	1975–2003	Malawi	1975–2003
Bhutan	1981–2003	Mali	1975–2003
Bolivia	1975–2003	Mauritania	1975–2003
Burkina Faso	1975–2003	Mongolia	1975–2003
Burundi	1980–2003	Morocco	1992–2003
Cambodia	1987–2003	Mozambique	1975–2003
Cameroon	1980–2003	Nepal	1980–2003
Central African Rep.	1980–2003	Nicaragua	1975–2003
Chad	1980–2003	Niger	1975–2003
Colombia	1975–2003	Nigeria	1980–2003
Comoros	1980–2003	Pakistan	1975–2003
Congo, Dem. Rep. of	1980–2003	Papua New Guinea	1975–2003
Congo, Republic of	1980–2003	Paraguay	1975–2003
Côte d'Ivoire	1980–2003	Peru	1975–2003
Djibouti	1980–2003	Philippines	1975–2003
Dominican Republic	1975–2003	Rwanda	1975–2003
Ecuador	1975–2003	Senegal	1975–2003
Egypt	1975–2003	Sierra Leone	1975–2003
El Salvador	1975–2003	Sri Lanka	1975–2003
Ethiopia	1980–2003	Sudan	1975–2003
Fiji	1975–2003	Swaziland	1975–2003
Gambia, The	1975–2003	Syrian Arab Republic	1975–2003
Ghana	1975–2003	Tajikistan	1992–2003
Guatemala	1975–2003	Tanzania	1975–2003
Guinea	1980–2003	Thailand	1975–2003
Guinea-Bissau	1980–2003	Togo	1975–2003
Guyana	1975–2003	Tunisia	1975–2003
Haiti	1975–2003	Turkey	1975–2003
Honduras	1975–2003	Uganda	1975–2003
Indonesia	1975–2003	Vietnam	1981–2003
Jamaica	1975–2003	Yemen, Republic of	1975–2003
Jordan	1975–2003	Zambia	1975–2003
Kenya	1975–2003	Zimbabwe	1978–2003

References

Arellano, Cristina, Aleš Bulíř, Timothy Lane, and Leslie Lipschitz, 2005, "The Dynamic Implications of Foreign Aid and Its Variability," IMF Working Paper 05/119 (Washington: International Monetary Fund).

Birdsall, Nancy, 2004, "Seven Deadly Sins: Reflections on Donor Failings," Working Paper No. 50 (Washington: Center for Global Development). Available via the Internet: http://www.cgdev.org/content/publications/detail/2737

Bulíř, Aleš, and A. Javier Hamann, 2003, "Aid Volatility: An Empirical Assessment," *IMF Staff Papers*, Vol. 50 (March), pp. 64–89. Available via the Internet: http://www.imf.org/External/Pubs/FT/staffp/2003/01/bulir.htm

Bulíř, Aleš, and Timothy Lane, 2004, "Aid and Fiscal Management," in *Helping Countries Develop: The Role of Fiscal Policy*, ed. by S. Gupta, B. Clements, and G. Inchauste (Washington: International Monetary Fund).

Commonwealth Secretariat/World Bank Task Force, 2000, "Small States: Meeting Challenges in the Global Economy," Report of a Joint Task Force (Washington: World Bank). Available via the Internet: http://wbln0018.worldbank.org/html/smallstates.nsf/(attachmentweb)/final/$FILE/final.pdf

Department for International Development and Her Majesty's Treasury, 2004, "The International Finance Facility" (London: HMT and DFID). Available via the Internet: http://www.hm-treasury.gov.uk/media/D64/78/IFF_proposal_doc_080404.pdf

HM Treasury, 2005, "G7 Finance Ministers Conclusions on Development," London, February 5. Available via the Internet: http://www.hm-treasury.gov.uk./otherhmtsites/g7/news/g7_statement_conclusions050205.cfm

Lensink, Robert, and Oliver Morrisey, 2000, "Aid Instability as a Measure of Uncertainty and the Positive Impact of Aid on Growth," *Journal of Development Studies*, Vol. 36 (February), pp. 31–49.

Lockhart, Clare, 2005, "From Aid Effectiveness to Development Effectiveness: Strategy and Policy Coherence in Fragile States," background paper prepared for the Senior Level Forum on Development Effectiveness in Fragile States, London, January 13–14. Available via the Internet: http://www.oecd.org/dataoecd/33/11/34258843.pdf

Organisation for Economic Co-operation and Development, 2003, "Harmonising Donor Practices for Effective Aid Delivery," DAC Guidelines and Reference Series (Paris: OECD, Development Assistance Committee). Available via the Internet: http://www.oecd.org/dataoecd/0/48/20896122.pdf

Pallage, Stéphane, and Michel A. Robe, 2001, "Foreign Aid and the Business Cycle," *Review of International Economics*, Vol. 9 (November), pp. 641–72.

———, 2003, "On the Welfare Cost of Economic Fluctuations in Developing Countries," *International Economic Review*, Vol. 44 (May), pp. 677–98.

———, and Catherine Bérubé, 2004, "On the Potential of Foreign Aid as Insurance," CIRPÉE Working Paper No. 04–04 (Montreal: Centre Interuniversitaire sur le Risque, les Politiques Économiques et l'Emploi). Available via the Internet: http://132.203.59.36/CIRPEE/cahierscirpee/2004/files/CIRPEE04-04.pdf

Ramey, Garey, and Valerie A. Ramey, 1995, "Cross-Country Evidence on the Link Between Volatility and Growth," *American Economic Review*, Vol. 85 (December), pp. 1138–151.

SESSION V

Aid, Debt, and Fiscal Policy

9

Debt and New Financing in Low-Income Countries

Looking Back, Thinking Ahead

CHRISTINA DASEKING AND BIKAS JOSHI*

I. Introduction

If financing for development is to be effective, it must reconcile the objective of meeting the large needs of poor countries with that of maintaining their debt at sustainable levels. Recognizing the need to overcome extreme poverty and spur sustainable development in low-income countries, the international community adopted the Millennium Development Goals (MDGs) in September 2000.[1] As the recent report of the UN Millennium Project (2005) highlights, attaining these comprehensive and ambitious targets will require substantial efforts by the recipient governments to improve their policies as well as considerable external financing.

At the same time, many poor countries have a history of severe debt problems that have imposed a heavy burden on their economies and ultimately led to the adoption, by the IMF and World Bank, of the Heavily Indebted Poor Countries (HIPC) Initiative in 1996, its enhancement in 1999, and proposals

---

*Both authors are at the International Monetary Fund. The authors would like to thank Mark Plant of the IMF and participants at the seminar on Foreign Aid and Macroeconomic Management, for valuable comments, and Vikram Nehru of the World Bank for helpful suggestions on an earlier draft of the first section of this paper.

[1] The MDGs are a set of development targets agreed by the international community, which center on halving poverty and improving the welfare of the world's poorest by 2015.

for additional debt relief, more recently. The challenge for development finance going forward is therefore twofold:

- to ensure that poor countries receive sufficient funds to meet their ambitious development goals and, at the same time,
- to avoid sowing the seeds of a future debt crisis.[2]

A central question in this context is what form financial aid should take. Should it take the form of pure grants, or of concessional loans, which combine a grant with a commercial component? While both have advantages and disadvantages, the main distinction is that for a given cost to donors, loans provide more upfront financing while grants avoid the risk of future debt problems. In light of this trade-off, the decision about the appropriate combination of grants and loans is not straightforward and needs to be tailored to individual country circumstances.

This paper, a general introduction to the issue, consists of two parts. The first is an empirical backward-looking exploration of the debt dynamics in low-income countries to analyze the relevant channels that have led to debt accumulation (and reduction) in the past. The second part is a forward-looking theoretical examination of the pros and cons of grants versus loans. Together, both parts shed light on the various elements and circumstances that bear consideration in determining an appropriate mix of grants and loans in development financing on a country-specific basis.

II. Explaining Past Trends in Debt Dynamics

A simple debt dynamics equation provides a convenient way to examine how various factors affect the evolution of the debt ratio:

$$\underbrace{\frac{NPV_t}{X_t}-\frac{NPV_{t-1}}{X_{t-1}}}_{\text{change in debt ratio}}=\underbrace{\frac{(i_t-\varepsilon_1)}{(1-\varepsilon_t)}\frac{NPV_{t-1}}{X_{t-1}}}_{\text{endogenous debt dynamics}}+\underbrace{\frac{(1-GE_t)}{x_t}}_{\text{multiplier}}\underbrace{(td_t-tr_1-fdi_t+\Delta r_t)}_{\text{financing gap}}$$

This equation (derived in Box 9.1) breaks down changes in the net present value (NPV) of a country's debt-to-export ratio into three main components:[3]

[2] This challenge of balancing large financing needs with maintaining sustainable debt levels is also at the core of the low-income country debt sustainability framework developed jointly by the staffs of the IMF and the World Bank. See IMF and World Bank (2004a, 2004b, and 2005).

[3] The NPV of the debt-to-export ratio is used for reasons of consistency with the HIPC Initiative, which applies a qualifying threshold of 150 percent for this ratio. While the above dynamics refer to total external debt, the HIPC Initiative applies to public and publicly guaranteed debt only, which is the bulk of external debt in most low-income countries.

Box 9.1. Representing Debt Dynamics in Low-Income Countries

Underlying discussions of debt sustainability is a basic debt dynamics equation, derived from the balance of payments identity, with all variables expressed in U.S. dollar terms:

$$D_t = (1+i_t)D_{t-1} + TD_t - Tr_t - FDI_t + \Delta R_t \tag{1}$$

where, D_t = nominal debt stock at the end of period t;
i_t = average effective interest rate in period t (interest payments in period t divided by the debt stock in the previous period);
TD_t = combined deficit in the trade and services account;
Tr_t = sum of official grants and other current transfers;
FDI_t = net non-debt creating (i.e., equity) capital inflows; and
ΔR_t = change in official reserves and other foreign assets (with a positive change implying an increase in reserves).

Equation (1) allows a simple interpretation of a country's debt dynamics: its gross external debt increases ($D_t - D_{t-1} > 0$) if its current account deficit ($TD_t + i_tD_{t-1} - Tr_t$), plus any reserve accumulation (ΔR_t), exceeds the level of net equity inflows (FDI_t).

Given the concessionality in loans extended to low-income countries, the net present value (NPV) of debt is the more relevant metric for evaluation. Equation (1) can be transformed into this form by adopting the concept of the grant element, *GE*. Note that the grant element is defined as the difference between the debt stock and the NPV of debt, expressed in percent of the debt stock:

$$GE_t = \frac{(D_t - NPV_t)}{D_t} \Leftrightarrow D_t = \frac{NPV_t}{(1-GE_t)} \tag{2}$$

Substituting in this manner for the nominal value of debt in equation (1) yields:

$$\frac{NPV_t}{(1-GE_t)} = (1+i_t)\frac{NPV_{t-1}}{(1-GE_{t-1})} + TD_t - TR_t - FDI_t + \Delta R_t \tag{3}$$

Multiplying the above equation by $\frac{(1-GE_t)}{X_t}$, where X_t denotes the U.S. dollar value of exports in period t, and ε_t the growth rate of exports, such that $X_t = (1+\varepsilon_t)X_{t-1}$, leads to the following equation for the NPV of the debt-to-export ratio in period t:

$$\frac{NPV_t}{X_t} = \frac{(1+i_t)}{(1+\varepsilon_t)}\frac{NPV_{t-1}}{X_{t-1}}\frac{(1-GE_t)}{(1-GE_{t-1})} + \frac{(1-GE_t)}{X_t}(TD_t - TR_t - FDI_t + \Delta R_t) \tag{4}$$

Assuming, for simplicity, that the grant element remains unchanged between periods *t-1* and *t*, and denoting by lower-case letters ratios in percent of GDP (e.g., $x_t = \frac{X_t}{GDP_t}$), equation (4) can be transformed into the following expression for the change in the NPV of the debt-to-export ratio:

$$\frac{NPV_t}{X_t} - \frac{NPV_{t-1}}{X_{t-1}} = \frac{(i_t - \varepsilon_t)}{(1+\varepsilon_t)}\frac{NPV_{t-1}}{X_{t-1}} + \frac{(1-GE_t)}{x_t}(td_t - tr_t - fdi_t + \Delta r_t) \tag{5}$$

Similar expressions can be derived for the debt dynamics in terms of GDP or revenue.

- The *external financing gap* captures most directly the tension between debt sustainability and new financing. A positive gap—defined as a deficit in the trade and services account (*td*) not financed by grants and other current transfers (*tr*), equity inflows (*fdi*), or reductions in foreign assets, including reserves (Δr)—adds to a country's external debt.
- The *multiplier* determines the impact of a given financing gap, expressed as a percent of GDP, on the NPV of the debt-to-export ratio. It is derived by dividing the gap by the export-to-GDP ratio (x) and multiplying by (1-GE)—where GE is the average grant element—to adjust for the concessionality of financing. Both low export ratios and small grant elements magnify the effect of the financing gap on the debt ratio.
- The *endogenous debt dynamics* describe the changes in the debt ratio that occur independent of new financing. They result from the difference between the (concessional) interest rate (i) and the growth rate of exports (ε) in the denominator of the debt ratio. The larger the initial debt ratio, the stronger this endogenous effect—which is beneficial in "normal" times, when export growth exceeds the concessional interest rate but works in the opposite direction, worsening an already high debt ratio, when export growth is very low or negative.

The equation implies that the debt-to-export dynamics in a given country are more favorable:

- the higher the country's growth rate of exports relative to the (concessional) interest rate, with the effect being magnified when the initial debt ratio is large;
- the smaller its financing gap;
- the higher the concessionality of its debt; and
- the more export-oriented it is, that is, the higher its share of exports in GDP.

The debt dynamics equation provides some interesting insights into past trends. Using data for 1993–2002 for a sample of 72 low-income countries, Table 9.1 summarizes the average experience of a "representative" country.[4]

- The endogenous debt dynamics of the representative low-income country were favorable, as export growth rates of 8.1 percent exceeded the average interest rate of 2.7 percent. This implies a decline in the NPV of the debt-to-export ratio of as much as 15 percentage points a year for a debt ratio of 300 percent (close to the historical average of 294 percent),

[4] The debt dynamics of the "representative" low-income country are obtained by computing cross-country averages for the individual variables of the debt-dynamics equation.

Table 9.1. Debt Dynamics in Low-Income Countries, 1993–2002[1]
(Annual average change in NPV of debt-to-exports ratio)

	Formula Based			Actual Change[2]	Unexplained Changes[3]
	NPV=100	NPV=150	NPV=300		
Endogenous dynamics	–5.0	–7.5	–15.0		
Multiplier times financing gap	5.0	5.0	5.0		
Total change in debt ratio	**0.0**	**–2.5**	**–10.0**	**–17.8**	**–8.2**
Memorandum items					
Multiplier, (1-*GE*)/*x*	2.2	2.2	2.2		
Financing gap (in percent of GDP)	2.3	2.3	2.3		

[1] Sample includes 72 of the low-income countries, defined as eligible for PRGF loans by the IMF.
[2] The actual average NPV of debt-to-exports ratio was about 294 percent over 1993–2002.
[3] Equivalent to the actual average change in the debt ratio per year minus the change implicit in the formula, calculated at the average NPV of debt-to-exports ratio of 294 percent (which is –9.7). Apart from data problems, the discrepancy can be explained, inter alia, by debt relief.

and 7½ percentage points for debt ratios at the HIPC threshold of 150 percent.

- The average financing gap during the past 10 years of about 2¼ percent of GDP and the multiplier of 2.2 implied average annual increases in the NPV of the debt-to-export ratio of 5 percentage points.
- Combining both effects, the representative country should have experienced favorable debt dynamics, even without debt relief, as long as the NPV of the debt-to-export ratio remained above 100 percent. Indeed, with an initial average debt ratio of 294 percent, the decline should have been quite rapid, at about 10 percentage points annually.

Perhaps contrary to common belief, actual debt ratios in low-income countries declined, on a simple-average basis, by 18 percentage points annually during the 10 years to 2002. The additional drop beyond what is explained by the debt equation reflects mainly the effect of debt relief, including that delivered through the HIPC Initiative. This obviously begs the question of why debt relief was necessary and the reason for the widespread perception that debt problems were not likely to be resolved on their own.

First, debt ratios were very high in the early 1990s. Therefore, even if the trend was favorable, debt-service payments were crowding out priority spending in other areas. Second, the analysis of a representative country obscures much of the variation across countries. As shown in Table 9.2, differences across countries, measured by standard deviations of the relevant parameters, are high. The multiplier in particular—which indicates sensitivity of a given

Table 9.2. Debt Dynamics in Low-Income Countries, 1993–2002
(In percent of GDP, unless otherwise indicated)

	Cross-Country Average	Cross-Country Std. Dev.
Interest rate, in percent (*i*)	2.7	2.7
Export growth, in percent (ε)	8.1	7.5
Grant element, in percent (*GE*)	29.2	12.9
Export ratio (*x*)	32.5	19.1
Trade and services deficit (*td*)	12.9	14.2
Transfers (*tr*)	8.4	8.5
FDI (*fdi*)	3.0	4.2
Increase in reserves (Δr)	0.8	2.9

country's debt-to-export ratio to changes in the financing gap—varies widely (Figure 9.1). Depending on the concessionality of financing available to the country and the relative size of its exports base, an identical current account shock (in percent of GDP) may have vastly different outcomes on the NPV of the debt-to-export ratio. In Guyana, for instance, an increase of 1 percentage point of GDP in the external financing gap leads to a rise in the debt-to-export ratio of only ¾ percentage points; in Burundi, on the other hand, the ratio rises by nearly 9 percentage points. Indeed, all five countries that experienced increases in their debt ratios of 200 percentage points or more over the 10-year period (Burundi, Central African Republic, Comoros, Eritrea, and Rwanda) had above-average multipliers.[5]

Arguably, the strongest case against optimism based on past trends is that the decline in average debt ratios was the result of a small group of countries that experienced very rapid export growth. This group includes such countries as Albania and Guinea Bissau, which recorded export growth rates of about 30 percent a year. An analysis of the debt dynamics based on the median (as opposed to the mean) of the relevant variables reduces the effect of such outliers and results in a much less favorable assessment—with a stable, as opposed to a declining, trend in the debt ratio. Furthermore, using GDP rather than exports as the denominator implies indeed a deteriorating debt ratio based on the debt-dynamics equation (that is, without considering debt relief).[6]

[5] The comparison of changes in the debt ratio is somewhat misleading to the extent that some countries have benefited from sizable debt relief.

[6] This result is consistent with the analysis presented in the recent review of IMF-supported programs, *The Design of IMF-Supported Programs*, IMF Occasional Paper No. 241 (Washington: International Monetary Fund). This study suggests that actual current account deficits in IMF-supported programs of low-income countries (under the IMF's Poverty Reduction and Growth Facility, PRGF) were higher than needed to stabilize the debt-to-GDP ratio of the median country.

Figure 9.1. Debt-to-Exports Multipliers in Low-Income Countries[1]

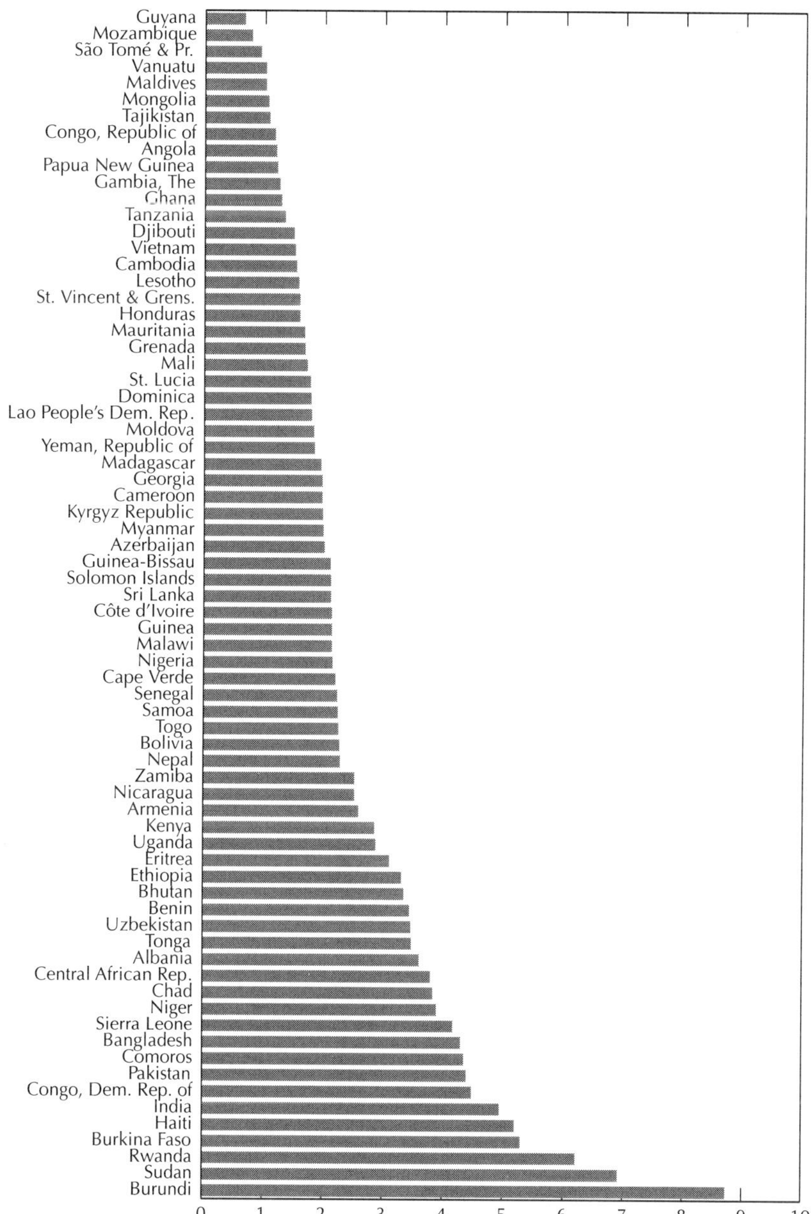

Source: IMF, World Economic Outlook; and World Bank, Global Development Finance.

[1]The multiplier measures the percentage point increase in the debt-to-exports ratio, due to a 1 percentage point of GDP increase in the external financing gap. It is defined as (1-grant element)/exports-to-GDP ratio, using 2001 grant elements and average exports-to-GDP rations over 2000-02.

An analysis of past debt dynamics, as well as a cursory examination of variation among countries, therefore reveals that borrowing at low concessional rates alone does not ensure stable or declining debt ratios. Although past average trends suggest favorable dynamics for low-income countries as a group, several cautionary notes arise:

- The debt dynamics in individual countries have differed greatly across countries and are also likely to display large variation in the future. While some countries have seen large improvements in their debt-to-export ratios, the median country would have only been able to stabilize its debt ratio at a relatively high level in the absence of debt relief. Moreover, export growth has generally been higher than GDP (and revenue) growth, implying a less favorable picture for the debt dynamics based on these alternative denominators.
- Efforts to attain the MDGs will undoubtedly entail high financing needs. If these are not met by additional grants, debt ratios are likely to deteriorate, with large variations across countries.
- As long as a country's export base is small, debt sustainability remains particularly fragile; a small shock could derail the debt dynamics, even with loans at highly concessional terms. The same holds for revenues in reference to the debt-to-revenue ratio. This underscores the need to strengthen export (and revenue) bases as primary insurance against deteriorations in debt dynamics.
- Aid flows tend to be volatile, particularly in highly aid-dependent countries; they also tend to be procyclical (Bulíř and Hamann, 2003). These fluctuations further underscore the fragility of a country dependent on external resource flows to finance development activities, and they point to the need for prudent debt management.

Based on these considerations, the goal going forward should be to generate significant upfront financing in order to help low-income countries attain their ambitious development targets without undermining debt sustainability. The remainder of the paper discusses how the terms of financing—that is, the mix between grants and loans—might be tailored most appropriately to support this goal.

III. Grants or Loans

Any discussion of the appropriate mix of grants and loans goes back to the classic economic problem of scarcity. Grant resources available for development finance are limited, but for a given resource cost to donors more upfront resources can be mobilized if aid is provided in the form of concessional loans (Box 9.2). Thus, pure grants are at one end of a spectrum of concessional

Box 9.2. Concessional Loans and Grants: Some Basic Features

Any concessional loan can be broken down into a commercial component, provided at market rates, and a grant component. The commercial component is the NPV of the loan, derived as the stream of debt-service payments, discounted by the (risk-free) market interest rate. The grant component (G) is the difference between the nominal loan amount (L) and the NPV (i.e., $L = G + NPV$) and reflects the cost to the donor of providing the concessional loan. Thus, a donor can either provide a pure grant of, say, $100, or "leverage" the grant through additional commercial resources—for example, by providing a loan of $200 with a grant element of 50 percent and a corresponding NPV of $100. While the cost to the donor is the same ($100), the loan allows for a larger provision of resources upfront ($200 instead of $100). But these additional resources are implicitly provided on commercial terms, potentially undermining the country's debt-servicing capacity.

In theory, a country is better off receiving a grant than a concessional loan with an identical grant component, if the rate of return on its investment is lower than the market rate (i.e., the discount rate used to derive the grant element). This is illustrated in the chart below, assuming that the resources are invested in a 40-year project with a constant rate of return of 3.5 percent. At a discount rate of 5 percent, this implies an NPV return of 75 cents for every invested dollar.

Comparison of Loan- and Grant-Financed Project
(Rate of return above concessional interest rate, but below discount rate)

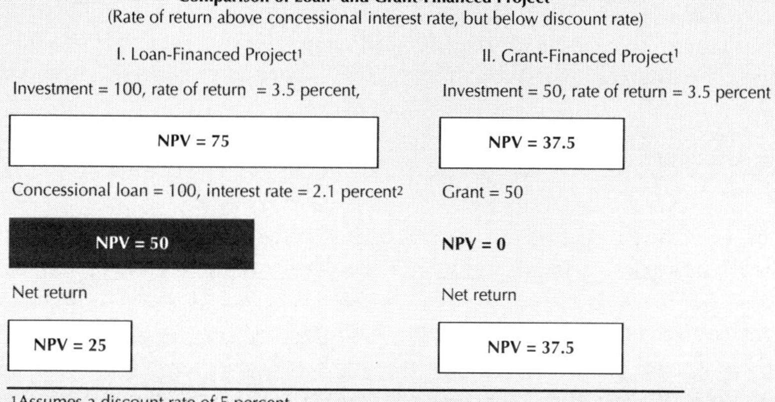

[1]Assumes a discount rate of 5 percent.
[2]Assumes a 40-year maturity period, with a bullet payment at the end.

The left-hand side shows the payoff resulting from an *investment of $100, financed by a concessional loan* with a grant element of 50 percent. In this case, the net return is $25 (i.e., $75 investment return minus $50 NPV of debt service).

The right-hand side shows the case of a pure *grant-financed investment of $50* (implying the same donor cost).

Although the gross return of the project is lower, at $37.50, no debt service is due, implying that the country is better off with the smaller grant-financed project. This result holds, as long as the rate of return on the project is lower than the discount rate. There may be other considerations beyond the direct (financial) rate of

(continued on page 228)

Box 9.2. Concessional Loans and Grants: Some Basic Features *(Continued)*

return, however, such as positive externalities and social considerations, that could qualify this result arguing for larger investments.

Finally, the country is still better off with the concessional loan than it would be with no financing at all. As long as the return on the project exceeds the concessional interest rate (2.1 percent in the example), the payoff is positive—although the financially wiser choice would still be a lower investment financed by a grant.*

*The example assumes a synchronized amortization and project-liquidation schedule (in this case at the end of the period) and no depreciation. If amortization payments occurred earlier, and depreciation was factored in, the implicit rate of return on the project would need to be higher than the concessional interest rate if the loan-financed project is to be financially beneficial.

finance. When grants are "leveraged," however—that is, distributed in the form of (larger) concessional loans—the additional resources are implicitly provided on commercial terms (equivalent to the NPV of the loan), which risks creating future debt-servicing problems. Donors must therefore decide how to distribute their scarce aid resources most efficiently, by weighing the benefit of large upfront financing against the risk of future debt problems.

The Case for Grants

Advocates of a grants-only approach stress the negative experience with loans to finance development.[7] They argue that the history of lending to low-income countries, even on highly concessional terms, has been marred by failure, as evidenced by a pervasive "lend-and-forgive" cycle. Grants, by their very own nature, carry no inherent debt sustainability risk—although the debt ratio, as discussed above, is still vulnerable to adverse movements in the denominator (exports, GDP, or fiscal revenue). Many grant advocates argue further that the ultimate need for debt relief is merely an opaque way of providing grants ex post.

In addition, a number of factors specific to low-income countries caution against the use of loans for development finance. The need to repay a loan requires the production of tradable goods or services—which could be exported or used to replace imports—in order to generate the necessary foreign exchange (the transfer problem). Many projects, particularly in the social area, may not

[7] The Meltzer Commission report (2000) recommended relying more on grants for development finance, with similar calls echoed recently by Bulow and Rogoff (2005), who highlight the deleterious effects of loan-financed development spending.

have an immediate tradable output, making them unsuitable as candidates for loans. In addition, returns on many projects accrue only over a long period, are highly uncertain, and may not be easily captured by the borrowing government—either directly or through additional tax revenue. Grants would thus seem to be the appropriate choice here.

The Case for Loans

Providing grants in lieu of loans, however, without an offsetting reduction in the amount of aid, may have important implications for the distribution of aid between current and future recipients. Given that loans are repaid, they generate a pool of future resources to be on-lent to other countries—allowing concessional loans to finance more projects over time than their grant equivalent.[8] Foregoing these reflows, while providing the same financing today, would require a massive ratcheting up in donor commitments in the future to the main development finance institutions, such as the International Development Association (IDA) of the World Bank, to match the level of currently envisaged resource flows.[9] Thus, an across-the-board switch from loans to grants of the same magnitude would increase uncertainties about the future availability of aid, as the intentions of current donor governments regarding their prospective contributions are not enforceable on future generations of policymakers.

The leverage of foreign aid through the use of concessional loans is also justified in the presence of market-information externalities. Most low-income countries are effectively cut off from the international capital markets, and the few that have sovereign ratings face high risk premiums on market borrowing. To the extent that these high premiums reflect limited market information, foreign aid can serve as a bridge to full-fledged market participation. Models of information externalities, such as that of Caplin and Leahy (1998), could be reinterpreted in this context; markets do not know if particular projects in developing countries are worthwhile, and financing from development agencies makes their worth clearer

---

[8] Cline (2003) cites the "economics of charity" reasoning of Schmidt (1964) to argue that loans are better than grants. However, this argument is based on the assumption that lenders are able to charge an interest rate that is not only below the rate of return on investment in the recipient country but also above the corresponding rate in the donor country. It is therefore not strictly applicable to development finance at concessional rates—although the general idea remains applicable to the commercial component of a concessional loan.

[9] According to the IDA website (http://www.worldbank.org/ida/), in 2003 alone, India borrowed $686.6 million. Given the grace period and long maturity of IDA loans, debt service on these loans will continue for a long time. Similarly, China, which "graduated" from IDA in 1999, will be servicing its debt for decades to come.

and acts, over time, to bring the risk premium down.[10] The abovementioned leveraging power of concessional loans implies that more projects may be financed across countries, thus enabling better transmission of such information content.

Incentive effects may also favor the use of loans as instruments of development finance. Advocates of loans have argued that the need to service them makes recipient countries more cautious about the use of these funds. In a dynamic setup, access to loans may also induce low-income countries to develop their debt management capabilities, further preparing them for participation in the international capital markets. Additionally, loans may be used to "cajole" recipient countries into making appropriate policy changes (Odedokun, 2004).[11]

Finally, the use of loans to leverage grant resources may be justified even if they often fail ex post. As concessional loans offer a way to convert limited grant resources into higher upfront financing, they enable low-income countries to undertake a larger number of projects than a grants-only approach would permit. Assuming there are many viable projects in the developing world, such a leveraging strategy may well be appropriate, even if some investments eventually fail and the country requires debt relief as a result. As long as successful projects—which could not have been financed through grants alone—provide the reflows to cover debt relief on failed projects and, at the same time, reduce future aid dependence, both recipients and donors are likely to benefit. In a sense, the additional financing generated by providing loans instead of grants can be interpreted as an investment by donors in a mutual fund that pools risks across countries. This reasoning qualifies the conclusion of grant advocates that the observed lend-and-forgive cycle warrants a shift from loans to grants; the validity of this argument, however, hinges on whether the prospect of debt relief itself alters recipient countries' behavior. If moral hazard is involved—such that efforts are reduced and funds are wasted deliber-

---

[10] Caplin and Leahy's (1998) model explores how information externalities may result in suboptimal investments for a long period of time and how, once information about the potential of that market is revealed, economic activity picks up. Their inspiration was the rejuvenation of lower Sixth Avenue in New York City, once Bed, Bath & Beyond—a large consumer goods store—established shop there, revealing information about the potential consumer base in that area. The model can be usefully interpreted in the context of low-income countries, where aid-financed investments reveal information about comparative advantage, thus leading to economic development and increased market access on reasonable terms.

[11] Advocates of the grants approach (Meltzer and Sachs, 2000) argue that grants would effectively provide a stronger incentive effect if they are designed such that funding is provided ex post, after an audit has been completed to make sure that a given project attained its objectives. Such incentives, they argue, would also lead to more selectivity in terms of projects chosen, reducing "loan-pushing" by donors. But since resources are generally required upfront, this approach may result in many projects not being undertaken at all.

ately in anticipation of debt forgiveness—then the lend-and-forgive cycle is indeed a problem and argues for a more conservative approach to loans and a larger use of grants. Depending on the importance of moral hazard relative to bad luck in explaining debt-servicing problems, it would be possible theoretically to devise an appropriate mix of grants and (concessional) loans.

In sum, an extreme solution, consisting of a grants-only approach, is unlikely to be the optimal choice. Given the need to finance development expenditure with a limited pool of grant resources, the optimal approach likely entails some combination of loans and grants. Determining the right mix, one that leverages available grant resources with the appropriate share of financing on commercial terms, however, requires a careful consideration of the specific circumstances.

Project-Based Approach

Based on the above considerations, a case could be made for tailoring the provision of grants and loans to individual projects. Instead of providing concessional loans, aid would be "unbundled" to finance through grants only those projects with high social value but uncertain or delayed returns—such as investment in education and health, including financing for HIV/AIDS medication and malaria vaccines. Other projects that are likely to generate sufficiently high and timely financial returns to the government—including a potentially wide range of infrastructure investments—could then be funded through loans on commercial terms to avoid an overall reduction in financing. Such a proposal, however, ignores that money is fungible. Unless there is perfect alignment between the preferences of donors and recipients, some projects that would have been undertaken in any event, financed by government funds, would be proposed for grant financing. The remaining savings could then be used for something less productive (or desirable from the donors' point of view), such as the purchase of another plane for the unprofitable national flag carrier. Thus, the split between grants and loans based on projects becomes a purely theoretical device, while it is ultimately the overall resource envelope and the terms of the combined financing package that matters.

The problems of fungibility associated with project loans may be alleviated by resorting to a particular form of targeted budget support—although not without creating other problems. Devarajan and Swaroop (1998) propose a Public Expenditure Reform Loan (PERL), under which governments would present their development expenditure plan to the World Bank (or, for that matter, other development agencies), which would then provide assistance (in the form of loans or grants, depending on the context) based on the merit of the proposals. This form of budget support, however, has its own set of problems. Giving donor agencies a mandate over a much wider set of projects—the whole development agenda of the government, in fact—risks compromising any domestic ownership. Moreover, the widened scope may greatly limit the ability of donors to monitor the use of development funds, thus undermining the purpose of this proposal, which is to overcome a misalignment between recipient and donor interests.[12]

Country-Specific Approach

Very few academic studies have systematically laid out economic rationales for the appropriate levels of aid concessionality, but those that have reach similar conclusions. In terms of empirical work, Odedokun (2004) examines the effect of concessionality on a borrowing country's fiscal discipline and the extent of borrowing. Odedokun finds that loans are better suited than grants for promoting a recipient government's budgetary discipline. He also finds that the rate of borrowing is positively correlated with the degree of concessionality, whether through longer grace periods or lower interest rates. Cordella and Ulku (2004) build a theoretical model in the presence of conflicts between donors' and recipients' objectives. They conclude that the level of loan concessionality that maximizes growth depends on the quality of a recipient country's policies and institutions, the level of initial income, and the level of existing debt obligations. Their results imply that more aid should be provided in the form of grants if the country already has high external debt ratios, is very poor, and has weak policies and institutions. Finally, using a dynamic contracting model where concessional lending is feasible up to a cutoff point (akin to IDA graduation), Koeda (2004) argues that—as long as over-borrowing in the earlier periods of highly concessional financing is contained—optimal concessional lending is better than its grants counterpart. When the caveat is not met, however, the country remains permanently near the cutoff point, remaining dependent on aid.

A number of studies have gone a step further, developing practical guidelines for providing aid. Collier (2005), for example, bases his analysis on the absorptive capacity of aid—described in Collier and Dollar (2001, 2002)—and derives a "poverty-efficient allocation of aid." Within that allocative envelope comes the division between loans and grants, with an increasing share of loans, and ultimate "graduation" to market financing, as a country develops. Radelet and Chiang (2003) propose an algorithm—consistent with the theoretical propositions of Cordella and Ulku (2004)—for determining aid allocation, based on the need for financing and the prospects for growth. The need would be determined by a range of economic and social indicators, while the prospects for growth could be estimated by looking at historical growth rates, "conservative" projections, and indicators of the quality of policies and institutions. Both

[12] Using a theoretical model, Cordella and Dell'Ariccia (2003) argue that budget support is preferable to project aid if total aid is small relative to the recipient's own resources and when the objective functions of the two parties are aligned.

the need for financing and prospects for growth then determine the composition of financing; poorer countries receive more of their financing in the form of grants while faster-growing countries, and those with sound policies and institutions, receive more in the form of loans. Radelet and Chiang modify these "clusters" with two additional qualifications: countries that are subject to volatility (in terms of, for example, export prices, political circumstances, and exchange rates), and those with high debt levels receive more funds in the form of grants.

The recently endorsed debt-sustainability framework for low-income countries, developed jointly by the staffs of the IMF and the World Bank, incorporates many of these considerations.[13] The objective of the framework is to provide guidance to low-income borrowers and their mainly official creditors and donors, in an effort to ensure that new financing in pursuit of the MDGs is consistent with a country's current and prospective ability to service debt. The design of the framework draws on the empirical findings of Kraay and Nehru (2004), corroborated by subsequent work of IMF staff (IMF and World Bank, 2004a). This empirical work suggests that the risk of "debt distress" depends predominantly on three factors: the debt stock itself, the quality of a country's policies and institutions, and the country's vulnerability to shocks. Consistent with these findings, and similar ones by other authors, as discussed above, the key features of the framework are: an assessment of debt sustainability informed by indicative debt-burden thresholds, linked to the quality of a country's policies and institutions; a standardized forward-looking analysis of the debt and debt-service dynamics under a baseline scenario and in the event of plausible shocks; and an appropriate borrowing (and lending) strategy, under which official creditors tailor the terms of new financing—that is, their lending and grant-allocation decisions—to an individual country's risk of debt distress.

IV. Conclusions

While the debate on the appropriate form of development finance and the trade-off between large financing needs and debt sustainability concerns is far from resolved, the above discussion suggests the following preliminary conclusions:

- The debt-to-export ratio of the average low-income country has fallen significantly over the past decade. The declining trend reflects, in large part, debt relief combined with very fast export growth in a few countries. Without debt relief, the median debt-to-export ratio would have remained broadly stable, and the debt-to-GDP ratio would have risen,

[13] The framework is described in IMF and World Bank (2004a and 2004b) and its endorsed operational features are clarified in IMF and World Bank (2005).

notwithstanding highly concessional interest rates. This highlights the fragility of the debt dynamics in low-income countries and underscores the case for adopting a country-specific approach to development finance.

- While a grants-only approach has clear advantages from the perspective of debt sustainability, it also has a number of important disadvantages. With competing claims on scarce donor resources, such an approach would imply a reduced level of aid—either for current or future recipients—relative to a mixed-financing approach.
- A tailoring of loans and grants to individual projects has some theoretical appeal, but it ignores the fungibility of aid resources. A potentially more promising approach, supported by empirical evidence, favors tailoring aid to individual country characteristics. Under this approach, the level of aid should be based on both need and absorptive capacity, while the terms—that is, the leveraging of grants through commercial loans—would be guided by a country's risk of debt distress. The latter is influenced by the country's growth prospects and, relatedly, the quality of its policies and institutions.
- The newly endorsed low-income country debt sustainability framework represents an important effort to make this approach operational, by linking the terms of new official financing to a country's risk of debt distress. The risk of debt distress is assessed on the basis of a forward-looking debt sustainability analysis and indicative debt-burden thresholds, which depend on the quality of a country's policies and institutions.

References

Bulíř, Aleš, and A. Javier Hamann, 2003, "How Volatile and Unpredictable Are Aid Flows, and What Are the Policy Implications?" IMF Working Paper 01/167 (Washington: International Monetary Fund).

Bulow, Jeremy, and Kenneth Rogoff, 2005, "Grants versus Loans for Development Banks," paper presented at the American Economic Association Meetings, Philadelphia, January.

Caplin, Andrew, and John Leahy, 1998, "Miracle on Sixth Avenue: Information Externalities and Search," *Economic Journal*, Vol. 108 (January), pp. 60–74.

Cline, William R., 2003, "HIPC Debt Sustainability and Post-Relief Lending Policy," Center for Global Development and Institute for International Development (unpublished).

Collier, Paul, 2005, "Loans and Grants: Coherence in Aid Instruments," in *Public Finance in a Globalizing World: Innovations in Theory and Practice*, ed. by Inge Kaul (Oxford: Oxford University Press).

———, and David Dollar, 2001, "Can the World Cut Poverty in Half? How Policy Reform and Effective Aid Can Meet International Development Goals" *World Development*, Vol. 29 (November), pp. 1782–802.

———, 2002, "Aid Allocation and Poverty Reduction," *European Economic Review*, Vol. 46 (September), pp. 1475–500.

Cordella, Tito, and Giovanni Dell'Ariccia, 2003, "Budget Support Versus Project Aid," IMF Working Paper 03/88 (Washington: International Monetary Fund).

Cordella, Tito, and Hulya Ulku, 2004, "Grants versus Loans," IMF Working Paper 04/161 (Washington: International Monetary Fund).

Devarajan, Shantayanan, and Vinaya Swaroop, 1998, "The Implications of Foreign Aid Fungibility for Development Assistance," Policy Research Working Paper No. 2022 (Washington: World Bank).

Gosh, Atish, and others, 2005, *The Design of IMF-Supported Programs*, IMF Occasional Paper No. 241 (Washington: International Monetary Fund).

International Monetary Fund, and World Bank, 2004a, *Debt Sustainability in Low-Income Countries: Further Consideration on an Operational Framework and Policy Implications* (Washington). Available via the Internet: http://www.imf.org/external/np/pdr/sustain/2004/091004.htm

———, 2004b, *Debt Sustainability in Low-Income Countries: Proposal for an Operational Framework and Policy Implications* (Washington). Available via the Internet: http://www.imf.org/external/np/pdr/sustain/2004/020304.htm

———, 2005, *Operational Framework for Debt Sustainability Assessments in Low-Income Countries—Further Considerations* (Washington). Available via the Internet: http://www.imf.org/External/np/pp/eng/2005/032805.htm

Koeda, Junko, 2004, "Grants or Concessional Loans? Aid to Low-Income Countries with a Participation Constraint" (unpublished; Los Angeles: University of California, Los Angeles).

Kraay, Aart, and Vikram Nehru, 2004, "When Is External Debt Sustainable?" Policy Research Working Paper No. 3200 (Washington: World Bank).

Meltzer, Allan H., and Jeffrey Sachs, 2000, "Reforming the IMF and the World Bank," *On the Issues*, American Enterprise Institute, March 8. Available via the Internet: http://www.aei.org/publications/pubID.11425,filter./pub_detail.asp

Meltzer Commission, 2000. International Financial Institution Advisory Commission Report. Available via the Internet: http://www.house.gov/jec/imf/meltzer.htm

Odedokun, Matthew, 2003, "Economics and Politics of Official Loans versus Grants," WIDER Discussion Paper No. 2003/04 (Helsinki: World Institute for Development Economics Research, United Nations University).

Radelet, Steve, and Hanley Chiang, 2003, "Providing New Financing to Low-Income Countries with High Levels of Debt: Some Considerations," Issue Paper on Debt Sustainability No. 2 (Washington: Center for Global Development).

Schmidt, Wilson E., 1964, "The Economics of Charity: Loans versus Grants," *Journal of Political Economy*, Vol. 72, No. 4, pp. 387–95.

UN Millennium Project, 2005, *Investing in Development: A Practical Plan to Achieve the Millennium Development Goals* (New York).

SESSION VI

The Roles of Aid, Governance, and the Political Economy

10

Aid, Governance, and the Political Economy

Growth and Institutions

SIMON JOHNSON AND ARVIND SUBRAMANIAN*

I. Introduction

Among the top priorities of the Millennium Development Goals (MDGs) is the eradication of "extreme poverty and hunger." Achieving this goal will no doubt require action on several fronts—but central to any such effort remains the generating of high and sustained growth.[1] What does this kind of growth require?

At least in part, growth needs so-called "institutions" or "good governance." There is little disagreement on this issue. For example, this is the first point (although the term used is "governance failures") which is used in explaining global poverty in the *UN Millennium Development Project Report*, coordinated by Jeffrey Sachs, and released in January 2005.[2] Growth is also central to points 1 and 2 in the latest document circulated by the Commission for Africa convened

*Both authors are in the IMF Research Department. Simon Johnson is on leave from MIT. The authors would like to thank Jonathan Ostry and Raghu Rajan for helpful comments on related work.

[1] See Kraay (2004): "In the medium- to long-run, most of the variation in changes in poverty can be attributed to growth in average income, suggesting that policies and institutions that promote broad-based growth should be central to the pro-poor growth agenda."

[2] *UN Millennium Development Project Report* (2005), Chapter 3: Why the World is Falling Short of the Goals; p. 31. Available via the Internet: http://unmp.forumone.com/

by Prime Minister Tony Blair.[3] The Davos *Global Governance Initiative Annual Report 2005* puts "improving governance to empower the poor and allow private enterprise to flourish" near the top of its lists of priorities.[4]

But what exactly are institutions (or what is governance?) and what do we know about the link from institutions to growth? This paper summarizes the current state of knowledge regarding the importance of economic and political institutions for growth. In particular, in Section II, we distinguish what is known about this relationship, and in Section III, what remains unknown or uncertain. In Section IV, we conclude by drawing implications for the international community and low-income countries.

II. Knowns

Post-1945 Growth Experience

Following are some key facts of the postwar experience with growth in the cross-section of countries.

First, there has been disappointingly little convergence in income per capita between poor and rich countries. Since 1950, few countries have grown spectacularly, but these have been the exception and are concentrated mostly in East Asia (Figure 10.1). In Africa, south of the Sahara, there was some respectable growth in the 1950s and 1960s, but only two countries (Botswana and Mauritius) have sustained a significant increase in per capita income. As a percent of U.S. GDP per capita, much of Latin America, with the notable exception of Chile, is where it was 50 years ago, having caught up to some extent through 1980 and then fallen back, despite significant reforms since 1985. Interestingly, there has been greater convergence between countries in health and educational attainment than in income per capita (see Figure 10.2).

A corollary of these developments is that much of the global reduction in poverty has been concentrated in Asia, with much less improvement in sub-Saharan Africa (Sala-i-Martin, 2003).

This lack of convergence during the last 50 years has occurred despite the widespread availability of high productivity technologies, a rapid increase in world trade, and unprecedented opportunities for countries to participate in global production chains.

Second, countries with worse average growth performance have also generally experienced more output volatility, that is, poor African countries typically have a standard deviation of their growth rate that is 2 or 3 times higher than

[3] See *Action for a Strong and Prosperous Africa* (2004). Available via the Internet: http://213.225.140.43/getting_involved/consultationdocument.htm

[4] See *Global Governance Initiative, Annual Report* (2005). Available via the Internet: http://www.weforum.org/pdf/ggi2005_low.pdf

Figure 10.1. GDP Per Capita by Country Groupings (1995 $)

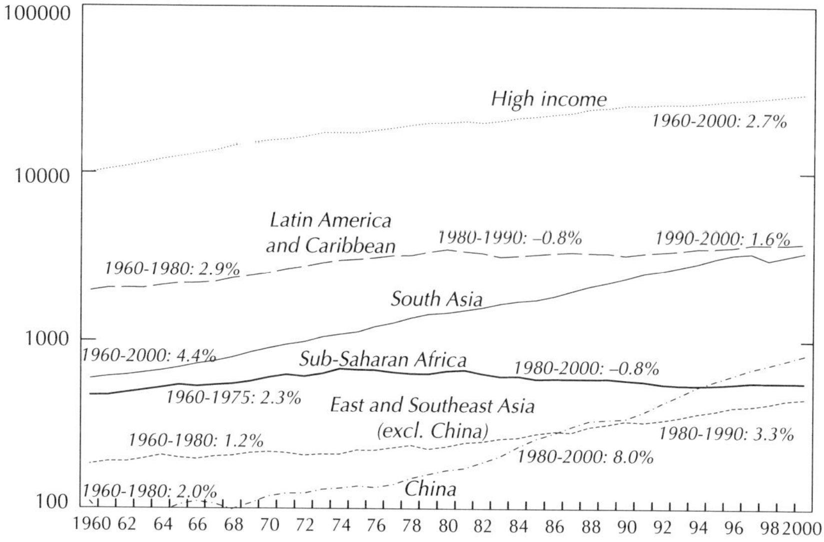

100000
10000
1000
100
High income
1960-2000: 2.7%
Latin America
and Caribbean
1980-1990: –0.8%
1990-2000: 1.6%
1960-1980: 2.9%
South Asia
1960-2000: 4.4%
Sub-Saharan Africa
1980-2000: –0.8%
1960-1975: 2.3%
East and Southeast Asia
(excl. China)
1960-1980: 1.2%
1980-1990: 3.3%
1980-2000: 8.0%
1960-1980: 2.0%
China
1960 62 64 66 68 70 72 74 76 78 80 82 84 86 88 90 92 94 96 98 2000

Source: Rodrik (2204).

Figure 10.2. Life Expectancy at Birth (1960–2000)

80
70
60
50
40
Life Expectancy at Birth
OECD
Latin America
Middle East
Asia
Africa
1960
1970
1980
1990
2000

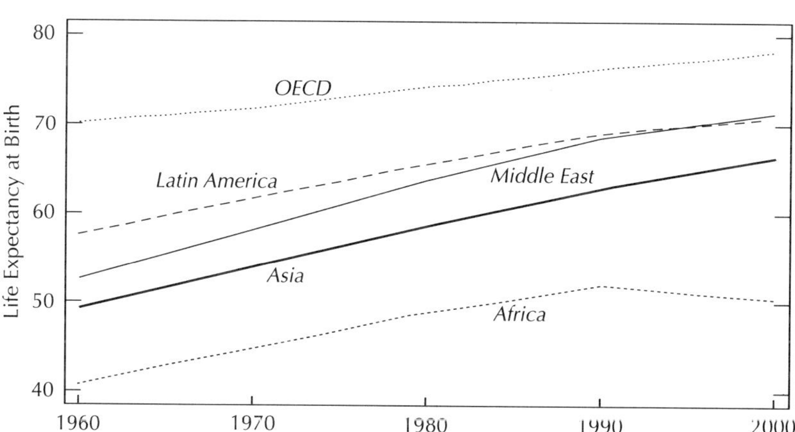

Source: Acemoglu and Johnson (2004).

Figure 10.3a. Growth and Volatility, All Countries (1960–2000)

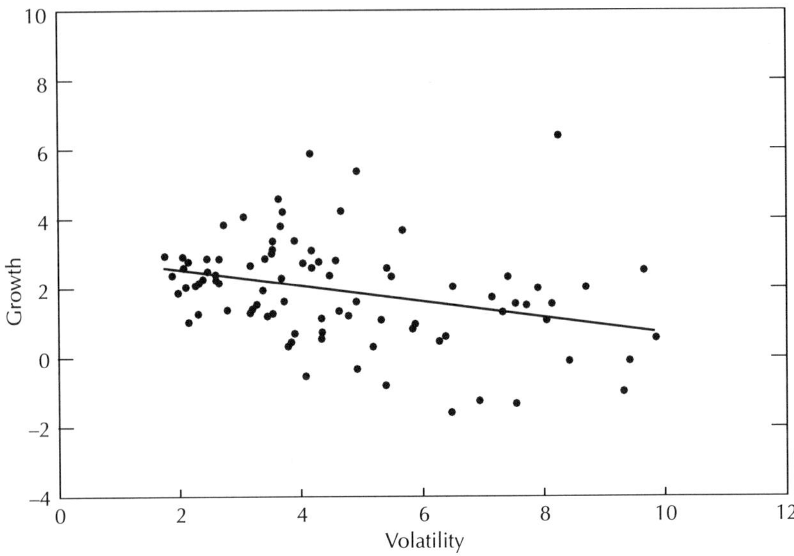

Source: Kose and others (2004).

rich European countries Figures 10.3a and 10.3b.[5] In fact, it is not unusual for 10 years or more of good growth to be wiped out by a few years of deep decline (e.g., the repeated experience in Latin America).[6] Many so-called growth accelerations, including some impressive performances in Africa during the 1960s, turned out not to be sustained.

Macroeconomic instability, in the form of high inflation or balance of payments crises or banking crises or an overvalued real exchange rate or some other form of economy-wide disruption, has consistently proved bad for growth (Easterly and Fischer, 2001). But macroeconomic stability by itself has not proved sufficient for sustained growth (e.g., Andean countries over the last decade, and some post-communist transition countries.)[7] Even when macroeconomic stability has been combined with structural reforms, the results have sometimes been disappointing—as in Latin America during the 1990s (Figure 10.4).

---

[5] This difference is largely not due to terms-of-trade fluctuations (Acemoglu and others, 2003) but to country-specific shocks (*World Economic Outlook 2005*). Ramey and Ramey (1995) first documented the connection between growth and its volatility.

[6] There is some evidence that after trade and financial liberalization, growth and volatility have become positively correlated (Prasad and others, 2004; Tornell, Ranciere, and Westermann, 2004). There is no doubt that stability of macroeconomic policies, including the avoidance of high inflation, has proved to be an important complement to sustained rapid growth.

Figure 10.3b. Growth and Volatility, Developing Countries (1960–2000)

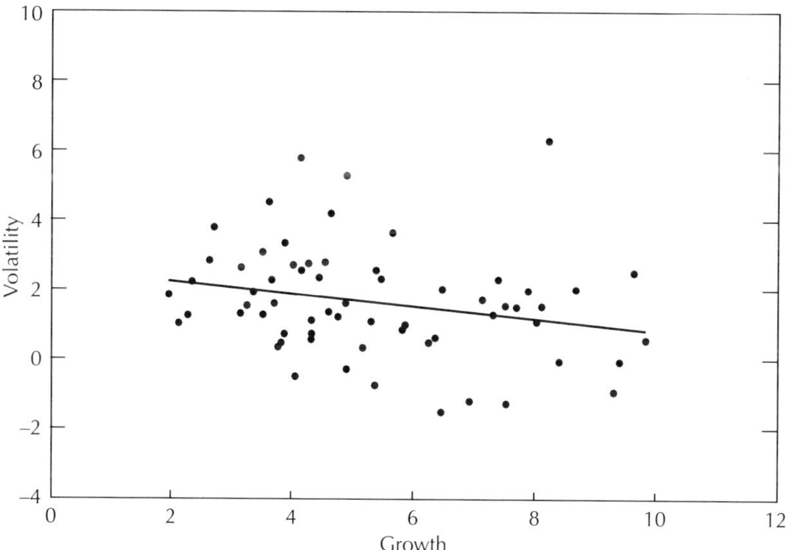

Source: Kose and others (2004).

Third, globalization of capital flows has in some instances helped growth, but there is no strong pattern in the cross-section[8]. But in other instances, where a country's system was fragile for other reasons, these capital flows may have contributed to economic instability (e.g., in Asia during 1997–98). In particular, serious crises can now be triggered by a loss of confidence and capital flows, even when the fiscal position and current account are in good shape.

In the light of this experience, economic thinking about growth has changed somewhat. The growth theory that was developed in the 1950s and 1960s stressed the need to accumulate factors of production—capital, and unskilled and skilled labor—and to increase the productivity with which these factors are used. But it left unanswered what has proved to be the more basic and essential question: under what conditions do countries accumulate factors and improve productivity? To answer this question, attention has turned increasingly to institutions along the lines of what we now outline.[9]

---

[7] See, for example, "Bolivia: Ex-Post Assessment of Longer-Term Engagement," February 2005. For an early reference to this point for post-communist countries, see Aslund, Boone, and Johnson (1996).

[8] See IMF (2001) for a survey of the evidence on the link between capital flows and growth.

[9] For a more detailed account of how ideas related to development have changed, see Easterly (2002). The danger, of course, is that the current focus on and consensus regarding institutions may turn out to be just another disappointing fad.

Figure 10.4. GDP Growth and Structural Reform Index for Latin America

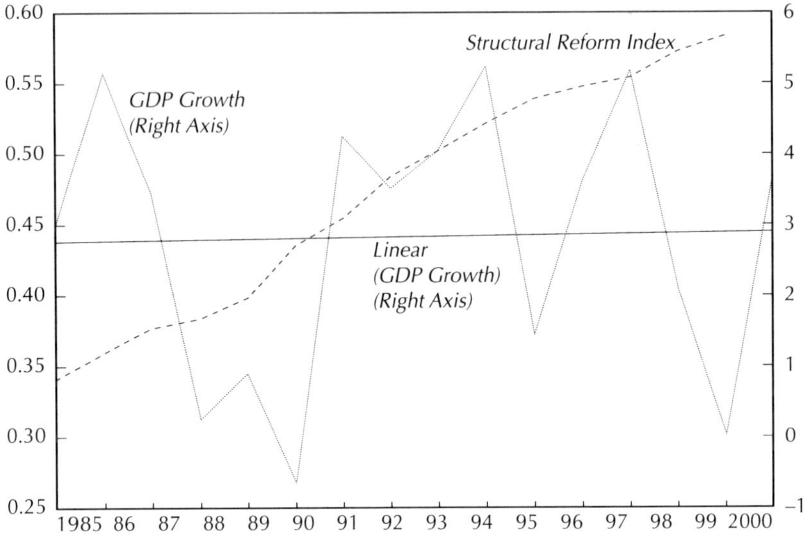

Source: Rodrik (2004).

Broad Economic Institutions[10]

One important dimension of governance is economic institutions. These come in two forms: broad and narrow. While distinction between the two may not always be easy to make in practice, the latter are more restricted in the scope of their impact. We return to narrow economic institutions later in this section. Here we focus on broad institutions.

Broad economic institutions are the set of laws, rules, and other practices that govern property rights for a broad cross-section of society. Good economic institutions create effective property rights for most people, which encompasses both protection against expropriation by the state (or powerful elites) and enforceable contracts between ordinary private parties. Although this definition is far from requiring full equality of opportunity in society, it implies that societies where only a small fraction of the population have well enforced property rights do not have good economic institutions.[11]

Property rights are essential if people are to invest in human and physical capital. Willingness to enter new lines of business is a particularly important

[10] The framework developed here and in the following sections builds directly on Acemoglu, Johnson, and Robinson (2004).

[11] In a number of resource-rich economies, property rights are clearly reasonably protected in the resource sectors themselves, as evidenced in the foreign investment. But in many such economies, similar protection may not exist economy-wide.

form of investment that has received some attention recently, but all forms of investment matter for development.[12]

Perhaps this point is self-evident—after all, who invests if they do not think it is worth the risks? While this may always have been an issue for people working on growth, there is now much more emphasis on the need for strong economic institutions.[13]

Bad economic institutions mean insecure property rights for most people. Insecure property rights can arise from expropriation by the state or powerful elites (often, but not exclusively, manifest in the form of corruption) or from severe political instability (e.g., failed states and conflict/post-conflict situations). Serious crime and the collapse of the state's capacity to maintain public order can undermine property rights surprisingly fast.

In addition to an understanding of economic institutions, policy and research require them to be measured. The Appendix at the end of the chapter reviews the available measures of broad economic institutions, which are far from perfect. In the case of institutions, perceptions are key—if governments can persuade potential and actual entrepreneurs that they will protect them, they can do well with relatively little in the way of formal rights. This is one interpretation of what has happened in China over the past 20 years.

However, perceptions eventually need to be underpinned by actual protections, that is, if someone tries to take over someone else's property, there is recourse or appeal of some meaningful kind.[14] Property rights are never perfect, and conflicts often emerge between alternative claimants on property. The issue is the extent to which property rights are protected, preferably by a fair and transparent process of dispute resolution.[15] The extent of recourse depends closely on political institutions.

Political Institutions

The second key dimension of governance is political institutions. Political institutions are the laws, rules, and other practices that determine how people get political power and what they do with it once they have it. Political insti-

[12] For one recent analysis of the importance of entry, see Laeven, Klapper, and Rajan (2004).

[13] For a nice synthesis, see the World Bank's *World Development Report 2002*, "Building Institutions for Markets."

[14] For disputes between private parties, the alternative mechanisms across countries have been documented and measured by Djankov, La Porta, Lopez-de-Silanes, and Shleifer in "Courts," Quarterly Journal of Economics, May 2003. These are part of the Doing Business database and website (see Appendix 1): http://rru.worldbank.org/DoingBusiness/ExploreTopics/EnforcingContracts/

[15] There are also difficult grey areas. For example, if a person obtained state property illegally, should they have the full protection of private property?

tutions place checks on those who hold political power, for example, by creating a balance of power in society. Without checks on political power, power holders are more likely to opt for economic institutional arrangements that benefit them and are detrimental for the rest of society. This makes political institutions highly sensitive and usually controversial within countries.

Economic institutions are typically deeply embedded in domestic political structures. A major issue, which we discuss further below, is the link between the two, and whether economic institutions can be substantially changed without changes in political institutions. If political structures, over which outsiders tend to have less influence, are the deeper problem, and all the difficulties with economic institutions are just symptoms, then actions by outsiders in this area (or in the more narrow domain of macroeconomics) may have less lasting impact.

Broad Institutions Are First Priority for Sustained Economic Prosperity

Economic and political institutions are of first order importance for growth in the medium to long run. This is not a new idea—in its modern form, it goes as far back as Douglass North—but in the last 10 years, the evidence has mounted that institutions have a large effect (Figure 10.5) on long-run growth (IMF, 2003).

If a country builds good institutions, entrepreneurs will invest in capital goods and ordinary people will invest in human capital. Empirical results accumulated recently show that the magnitude of the impact is substantial. For example, an improvement in sub-Saharan Africa's level of institutional development from its current average to the mean of developing Asia would imply an 80 percent increase in its per capita income (from $800 to more than $1,400).

Note that good institutions are not necessarily the same thing as "free markets". Markets may be free of government intervention but highly skewed toward the rich and powerful. If the playing field is uneven, there will be little entry into the formal sector and a few large unproductive firms will dominate the economy. Indeed, good institutions entail strong and effective government capability that allows markets to be created and to flourish. If physical infrastructure is the hardware of an economy, strong institutions are its essential software.

Broad Institutions Also Help Explain Macroeconomic Instability and Many Crises

There is more volatility and instability—both in real terms and in terms of inflation—when economic and, especially, political institutions are weak Figures 10.6a and 6b?[16] This is especially true in relation to shocks, where there is evidence that shocks are more damaging where political institutions are weak.[17]

[16] See Acemoglu and others (2003); Rodrik (1999); Haman and Prati (2002); Satyanath and Subramanian (2004); and Rajan (2004).

[17] Rodrik (1999) argues that weak political institutions mean that societies cannot handle the disputes that arise after negative shocks.

Figure 10.5. Relationship Between Income and Institutions

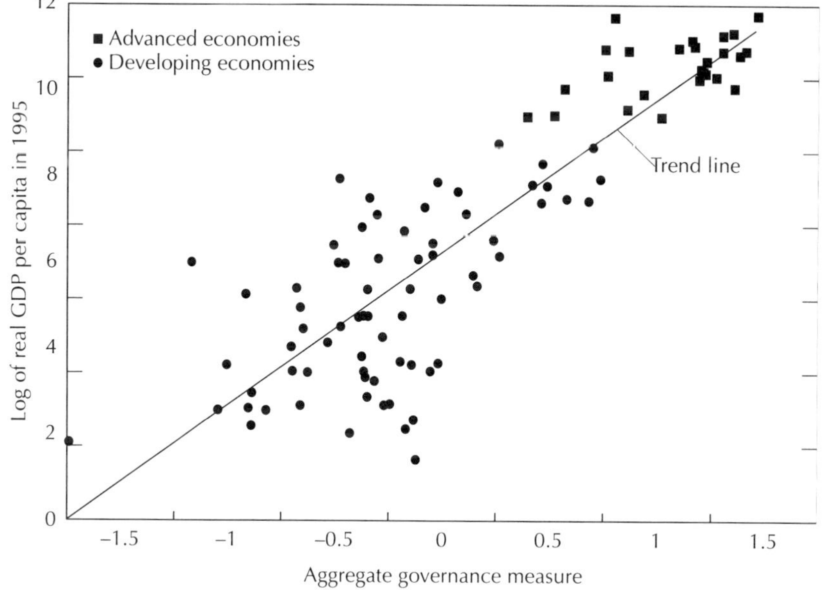

Source: WEO (2003).

The reason why political institutions in particular play an important role in relation to instability is that they determine the distribution of resources within society. For example, in the wake of shocks, the ability of countries to respond depends on economic adjustment. Strong political institutions facilitate a smooth or equitable distribution of the burden of adjustment in society, which will lead to stability. Distributional conflicts, which are likely when political institutions are weak, on the other hand, will aggravate instability.

The differential responses of Korea and Thailand versus Indonesia in the aftermath of the Asian financial crisis are also consistent with the importance of political institutions in response to shocks (see Fischer, 2002).[18] Even though democratic institutions had developed recently, they helped the two countries adjust in several ways: by facilitating a smooth transfer of power to a new set of politicians;[19] by providing mechanisms to enable policymakers to fashion the

[18] For an innovative evaluation of what happened in Indonesia toward the end of the Suharto regime, see Fisman (2001).

[19] In Thailand, Mr. Yongchaiyudh resigned in the wake of the crisis, and power transitioned smoothly to Prime Minister Leekpai. In Korea, the veteran opposition leader, Kim Dae-Jung, was elected to office as the crisis broke. Both these candidates were seen as representing a break from the past.

Figure 10.6a. Relationship Between Exchange Rate Instability and Political Institutions

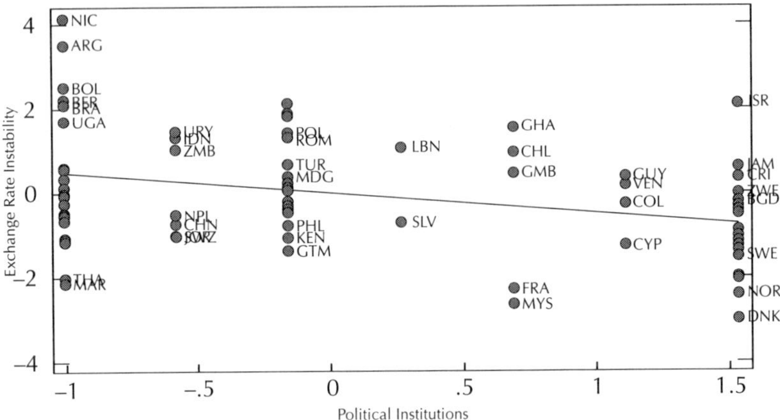

Figure 10.6b. Relationship Between Inflation Instability and Political Institutions

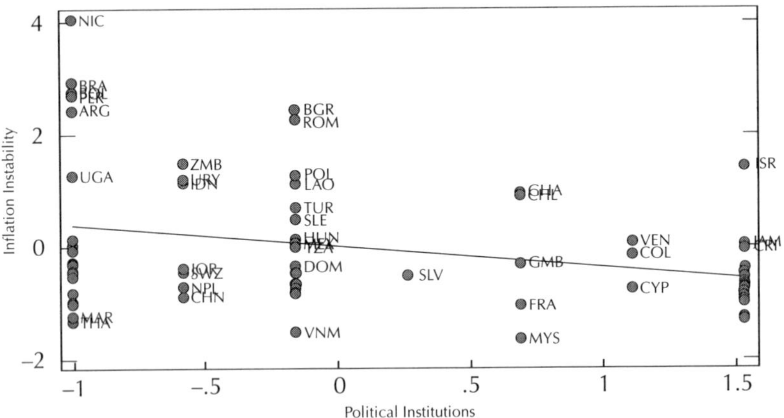

Source: Satyanath and Subramanian (2004).

consensus needed to undertake the necessary policy adjustments;[20] and by providing mechanisms of "voice," obviating the need for riots, protests, and other disruptive and economically costly actions (Rodrik, 1999).

Another famous example of political institutions having had an effect on crises has been documented by Sen (1981) in his analysis of famines. He argues

[20] In the case of Korea, the opposition's consent to the IMF's letter of intent was seen as representing a social consensus on the need for reforms.

that the contrasting experiences of China and India in avoiding famines stemmed from the greater degree of transparency in India's political institutions, which allowed quicker public awareness of the problem and speedier responses to it.

But Institutions Do Not Explain Growth Fluctuations in the Short Run

The growth record clearly indicates that countries can grow in the short run with weak institutions. In other words, institutions are not crucial in relation to short-run growth. Igniting growth may not be particularly difficult, but sustaining it is difficult without good institutions.[21] Growth spurts or transitions often happen by chance or due to other triggers; for example, because the terms of trade improve for a natural resource producer, or because there is a change in government, or an end to civil war. They do not even seem to require major policy reforms.[22]

One particularly interesting episode took place during the end of the nineteenth and the early twentieth centuries. Some of the fastest growing countries had weak institutions, such as Argentina, Mexico, and Russia. But each of them then experienced a major political and economic disruption that derailed growth.

There are two reasons for this disruption. First, the elite can do a great deal for itself and among itself. Webs of personal connections can sustain investment even when the general environment is unstable.[23] The key point is that elites do not expropriate everyone all the time. It depends on the alternatives. For example, related lending by a bank to its owners may work fine during periods of prosperity. But these arrangements are quite vulnerable to collapse.

Second, elite expropriation may get worse as an economy experiences a sustained credit boom. This would be the case, for example, if there were less pressure to control corruption when times are good (e.g., when oil prices are high, this is probably the case with some oil producers). Alternatively, or in addition, when there is a shock that shortens time horizons and reduces the value of repeated game interactions, elites may engage in a grab for resources.

---

[21] One manifestation of this differential impact of institutions is that measures of institutional quality are more robust in regressions involving the level of income than in growth regressions.

[22] There is a lot of randomness in growth experiences, that is, a large component that is hard to explain with any kind of regression analysis. See Hausmann, Pritchett, and Rodrik (2004). In the case of India, for example, growth was ignited in the early 1980s even in the absence of significant policy reform by an apparent attitudinal shift on the part of the government toward the private sector (Rodrik and Subramanian, 2005). Srinivasan (2005) contests this interpretation of events in India.

[23] For the fascinating historical case of Mexico, see Haber, Razo, and Maurer (2003), and also the review by Bates (2004). Of course, it is not clear that a modern country could pull off the same kind of record.

Figure 10.7. Evolution of Democracy (1960–2000)

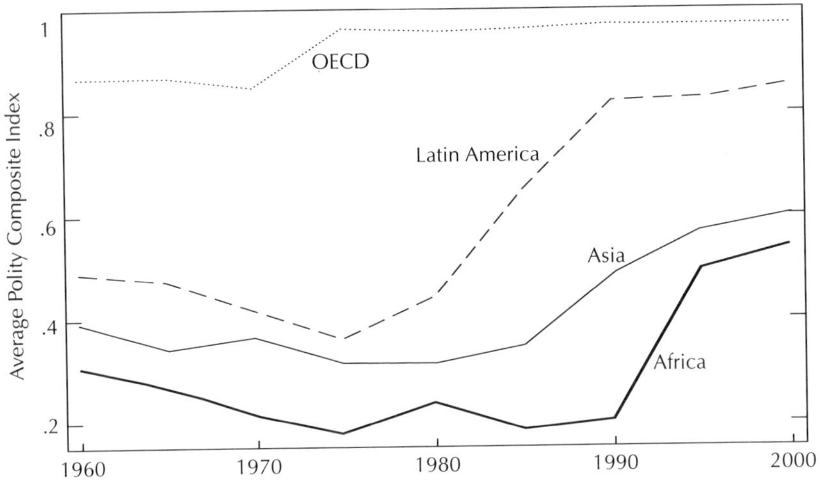

Source: Acemoglu and others (2004).

Institutional Persistence and Change

Institutions persist; that is, institutions tomorrow are very likely to be quite similar to institutions today. The most likely explanation is that they suit the interests of those with power. One example of this was the relatively slow pace of reforms in the Commonwealth of Independent States (CIS) during the reform process, compared with the more rapid change in the Central and Eastern European countries. Institutions are also persistent because they are the result of historical factors, which are difficult to overcome.[24]

But institutional persistence is not institutional predetermination. In fact, historical variables typically explain about a fourth of the variation in measures of institutions today. This means that much of the variation does not come from history. For example, between the 1970s and 1990s, there have been some very notable changes in the quality of institutions (see Figure 10.7 for political institutions). One indicator of institutional quality is the index measuring the constraint on the executive. Twenty countries improved their institutional quality ratings by more than 40 percent. Of course, how institutional change

[24] Two examples illustrate the role of historical factors. Banerjee and Iyer (2004) document the role of land tenure systems in pre-colonial India in affecting current institutions in agriculture. Nunn (2004) finds strong evidence that the Atlantic and Indian Ocean slave trade between 1400 and 1900 has adversely affected Africa's growth performance in the last 40 years.

can be effected is a difficult question—perhaps at the core of many current debates about growth and development—but that they can change and have lasting effects on development should not be in doubt.

Effective institutional change is often fairly gradual, that is, taking place over 10–20 years or even longer. It often comes about in a fairly piecemeal fashion, where changing one dimension makes it more appealing to change another complementary dimension. Most countries changed their institutions substantially during the eighteenth and nineteenth centuries. During the twentieth century, for various reasons, institutions around the world have changed less dramatically, but they have changed in many instances—for example, in all the East Asian countries that have sustained rapid growth. Occasionally, though, institutions, especially political institutions, can change suddenly, brought about by the collapse of the previous regime. Notable recent examples include the collapse of the former Soviet Union, and the change in post-conflict states such as Timor-Leste, Kosovo, Afghanistan, and Iraq.

III. Uncertainties

Relationship Between Political and Economic Institutions

Rents themselves may be partly endogenous, but good economic institutions are more likely to arise and persist when there are only limited rents that power holders can extract from the rest of society (e.g., when there are limited natural resources), since such rents would encourage them to opt for a set of economic institutions that make the expropriation of others possible.

Good economic institutions are more likely to arise when political power is in the hands of a relatively broad group with significant investment opportunities. The reason for this result is that, everything else equal, in this case, power holders will themselves benefit from secure property rights.

This puts political institutions at the center of the story. But what is the exact relationship between political and economic institutions? We know little about this relationship. Economic institutions may improve first, followed by political institutions—this has been the experience in much of East Asia and Chile. The converse—namely, strong political institutions leading economic ones—has been true for Botswana and Mauritius, the only two countries in sub-Saharan Africa that have enjoyed sustained growth. Indeed, there is very little correlation between economic and political institutions between 1980 and 2000 for countries around the world (see Figure 10.8a, which plots the correlation between changes in economic and political institutions between 1980 and 2000).

In Africa, there has been an improvement in political institutions—that is, more democracy—but whether this will necessarily translate into better economic institutions remains to be seen; the simple correlation between economic and political institutions is insignificantly small (see Figure 10.8b on Africa).

Figure 10.8a. Change in Political and Economic Institutions, All Countries (1980–2000)

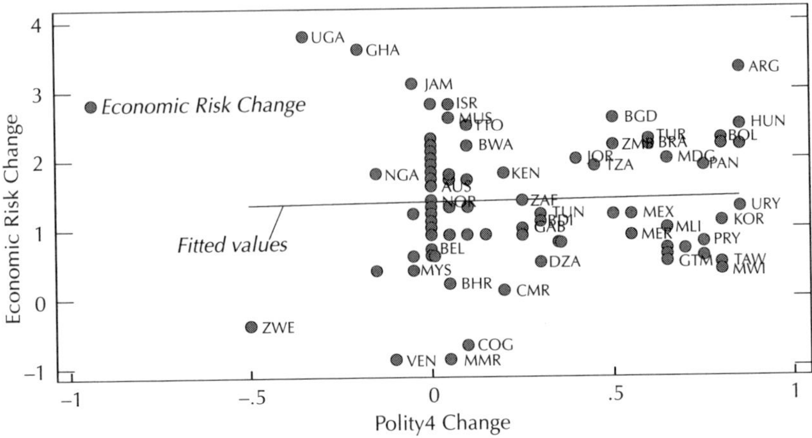

Figure 10.8b. Change in Political and Economic Institutions, Africa (1980–2000)

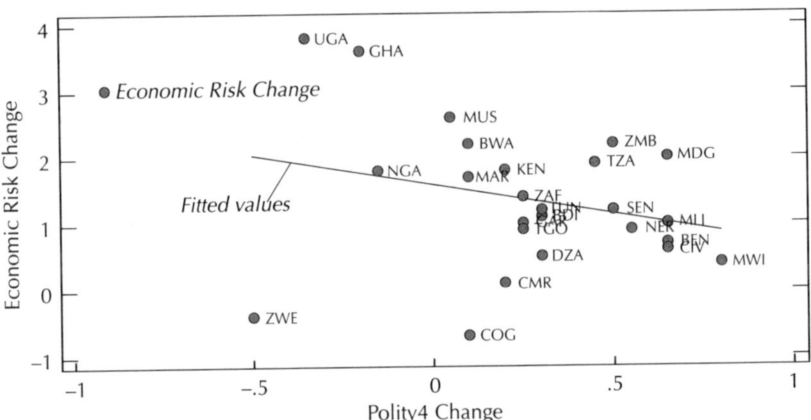

Source: Authors' calculations.

Indeed, as Figure 10.9 shows, economic institutions, after having improved in the early 1990s, have leveled or perhaps even deteriorated—so there is little sign of convergence in economic institutions.

How Do Institutions Change?

That institutions change is clear. But understanding change, and more specifically, identifying the policy actions or levers for change is perhaps one of the

Figure 10.9. International Country Risk Guide: Rule of Law Indicator
(Sources range from 0, high business risk due to poor observance of law and order to 6, low business risk)

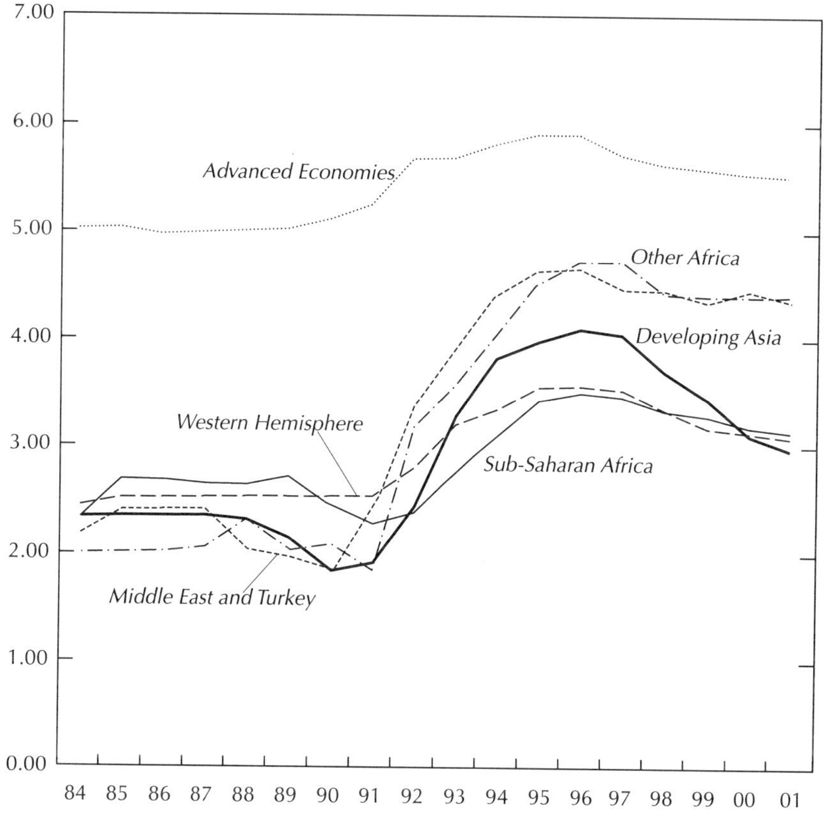

Source: WEO (2003).

key unknowns in development. A number of forces may lie behind institutional change. The first is the desire of the elite to preempt problems with other groups in society. One example would be the extension of the franchise in nineteenth century Europe (Acemoglu and Robinson, 2001). But as remarked earlier, more often than not, elites have a strong interest in maintaining the status quo, especially if there are rents to be extracted from current arrangements.

A second reason for change is some extreme event or crisis, such as a revolution or some other form of uprising by groups that do not have political power. The French, Russian, and Chinese Revolutions are leading examples, although each of them obviously led to different institutional arrangements. The breakdown of the former Soviet Union is another example of extreme political change. Even in postwar data, there is evidence that political institutions change due to crises.

Institutional change may be easier when there is economic growth; thus losers can more easily receive at least partial compensation.[25] So economic growth per se should promote better institutions. Also, if good institutions and governance are superior goods, there will be greater demand for them as incomes rise, suggesting another channel of impact from growth to institutions. Therefore, is it the case that rising per capita income itself leads to better institutions? This is a long-standing view in political science and economics, for example, articulated clearly in the work of Lipset (1959).

There has been both a general trend toward democratization and economic growth over the past 200 years. These trends have continued, in broad terms, since 1950. However, if we look at the within-country variation, there is no relationship between growth and the extent of democracy.[26] In other words, growth by itself does not lead to democracy, at least in the post-World War II period. Even within East Asia, Korea and Indonesia offer contrasting experiences of institutional change in response to growth. But one robust stylized fact is that countries above a certain threshold level of income (perhaps $6,000) have not experienced the overthrow of democracy (Przeworski, 1991).

Another driver of institutional change could be good leaders. Jones and Olken (2004) present important new evidence supporting this point; they also show that good leaders have more of an impact when institutions are weak.

Yet another driver of institutional change appears to be natural resource discoveries. The problem with them is that they yield enormous rents to a small elite that has no interest in broader economic development. In such a situation, a resource boom may actually undermine institutional development as the now more economically powerful elite has less incentive to develop a broad tax base or more generally improve property rights for a broad cross-section of society.[27]

The above makes clear that a wide variety of factors can cause institutional change. Moreover, most of the factors identified—crisis, revolutions, growth, natural resources, and leaders—are typically not easy to influence (for example, how can a country chose "good leaders?") and provide frustratingly little guidance on what policy levers can be used to effect institutional change.

---

[25] Lau, Roland, and Qian (2000) make a nice version of this argument for China, although their emphasis is more on the sequencing of reform.

[26] Technically speaking, this describes results from a fixed-country and time-effects panel regression. See Acemoglu, Johnson, Robinson, and Yared (2004a).

[27] Ross (2001) and Sala-i-Martin and Subramanian (2003) document the adverse impact of natural resources on institutional quality.

Can Outsiders Change Economic and Political Institutions?

This is a very important question, especially for the international community, which through a combination of assistance and conditionality seek to change institutions and outcomes in aid-receiving countries. It is especially important for interventions in low-income countries through the PRSP (Poverty Reduction Strategy Paper) process, because in these cases, there are explicit institution-related interventions. For example, PRSPs require extensive "process" requirements, in terms of participation and consultation.

Historically, external military action, including colonialism, has been a primary way in which some countries have shaped the institutions of other countries. But colonialism imposed various forms of expropriation, and with a few exceptions, it established bad institutions.[28]

Of course, outsiders can have an important impact in preventing, minimizing, or resolving conflict (the interventions in Bosnia and Sierra Leone being two recent examples). But whether they can play a crucial role in the positive engineering of institutions remains unclear.

One recent example of change from the outside is accession to the European Union (EU). Countries that have joined the EU have changed their institutions in far-reaching and fundamental ways to comply with EU norms—the famous *acquis communautaire*. There are, however, significant differences between EU accession and Bank-IMF programs (Roland, 2003). First, the lure of accession to the EU can be so overwhelming, going beyond financial assistance to benefits in the realm of politics (e.g., the consolidation of democracy in Spain and Portugal, the move away from the Soviet sphere of influence for many of the former Soviet Union and Eastern European countries) to market access benefits in goods, services, and labor mobility, so as to provide the necessary incentive to countries to undertake institutional reform. The ownership-conditionality dilemma that fundamentally afflicts IMF-Bank involvement is thus largely resolved because the lure of prospective benefits provides adequate incentives for serious ownership. Second, the mechanisms for ensuring compliance with norms pre-entry are very strong in the EU (Roland, 2003).[29]

---

[28] The origin of the term colonization lies with the idea of sending settlers—something that Greek cities, for example, did around the Mediterranean in ancient times. Settlers tend to take the institutions of their home country or even improve them (as labor tends to be freer in new settlements, so it acquires greater rights). The quality of institutions in former European colonies is higher where settlements were more important (Acemoglu and others, 2001).

[29] Arguably, the IMF has played an important constructive role in facilitating accession to the EU in many instances. Particularly for countries that did not need IMF resources and where policymakers had a clear picture of what needed to be done, the IMF's role in large part was to validate and endorse, as well as to provide implicit insurance in case a shock knocked the country off track.

Another often-cited example of a successful external anchor is the World Trade Organization (WTO). In the case of China, the goal of WTO accession encouraged authorities to undertake significant reforms of the trade system, the restructuring of state-owned enterprises, and encouraging the removal of internal trade barriers such as obstacles to labor migration. But this has been more the exception than the rule. For the vast majority of developing countries, the WTO has not played the role of anchoring domestic policies reflected in the fact that countries' actual trade policies—in both manufacturing and services—are more liberal and open than what they have committed in the WTO.[30]

Thus, unless there are substantial benefits that outsiders can offer, it remains a big challenge for positive institutional change to be driven from the outside.

Form vs. Function

A related issue, which is of great operational significance, is whether we can know good institutions by particular forms, or whether we have to look at the functions that these institutions are playing.

For each of the functions performed by institutions, there is an array of choices about their specific form. What type of legal regime should a country adopt—common law, civil law, or some hybrid? What is the right balance between competition and regulation in overcoming some of the standard market failures? What is the appropriate size of the public sector? How much discretion and how much flexibility should there be in arrangements for the conduct of fiscal, monetary, and exchange rate policies?

Unfortunately, economic analysis provides surprisingly little guidance in answering these questions. Indeed, there is growing evidence that desirable institutional arrangements have a large element of context specificity, arising from differences in historical trajectories, geography, political economy, or other initial conditions. This could help explain why successful developing countries have almost always combined unorthodox elements with orthodox policies. East Asia combined "outward orientation" with industrial intervention. China grafted a market system on top of a planned economy rather than eliminating the latter altogether. Much of the growth in "private" investment in China during the 1980s and early 1990s came from township village enterprises (TVEs), which embodied a unique system of property rights. It could also account for why major institutional differences persist among the advanced countries of North America, Western Europe, and Japan—in the role of the public sector, the nature of the legal systems, corporate governance, financial markets, labor mar-

[30] See Mattoo and Subramanian (2004), who provide evidence of the substantial wedge between the stance of developing countries' actual trade policies and what they have "bound," that is, committed in the WTO.

kets, and social insurance mechanisms, among others. Moreover, institutional solutions that perform well in one setting may be inappropriate in another setting without the supporting norms and complementary institutions. In other words, institutional innovations may not necessarily travel well.

As far as we know, a wide variety of different institutional forms can serve the same useful functions, that is, there is not one recipe for good institutions. For example, the discussion of whether French institutions are bad for economic performance is largely a red herring.[31] There are different ways to construct the institutions that are consistent with a high level of productivity. It is very hard, and probably not helpful, to argue whether Japan or Germany or France or any other country has "the" ideal institutions. Countries can and do develop their own institutions. There is definitely not a one-size-fits-all solution.

Furthermore, it is also unlikely that we have seen the full range of institutional innovations. We are also not confident that we will always recognize sensible innovations when we see them.

Relationship Between Broad and Specific Institutions

Much of the international community's work—lending and technical assistance—involves creating or changing specific institutions—central banks, regulatory bodies, public expenditure management systems, etc. The question to ask is whether these specific institutions can be changed if the more basic institutions are weak. In relation to monetary policy, for example, there is the issue of whether independent central banks contribute to low inflation because of being an efficient commitment device (Kydland and Prescott, 1977) or whether they represent the outcome of a prior political and social consensus reflected in strong political institutions in favor of low inflation.[32]

Similarly, can corruption in customs, that is, customs reform, be addressed independently of the state of corruption in the public sector as a whole?[33] Can revenue authorities perform better than conventional tax agencies? Can financial development lead to growth when more fundamental institutions remain weak? These are considerable uncertainties, and yet very important if donors' intervention, even in their areas of expertise, is to be effective.

Overall, we can recognize institutional change when it occurs, but realistically, this happens often only with a time lag. We know little about how to systematically change or induce change in institutions. This is an important gap in our knowledge.

---

[31] See Acemoglu and Johnson (2003). This point remains controversial.

[32] Subramanian and Satyanath (2004), provide evidence in favor of the latter.

[33] Yang (2004) provides evidence that institutional reform, such as the appointment of preshipment inspection companies to manage customs, may not have the desired effect.

Relationship Between Policies and Institutions

There is strong evidence that institutions affect policies and policy effectiveness. For example, the strength of political institutions is an important determinant of the success of disinflation programs (Hamann and Prati, 2002). An even more stark example relates to oil-exporting countries such as Nigeria, where the basic principle of saving while oil prices are low and drawing upon savings when prices decline had been studiously avoided for decades despite IMF-Bank conditionality. The underlying governance did not make prudent fiscal policy feasible. Similarly, weak financial regulation and supervision lead to excessive risk-taking, exposing countries to major financial crises.

From the perspective of changing institutions, however, a key question is whether policies can change institutions. Is there something that governments can do that will foster the development of institutions? It is clear that if attempts to improve competition are successful (i.e., if such attempts are not thwarted by the very institutions that are sought to be changed), they can have a major positive effect on institutions, provided and especially if the opportunities fall substantially into the hands of entrepreneurs outside the established elite. Domestic competition and trade reform are policies that fall into this category (see Djankov and others, 2001; World Bank, 2003; and Wei, 2000).

Another important area where policies can have an impact on institutions is tax policy. On the one hand, the experience with natural resources and aid suggests that when governments are relieved of the pressure to tax citizens, long-run institutional development suffers. The incentives for two-way engagement between governments and citizens/taxpayers are undermined. Citizens have less incentive to hold governments accountable because of not being taxed.

On the other hand, taxes—especially high and complicated taxes—can also undermine entrepreneurial development. There has been a great deal of discussion recently on the regulatory barriers to entry, that is, the costs that entrepreneurs have to pay in order to register their businesses and operate officially. But the most obvious cost is simply that, once registered, these entrepreneurs have to pay taxes. If taxes are high, entrepreneurs may stay underground. Underground business is very unlikely to be an effective lobby for improving institutions.[34]

Transparency and information dissemination can clearly have a positive impact on institutional outcomes. Transparency can also be part of the broad institutional framework; for example, a free and privately controlled press, which may help reduce corruption and government effectiveness (see work by

---

[34] See the discussion of recent Ukrainian experience in the IMF's September 2004 *World Economic Outlook*. The World Bank's *Doing Business* indicators do not currently include measures of tax rates faced by entrepreneurs. However, these will likely soon be added to their dataset.

Sen, 1981, on famines), or can relate to specific contexts. Evidence for the latter is provided by Ritvikka and Svennson (2004) for Uganda, di Tella and Schargrodsky (2001) for public procurement, and Glennerster and Shin (2004) for the case of data dissemination standards promoted by the IMF.

Aid, Institutions, and Growth

What do we know about the impact of aid on institutions and growth? The literature on aid and growth is mired in controversy. Burnside and Dollar (2000) made the claim that aid is not unconditionally beneficial but can help where recipient country policies are good. Easterly (2003) and Easterly and others (2004) contest these claims, arguing that the results are not at all robust. Recently, Clemens and others (2004) argue that short-term aid has a positive effect on growth, which still leaves open the question of the long-run impact, which is of central concern to policymakers. Rajan and Subramanian (2005) depart from the question of whether aid helps in examining the question of the channels through which aid might help or hurt growth. They find strong evidence of an adverse impact of aid on an economy's competitiveness and hence on long-run growth.

There is the related question of the impact of aid on institutions, which development practitioners have loosely articulated as "aid-dependence"—the incentive effects of aid on those in power to reform policies and institutions. The obvious analogy is with natural resource revenues, which are known to undermine institutions. Clearly, during the cold war period, examples of aid propping up "our guy" were not difficult to find. There is relatively little research on whether this phenomenon was more widespread and discernible in the cross-country evidence. If it were, there may be reason to believe (or not) that strategic considerations will play less of a role in the future, and that aid may not have a corrosive effect on institutional quality going ahead.

Overall, a careful reading of the evidence suggests that it is difficult to take comfort in the view that aid, or at least aid as we know it, can build institutions and sustain long-run growth.

IV. Implications for the International Community and Aid Recipients

This section draws some implications from the above analysis.

(1) Perhaps the most important implication is in delineating the limits of the possible. Given that basic economic and political institutions are important for growth, that they take a long time to change, and that they cannot easily be altered from the outside (something supported by the mixed record of conditionality), and even if they could, the relevant levers (for example, basic economic and political institutions) are outside the scope of the international

community's mandate and competence, there is a fundamental problem regarding expectations and time horizons.

Accordingly, there is the risk that donors may be setting inappropriate expectations in terms of how much growth and how quickly. The horizon over which progress can be realistically made and assessed is likely to be far greater, for example, than that of the typical Poverty Reduction Strategy Paper.

(2) The international community has an important role to play in helping maintain macroeconomic stability, prevent crises, or manage recoveries. The evidence suggests that developing countries, especially those in Africa, are especially prone to volatility. Mitigating volatility may not in itself deliver high growth, which again argues for a moderation of expectations about high growth over short time horizons.

However, not mitigating volatility may entail large costs in terms of institutional deterioration and failure, and hence long-run growth. In Africa, for example, rainfall-related shocks have a sizable impact on the probability of civil war (Miguel and others, 2004). Limiting the impact of these shocks would therefore seem to be an important role for the international community to play.

A shocks facility for low-income countries would, in effect, provide insurance to countries affected by shocks. This insurance could be provided at highly concessional rates (perhaps even as grants), given the income level of countries and the magnitude of the shocks, especially if the adverse incentive problems can be avoided through appropriate design of the facility.

(3) Donors could talk more openly about the problems of economic governance and serve as an honest and independent assessor of governance. This assessment of governance could be based in part, but not exclusively, on existing governance indicators. These are complex phenomena with important nuances that vary across countries. Measures of institutions change more slowly than the reality and may not reflect what is actually happening. Hence, donor assessments will have to be supplemented with other data. One useful indicator to which more attention could be paid is private sector investment.[35]

Without a high level of investment in the productive sector, it is not possible to sustain growth. If there are problems with governance, presumably it will be manifest in investment. If a country can find ways to sustain, say over 10 years, high private sector investment with weak governance, that is fine. However, we should constantly warn countries that private sector investment can and does collapse suddenly unless it is underpinned with strong institutions.

(4) Given the idiosyncratic and context-specific nature of institutional change, there may be a role for legitimate experimentation by countries with regard to economic institutions and policies. Of course, this is easier said than

[35] Focusing on growth outcomes is less attractive, because these contain a lot of noise. Also, there are ways to boost growth in the short- to medium-run; for example, through high levels of public spending, and this may prove unsustainable.

done because distinguishing good from bad experimentation may be difficult to identify in practice.

Take two examples from recent history, where there was some heterodoxy in policy reform. In the case of China, the township and village enterprises (TVEs) were for some time the drivers of industrial growth. In the case of Mauritius, two-track reforms were pursued with a protected import sector, and an outward-oriented enclave in the form of export processing zones with special benefits. These are not experiments that U.S. economists would have obviously endorsed. There are other instances where U.S. economists' assessment and endorsement proved correct (Chile, Korea). And yet others where despite outside endorsement of reforms did not lead to the expected growth outcomes (the Andean Region). How should donors distinguish these cases, and are there early indicators that would help them to do so?

(5) Insofar as transparency is a key element of institutions, donors should consider making transparency in public finances, and norms, more routinely integral to conditionality. This is particularly appropriate for natural resource-based countries, where there are a few relatively centralized sources of government revenue. Transparency in this area can presumably have significant macroeconomic consequences. Transparency could include observance of Reports on the Observance of Standards and Codes (ROSCs), adherence to relevant international standards (such as the U.K. Extractive Industries Transparency Initiative), and open public expenditure management systems. Recent steps in this direction in Angola and Republic of Congo (Brazzaville) appear legitimate in the eyes of all, and are arguably consistent with donors' mission and expertise.

(6) The importance of institutions also raises challenging questions about conditionality. If institutions are indeed the deep determinants of development, then policies traditionally subject to conditions—fiscal, monetary, exchange rates, structural reforms—cannot be evaluated simply by looking at their intended effects. When the underlying institutions are not being changed in the appropriate way, conditionality on policies may be ineffective. Therefore, the exclusive focus in conditionality on "getting policies right" may need to be rethought.

Clearly, a response of setting conditionality on institutions or institutional change per se may not be feasible either. For one, conditionality on basic institutions may be considered overly intrusive, while conditionality on the range of narrower institutions may run counter to the September 2002 guidelines calling for parsimony in conditionality.

One alternative to detailed policy conditionality is to find the right institutional preconditions for lending. Spotting opportunities—for example, through a tough ex ante screening process (based, say, on an assessment of institutional strength) combined with less onerous ex post conditionality—may be worth considering. Such a move could also have another advantage.

Detailed conditionality can may be inconsistent with the spirit of ownership, which properly defined necessarily involves allowing countries a certain measure of freedom to find appropriate institutional and policy solutions to development problems. The U.S. Millennium Challenge Account tries to incorporate this principle of ex ante screening of institutional conditions.

Another alternative to addressing the dilemma of conditionality is to draw upon the EU example. The key point here is whether the international community can offer—for example, through a seal of approval that investors would respond to—benefits that countries might consider attractive enough to want to change domestic institutions without the need for onerous conditionality. That remains to be seen.

Even if the international community itself did not serve as an anchor, the presence of other anchors for countries could be helpful. For many of the FSU and Central and Eastern European countries, the IMF's role has been—in part—one of helping manage the economic transition until the anchor of the EU was in sight. The question is whether the poorer developing countries can find such an anchor. Outside of the European region, broadly defined, the EU is unlikely to play this role. The WTO can play this role for some countries, but not likely for most, and even then the anchor would only guide trade policy. Unless an anchor can be created for Latin America, Africa, and perhaps some parts of Asia, the ability of any outside organization to play an important validating role may be quite limited.

(7) Another challenge relates to post-conflict situations. Should countries in these situations be treated differently? There are two views.

The first view is that requiring these countries to immediately improve their institutions is arguably unreasonable. An alternative would be grants with light conditionality, with help on all macroeconomic management issues, and a graduation to lending only when institutions have improved sufficiently.

A second view is, to the contrary, that post-conflict situations allow outsiders to have a great deal of impact on public expenditure management systems and other issues that fall within the scope of our technical assistance mandate. This may be possible, but much of the previous discussion cautions against the idea that we know enough to enter into broader institutional engineering or that such attempts can be successful when the basic institutions are weak.

V. Conclusion

The problem is not that we do not know what is needed for growth. There is nothing much wrong with advocating macroeconomic stabilization, trade liberalization, deregulation, and privatization—provided institutions are strong. However, these policies may be insufficient for growth when institutions are weak.

Such policies are also presumably much harder to implement when institutions are weak. The experience of Latin American reforms since the mid-1980s (see

Figure 10.4 on Latin America), and of Africa, over a longer period, are suggestive of the importance of institutions. Probably everyone involved in development had a good sense of the importance of institutions long before the 1990s. However, recent experience has strengthened our intuition and deepened our understanding on this point.

But the reality is that there are considerable uncertainties in our knowledge about how institutional change can be promoted, if at all. And the policy levers that outsiders can control or influence to promote institutional development may be limited. This calls for a moderation of expectations about what can be delivered on growth and poverty reduction and a greater openness to experimentation on policy and institutional choices by countries. Of course, this experimentation needs to stay within the bounds of what can be considered reasonable and consistent with good economic governance.

Appendix

Measuring Economic Institutions

One entirely reasonable concern regarding the recent emphasis on institutions is the lack of uncontroversial measures. This is not surprising considering both the recent nature of empirical work on this subject, as well as the conceptual issues involved.

Brief History of the Indicators

The modern empirical work on economic institutions goes back to Mauro (1995), who used expert assessments of the investment environment.[36] The key findings from this early literature were that perception-based expert assessments of corruption and the rule of law were significantly correlated with growth performance. Barro and Sala-i-Martin (1995) also found that the rule of law was highly significant in standard growth regressions.

Since then, there has been a great deal of work on these kinds of indicators.[37] Much of this has been pulled together and evaluated by a group at the World

---

[36] Knack and Keefer (1995) is another important early reference.

[37] Kaufmann and Recanatini (2005) provide an overview of alternative methodologies and tools to measure governance and institutions. Because of the complexity of governance, there is a variety of tools and indicators that have been developed recently. A detailed inventory of the indicators is available at: http://www1.worldbank.org/publicsector/indicators.htm and http://www.worldbank.org/wbi/governance/govdatasets/external.html. Major contributions—in terms of substance and in stimulating the debate on indicators—were made by, among others, Transparency International, Freedom House, and the Heritage Foundation.

Bank headed by Daniel Kaufmann and Aart Kraay (see Kaufmann, Kraay, and Loido-Zobaton, 1999). They have compiled a set of comparable cross-country governance indicators, using a clear methodology.[38] The six indicators provide country-level information on government effectiveness, rule of law, and control of corruption, voice, political stability, and regulatory quality. In addition, the authors calculate the confidence intervals (or "margins of error") for each indicator.

There are also some long-standing measures of political institutions, such as the Polity IV dataset and, more recently, measures of State Failure put together at the University of Maryland by Marshall and Jaggers. Their website is: http://www.cidcm.umd.edu/inscr/polity/. The World Bank has also put together a useful database (Beck and others, 2001): http://www.worldbank.org/research/bios/pkeefer.htm.

Conceptual Issues

There are three main concerns with currently used indicators of institutions, which are subjective and perceptions-based, that is, the result of someone's assessment, rather than something that is objectively measurable.

The first issue is that outside expert assessments may be colored by biases of various kinds. However, what really matters is the assessment of people making investment decisions (and people who advise them), thus the focus on opinions is not irrelevant. These subjective measures are correlated with a firm's own assessments.[39]

The second issue is that subjective assessments move around in response to events often more than is warranted, which can be addressed by looking at averages over time. These concerns create two problems for econometric work. First, they lead to error in the measurement of the underlying variable. Second, because perceptions are influenced by the outcome of interest (investors will say there is good protection of property rights when there is much investment), there is "endogeneity" bias. In other words, we cannot distinguish whether to interpret an improvement in perceptions as a true underlying development or simply a consequence of higher investment.

There is a third concern with perceptions-based measures relating to prescription. Suppose that the previous concerns were somehow addressed and the analysis pointed to the need to improve institutions. But translating this conclusion into policy actions would be very difficult because the prescription

[38] These indicators are constructed using information from about 20 different sources compiled by 18 different organizations. The information is then summarized and translated into six aggregate indicators using an unobserved component model.

[39] The revised version of Acemoglu and Johnson (2003) documents this using the World Business Environment Survey.

would be to improve "investor perceptions," asking the question of how this might be done in the first place.

The alternative to such complex and perceptions-based indicators is to develop objective measures of quality of governance.[40] This is an appealing agenda, and substantial progress has been made in developing sensible indicators, particularly in the World Bank's *Doing Business* project,[41] the Investment Climate Assessment, and the World Bank Institute Governance and Anti-corruption Diagnostic Surveys. The World Business Investment Surveys, in particular, focus on a multiplicity of stakeholders, such as public officials, households, and business people. Their objective is to gather specific, objective information about strengths and weaknesses within the country's institutions and use it as input to concrete anticorruption strategy in the country level.[42]

Overall, it appears that the field of measurement in its early stages—and considerable work—remains to be done. Governance evaluations are still, and likely to remain, more art than science.

References

Acemoglu, Daron, 2003, "The Form of Property Rights: Oligarchic vs. Democratic Societies," NBER Working Paper No. 10037 (Cambridge, Massachusetts: National Bureau of Economic Research).

———, and Simon Johnson, 2003, "Unbundling Institutions," NBER Working Paper No. 9934 (Cambridge, Massachusetts: National Bureau of Economic Research).

———, 2004, "Disease and Development: The Effect of Life Expectancy on Economic Growth," presentation, Harvard/MIT Development Seminar, December.

———, and James A. Robinson, 2001, "The Colonial Origins of Comparative Development: An Empirical Investigation," *American Economic Review*, Vol. 91 (December), pp. 1369–401.

———, 2003, "Disease and Development in Historical Perspective," *Journal of the European Economic Association*, Vol. 1 (April), pp. 397–405.

———, 2004, "Institutions as the Fundamental Cause of Long-Run Growth," NBER Working Paper No. 10481 (Cambridge, Massachusetts: National Bureau of Economic Research).

[40] But the leading objective indicators have proved not to be correlated with growth outcomes.

[41] See http://rru.worldbank.org/DoingBusiness.

[42] The key instruments used are detailed, country-specific surveys of thousands of households, business people, and public officials. These tools are designed to provide the basis of technical discussions for policymakers and civil society for policy formulation, complementing the traditional sources such as experts' opinions or case study analysis. Furthermore, the combined surveys of households, business people, and public officials permit consistency checks of the results. These surveys utilize experience-based (rather than 'opinions') type of questions, hopefully reducing the element of subjectivity.

———, and Yunyong Thaicharoen, 2003, "Institutional Causes, Macroeconomic Symptoms: Volatility, Crises and Growth," *Journal of Monetary Economics*, Vol. 50 (January), pp. 49–123.

Acemoglu, Daron, Simon Johnson, James A. Robinson, and Pierre Yared, 2004, "Revisiting the Determinants of Democracy" (unpublished).

———, 2005a, "Income and Democracy?" MIT Department of Economics Working Paper No. 05-05 (Cambridge, Massachusetts: Massachusetts Institute of Technology).

———, 2005b, "From Education to Democracy?" NBER Working Paper No. 11204 (Cambridge, Massachusetts: National Bureau of Economic Research).

Acemoglu, Daron, and James A. Robinson, 2001, "A Theory of Political Transitions," *American Economic Review*, Vol. 91 (September), pp. 938–63.

Alcalá, Francisco, and Antonio Ciccone, 2004, "Trade and Productivity," *Quarterly Journal of Economics*, Vol. 119 (May), pp. 613–46.

Artadi, E. V., and Xavier Sala-i-Martin, 2003, "The Economic Tragedy of the XXth Century: Growth in Africa," NBER Working Paper No. 9865 (Cambridge, Massachusetts: National Bureau of Economic Research).

Aslund, Anders, Peter Boone, and Simon Johnson, 1996, "How to Stabilize: Lessons from Post-Communist Countries," *Brookings Papers on Economic Activity: 1*, Brookings Institution.

Bairoch, Paul, 1998, *Cities and Economic Development: From the Dawn of History to the Present*, trans. by Christopher Braider (Chicago: University of Chicago Press, rev. ed.).

Banerjee, Abhijit V., and Lakshmi Iyer, 2002, "History, Institutions and Economic Performance: The Legacy of Colonial Land Tenure Systems in India," MIT Department of Economics Working Paper No. 02-27 (Cambridge, Massachusetts: Massachusetts Institute of Technology).

Barro, Robert J., and Rachel McCleary, 2003, "Religion and Economic Growth," NBER Working Paper No. 9682 (Cambridge, Massachusetts: National Bureau of Economic Research).

Barro, Robert J., and Xavier Sala-i-Martin, 1995, *Economic Growth* (New York: McGraw-Hill).

Bates, Robert H., 2004, "On The Politics of Property Rights by Haber, Razo, and Maurer," *Journal of Economic Literature*, Vol. 42 (June), pp. 494–500.

Beck, Thorsten, George Clarke, Alberto Groff, Philip Keefer, and Patrick Walsh, 2001, "New Tools in Comparative Political Economy: The Database of Political Institutions," *World Bank Economic Review*, Vol. 15, No. 1, pp. 165–76.

Bleakley, Hoyt, 2005, "Malaria Eradication in Columbia and Mexico: A Long-Term Follow-Up" (unpublished).

Braudel, Fernand, 1972, *The Mediterranean and the Mediterranean World in the Age of Philip II*, trans. by Siân Reynolds (New York: Harper and Row).

Chandler, Tertius, 1987, *Four Thousand Years of Urban Growth: An Historical Census* (Lewiston, New York: St. David's University Press).

Clemens, Michael, Steven Radelet, and Rikhil Bhavnani, 2004, "Counting Chickens When They Hatch: The Short-Term Effect of Aid on Growth," Working Paper No. 44 (Washington: Center for Global Development).

Commission for Africa, 2004, "Action for a Strong and Prosperous Africa," Consultation Document (Secretariat to the Commission for Africa). Available via the Internet: http://www.commissionforafrica.org/english/consultation/introduction.html

Dell'Ariccia, Giovanni, Enrica Detragiache, and Raghuram Rajan, 2004, "The Real Effect of 18 Banking Crises" (unpublished; Washington: International Monetary Fund).

Di Tella, Rafael, and Ernesto Schargrodsky, 2001, "The Role of Wages and Auditing During a Crackdown on Corruption in the City of Buenos Aires." Available via the Internet: http://papers.ssrn.com/sol3/papers.cfm?abstract_id=269490

Diamond, Jared M., 1997, *Guns, Germs, and Steel: The Fates of Human Societies* (New York: W. W. Norton & Co.).

Djankov, Simeon, Rafael La Porta, Florencio Lopez-de-Silanes, and Andrei Shleifer, 2001, "The Regulation of Entry," CEPR Discussion Paper No. 2953 (London: Centre for Economic Policy Research).

———, 2003, "Courts," *Quarterly Journal of Economics*, Vol. 118 (May), pp. 453–517. Available via the Internet: http://rru.worldbank.org/PapersLinks/Open.aspx?id=3513

Do, Quy-Toan, and Lakshmi Iyer, 2003, "Land Rights and Economic Development: Evidence from Viet Nam," Policy Research Working Paper No. 3120 (Washington: World Bank).

Easterly, William, 2001, *The Elusive Quest for Growth: Economists' Adventures and Misadventures in the Tropics* (Cambridge, Massachusetts: MIT Press).

———, 2003, "Can Foreign Aid Buy Growth?" *Journal of Economic Perspectives*, Vol. 17 (Summer), pp. 23–48.

———, and Stanley Fischer, 2001, "Inflation and the Poor," *Journal of Money, Credit and Banking*, Vol. 33, No. 2 part 1, pp. 160–78.

Easterly, William, Ross Levine, and David Roodman, 2003, "New Data, New Doubts: Revisiting 'Aid, Policies and Growth,' " Working Paper No. 26 (Washington: Center for Global Development).

Eschenbach, Felix, 2004, "Finance and Growth: A Survey of the Theoretical and Empirical Literature," Discussion Paper No. 2004-039/2 (Rotterdam: Tinbergen Institute).

Fischer, Stanley, 2002, "Financial Crises and Reform of the International Financial System," NBER Working Paper No. 9297 (Cambridge, Massachusetts: National Bureau of Economic Research).

Fisman, Raymond, 2001, "Estimating the Value of Political Connections," *American Economic Review*, Vol. 91 (September), pp. 1095–102.

Friedman, Eric J., Simon Johnson, and Todd Mitton, 2003, "Propping and Tunneling," *Journal of Comparative Economics*, Vol. 31 (December), pp. 732–50.

Glennerster, Rachel, and Yongseok Shin, 2003, "Is Transparency Good for You and Can the IMF Help?" IMF Working Paper 03/132 (Washington: International Monetary Fund).

Global Governance Initiative, 2004, *Annual Report*, World Economic Forum. Available via the Internet: http://www.weforum.org/pdf/ggi2005_low.pdf

Haber, Stephen, Armando Razo, and Noel Maurer, 2003, *The Politics of Property Rights: Political Instability, Credible Commitments, and Economic Growth in Mexico, 1876–1929* (New York: Cambridge University Press).

Hamann, A. Javier, and Alessandro Prati, 2002, "Why Do Many Disinflations Fail? The Importance of Luck, Timing, and Political Institutions," IMF Working Paper 02/228 (Washington: International Monetary Fund).

Hausmann, Ricardo, Lant Pritchett, and Dani Rodrik, 2004, "Growth Accelerations," NBER Working Paper No. 10566 (Cambridge, Massachusetts: National Bureau of Economic Research).

Hibbs, Douglas A., Jr., and Ola Olsson, 2004, "Geography, Biogeography, and Why Some Countries Are Rich and Others Are Poor," *Proceedings of the National Academy of Sciences*, Vol. 101, No. 10, pp. 3715–20.

International Monetary Fund, 2001, *World Economic Outlook* (Washington).

———, 2003, *World Economic Outlook* (Washington).

———, 2004, *World Economic Outlook* (Washington).

———, 2005, *World Economic Outlook* (Washington).

Jones, Benjamin F., and Benjamin A. Olken, 2004, "Do Leaders Matter? National Leadership and Growth Since World War II" (March). Available via the Internet: http://papers.ssrn.com/sol3/papers.cfm?abstract_id=524042

Kaufmann, Daniel, Aart Kraay, and Pablo Zoido-Lobatón, 1999, "Aggregating Governance Indicators," Policy Research Working Paper No. 2195 (Washington: World Bank).

Kaufmann, Daniel, and Francesca Recanatini, 2005, "Measuring Governance: Tools and Methods for Policy Advice and Capacity Building" (unpublished).

Khwaja, Asim Ijaz, and Atif R. Mian, 2004, "Do Lenders Favor Politically Connected Firms? Rent Provision in an Emerging Financial Market" (December). Available via the Internet: http://ssrn.com/abstract=631703

———, 2006, "Unchecked Intermediaries: Price Manipulation in an Emerging Stock Market," *Journal of Financial Economics*, Vol. 78 (October), pp. 203–41.

Klapper, Leora, Luc Laeven, and Raghuram Rajan, 2004, "Business Environment and Firm Entry: Evidence from International Data," NBER Working Paper No. 10380 (Cambridge, Massachusetts: National Bureau of Economic Research).

Knack, Stephen, and Philip Keefer, 1995, "Institutions and Economic Performance: Cross-Country Tests Using Alternative Institutional Measures," *Economics and Politics*, Vol. 7, pp. 207–27.

Kraay, Aart, 2004, "When Is Growth Pro-Poor? Cross-Country Evidence," IMF Working Paper 04/47 (Washington: International Monetary Fund).

Kydland, Finn, and Edward Prescott, 1977, "Rules Rather Than Discretion: The Inconsistency of Optimal Plans," *Journal of Political Economy*, Vol. 85, No. 3, pp. 473–91.

La Porta, Rafael, Florencio Lopez-de-Silanes, and Guillermo Zamarripa, 2003, "Related Lending," *Quarterly Journal of Economics*, Vol. 118 (February), pp. 231–68.

Laeven, Luc, Daniela Klingebiel, and Randy Kroszner, 2002, "Financial Crises, Financial Dependence, and Industry Growth," Policy Research Working Paper No. 2855 (Washington: World Bank). Available via the Internet: http://ssrn.com/abstract=320142

Landes, David S., 1998, *The Wealth and Poverty of Nations: Why Some Are So Rich and Some So Poor* (New York: W. W. Norton).

Lau, Lawrence, Yingyi Qian, and Gérard Roland, 2000, "Reform without Losers: An Interpretation of China's Dual-Track Approach to Transition," *Journal of Political Economy*, Vol. 108 (February), pp. 120–43.

Levine, Ross, 1997, "Financial Development and Economic Growth: Views and Agenda," *Journal of Economic Literature*, Vol. 35 (June), pp. 688–726.

Lipset, Seymour Martin, 1959, "Some Social Requisites of Democracy: Economic Development and Political Legitimacy," *American Political Science Review*, Vol. 53 (March), pp. 69–105.

Maddison, Angus, 2001, *The World Economy: A Millennial Perspective* (Paris: Organisation for Economic Co-operation and Development).

———, 2003, *The World Economy: Historical Statistics* (Paris: Organisation for Economic Co-operation and Development).

Marshall, Monty G., and Keith Jaggers, 2003, "Polity IV Project: Political Regime Characteristics and Transitions, 1800–2003," Polity Country Reports 2003 (College Park, Maryland: University of Maryland).

Mattoo, Aaditya, and Arvind Subramanian, 2004, "The WTO and the Poorest Countries: The Stark Reality," IMF Working Paper 04/81 (Washington: International Monetary Fund).

Mauro, Paolo, 1995, "Corruption and Growth," *Quarterly Journal of Economics*, Vol. 110 (August), pp. 681–712.

Miguel, Edward, Shanker Satyanath, and Ernest Sergenti, 2004, "Economic Shocks and Civil Conflict: An Instrumental Variables Approach," *Journal of Political Economy*, Vol. 112 (August), pp. 725–53.

North, Douglass C., 1990, *Institutions, Institutional Change, and Economic Performance* (New York: Cambridge University Press).

———, and Robert P. Thomas, 1973, *The Rise of the Western World: A New Economic History* (Cambridge, United Kingdom: Cambridge University Press).

Nunn, Nathan, 2003, "The Legacy of Colonialism: A Model of Africa's Underdevelopment," Working Paper (Toronto: University of Toronto). Available via the Internet: http://www.uoguelph.ca/~sday/cneh-rche/pdfs/nunn.pdf

———, 2004, "Slavery, Institutional Development, and Long-Run Growth in Africa, 1400–2000," Working Paper (Toronto: University of Toronto).

Prasad, Eswar S., Kenneth S. Rogoff, Shang-Jin Wei, and M. Ayhan Kose, 2004, "Financial Globalization, Growth and Volatility in Developing Countries," NBER Working Paper No. 10942 (Cambridge, Massachusetts: National Bureau of Economic Research).

Pritchett, Lant, 2006, "Does Learning to Add Up Add Up? The Returns to Schooling in Aggregate Data," in *Handbook of Education Economics* (forthcoming).

Przeworski, Adam, 1991, *Democracy and the Market: Political and Economic Reforms in Eastern Europe and Latin America* (New York: Cambridge University Press).

Putnam, Robert D., Robert Leonardi, and Raffaella Y. Nanetti, 1994, *Making Democracy Work: Civic Traditions in Modern Italy* (Princeton, New Jersey: Princeton University Press).

Raddatz, Claudio E., 2003, "Liquidity Needs and Vulnerability to Financial Underdevelopment," Policy Research Working Paper No. 3161 (Washington: World Bank).

Rajan, Raghuram G., 2004, "Dollar Shortages and Crises," NBER Working Paper No. 10845 (Cambridge, Massachusetts: National Bureau of Economic Research).

———, and Luigi Zingales, 1998, "Financial Dependence and Growth," *The American Economic Review*, Vol. 88 (June), pp. 559–86.

Ramey, Garey, and Valerie A. Ramey, 1995, "Cross-Country Evidence on the Link Between Volatility and Growth," *American Economic Review*, Vol. 85 (December), pp. 1138–51.

Ranciere, Ramon, Aaron Tornell, and Frank Westermann, 2003, "Crises and Growth: A Reevaluation," NBER Working Paper No. 10073 (Cambridge, Massachusetts: National Bureau of Economic Research); also under review *American Economic Review* and featured in the Economic Focus section of *The Economist* (December 11, 2003).

Reinikka, Ritva, and Jacob Svensson, 2004, "Local Capture: Evidence from a Central Government Transfer Program in Uganda," *Quarterly Journal of Economics*, Vol. 119 (May), pp. 679–706.

Rodriguez, Francisco, and Dani Rodrik, 1999, "Trade Policy and Economic Growth: A Skeptic's Guide to Cross-National Evidence," NBER Working Paper No. 7081 (Cambridge, Massachusetts: National Bureau of Economic Research).

Rodrik, Dani, 1999, "Where Did All the Growth Go? External Shocks, Social Conflict, and Growth Collapses," *Journal of Economic Growth*, Vol. 4 (December), pp. 385–412.

———, 2006, "Growth Strategies," in *Handbook of Growth* (forthcoming).

———, and Arvind Subramanian, 2004, "From 'Hindu Growth' to Productivity Surge: The Mystery of the Indian Growth Transition," NBER Working Paper No. 10376 (Cambridge, Massachusetts: National Bureau of Economic Research).

Roland, Gerard, 2004, "After Enlargement: Institutional Achievements and Prospects in the New Member States," paper presented at the third European Central Bank conference, "The New EU Member States: Convergence and Stability," Frankfurt, October (final version, December).

Ross, Michael L., 2001, "Does Oil Hinder Democracy?" *World Politics*, Vol. 53 (April), pp. 325–61.

Sachs, Jeffrey, and others, 1995, "Economic Reform and the Process of Global Integration," *Brookings Papers on Economic Activity: 1*, Brookings Institution, pp. 1–118.

Sachs, Jeffrey D., John W. McArthur, Guido Schmidt-Traub, Margaret Kruk, Chandrika Bahadur, Michael Faye, and Gordon McCord, 2004, "Ending Africa's Poverty Trap," *Brookings Papers on Economic Activity: 1*, Brookings Institution, pp. 117–216.

Sala-i-Martin, Xavier, and Arvind Subramanian, 2003, "Addressing the Natural Resource Curse: An Illustration from Nigeria," NBER Working Paper No. 9804 (Cambridge, Massachusetts: National Bureau of Economic Research).

Satyanath, Shanker, and Arvind Subramanian, 2004, "What Determines Long-Run Macroeconomic Stability? Democratic Institutions," IMF Working Paper 04/215 (Washington: International Monetary Fund).

Sen, Amartya Kumar, 1981, *Poverty and Famines: An Essay on Entitlement and Deprivation* (Oxford: Clarendon Press; New York: Oxford University Press).

Srinivasan, T. N., 2004, "Comments on Dani Rodrik and Arvind Subramanian, 'From "Hindu Growth" to Productivity Surge: The Mystery of the Indian Growth Transition,' " (Washington: International Monetary Fund). Available via the Internet: http://www.imf.org/external/pubs/ft/staffp/2004/00-00/sriniv.pdf

Tabellini, Guido, 2005, "Culture and Institutions: Economic Development in the Regions of Europe," IGIER Working Paper No. 292 (Milan: Innocenzo Gasparini Institute for Economic Research).

UN Millennium Development Project, 2005, *Investing in Development: A Practical Plan to Achieve the Millennium Policy Development Goals* (New York). Available via the Internet: http://www.unmillennium project.org/reports/fullreport.org

Weber, Max, 1930, *The Protestant Ethic and the Spirit of Capitalism*, trans. by Talcott Parsons (London: G. Allen and Unwin).

Wei, Shang-Jin, 2000, "Natural Openness and Good Government," NBER Working Paper No. 7765 (Cambridge, Massachusetts: National Bureau of Economic Research).

World Bank, 2002, *World Development Report 2002: Building Institutions for Markets* (Washington). Available via the Internet: http://econ.worldbank.org/wdr/WDR2002

———, 2003, *World Development Report 2003: Sustainable Development in a Dynamic World: Transforming Institutions, Growth, and the Quality of Life* (New York: Oxford University Press). Available via the Internet: http://econ.worldbank.org/wdr

Yang, Dean, 2002, "Can Enforcement Backfire? Crime Displacement in the Context of Customs Reform in the Philippines," Ford School of Public Policy Working Paper No. 2002-09 (Ann Arbor: University of Michigan).

Zettelmeyer, Jeromin, Ravi Balakrishnan, Alessandro Giustiniani, Paulo Medas, and Jesmin Rahman, 2005, "Bolivia: Ex-Post Assessment of Longer-Term Program Engagement, 'maturubo@centralbank.go.ke' " IMF Country Report No. 05/139 (Washington: International Monetary Fund).

Seminar Program

Monday, March 14

Opening Ceremony

Introduction
Abdoulaye Bio-Tchané, Director, African Department, IMF

Welcoming Remarks
Luisa Dias Diogo, Prime Minister, Republic of Mozambique

SESSION I

Aid, Growth, and Poverty Reduction
What Should Aid Be Trying To Achieve? How Good Is The Record?

Chair
Peter Heller, Deputy Director, Fiscal Affairs Department, IMF

Paper on Aid and Growth
Steven Radelet, Senior Fellow, Center for Global Development

Paper on Aid and Poverty Alleviation
Aart Kraay, Senior Economist, Development Research Group, World Bank

Discussant
Arvind Subramanian, Division Chief, Research Department, IMF

General Discussion

Luncheon Address

Gudrun Kochendörfer-Lucius, Managing Director, Internationale Weiterbildung und Entwicklung (InWEnt)

SESSION II

Aid Absorption
Recognizing and Avoiding Macroeconomic Hazards

Chair
Anupam Basu, Deputy Director, African Department, IMF

Analytical Overview Paper
David Bevan, Fellow of St. John's College and Research Associate, Centre for the Study of African Economies, University of Oxford

Case Study
Andrew Berg, Division Chief, Policy Development and Review Department, IMF

Case Study
Mark Sundberg, Lead Economist, Development Policy, World Bank

Discussant
Alan Gelb, Director, Development Policy, World Bank

General Discussion

Dinner Address

Charles Soludo, Governor, Central Bank of Nigeria

Tuesday, March 15

SESSION III

Exogenous Inflows and Real Exchange Rates
Theoretical Quirk or Empirical Reality?

Chair
T. N. Srinivasan, Samuel C. Park, Jr. Professor of Economics, Yale University

Paper
Christopher Adam, Research Associate, Centre for the Study of African Economies, and University Lecturer in Development Economics, Fellow of St. Cross College, University of Oxford

General Discussion

SESSION IV

Aid, Volatility, and Stabilization Policy. Does Aid Smooth Absorption or Exacerbate Shocks?

Reliability and Counter-Cyclicality

Chair
Catherine Pattillo, Senior Economist, African Department, IMF

Paper
Aleš Bulíř, Senior Economist, Policy Development and Review Department, IMF

General Discussion

SESSION V

Aid, Debt, and Fiscal Policy

Chair
Nancy Birdsall, President, Center for Global Development

Paper
Bikas Joshi, Economist, Policy Development and Review Department, IMF

General Discussion

Luncheon Address

Donald Kaberuka, Minister of Finance and Economic Planning, Rwanda

SESSION VI

Aid, Governance, and the Political Economy

Chair
Paul Isenman, Head, Development Policy Division, Development Cooperation Directorate, Organisation for Economic Co-operation and Development

Paper
Arvind Subramanian, Assistant Director, Research Department, IMF

General Discussion

SESSION VII

Roundtable Discussion

Chair
Leslie Lipschitz, Director, IMF Institute, IMF

Panelists
Goodall Gondwe, Minister of Finance, Malawi

Peter Grant, Director, Europe, Trade and International Financial Institutions Division, Department for International Development (DFID)

Charles Soludo, Governor, Central Bank of Nigeria

T.N. Srinivasan, Samuel C. Park, Jr. Professor of Economics, Yale University

General Discussion

List of Participants and Observers*

Adam, Christopher
University Lecturer and Research Associate, Center for the Study of African Economies, University of Oxford

Ashong, Samuel Niinoi
Minister of State for Economic Planning, Ministry of Finance and Economic Planning, Ghana

Bakary, Semiou
Director of Debt Operations, Ministry of Finance, Benin

Basu, Anupam
Deputy Director, African Department, IMF

Berg, Andrew
Division Chief, Policy Development and Review Department, IMF

Bevan, David
Research Associate, Centre for the Study of African Economies, University of Oxford

Bio-Tchané, Abdoulaye
Director, African Department, IMF

Birdsall, Nancy
President, Center for Global Development, Washington, D.C.

Bojang, Karamo
Permanent Secretary, Department of State for Finance and Economic Affairs, The Gambia

Bosten, Emmy
Office of the IMF Resident Representative, Mozambique

Bulíř, Aleš
Senior Economist, Policy Development and Review Department, IMF

Calu, Massiquina
Office of the IMF Resident Representative, Mozambique

Chambuca, Anabela
Economist, Public Debt Department, Mozambique

*Titles and affiliates are those that were in effect at the time of the seminar (March 2005). The list does not include observers who did not register for the seminar.

Chang, Manuel
Minister of Finance, Mozambique

Cisse, Hamza A.
Director, President's Cabinet, West African Economic and Monetary Union, Burkina Faso

Couto, Pedro
Director, Studies Cabinet, Mozambique

Crowards, Tom
Economic Adviser, Macroeconomic Growth Team, Policy Division, DFID, United Kingdom

Dauda, Joseph Bandabla
Minister of Finance, Sierra Leone

De Abreu, Antonio Pinto
Administrator, Banco de Mozambique

De Lima, Pedro
Senior Economist, European Investment Bank

De Sousa, Amilcar
Third Secretary, Ministry of Foreign Affairs, Mozambique

De Sousa, Clara
Administrator, Banco de Mozambique

Diogo, Luisa Dias
Prime Minister, Mozambique

Gelb, Alan
Director for Development Policy, World Bank

Gondwe, Goodall E.
Minister of Finance, Malawi

Grant, Peter
Director, International Division, DFID, United Kingdom

Guereneia, Aiuba
Minister of Development and Planning, Mozambique

Hadorn, Adrian
Ambassador of Switzerland to Mozambique

Heller, Peter
Deputy Director, Fiscal Affairs Department, IMF

Isard, Peter
Senior Advisor, IMF Institute

Isenman, Paul
Chief of Policy Coordination Division, Organisation for Economic Cooperation and Development, France

Itsede, Chris
Director General, West African Institute for Financial and Economic Management, Nigeria

Jatta, Famara L.
Governor, Central Bank of The Gambia

Joshi, Bikas
Economist, Policy Development and Review Department, IMF

Kaberuka, Donald
Minister of Finance and Economic Planning, Rwanda

Karimoune, Kassoum
Director of Economic Forecasting, Ministry of Finance, Niger

Keita, Margaret
Secretary of State, Department of State for Finance and Economic Affairs, The Gambia

Kerow, Billow
Economics Spokesman, Kenyan African National Union

Kitay, Mavuela Ma
Director of the Treasury, Congo, Dem. Rep. of

Kochendörfer-Lucius, Gudrun
Managing Director, InWEnt, Germany

Kraay, Aart
Lead Economist, Development Research Group, World Bank

Krueger,Thomas
Senior Advisor, African Department, IMF

Laice, Antonio
Director, National Treasury Directorate, Mozambique

Lipschitz, Leslie
Director, IMF Institute

Loforte, Thelma
Domain Manager, Swiss Agency for Development and Cooperation

Loum, Lamine
Former Prime Minister, Senegal

Lucas, Isaltina
Director, Economic Division, National Treasury Directorate, Mozambique

Maleiane, Adriano
Governor, Bank of Mozambique

Manu, Essimbo Numayeme
National Committee for Monitoring Economic Reforms, Congo, Dem. Rep. of

Martin, Matthew
Debt Relief International

Maruping, Mothae
Executive Director, Macroeconomic and Financial Management Institute of Eastern and Southern Africa, Zimbabwe

Masawe, Joseph
Senior Advisor to Executive Director, IMF

Massangai, Felix
Senior Technician, International Relations Section, Public Debt Department, Mozambique

Mausse, Argentina
Director, International Cooperation Division, National Treasury Directorate, Mozambique

Meyer, Ronald
Head of Cooperation, German Embassy in Mozambique

Mourmouras, Alex
Deputy Division Chief, IMF Institute

Musokotwane, Situmbeko
Secretary of the Treasury, Ministry of Finance and National Planning, Zambia

Nhalidede, Angelo
Economist, Public Debt Department, Mozambique

Njankuou Lamere, Daniel
Minister Delegated, in Charge of Programs, Ministry of Finance, Cameroon

Nsubuga, David
Economic Advisor, Ministry of Finance, Uganda

Okleirigh, Earnan
Department of Foreign Affairs, Ireland

Patel, Yasmin
Senior Advisor, Executive

Director's Office, IMF

Pattillo, Catherine
Senior Economist,
African Department, IMF

Paulo, Manuel
Chief, International Cooperation
Department, Mozambique

Rabiou, Albert Boura
Department of Economic Policy,
West African Economic and
Monetary Union, Burkina Faso

Radelet, Steven
Senior Fellow, Center for Global
Development, Washington, D.C.

Sandhop, Carsten
Director, KfW Office,
Mozambique

Sanou, Bolo
Director, International Relations
Division, Research Department,
Central Bank of
West African States, Senegal

Santos, Otília
Director, Public Debt Division,
National Treasury Directorate,
Mozambique

Soludo, Charles
Governor,
Central Bank of Nigeria

Srinivasan, T. N.
Samuel C. Park, Jr. Professor of
Economics, Department of
Economics, Yale University

Subramanian, Arvind
Division Chief,
Research Department, IMF

Sulemane, Jose
Director, National Directorate of
Planning and Budget,
Mozambique

Sumar, Isabel
Chief, Foreign Debt Department,
Mozambique

Sundberg, Mark
Economist, Development
Economics, World Bank

Taube, Gunther
Department Head, InWEnt,
Germany

Toure, Bassary
Former Minister of Finance, Mali

Vanden Broeke, Simon
Economic Adviser, Office of
DFID, Mozambique

Wagué, Sambou
Technical Advisor,
Economic Reform Programs,
Ministry of Finance, Mali

Yao Sahi, Kablan
National Director, Central Bank
of West African States,
Côte d'Ivoire

Yontcheva, Boriana
Economist, IMF Institute

Zongo, Tertius
Ambassador of Burkina Faso to
the United States